Time to Begin Anew

The Bucknell Studies in Eighteenth-Century Literature and Culture

General Editor: Greg Clingham, *Bucknell University*

Advisory Board: Paul K. Alkon, *University of Southern California*
Chloe Chard, *Independent Scholar*
Clement Hawes, *Southern Illinois University*
Robert Markley, *University of West Virginia*
Jessica Munns, *University of Denver*
Cedric D. Reverand II, *University of Wyoming*
Janet Todd, *University of East Anglia*

The Bucknell Studies in Eighteenth-Century Literature and Culture aims to publish challenging, new eighteenth-century scholarship. Of particular interest is critical, historical, and interdisciplinary work that is interestingly and intelligently theorized, and that broadens and refines the conception of the field. At the same time, the series remains open to all theoretical perspectives and different kinds of scholarship. While the focus of the series is the literature, history, arts, and culture (including art, architecture, music, travel, and history of science, medicine, and law) of the long eighteenth century in Britain and Europe, the series is also interested in scholarship that establishes relationships with other geographies, literatures, and cultures of the period 1660–1830.

Titles in This Series

Tanya Caldwell, *Time to Begin Anew: Dryden's* Georgics *and* Aeneis

Mita Choudhury, *Interculturalism and Resistance in the London Theatre, 1660–1800: Identity, Performance, Empire*

James Cruise, *Governing Consumption: Needs and Wants, Suspended Characters, and the "Origins" of Eighteenth-Century English Novels*

Edward Jacobs, *Accidental Migrations: An Archaeology of Gothic Discourse*

http://www.departments.bucknell.edu/univ_press

Time to Begin Anew

Dryden's *Georgics* and *Aeneis*

Tanya Caldwell

Lewisburg
Bucknell University Press
London: Associated University Presses

Associated University Presses
440 Forsgate Drive
Cranbury, NJ 08512

Associated University Presses
16 Barter Street
London WC1A 2AH, England

Associated University Presses
P.O. Box 338, Port Credit
Mississauga, Ontario
Canada L5G 4L8

The paper used in this publication meets the requirements of the American National Standard for Permanence of Paper for Printed Library Materials Z39.48-1984.

Library of Congress Cataloging-in-Publication Data

Caldwell, Tanya, 1969–
    Time to begin anew : Dryden's Georgics and Aeneis / Tanya Caldwell.
        p.   cm.
    Includes bibliographical references (p.) and index.
    ISBN 0-8387-5435-X (alk. paper)
    1. Virgil — Translations into English — History and criticism.   2. Didactic poetry, Latin — Translations into English — History and criticism.   3. Epic poetry, Latin — Translations into English — History and criticism.   4. Dryden, John, 1631–1700 — Knowledge — Translating and interpreting.   5. Dryden, John, 1631–1700 — Knowledge — Language and languages.   6. Translating and interpreting — England — History — 17th century.   7. Latin language — Translating into English — History.   8. Aeneas (Legendary character) in literature.   9. Agriculture in literature.   10. Rome — In literature.   11. Virgil. Georgica.   12. Virgil. Aeneis.   I. Title.
PA6825 .C347   2000
873'.01 — dc21   99-089592

PRINTED IN THE UNITED STATES OF AMERICA

For Reg Berry,
sine quo non

Contents

Acknowledgments

Many individuals and several institutions have supported this project and made it possible. Grants and research aid have come from the Canadian Commonwealth Scholarship and Fellowship Programme, the American Society for Eighteenth-Century Studies, The William Andrews Clark Memorial Library, the Georgia State University English Department, and the University of Toronto libraries. Parts of chapters 1 and 3 have appeared in *Eighteenth-Century Life* and *The Eighteenth Century: Theory and Interpretation* respectively; I am grateful to the editors of those journals for permission to reprint material. I owe an unrepayable debt to Reginald Berry, who introduced me to Dryden and his translations and whose example and input have been more influential than he can know. To him the book is fondly dedicated. In the first and most crucial stages of this project Brian Corman and, later, Steven Zwicker gave invaluable guidance and unflagging support. Others have read and offered advice about various sections and aspects of the book. Thanks especially to Reiner Smolinski and Robert Markley, as well as to Patricia Brückmann, Greg Clingham, Hugo de Quehen, Jake Fuchs, Brean Hammond, Mecthilde O'Mara, Malinda Snow. All errors and omissions are, of course, my own. For constant love, support, and encouragement I am thankful to my husband, Reiner Smolinski, and to my parents, Nan and Bill Caldwell, who are always there for me even when, geographically, they are not.

Introduction: All of a Piece

In Swift's *Battle of the Books*, Dryden makes an appearance as a Moderns cavalier. Coming face to face with Vergil, he talks him into an exchange of armor and horses. He cuts a ridiculous figure, however, for the Ancient's "glittering armour" neither fits nor becomes him, and "when it came to the trial, Dryden was afraid and utterly unable to mount."[1] In placing Dryden's *Aeneis* at the heart of the Ancients vs. Moderns debate and presenting Dryden as an aspiring but hopelessly doomed Ancient, Swift pinpoints the tension at the center of the epic translation: its commitment both to an (idealized) heroic past and to an unheroic present. He also acknowledges its significance as a product of a watershed moment in English history and literature. Yet these two vital aspects of Dryden's *Vergil* have been overlooked since the day of its publication, and Dryden has been condemned for his incompetence as translator by considerably lesser classicists than Swift—and than Dryden himself. The discounting of translation as a legitimate literary mode aside, a single factor seems to be responsible for the misunderstanding and neglect of what is not only one of Dryden's most powerful and important works but a crucial document in the history of generic developments between the seventeenth and eighteenth centuries. The gulf between Dryden's translation and earlier seventeenth-century portrayals of Vergil and notions of the heroic has been attributed to Dryden rather than to the historical and literary contexts from which his *Georgics* and *Aeneis* arise. Swift's portrait, quite simply, is unfair and misleading. The problem was not that Vergil's armor did not fit Dryden, rather that it was out of date. As Brean Hammond has most recently pointed out, the key issue in the debate that was rooted in cultural and political turmoil is not the superiority of Moderns or Ancients but the relevance and relation of the present to the past.[2] This crisis over the use and usefulness of history is also at the center of Dryden's *Vergil*, which is as much a product of an age of transition as the Ancients/Moderns controversy itself.

When he set about translating Vergil's works, Dryden had just been deposed from what he viewed as his rightful positions as poet laureate and historiographer royal. He was also ill, feeling his age, in extreme

11

financial exigency and, as a prominent Catholic and Jacobite supporter, in a difficult political and social position. He saw no reason, however, to relinquish his life-long work as the nation's guardian and caretaker. Like his other post-1688 works, his Vergil translations consequently employ, or attempt to employ, his wonted techniques, for as he renders Vergil English he searches the Ancient's works for insights into contemporary problems. In the process, he imbues his translation with disguised political and social commentaries, which have not escaped the notice of critics who, in the past two decades, have drawn attention to Dryden's post-1688 plays, essays and translations.[3] Steven Zwicker, in particular, has clearly demonstrated that Dryden's *Aeneis* is an important document in the "Arts of Disguise" which dominated the last part of the century. What has not been highlighted is the importance of the generic issues at work in the *Aeneis* especially. As Dryden turns yet again to Vergil's heroic codes and to current notions of historical and political continuity to address contemporary English literary and political crises, Vergil's epic fragments under his fingertips. The purpose of this study is to demonstrate that Dryden's inconsistent, distinctly unheroic and profoundly uncertain translation is a product not simply of his own disillusionment or sense of displacement (though it is certainly that) but of a decade that heralded the end of one age while groping toward a new. Accordingly, the aim here is also to show that Dryden's compromised and irresolute *Vergil* illuminates the historical and generic negotiations and processes by which characteristically eighteenth-century literary forms emerged from seventeenth-century literary modes and notions of literature.

Less than three years after what was for Dryden the not so Glorious Revolution the ex-poet laureate set down guidelines for the English epic he himself clearly did not have the heart to write. Claiming in his "Discourse Concerning the Original and Progress of Satire" (1693) that any Modern with the requisite "Genius" and other "Qualifications" might "build a Nobler, a more Beautiful and more Perfect Poem, than any yet extant since the Ancients," Dryden proposes a "Model."[4] To equal or surpass the achievements of the Ancients, he claims, all "Christian Poets" need do is peruse the Old Testament and accommodate "what there they find, with the Principles of *Platonique* Philosophy, as it is now Christianis'd" (4:19). He then reflects on the subject matter he himself might choose: "King *Arthur*, Conquering the *Saxons*; which being farther distant in Time, gives the greater Scope to my Invention: Or that of *Edward* the Black Prince in subduing *Spain*, and Restoring it to the Lawful Prince, though a Great Tyrant, *Don Pedro* the Cruel" (4:22). Among reasons for this last choice is "the Magnanimity of the *English* Hero . . . together with the Characters of the chiefest *English* Persons;

wherein, after *Virgil* and *Spencer*, I wou'd have taken occasion to represent my living Friends and Patrons of the Noblest Families, and also
shadow'd the Events of future Ages, in the Succession of our Imperial
Line" (4:23).

In proposing to bring together great figures from an English past and
an English present and to establish both in the framework of sacred
history for the instruction and delight of posterity, Dryden holds up the
blueprint continually employed not just by himself but throughout the
seventeenth century. Informing and shaping this blueprint is a conviction in the typology of history. This view is most clearly expressed in
Dryden's 1683 "Life of Plutarch" where he calls history

> a Prospective-Glass carrying your Soul to a vast distance, and taking in the
> farthest objects of Antiquity. It informs the understanding by the memory:
> It helps us to judge of what will happen, by shewing us the like revolutions
> of former times. For Mankind being the same in all ages, agitated by the
> same passions, and mov'd to action by the same interests, nothing can come
> to pass, but some President of the like nature has already been produc'd. . . .
> (17:270)

The importance to future actions of examining "like revolutions of former times" is now underlined: "God, tis true with his divine Providence,
over-rules and guides all actions to the secret end he has ordain'd them"
(17:271).

Dryden's notions of secular typology as manifested here and in his
other works of the Stuart era reflect what Michael McKeon sees as the
seventeenth-century "concrete historicity of typological thought." This
came into being when "Protestantism elevated typology as the authoritative means of exegesis," and, by employing the language of Scripture,
it extended "its reference to include not only Old Testament but contemporary and individual 'history,' the immediately accessible material
of local political conflict or private emotional upheaval." Finally, "[l]ike
Bacon's 'natural matter,' history is seen to be 'impressed and defined'
by 'the creator's own stamp.' "[5] Dryden's mounting distress over the
corruption of the biblical logos, which such interpretation involved, ultimately led him, willy nilly, away from the typological *modus operandi*
he had employed with such authority and ease in, for example, *Absalom
and Achitophel* (1681). Joseph Levine presents the passage quoted above
from Dryden's Plutarch as the poet's definitive word on the nature of
history, and refers to the thoughts as "commonplace," "conventional"
and "a view that nearly everyone shared."[6] Indeed, Dryden himself in
the "Discourse" and in the dedication of his *Aeneis* reiterates his earlier
claims about the cyclical movement of history. Yet the difference be-

tween his pre- and post-1688 poetry reveals both the poet's departure in the 1690s from his former emphasis on the teleology of history and his change in attitude toward the function of literature.

These shifts occur within his late translations, which concede the onset of a new era while clinging tenaciously to old ideologies. They are made possible by Dryden's Platonism, which, as the "Discourse" indicates, is a major—but understudied—force behind his particular brand of typology. At the heart of all his translations and use of former writers in his original works is the belief he expresses in his "Life of Plutarch" and was to stress after 1688: humankind is "the same in all ages, agitated by the same passions, and mov'd to action by the same interests." Richard Popkin's discussion of Gerard Vossius and his follower Ralph Cudworth, whose beliefs concur with those of the Florentine and Cambridge Platonists, demonstrates how this view is also central to the theories of seventeenth-century Platonists. Vossius's major work, Popkin argues,

> is a handbook of mythology, ancient and modern. The author contended that various mythologies are picturesque descriptions of historical events, of natural phenomena and of social conditions. Vossius sought to uncover what led to the formation of these myths, and to idolatrous practices. He did this . . . as a literary humanist, sifting out texts rather than facts and artifacts.[7]

Building on Vossius's work and equally accepting the "*prisca* theology view that a clear divine revelation was given to Moses that trickled down, and became corrupted in pagan views," Cudworth insisted that a "taxonomy of human beliefs about God and the world . . . led to Christian and not just natural belief." Popkin summarizes:

> Although we might not have rational comprehension of God, and how He or She operates in Nature and History, we can conceive in terms of the way people have thought and written of God, and the way Nature appears to operate that God exists, and that the Judeo-Christian revelation is correct.[8]

The Platonists' debates provide an illuminating background to Dryden's theory of poetry and translation (which he saw as just as much an act of creation as an "original" poem). The common ground is the implied sacred nature of any true poetic endeavor whether heathen or Christian. As this study of Dryden's *Vergil* demonstrates, belief in the divinity of true poetry in any age is both the driving force behind and major source of consolation in Dryden's works from the late 1680s on. It is also the hinge on which the changes in his late works swing. As he struggles to continue his life's work, outcast and baffled by a rapidly and irrevocably changing world, Dryden's former emphasis on the his-

torical moment and his confidence that God is working "all actions to
the secret end he has ordain'd them" becomes emphasis on the sacred
nature of great works of the past. Like Vossius, he turns more and more
for answers to the texts of kindred poetic spirits rather than to facts and
artifacts—or to the types and antitypes of Christian history. This shift
is already apparent in the discrepancy between the *ars poetica* outlined
in the "Discourse" and the translations which follow it.

In his "Discourse" Dryden again employs the typological methodology he advocates. Still ostensibly giving advice, he notes that the "Judicious Writer" must also "add the opposition of ill Spirits to the good,"
for the cosmic battle is ongoing, "A great Testimony of which we find
in Holy Writ, when God Almighty suffer'd *Satan* to appear in the Holy
Synod of the Angels" (4:21). In his translation of Persius's third satire,
Dryden makes quite clear that the antitype to Satan he has in mind is
William III. He translates freely:

> Great Father of the Gods, when, for our Crimes,
> Thou send'st some heavy Judgment on the Times;
> Some Tyrant-King the Terrour of his Age,
> The Type, and true Vicegerent of thy Rage;
> Thus punish him. . . .
>
> (65–69)

By presenting the Dutch prince, in this way, as simply another "ill
Spirit" or "Type" in the revolutions of Judaeo-Christian history, Dryden attempts to console himself and his readers—or at least his fellow
Jacobites. Both the sentiment (the desire for political stability) and the
authority (the typological framework) of the lines are those Dryden had
used many times, those of, say, *Absalom and Achitophel*. Again the reminder is (as he puts it in the "Discourse") that God "can work Good
out of Evil, as he pleases; and irresistibly sways all manner of Events
on Earth, directing them finally for the best, to his Creation in General,
and to the Ultimate End of his own Glory in Particular" (4:20). The
power of the satiric translations, however, lies not in their attempt to
explain low points of Roman and English history in typological terms
but in Dryden's communion as translator with the spirits of Juvenal
and Persius so that their wrath enhances his own. The intensity of his
anger is such, in fact, that the consolation of the "Discourse" is forgotten.

The same slippage between ideology and the translation itself occurs
in Dryden's *Vergil*. Here, however, the consequences are greater and
more telling. In his instructions in the "Discourse" Dryden presents
Vergil as an example of the way Platonic philosophy can be accommo-

dated to "Christian use": in other words, to the ends of secular typology
(4:21). In making the statement, he is fully aware of the long line of
English and French translators and commentators who had employed
Vergil as a political guidebook in times of crisis. When he attempts to
make Vergil speak to the issues of 1690s England, however, Dryden
discovers that Vergil's heroic codes and those of his previous translators
and interpreters no longer have contemporary parallels.[9] As a result,
epic is imbued with satire, Vergil's heroic becomes mock-heroic, and
any attempt to make typological sense of contemporary history col-
lapses into profound *aporia*.[10]

As the following chapters argue, the dilemma was one that Dryden
really only confronted (and that gradually) as he worked through his
Vergil; at its center is the problem he lamented in the "Discourse" and
saw as the force curbing his poetic powers: "the Change of the Times"
(4:23). McKeon, J. Paul Hunter and other significant commentators
on the emergence of literary forms that developed into the novel have
demonstrated that self-assured seventeenth-century literary modes and
their typological foundations were gradually undermined and disman-
tled as the multisourced empiricism of "true history" challenged their
authority.[11] Dryden's own "Life of Plutarch" highlights the empiricism
that was an intrinsic part of seventeenth-century secular typology when
he claims that the importance of examining "like revolutions of former
times" lies in "having the causes before our eyes [so that] we cannot
easily be deceiv'd in the effects, if we have judgment enough but to
draw the parallel" (18:270–71). After 1688, however, the world visibly
changed so rapidly that (as chapter 3 will illustrate) the always-existing
gap between historical reality and aristocratic ideology, which was en-
shrined in established genres, widened to such a degree that Vergil
could no longer be used, as he had been by earlier seventeenth-century
translators and commentators, to bridge that gap and enfold history
within a divinely-authorized framework. In other words, there no
longer seemed to be any parallels between the present and the (heroic)
past and therefore no way of projecting the present into the future by
continuing patterns elucidated by the past.

This demise of the heroic and of the world in which it reigned is manifested in a trend, of which Dryden's unheroic *Vergil* is a single document. Hammond points to the epic "plausibility crisis," which "affects
the way the classical world is represented in original writing and in the
translation of epic."[12] His discussion of the burlesque renditions of the
classical world that poured off the press and filled the stages in the late-
seventeenth and early-eighteenth centuries is underscored by his argument that mock-heroic even provides the "missing-link between the
epic and the novel."[13] This in-between literary mode peaked, he notes,

at a moment of generic confusion: "Typically, the forms of the 1690s are mixed: tragicomic, sentimentalised drama and fiction that admits realistic elements into romance paradigms."[14] If considered in the context of the political and social uncertainties of the 1690s (a major concern of this study), such an observation highlights the way in which generic and social and political instability are linked.[15]

Yet, while the 1690s have been highlighted as a turning-point in English politics and culture, the literature of this period has been largely overlooked, even in studies of the emergence or origins of the novel. Hunter argues that by the 1690s the nature of the print world and its relation to society had changed, and he sees the decade as the first wave of novel writing, the second and most important wave occurring in the 1740s. In his study of the political and cultural origins of the English novel, McKeon acknowledges that for many "the most important event of the century was the Glorious Revolution and its attendant innovations in finance."[16] Indeed, the impact on the national psyche of these "innovations" has been best elucidated by J. G. A. Pocock's study of the effects of the excitement and fears precipitated by the financial revolutions of the mid-1690s.[17] The literature itself of this watershed period continues to be overlooked, however. The reason undoubtedly lies in the approach outlined by McKeon: "To formulate the problem of the origins of the novel in terms of how one dominant prose form 'became' another is really to ask how romance responded to the early modern historicist revolutions."[18] In fact, as Hammond recognizes, many more clues to this important "problem" can be found in poetry and drama. If the question at hand is generic instability and the formulation of a new genre, it makes sense, after all, to examine what is happening in modes which most rigidly uphold generic laws: poetry and drama.

What makes Dryden's *Vergil* such a crucial document in this period is not just that it sheds light on the demise of the heroic and the related destabilization of genres, but that its own crises derive from the issue at the heart of the 1690s crises: genealogy. McKeon pinpoints what he sees as the force behind "aristocratic ideology," which shaped the seventeenth century and its literature: "the conviction that a stable social order is a dependable guide to the greater moral order, and in a patrilinear culture based upon degrees of status, social order is a function of genealogy."[19] Such a conviction is behind all Dryden wrote in support of the Stuart monarchies, and, as the following chapters argue, it is the conviction with which he set about translating Vergil. McKeon's observations concerning the significance of Vergil to English tradition suggest why the Roman poem was, finally, more appropriate epic subject matter in the 1690s than the topics Dryden had proposed in his "Discourse": "The Arthurian *matière de Bretagne* had . . . dubious roots.

The genealogy established at the fall of Troy, on the other hand, provided a national lineage not only for the followers of Aeneas but also, through Priam, for the barbarian tribes that roamed and settled the rest of Europe."[20] The desire expressed in the "Discourse" to follow "*Virgil and Spencer*" in representing "my living Friends and Patrons of the Noblest Families, and also [shadow] the Events of future Ages, in the Succession of our Imperial Line" is just one expression of Dryden's urge to uphold English mythical and historical genealogies at a time when patrilinear authority had been fundamentally undermined. His reference to Spenser is a reminder of the British genealogy (immortalized by *The Faerie Queene*) that traced its roots to the myth of Troy. In the dedication of his *Aeneis* Dryden is again careful to place himself in an English heroic tradition in which he is successor to Spenser. The translation itself establishes its position in that tradition and so emphasizes its national task through numerous echoes of Spenser and other English and French royalist writers. Yet when the *Georgics* and *Aeneis* confront events of the 1690s the rupture of time-honored traditions becomes obvious.

Useful here—and throughout this study—are Bakhtin's observations on the cultural and literary circumstances in which the demise of the heroic coincides with the rise of literary forms and characteristics that are subsequently called novelistic. While Bakhtin can be disturbingly absolutist, presenting, as he does, a simple epic world, his discussion of the differences between and processes which link epic and novel shed light on the progressive collapse of generic certainties not only in Dryden's *Aeneis*, but, as Hammond argues, characteristically in poetry and drama of the 1690s. The key point in Bakhtin's consideration of epic and novel concerns the displacement of epic emphasis on sacrosanct tradition (which he sees as "immanent in the very form of the epic") by novelistic "contact with the spontaneity of the inconclusive present."[21] As he argues, the "world of the epic is the national heroic past: it is a world of 'beginnings' and 'peak times' in the national history, a world of fathers and of founders of families, a world of 'firsts' and 'bests'."[22] This world breaks down when it comes into contact with "the present day with all its inconclusiveness, its indecision, its openness, its potential for re-thinking and re-evaluating."[23]

On Bakhtinian terms the crises faced by the *Aeneis* and the features which make it unheroic indicate the dawning of an age of noveldom. Unable to reconcile events of the 1690s, specifically William III's reign, with the heroic tradition "immanent" in Vergil's epic as it had been read in the seventeenth century, Dryden is forced, against his will, to violate what Bakhtin sees as the three constitutive features of epic. He denies the possibility any longer of creating "a national epic past" by arguing that the present is not worthy of being memorialized for the benefit of posterity. He portrays the disintegration of "national tradition" as he laments the fall of the Stuart monarchy. And he transgresses the "absolute epic distance separating the epic world from contemporary reality" by infusing his poem with satire.[24] As a result, the translation becomes irresolute, inconsistent and fragmented: what Bakhtin would call novelistic.

The dilemmas of the *Aeneis*, then, are those of a new age, and chapter 4 especially will stress the complexity of the problems confronting Dryden in a decade plagued not only by deeply disturbing issues of kingship, authority and national law, but by exhausting and seemingly pointless wars.[25] The poet's solutions are equally those of a new age, however. In negotiating the collapse of (historical) monarchic genealogy and—in his view—of national stability, Dryden ultimately turns for consolation and authority to poetic genealogies, stressing his own perpetuation of a legitimate descent of kindred poetic spirits. As his communion with Juvenal and Persius in 1693 indicates, this change is already apparent in his translations and contributions to poetic miscellanies in the early 1690s. It culminates in *Fables*, the driving force behind which (as the preface makes clear) is Dryden's sense of affinity with spirits from the past. The movement toward a new mode of national literature exemplified in *Fables* begins in earnest, if unintentionally, in the *Aeneis*, however.[26] Dryden's insistence on his bond with Vergil in the dedication of his translation elicited Swift's wrath; for, as he encounters Vergil in the Battle of the Books, "Dryden, in a long harangue, soothed up the good Ancient, called him 'father', and by a large deduction of genealogies made it plainly appear that they were nearly related."[27] Yet in recognizing (both in the dedication and translation) the fundamental differences between the historical circumstances under which he and Vergil were writing while arguing his kinship with the Roman poet, Dryden anticipates prevailing features of eighteenth-century literature in its attitude towards the authority of the past.

Apprehending, in the process of translation, that history can no longer provide assurance about the place of humanity in God's greater scheme, Dryden ceases finally to stress the significance of any historical moment; instead he finds authority and consolation in the laws and traditions of poetry. Simply to commune with the spirits of Vergil, Spenser, Milton, Denham, Segrais and the many other poets whose presence can be felt in his *Vergil* is to tap the spring in which truths about human nature lie and to which all true poets have access. In this way moral guidance may be offered to the individual reader where directions for the nation cannot. The historicity of Dryden's text and of its ancestors is still crucial, however. For, while the poets' truths are beyond the reach of time's corrosive powers, their works either arise from or record the experiences, difficulties, joys, values, or concerns of a particular moment in time. The difference now is that Dryden is interested in comparing and contrasting, weighing and differentiating various tales rather than searching for patterns and finding consolation in recurring cycles.[28] This change in approach and imperatives is not unique to Dryden, however. The emphasis in the *Aeneis* on liberation from time at the expense of the importance of the historical moment embodies the difference between epic and novel, between seventeenth-century relative certainties and eighteenth-century profound uncertainties.[29] In downplaying his wonted emphasis on preparing for the nation's future by looking at its past and by focusing instead on the light shed on moral truths by ancient (and not so ancient) voices, Dryden sets the stage for the dawning century.

Certainly his need to set his *Aeneis* firmly in a semimystical tradition, which he achieves through the translation's awareness of its ancestry, and his simultaneous concern over how an individual should or can behave in a chaotic, mutable present has parallels in (for example) the works of Swift, Defoe, and Fielding. Like Dryden's epic framework, Defoe's seventeenth-century settings and Swift's and Fielding's epic backdrops provide a background against which the moral character of the hero and his or her world can be measured, even while that background is mocked as belonging to a bygone era. Dryden also foreshadows works of the next age (most notably Fielding's and Swift's) in giving ultimate power to the author rather than to history, secular or divine. His fragmented translation and exchanges in the *Aeneis* with whatever voices he chooses to call upon—like his later manipulation in *Fables* of handpicked poets—control the text and consequently the reader's access to the past. His authority as poet is essentially that of Fielding's and Swift's domineering narrators and commentaries and Defoe's independent narrators: history and the content of the text are at the mercy of the omnipotent author, rather than the author following the dictates of typological and generic authority.

Trailblazing, whether deliberate or (as in Dryden's case) forced upon the pioneer, comes at a cost, however. The inherently skeptical and innovative methodologies of Dryden's *Vergil* are directly responsible for the misunderstandings that have surrounded it for three centuries. Because, for the first time, his intense investigation of questions of kingship and government within a clearly contemporary context offers no answers, for example, the *Aeneis* has been seen as Dryden's acceptance of and reconciliation with William and Mary's regime.[30] This study focuses throughout on the profundity of Dryden's commitment to the Stuarts and ideologies associated with monarchy by divine right. A couple of prefatory comments on the translation's strongly Jacobite context seem useful, however. For a start, the *Vergil* is framed by Dryden's late plays and *Fables* (1700), all of which contain unmistakable and bitter invective against England's new government and monarchy. It seems unlikely to say the least that pro-Williamite politics or even a lukewarm acceptance of the new status quo could shape a work that falls between (for example) *Amphitryon*, with its thinly-disguised indictment of the Dutch prince as a debauched usurper, and, say, "Palamon and Arcite" with its enraged outburst against "Jove's usurping Arms" supported by "all the Pow'rs who favour Tyranny; / And all the Standing Army of the Sky."[31] The bitter poet's unwavering loyalty to his rightful king is also revealed in a letter to the Earl of Chesterfield in February 1697. Explaining the delay in the publication of his *Vergil*, he laments: "I have hinder'd it thus long in hopes of his return, for whom, and for my Conscience I have sufferd, that I may have layd my Author at his feet: But now finding that Gods time for ending our miseries is not yet, I have been advis'd to make three severall Dedications. . . ."[32] These dedications were all to prominent non-Williamites: a fact which surely highlights Dryden's obstinacy in refusing to dedicate his epic translation to England's new king.

His letters also reveal his resistance to an age of consumer-dictated publication, which, like the nonheroic elements of his translation, represented, finally, the defeat of an aristocratic, patronage-based world by the new social and political climate of which his *Vergil* was such a part. In September 1697, he confides to his sons his personal feelings concerning the enormously successful subscription publication of his translation: "My Virgil succeeds in [the World beyond its desert or my Expectation. You] know the profits might have been more, but neither my conscience nor honour wou'd suffer me to take them: but I can never repent of my Constancy; since I am thoroughly perswaded of the justice of the laws, for which I suffer" (*Letters*, 94). Quoting Samuel Johnson's assertion that Dryden's *Vergil* is "the first considerable work for which this expedient [of printing by subscription] was employed," the editors of the California *Dryden* point out that while Milton's *Paradise Lost* and other publications (including a second, 1654 edition of Ogilby's *Vergil*) had been by subcription or solicitation, yet "Johnson's emphasis is exactly right, for the true significance of the Dryden-Tonson enterprise in 1697 was a watershed in the economic liberation of authorship from the exclusive reliance on the stage, on patronage or on politics, which had theretofore prevailed" (6:848). In every sense then, Dryden's *Vergil* was a significant participant in, even a precipitator of, interrelated social, political, economic and consequently ideological, and literary changes that were irrevocable by the 1690s. Yet, as his letters and his nostalgic translations indicate, in every sense Dryden resisted those changes, clinging to the last to the hierarchical, time-honored, patriarchal world embodied by idealized Stuart monarchy and its "laws."[33]

The translation's commitment to the new world of professional writing and to the political and social demands of which that world was symptomatic has also led critics, unaccountably, to forget how immersed in the Classics Dryden was, and to accuse him of ignorantly mistranslating Vergil. A clearly baffled Luke Milbourne and William Benson, to name just two of Dryden's first condemners, seem completely to have forgotten about Dryden's extensive Latin training under Busby at Westminster and at Trinity College, Cambridge. Nor, apparently, did it occur to them that *Annus Mirabilis* (for example) stands as proof of Dryden's full comprehension of Vergil's significance to seventeenth-century England. In any case, the philological achievement of the *Aeneis* is documented by the numerous translations and editions that Dryden drew on, and, as in the case of *Fables*, the input from these widely diverse sources highlights the work's uniqueness and commitment to its time and task.[34] Looking back on the accomplishments of the great minds of the past, the *Aeneis* builds on their legacy while recognizing—ultimately—the need to move into the future. Far from being evidence of incompetency or misunderstanding, Dryden's deviations from Vergil and his predecessors rather highlight his own intentions. Perhaps the most telling incidents occur when he either ignores or contradicts a note by the editor of his main Latin text: the 1682 second edition of Carolus Ruæus' "Delphin" *Vergil*, first published in Paris in 1675.[35]

The process begun in the *Aeneis* culminates in *The Secular Masque*, written just before Dryden's death in 1700. The cast of deities joins in the final chorus to celebrate the new century:

> All, all, of a piece throughout;
> Thy Chase had a Beast in View;
> Thy Wars brought nothing about;
> Thy Lovers were all untrue.
> 'Tis well an Old Age is out,
> And time to begin a New.
>
> (86–91)

According to Sir Walter Scott, "the poet alludes to the sylvan sports of James I, the bloody wars of his son, and the licentious gallantry which reigned in the courts of Charles II and James, his successor."[36] Whatever the specifics involved, in these lines Dryden finally yields to history's tide: looking nostalgically at the past, his chorus acknowledges its pastness and expresses hope for a new age. At this point in 1700, however, Dryden was aware that he would have no part of that future other than the legacy he had left for it, and it is significant that the last lines he wrote incorporate the refrain that runs through his works: all of a piece throughout. Despite three hundred years of charges against him for expedient allegiances and an expedient conversion, and despite his own profound uncertainty after 1688, Dryden's nostalgia for and adherence to ideologies and convictions he had expressed as early as 1660 are evident in his late translations, particularly in his *Georgics* and *Aeneis*. Here he begins consciously revisiting old ground, and in so doing achieves consistency and wholeness for his works as a body even as he highlights the inconsistencies of history.

Throughout, this study looks in detail at many passages from the translation, considering them alongside the Latin of the annotated 1682 Delphin text and highlighting echoes and allusions from Dryden's own earlier works and from the numerous English and French poets and commentators he takes into account. Chapters 1 and 2 treat Dryden's theory of translation and view of translator and original poet as equals separated by time and circumstance. The discussion of the translation itself begins in chapter 1 with Dryden's third *Georgic*, the poem in which he contemplates Vergil's epic plans and promises and acknowledges the anachronism of the heroic in contemporary England. Chapter 2 examines the remaining *Georgics*, illustrating that in these translations Dryden attempts to reestablish his powers and emphasizes the common roots of poetry and nature as he prepares for his unheroic epic. Chapter 3 focuses on *Aeneis I*, which performs a similar function to his *Georgics* as it explores ways of utilizing the *Aeneid*'s codes and those of its Renaissance interpreters to address issues of a world in which those codes have no parallels. The final two chapters examine the remaining books, mapping the disillusionment that overtakes the translation as Dryden becomes increasingly cynical about the present even as he realizes the need to relinquish old ideologies and explore new. While the aim here ultimately is to show how Dryden's late translations, especially his *Vergil*, shed new light on his *oeuvre* and the importance of his usually overlooked late works, it is also to argue that the aged poet's struggles in his last decade were the struggles of his contemporaries, and his fragmented translation a reflection of the fragmentation of history and literature in a period of transition.

Time to Begin Anew

1

On Equal Terms with Ancient Wit Engaging

THE LANGUAGE OF THE SKY

O pierlesse Poesye, where is then thy place?
If nor in Princes pallace thou doe sitt:
(And yet is Princes pallace the most fitt)
Ne brest of baser birth doth thee embrace.
Then make thee winges of thine aspyring wit,
And, whence thou camst, flye backe to heauen apace.
—Spenser, *The Shepheardes Calender*

In 1724 and 1725, Dryden's *Georgics* II and I respectively were reprinted alongside the Latin texts and translations by William Benson. Both editions were prefaced by Benson's essays on "Virgil's Husbandry" and made complete by the addition of "Notes Critical, and Rustick." Their declared purpose was to vindicate the "Injustice" done the Roman poet by Dryden "in every respect possible," and to repair some of the damage resulting from his "perfect Ignorance of the Subject which *Virgil* treats of."[1] Nor was Benson the first to express outrage that a man who had probably never owned so much as a pair of pruning shears should undertake to translate what Dryden himself described as "the best Poem of the best Poet" (5:137).

In his *Notes on Dryden's Virgil, 1698*, Luke Milbourne quotes and angrily affirms the confession made in Dryden's dedication of his *Georgics*: "*I have too much injur'd my great Author, I would have Translated him, but fear, according to the literal* French *and* Italian *Phrases I have traduced him.*" This "*Acknowledgement* is true," Milbourne declares, "for never was *Poet* so abus'd, nor *Mankind* so impos'd on, by a *Name* before."[2] He goes on to assert that "this *Virgil* is far the *worst* of all, a Poem neither *tolerable* when Read *alone*, nor when compar'd with what he calls, or few would believe, was the *Original*." As Benson was to do later, Milbourne includes in his volume his own translation of *Georgics* I as he attempts to

27

salvage Vergil's reputation and to demonstrate the nature of "a *true Georgic*, that is, *an exact Art of Husbandry*."[3]

From his earliest to his last works, however, Dryden reveals that he considered himself the most important kind of husbandman. While he may not have known (as Vergil did) what to do with a hoe, he clearly saw his position as the nation's leading poet as one that made him a cultivator of the land: protector of England's health, reaper of her fruit and sower of seeds of her glory.[4] In the "Account" of *Annus Mirabilis* in the letter to Sir Robert Howard (1667), for example, Dryden alludes to Vergil's *Georgics* as he describes his subject material and the nature of his task: "*Omnia sponte sua reddit justissima tellus*. I have had a large, a fair and a pleasant field, so fertile, that, without my cultivating, it has given me two Harvests in a Summer, and in both opress'd the Reaper" (1:52). The georgic imagery used here is present in the poem itself, most significantly as Dryden describes the king's actions following the fire:

> The Father of the people open'd wide
> His stores, and all the poor with plenty fed:
> Thus God's Annointed God's own place suppli'd,
> And fill'd the empty with his daily bread.
>
> (1141–44)

The portrayal of Charles as (semidivine) husbandman doling out his plenty from stores built up in a better season is reinforced by the image drawn a few lines earlier as he "thanks [God] low on his redeemed ground." Placed between these two images, the simile describing the growth of "spreading gladness" in English hearts at their salvation emphasizes the fertility—and security—of the nation under the guidance of its devout and humble husbandman-king:

> As when sharp frosts had long constrain'd the earth,
> A kindly thaw unlocks it with mild rain:
> And first the tender blade peeps up to birth,
> And straight the green fields laugh with promis'd grain.
>
> (1133–36)

God has created the miracle, yet it is granted in response to the prayers of the king, who, as God's anointed and a careful husbandman, is seen as performing in the chosen land a role analogous to that played by God as tender of the vineyard of Israel.[5] By describing his own task in terms used of the king's, Dryden subtly suggests the equation of the power of poet and monarch as sowers, tenders and reapers of England's glory. The poem, after all, celebrates events seen by Dryden's contemporaries as signs of divine displeasure. Like Charles, Dryden has produced victory from defeat, reaped glory from a soil blighted by shame.

Twenty years later in a much grimmer political atmosphere, James II is also portrayed as a "Plain good Man" (3:188.907), who, "as Heav'n encreas'd his Store, / Gave God again, and daily fed his Poor" (3:189.938–39). Still, too, Dryden sees his own role as parallel to his king's. Glancing at the difficulty of his task in the volatile political atmosphere of 1688, he reflects in *Britannia Rediviva* that "Poets are not Prophets, to foreknow / What Plants will take the Blite, and what will grow." Yet, he implies, since God's "Footsteps may be found" even in England's plagued and storm-beaten soil, both poet and king must toil on in the service of God and nation (71–73). As the blight of the Glorious Revolution struck the land, however, the ex-poet laureate clearly found it more and more difficult to reap gain from what he viewed as England's increasingly rank soil.

Throughout the 1690s, Dryden stresses the pain and hardships of his labor. In the dedications of his post-1688 plays particularly, he points to the difficulties of writing and to the barrenness of literature and the political situation, and in the prologue to *Amphitryon* he describes himself not as a farmer but as a "lab'ring Bee" (1). Yet the continuing importance to him of his georgic task is apparent in the world-weary comments made in the dedication of *Eleanora*:

> They say my Talent is Satyre; if it be so, 'tis a Fruitful Age; and there is an extraordinary Crop to gather. But a single hand is insufficient for such a Harvest: They have sown the Dragon's Teeth themselves; and 'tis but just they shou'd reap each other in Lampoons. (3:234)

This oft-quoted passage is almost invariably seen as epitomizing Dryden's bitterness in "this Bad Age" (3:246.368). Yet its georgic imagery also incorporates the hope that he never lost sight of. "[A]lways a poet," Dryden strove continually in the 1690s to weed the rank land as others in William III's "stupid Military State" were busy, Cadmus-like, sowing dragons' teeth (*Letters*, 109; 4:463.53).

The image in the *Amphitryon* prologue of the bee whose "Honey-bag, and Venome, lay so near" is an important one, for it sums up Dryden's double-fold task in his 1690s translations. These works invariably contain a satiric sting, yet equally important are their poetic beauty, freshness and vigor. In the dedication of his *Aeneis*, Dryden would claim that he had followed Spenser and other predecessors as "the Magna Charta of Heroick Poetry; [for I] am too much an *English*-man to lose what my Ancestors have gain'd for me" (5:331). An important article in that Magna Charta was the *imitatio Vergilis* tradition as it had been cast by

Spenser, who followed such earlier Renaissance commentators as Scaliger and Landino. As William Sessions points out, the Georgics were perhaps the key element in this forceful and ubiquitous tradition, for Vergil's "essential strategy" is laid out in these poems, which urge a "series of difficult labors in historical time" for the future glory of a nation.[6] The georgic labors of all Dryden's political poems, which advocate effort in the present for the future, demonstrate his awareness of his place in that tradition, and, as he confronts the tensions so highly-wrought by the late 1680s, he again turns instinctively and compulsively to Vergil even before he applies himself to the complete translation. Attempting to reestablish the "better melodie" that Cuddie had long ago called out for in Spenser's *Shepheardes Calender*,[7] Dryden's poems from *The Hind and the Panther* through his actual *Georgics* derive solace and vigor from their own conviction that poetic renewal and growth work hand-in-hand with natural renewal and growth, and, like Spenser's *Shepheardes Calendar*, they insist that georgic toils performed by true poets can overcome historical disaster. As the following discussion will demonstrate, however, as they respond to contemporary politics and problems they authorize changes in the function of literature and of history in literature that signal a movement away from a Spenserian world view and deny the possibility of an heroic *Aeneis* from the start.

Following hard on the heels of the 1693 group translation of Juvenal, *Examen Poeticum: Being the Third Part of Miscellany Poems* appeared in 1693.[8] As the California editors note, "Dryden's source here, as the two mottoes prefixed to the volume make clear, is Virgil's *Georgics*, where examen means a swarm of bees; thus the volume's title, 'A Poetic Swarm of Bees,' alludes to the contents as honey garnered from various sources" (4:695–96). In the dedication of this volume Dryden complains bitterly about the "Writers of this Age" and their attempts to destroy "our Poetical Church and State" (4:366). The miscellany itself works to fortify and cultivate that state by garnering honey—or translations and original poems—from rising talents like Congreve and Addison as well as from such authorities as Nat Lee and, of course, Dryden himself. The collection is dominated perhaps by Dryden's new Ovid translations, which furnish it with "buddes" from "old stocke," yet earlier poems are also replanted here to bear fruit for a new age. Included, for example, are Dryden's *To the Dutchess on her Return from Scotland, in the Year 1682, To the Pious Memory of the Accomplisht young Lady, Mrs Anne Killigrew* [1685] and *A Song for St. Cecilia's Day, 1687*. Each of these poems deals with the profanation of God's "Heav'nly Gift of Poesy" by contemporary immorality and political and social discord (3:111.57), yet each also stresses poetry's ultimate transcendence of earthly woes.

Emphasis on poetic and georgic toil continues with Dryden's contributions to Tonson's miscellany of the following year, 1694: accompanying the poem to Godfrey Kneller, where he places himself in a "Godlike Race" (76), Dryden's third *Georgic* provides a preview of the 1697 *Vergil* and promises his own ongoing labors. The importance of his efforts and those of other "Godlike" artists had just been highlighted in the tribute *To my Dear Friend Mr. Congreve, On his Comedy, call'd, The Double Dealer,* written between the 1693 and 1694 miscellanies. Looking back over his previous georgic toils, Dryden denounces the "present Age of Wit." Our "syres," he declares, "Fought [as] they Writ":

> Theirs was the Gyant Race, before the Flood:
> And thus, when Charles Return'd, our Empire stood.
> Like Janus he the stubborn Soil Manur'd,
> With Rules of Husbandry the rankness cur'd:
> Tam'd us to manners, when the Stage was rude;
> And boistrous English Wit, with Art indu'd.
> Our Age was cultivated thus at length;
> But what we gain'd in skill we lost in strength.
>
> (1–12)

The poem reflects with nostalgia on the loss described by *Threnodia Augustalis* (1685) of the "Royal Husbandman," who, reviving the "drooping Arts" in England's "fruitful" but "uncultivated" soil, "Plough'd, and Sow'd, and Till'd, / The Thorns he rooted out, the Rubbish clear'd, / And Blest th'obedient Field" (346–59). It ends, however, with Dryden's exhortation to Congreve to "Maintain Your Post" and "shade those Lawrels which descend to You" (64, 75). The labors to which he has devoted his life not only can be but must be continued he argues. While the monarchical line has been disrupted and a dunce crowned with the laureate's wreath ("*Tom* the Second reigns like *Tom* the first" [4:433.48]), true poetical lines are immune to historical disaster, and Dryden's ancestry will be maintained by such poetical sons as Congreve, whose "Genius" can restore poetry's lost vigor and let it "flye backe to heauen apace."

Dryden's insistence, from his first works to his last, on the georgic nature of his poetry reveals that his strong sense of kinship with Vergil stemmed from his discovery in the Roman's works of the kind of "translatability" (*Übersetzbarkeit*) that Walter Benjamin sees as an "essential quality of certain works." As Benjamin adds, this "is not to say that it is essential [such works] be translated; it means rather that a specific significance inherent in the original manifests itself in its translatibility."[9] The specific significance of Vergil's *Georgics* to Dryden's works clearly lay in his own undertaking of what the seventeenth century saw as Vergil's life work: "the rendering," as Sessions puts it, "of a series of cultivating labors with the purpose of redeeming a land and a history from the effects of time's disorders."[10] The agricultural beginnings of both England and Rome obviously reinforced Vergil's usefulness to Dryden as he contemplated growing British imperialism. David Ross comments that "there is a special Italian reason for the *Georgics*: the Romans were a people who remained close to their pastoral and agricultural origins in many important ways."[11] Dryden's frequent allusions to Vergil's *Georgics* in his English poems and the allusions in his own *Georgics* to a number of English poets stress the traditions which root England and her poetry firmly in the land.[12] Yet the echoes from the *Eclogues* and *Aeneid* that also permeate his works indicate that he continually heard Vergil crying out for translation, and the authority and consolation he found in the Roman poet was founded on more than appropriate subject matter. Dryden considered himself and Vergil equals separated by time, and felt that through spiritual commerce with the Ancient he himself could gain access to the sacred truths inherent in his works.

Seeing himself as a seventeenth-century British Vergil, he approached his 1697 translations, as he had his Vergilian-style political poems, believing that his task was not so much to transmit subject matter as to invoke Vergil's spirit in updated material. Like *Astræa Redux* and *Annus Mirabilis*, his own *Eclogues*, *Georgics* and *Aeneis* would become a point in the afterlife of Vergil's originals, a part of their ongoing history, for, as Benjamin observes, translations "that are more than transmissions of subject matter . . . do not so much serve the original as owe their existence to it." As such, "translation [*Übersetzung*] issues from the original—not so much from its life as from its afterlife [*Überleben*]."[13] In Dryden's translations, just as in his poems inspired by Vergil, then, Vergil's voice is still very much alive and relevant while his works, paradoxically, have died in a way, for "in its afterlife—which could not be called that if it were not a transformation and renewal of something living— the original undergoes a change." This change accounts for the lack of faithfulness to the originals for which critics have constantly condemned Dryden's *Vergil*, and, like the Vergilian resonances in his original poems, the work illustrates Benjamin's point that in translation "kinship does not necessarily involve likeness."[14]

Dryden's view that a translation belongs as much to the age in which it is written as an original poem is not only apparent in his works themselves: over two decades he reiterates the liberation of his translations from the original works to which they owe their existence. In the preface to *Sylvae* (1685), he claims of his first actual Vergil translations that they are "of a piece with [Vergil's poetry], and that if he were living, and an *Englishman*, they are such, as he wou'd probably have written" (3:4). A similar assertion ends the discussion of his Juvenal translations in 1693: "[We] have endeavour'd to make [Juvenal] speak that kind of *English*, which he wou'd have spoken had he liv'd in *England*, and had Written to this Age" (4:89). The point is made again with regard to the 1697 *Vergil*: "I have endeavour'd to make *Virgil* speak such *English*, as he wou'd himself have spoken, if he had been born in *England*, and in this present Age" (5:330–31). In each of these statements, Dryden recognizes that a translation must be clothed in contemporary dress if it is to be meaningful; he also recognizes that just as in an original poem a translator is working over the same material that poets have treated in every age.[15] Both points are highlighted in his last words on translation. Contemplating Chaucer's pilgrims in the preface to *Fables*, he observes:

> We have our Fore-fathers and Great Grand-dames all before us, as they were in *Chaucer*'s days; their general Characters are still remaining in Mankind, and even in *England*, though they are call'd by other Names. . . . For Mankind is ever the same, and nothing lost out of Nature, though every thing is alter'd. (Kinsley, 1455)

The view that Nature is always the same and present in all timeless works is central to Dryden's belief that only a true poet can translate true poetry, and, in his insistence on his own Vergilian powers, he implies that though shrouded in the veils of history his own poetry emanates from the same sacred source as Vergil's.

Here Benjamin's theories are again illuminating, for Dryden also believed that his translations were yoked to the original poem by a "shared nucleus . . . best defined as the element which does not lend itself to translation." Like Benjamin, he seemed to view this nucleus governing both original and translation as located in a transcendent realm, to which both poet and translator have access. Benjamin posits the existence of a "tensionless and even silent depository of ultimate truth which all thought strives for." The language of this truth is the *"reine Sprache"*: one pure, true language for which all other language yearns. To explain, he quotes Mallarmé: "Les langues imparfaites en cela que plusieurs, manque la suprême: penser étant écrire sans accessoires, ni chuchotement mais tacite encore l'immortelle parole, la diversité, sur terre, des idiomes empêche personne de proférer les mots qui, sinon se trouveraient, par une frappe unique, elle-même matériellement la vérité."[16] Dryden's own belief in the existence of ultimate truth discernible despite "la diversité, sur terre, des idiomes" underlies what Judith Sloman calls his "logos theory of translation." As she argues, for Dryden all "poetry involves translating ideas from the realm of ideas into whatever human language the translator works in, and translation between two poets is mediated through these ideas."[17]

Like Benjamin's, Dryden's transcendent realm is a sacred one; yet for him it is here that the aesthetic and the sacred are married. All true poetic spirits whether heathen or Christian had access to this realm; in it true poetic spirits conversed and from it all true poetry derived.[18] In the preface to *Religio Laici*, he asserts that it will not "enter easily into my belief, that before the coming of our Saviour, the whole World, excepting only the *Jewish* Nation, shou'd lye under the inevitable necessity of everlasting Punishment, for want of that Revelation, which was confin'd to so small a spot of ground as that of *Palæstine*" (2:99). Dryden found evidence in heathen poetry of an apprehension of the "one Supream Agent or Intellectual Being which we call God" (2:100), and Vergil, the author of the Messianic eclogue, was, of course, was the most "Christian" of all heathen poets.

In the preface to *Annus Mirabilis*, Dryden claims of Vergil, "We see the Soul of the Poet, like that universal one of which he speaks, informing, and moving through all his Pictures" (1:54). In the preface to *Sylvae* (1685), he implies that his own calling as a poet allows him also to hear, through the noise created by diversity of idiom and linguistic multivalence, the language of the universal spirit by which all true poetic souls are informed. Where I have "added and omitted," he says,

> I have thought that I discover'd some Beauty yet undiscover'd . . . which none but a Poet cou'd have found. . . . And where I have enlarg'd them, I desire the false Criticks wou'd not always think that those thoughts are wholly mine, but that either they are they are secretly in the Poet, or may be fairly deduc'd from him: . . . my own is of a piece with his. (3:4)

Like Benjamin who realizes that "[f]idelity in the translation of individual words can almost never fully reproduce the meaning they have in the original,"[19] Dryden recognizes (as he had in his Vergil imitations) that it is often necessary to add, omit, enlarge or substitute words, images or effects when transferring beauty or sentiment from one human language to another. For Dryden as for Benjamin, however, the exercise itself of translation affirms the existence of a transcendent realm.

Benjamin's image of pure language as a broken vessel is useful here:

> Fragments of a vessel which are to be glued together must match one another in the smallest details, although they need not be like one another. In the same way a translation, instead of resembling the meaning of the original, must lovingly and in detail incorporate the original's mode of signification, thus making both the original and translation recognizable as fragments of a greater language, just as fragments are part of a vessel.[20]

The desire of the translator to match fragments of language and the possibility of doing so point to the existence of a lost and universally yearned-for parent language in which truth is embodied. As Dryden contemplates Vergil's works in his pre-1688 poems, the broken fragments are those of sacred history and to piece them together is to piece together the story of Judeo-Christian history. That is, by incorporating contemporary material into Vergil's original "mode of signification" and matching together segments of English and Roman history, he not only draws didactic comparisons between those histories, but, more importantly, imbues both his own and Vergil's text with typological significance. Because of the implied exchange of poetic voices, Dryden is not merely copying pleasing images; he is indicating that "informing and moving through all his Pictures," as through those of Vergil before him, is the spirit of the supreme intellectual being, who "with his divine Providence, over-rules and guides all actions to the secret end he has ordain'd them" (17:271). As the pieces come together, Dryden also discovers what George de F. Lord sees as the source of hope in his "political poems from *Astræa Redux* (1660) to *Absalom and Achitophel* (1681)": "a central myth of renewal and restoration following a crisis of civil war, defeat, destruction or exile."[21] After 1688, however, the pieces of Roman and English history no longer fit together. Bewildered, Dryden turns from history to mythology. As he fits together his fragmented stories with pieces from kindred poetic spirits he still discovers a central myth of renewal and restoration following historical disaster; the fabric of this myth, however, is the sacred language of the sky which all true poets speak and which is rooted in nature, and the consolation poured forth from the reconstructed vessel is not the political wisdom and guidance offered by historical typology but moral truth and the assurance of poetic and natural renewal and growth.

Dryden's movement toward emphasis on nature's cycles and regeneration and away from confidence in history's cycles is apparent in his last poem as poet laureate and spokesperson for the Stuart regime. At the heart of *Britannia Rediviva* (1688)—a celebration of the birth of James II's and Mary's son—is the image of a new age dawning with a new century: "Betwixt two Seasons comes th'Auspicious Heir, / This Age to blossom, and the next to bear" (17–18). Once more, then, a "central myth of renewal and restoration" is set against historical chaos, with which the poet is equally concerned. Yet, as the title of the poem and its epigraph from Vergil's *Georgics* suggest, national restoration is much more closely connected than ever before with the promise of regeneration inherent in nature. References to Scripture and sacred history still provide a typological background, but imagery of nature and georgic toil and allusions to Vergil's *Georgics* dominate the poem and supply its assurance. Not only is the birth of "th'Auspicious Heir" inextricably linked with the turning of the seasons, but to look on his "Manly" face is "to look / On the fair Frontispiece of Nature's Book" (105–7). The comfort offered subdues the fear underlying the poem that it and its subject, the prince and Jacobite monarchy, will fall prey to "Blite" (72). The plagues and storms of contemporary history may assail the nation, but the seasons always turn "breeding / Lilacs out of the dead land."

Even before exerting their influence on *Britannia Rediviva*, Vergil's *Georgics* (as Earl Miner notes) are an important force in *The Hind and the Panther* (1687), which is also dominated by images of planting, tending and toiling.[22] As Zwicker comments, the poem stands out from Dryden's other works as a chinese box of myth, allegories and enigmas. Its elusiveness and complexity, he concludes, reflect the "larger puzzles and paradoxes" in which the poet found himself in the late 1680s.[23] The significance of *The Hind and the Panther* on Dryden's road to his translations is that at the moment he seeks refuge in both nature and myth, he first makes "the bold assimilation of poet to savior" which shapes all his subsequent works.[24] Accordingly, the poem also anticipates the methods and concerns of his 1690s works, most importantly their reliance on the truth inherent in old tales and their consciousness of a poetic apostolic tradition.

At the beginning of the third section Dryden reflects on the mode he has chosen:

> Much malice mingl'd with a little wit
> Perhaps may censure this mysterious writ,
> Because the Muse has peopl'd *Caledon*
> With *Panthers*, *Bears*, and *Wolves*, and Beasts unknown,
> As if we were not stock'd with monsters of our own.
> Let *Æsop* answer, who has set to view,
> Such kinds as *Greece* and *Phrygia* never knew;
> And mother *Hubbard* in her homely dress
> Has sharply blam'd a *British Lioness*,
> That *Queen*, whose feast the factious rabble keep,
> Expos'd obscenely naked and a-sleep.
> Led by those great examples, may not I
> The wanted organs of their words supply?
> If men transact like brutes 'tis equal then
> For brutes to claim the privilege of men.
>
> (3:161.1–15)

Attention is drawn to the marriage of sacred and secular: the poem is at once "mysterious writ" and beast fable. By demonstrating that precedents for his work can be found in the oral (and later written) tradition of Æsop as well as in the English traditions of Chaucer, Spenser and the Reformation, Dryden applies to poetry the Hind's earlier argument:[25]

> Before the Word was written, said the *Hind*:
> Our Saviour preach'd his Faith to humane kind,
> From his Apostles the first age receiv'd
> Eternal truth, and what they taught, believ'd.
> Thus by tradition faith was planted first.
>
> (3:148.305–10)

In effect, he argues that in poetry too "following ages leaning on the past, / May rest upon the Primitive at last" (3:150.355–56). The "Eternal truth" first planted orally by Æsop (and, as we learn in part 3, by Homer) has been transmitted through the ages to Dryden's own poem. Such truth can be traced because the poets' and the Hind's stories all contain echoes of the single eternal language in which it is planted. Dryden's role as secular apostle is underscored at the climax of the poem, when the Hind, "looking upward to her kindred sky, / As once our Saviour own'd his Deity, / Pronounc'd his words — *she whom ye seek am I*" (3:151.396–98). Since the Hind's words are Christ's, as the narrator of her story, Dryden assumes the task of the Apostles to whom, as he implies in lines 305–10 quoted above and as Spinoza had asserted in 1670, "God manifested Himself . . . through the mind of Christ."[26] The equation of his poetic with the Hind's sacred power is reinforced in part 3 when she recognizes that poets too are inspired by and speak the language of her "kindred sky": "*Homer*, who learn'd the language of the sky, / The seeming *Gordian* knot would soon unty" (3:185.821–22). By suggesting the sanctity of his own powers in this politico-theological poem, Dryden indicates that he himself is one of those "Guardian Angels," who, he claims in his "Discourse," are "appointed by God Almighty, as his Vicegerents, for the Protection and Government of Cities, Provinces, Kingdoms, and Monarchies; and those as well of Heathens, as of true Believers" (4:19). Given the importance to him at this time of a poetic apostolic tradition, he was perhaps thinking here of Spinoza's reminder that "Moses admitted, indeed, that there were beings . . . who acted as God's vicegerents — that is beings to whom God had given the right, authority, and power to direct nations and care for them."[27] In any case, Dryden argues in *The Hind and the Panther* that his right to direct the nation derives from his ability to commune (in the language of the sky) with his poetic ancestors, and he is careful to place himself at the end of a line of sacred fathers, for "pure" poetic tradition is transmitted in a legitimate "lineal course" (3:157.615), just as the

"pure" traditions of the church are passed on "from sire to son . . . /
Where ev'ry age do's on another move" (3:146.213, 217–18).[28]

When Dryden turned to his translations of Vergil's *Georgics*, then, he
was simply continuing the labors he had pursued throughout his career
and with particular vigor and determination in the late 1680s and early
1690s. Because he clearly viewed true poetic endeavor as a perpetuation—or translation—of the toils of poetic forefathers, his translations
of Vergil's *Georgics* were, from the start, no less English *Georgics* than
(say) Spenser's Vergilian toils. As the following discussion of *Georgics*
III will demonstrate, however, when Dryden confronts Vergil's heroic
in this poem and is forced to contemplate the relevance and usefulness
in the 1690s of the English *imitatio Vergilis* tradition, he apprehends—
though he cannot yet accept—the impossibility of upholding this histor-
ically-based legacy. Unlike Vergil and unlike Spenser, Dryden (as a
Jacobite and adherer to the divine right of monarchy) could not look
to the future in hope; nor, therefore, could he advocate labors in historical time for the glory of the future as he had in poems like *Astræa Redux*,
Annus Mirabilis and *Absalom and Achitophel*. Instead, as he had begun to
do in *The Hind and the Panther*, he stresses the common roots of poetry
and nature, deriving and offering solace from the fact that both are immune to the destructive forces of history. In so doing he lays the foundations of his own *Georgics* and his *Aeneis*, where his unwilling rejection
of the heroic has implications that go far beyond Dryden's own works.

Satire Will Have Room, Where'er I Write

> But ah *Mecænas* is yclad in claye,
> And great *Augustus* long ygoe is dead:
> And all the worthies liggen wrapt in leade,
> That matter made for Poets on to play.
> —Spenser, *The Shepheardes Calender*

While the dedication of the *Georgics* expresses concern that the translations injure Vergil, Dryden had earlier admitted, "I have labour'd and I
may say I have cultivated the Georgiques with more care than any other
part of [Vergil], and I think myself with more success" (*Letters*, 86). The
programmatic introduction of *Georgics* III outlines the nature of that
cultivation: the pruning and planting which led to the changes in Vergil's landscape that Dryden feared would be construed as "traduction"
(5:137). As noted above, *The Third Book of Virgil's Georgicks* first appears
in Tonson's *The Annual Miscellany for the Year 1694: Being the Fourth Part*

of Miscellany Poems, where it reinforces Dryden's georgic toils in the aftermath of the Glorious Revolution. Yet Dryden was also aware of its importance "as an Essay" and "an Example" of the complete *Vergil* (*Letters*, 64). He chose this particular *Georgic* because Vergil's announcement of epic plans allowed him to draw attention to his own position in 1690s England and to introduce his *Vergil* as fully implicated in contemporary concerns as well as in the timeless question of poetry's place in society.

The cultivation of English poetry undertaken by the "lab'ring Bees" of *Examen Poeticum* is the opening subject of Dryden's third *Georgic*. The first lines reveal that just as in "To Sir Godfrey Kneller," his only other poem in the 1694 miscellany, Dryden is again concerned with the status of poetry in "these Inferiour Times" (4:465.118):

> Thy Fields, propitious *Pales*, I reherse;
> And sing thy Pastures in no vulgar Verse,
> *Amphrysian* Shepherd; the *Lycæan* Woods;
> *Arcadia's* flow'ry Plains, and pleasing Floods.
> All other Themes, that careless Minds invite,
> Are worn with use; unworthy me to write.
>
> (1–6)[29]

As Vergil's opening lines call upon "mighty" deities, a prayer-like incantation is effected by his repetition of the vocative second-person pronoun: "Te quoque, magna Pales, et te memorande canemus / Pastor ab Amphryso: vos sylvæ amnesq; Lycæi."[30] Lauderdale's "Thou mighty Pales, and ye Gods . . . You great Apollo"[31] is typical of previous translators' attempts to recreate Vergil's reverent address. Only Dryden makes a territorial claim: his focus is on "Fields," and his verse will celebrate "Pastures". The verb "reherse," which signals the retelling of an old story, indicates that these are to be fabulous fields and pastures, and the emphasis on poetry itself becomes clear in the rendering of Vergil's appeal to (what is literally) "You woods and streams of Arcadia."

As Ruæus's note implies, Vergil is requesting fruitfulness in his land and his poetry: his invocation to Arcadia's waters and trees provide a reminder that the spirit of Pan, whose name is also Lycæus, permeates the countryside (n. 2). The only basis for Dryden's "flow'ry Plains" and "pleasing" Floods is surely the Arcadias of the pre–civil war Jacobean and Caroline court poets. The English concern of these lines is underlined by the rearrangement of Vergil's balanced tripartite appeal so as to include among Apollo's pastures "*Lycæan* Woods" and "*Arcadia's* flow'ry Plains, and pleasing Floods." In his note to "Pastoral 3d." Dryden comments that "*Phoebus*, not *Pan*, is here call'd the God of Shepherds: The

Poet alludes to the same Story, which he touches in the beginning of the Third *Georgic*" (6:811). His reason for drawing attention to "*Phoebus*, not *Pan*" as the deity present in what is now his poem may lie in his "May Day" song of the early 1690s. As Anne Barbeau Gardiner argues, that poem's exiled Pan is quite clearly James II.[32] By placing "*Lycæan* Woods" and Arcadian fields (or Pan's territory) under the care of Apollo Dryden suggests here too the absence of Pan's nurturing presence.[33] His connection of *Georgics* III with the pastorals may also indicate that the "Fields" of this poem are those "pleasing Fields and Native Home" of *The First Pastoral*, where the banished Meliboeus seems to represent Dryden himself: "exile[d]", as Miner put it, "in his own land" and forced to speak out through translation.[34]

Dryden is pointing, then, to England's special need for Apollo's protection. The evocation of "*Arcadia*'s flow'ry Plains" perhaps even provides a nostalgic reminder of Ben Jonson's and Inigo Jones' court masques where the monarch appeared, amidst a dance of nymphs, floods and flowers, if not always as Pan yet still as "a god of power, the center of a universe."[35] Despite Pan's (or James II's) absence, however, Dryden is confident in his verse's power. He opens with an assertion of subject matter, not, as Vergil does, with a plea for inspiration, and the replacement of Vergil's "mighty" Pales with his own "propitious" Pales suggests that his verse is sanctioned by a providential power.[36] The importance of his own powers as Apollo's spokesperson is highlighted in lines 5–6.

Dryden's voice makes itself felt in line 2 where the announcement of a song "in no vulgar Verse" is a reminder both of his earlier allusion to himself as a "Mortal Muse," who will "rehearse" Anne Killigrew's "Praise" in "no ignoble Verse" (16–17), and of his plea that Eleanora accept the "Tribute of no vulgar Muse" (360). His subsequent rejection of "Themes" that occupy "careless minds" reinforces his presence; over and again after 1688 he laments being "worn with Cares" (4:434.66). (Lauderdale translates Vergil's "vacuas . . . mentes" [3] as "the thoughtless Croud" [6]; May has "light minds."[37]) Having made *Georgics* III as much his poem as Vergil's, Dryden then points to his own georgic task. The interpolated refusal to undertake what is "unworthy me to write" has no precedent in previous translations; it does, however, recall the opening of *Paradise Regained* with its promise "to tell of deeds" that are "Worthy t'have not remaind so long unsung." As Milton does there, Dryden could also claim to have in a way "ere while the happy Garden sung," and, as Milton perhaps did, Dryden clearly felt an affinity with the "glorious Eremite."[38] *Georgics* III, then, announces poetic labors in a postlapsarian age; it also immediately points to the difficulties Dryden faced.

Vergil's "Tentanda via est, qua me quoq; possim / Tollere humo, victorque virum volitare per ora" (8–9) ("I must attempt a path by which I too can lift myself heavenward and, as victor, fly on human lips") becomes in Dryden: "New ways I must attempt, my groveling Name / To raise aloft, and wing my flight to Fame" (13–14). His emphasis on innovation ("New ways") has roots only in his own thinking and works in the 1690s. It recalls his assumption of Daedalian arts in his rendition of Juvenal's third satire:

> Then thus *Umbricius*, (with an Angry Frown,
> And looking back on this degen'rate Town,)
> Since Noble Arts in *Rome* have no support,
>
> .   .   .   .
>
> 'Tis time to give my just Disdain a vent,
> And, Cursing, leave so base a Government.
> Where *Dedalus* his borrow'd Wings laid by,
> To that obscure Retreat I chuse to fly.
>
> (37–39, 43–46)

The embittered Umbricius is clearly a mouthpiece for Dryden himself.[39] His intention to take up Daedalus' "borrow'd Wings" (Juvenal has "*fatigatas*" or "weary" wings [25]) and fly to "that obscure Retreat" (Dryden's interpolation) points to Dryden's own decision to "borrow" cunning arts and fly (as Daedalus did from the base "Government" of a tyrant) to the obscure retreat of translation.

The personal and political implications of the opening section of *Georgics* III certainly suggest that Dryden had the Juvenal passage in mind here. The same complaint about "Noble Arts" having no support in "this degen'rate Town" is implicit in the poet's "care"-burdened task,[40] while a refusal to comply with "so base a Government" is inherent in the adjective "groveling," which subtly contrasts Dryden and Vergil. In the "Discourse," Dryden condemns Horace for his "groveling," in effect accusing him of being "a Temporizing Poet, a well Manner'd Court Slave" (4:64–65). If he is thinking here of the cruel conjectures after 1688 that he would reconvert,[41] he is also aware, as Sloman points out, that his own name is "anything but 'groveling' at this time," and that by 1694 even his worst enemies could hardly accuse him of pandering to William III's court.[42] By means of irony, then, the lines make a distinction between Vergil's task (as a temporizing poet) and Dryden's, which still requires the satiric sting and disguised arts of the Juvenal translations.

Having drawn attention to his role as noble poet in a "degen'rate" regime (the old Lycæan woods), Dryden goes on to establish a distinction between himself and William III. As Sloman notes of lines 13–14, "the image of conquest, which is in the original, suggests a parallel between William III's military activities and Dryden's literary activities."[43] It seems likely, however, that Dryden chose here to ignore Vergil's "victor" so as to distance himself from the military conqueror that he subsequently satirizes. As he translates Vergil's announcement of epic plans he sets up a contrast between his own socially beneficial toil and the destructiveness of what he refers to in "To Sir Godfrey Kneller" as a "Stupid Military State" (53).

He begins by shifting Vergil's focus on epic to his own on translation:

> Primus ego in patriam mecum (modo vita supersit)
> Aonio rediens deducam vertice Musas:
> Primus Idumæas referam tibi, Mantua, palmas:
> Et viridi in campo templum de marmore ponam.
>
> (10–13)

becomes

> I, first of *Romans* shall in Triumph come
> From conquer'd *Greece*, and bring her Trophies home:
> With Foreign Spoils adorn my native place;
> And with *Idume*'s Palms, my *Mantua* grace.
> Of *Parian* Stone a Temple will I raise.
>
> (15–19)

Dryden has omitted Vergil's "modo vita supersit," which points to future intentions "if life enough remain"; his own concern is with these translations. His promise to bring back (interpolated) "Foreign Spoils" from "conquer'd Greece" rather than "lead the muses from Aonian heights" (a literal translation) recalls his tribute "To the Earl of Roscommon, on his Excellent Essay on Translated Verse." There, in very similar terms, he describes the development of translation: "For conquering *Rome* / With *Grecian* Spoils brought *Grecian* Numbers home" (7–8). There, too, translation is husbandry, for poetry is a "noble Plant" whose seeds were "translated first" from the East and "in *Grecian* Gardens nurst" (1–4). By alluding to that poem Dryden also aligns himself as translator with Roscommon, who "The Muses Empire . . . restor'd agen, / In *Charles* his Reign" (28–29). For, the implied parallel between his work and Roscommon's is reinforced by the concern the *Georgics* passage shares with that poem for illustrating the "Manly sweetness" of English verse and for demonstrating that if well cultivated it can achieve, like Italian verse, "all the Graces a good Ear affords" (25, 18).

Dryden's notion of grace is interpolated, and by turning Vergil's

apostrophe "to you Mantua" into a reference to "my Mantua" he indicates that he indeed has his own Mantua, or England, in mind. Certainly, the idea of gracing his native land with poetic temples is at the
heart of "To Congreve" published at the same time as *Georgics* III. There
he praises the playwright because "Firm *Dorique* Pillars found Your
solid Base: / The Fair *Corinthian* Crowns the higher Space; / Thus all
below is Strength, and all above is Grace" (17–19). Grace and native
English strength are achieved in these lines, as in lines 17–19 of *Georgics*
III, through the domination of "*Teuton* Monosyllables," which also form
their triplet endings. In the dedication of the *Aeneis*, Dryden comments
that "Poetry requires Ornament, and that is not to be had from our Old
Teuton Monosyllables" (5:336). Yet, as Winn observes, "the wonderful
muscularity of . . . parts of the *Virgil* comes from his fondness for '*Teuton*
Monosyllables,' especially in his verbs."[44] Here the combination of
Latin and Saxon vocabulary (that Winn also notes as a virtue of the
translations) demonstrates Dryden's point in the dedication that "I
Trade both with the Living and the Dead for the enrichment of our
Native Language" (5:336). The criticism of William III's expensive
continental wars implicit there in his subsequent observation, "I carry
not out the Treasure of the Nation, which is never to return; but what
I bring from *Italy*, I spend in *England*," also seems to underlie his interpolation of "Foreign Spoils" here. Dryden's own "Triumph" will enrich
and strengthen his native place, while William III's costly and dubious
victories continue to drain England's treasury.

The pitting of poetic powers against military is developed as Vergil's
plans to glorify Octavian Caesar are overturned. Dryden first distances
himself from Vergil's Caesar. Vergil's dative personal pronouns and chi-
astic syntax accentuate the interdependence of his glory and Caesar's:
"In medio *mihi* Caesar erit, templumque tenebit. / *Illi* victor *ego*, et Tyrio
conspectus in ostro" (emphasis added) (16–17). Lauderdale's expan-
sion of the second line captures the sense of the Latin: "While I in purple Robes as Victor shine, / And to his Glory render Rites divine"
(22–23). Admitting his restrictions as a translator, Dryden grants, "Full
in the midst shall mighty *Cæsar* stand: / Hold the chief Honours; and
the Dome command. / Then I, conspicuous in my *Tyrian* Gown, / (Sub-
mitting to his Godhead my Renown)" shall preside over games (23–26).
Rather than being an integral part of the scene in the temple on the
bank of winding Mincius, however, Dryden's Caesar rudely intrudes
upon his idyllic Arcadia, "Where the slow *Mincius* through the Vally
strays: / Where cooling Streams invite the Flocks to drink; / And Reeds
defend the winding Waters Brink" (20–22). Although Milbourne calls
line 21 "a Patch on a Face which needed it not" (175), Dryden's mean-
dering and lyrical lines create an inviting poetic world which is dis-

rupted with a jolt as "mighty Caesar" enters unannounced at line 23 wielding his "Honours" and (interpolated) commands. The notion of a power conflict is emphasized in the *"impertinent Parenthesis"* interpolated at line 26.[45] Here, however, Dryden undermines Caesar's authority. While he may be forced as translator and as ex-poet laureate and English subject to watch a military leader "Hold the chief Honours" and intrude upon his poetic ambitions, Dryden is confident in the legitimacy of his own powerful "Godhead."

The yoking of "Gown" and "Renown" effected by the couplet (Vergil's emphasis on "Tyrian purple" has been sacrificed for a focus on the "Gown") picks up an issue from the dedication of *Examen Poeticum*: "Why am I grown Old, in seeking so barren a Reward as Fame? The same Parts and Application, which have made me a Poet, might have rais'd me to any Honours of the Gown, which are often given to Men of as little Learning and less Honesty than myself" (4:363). The same discontent over his hardships and loss of his laureateship undoubtedly pervades these lines.[46] However, the couplet also echoes that which celebrates Roscommon's poetic achievement: *"Roscommon* first in Fields of Honour known, / First in the peaceful Triumphs of the Gown" (70–71). The same conviction in "Honour known" or won from "peaceful Triumphs of the Gown" underlies the yoking of "Gown" and "Renown" here, and the irony of the poet's submission of his renown to Caesar's "Godhead" is highlighted by the following lines in which ephemeral earthly victories are contrasted with the poet's divinely-sanctioned "Gown" or fame.

As Milbourne notes, Dryden's comment that his "Games" shall be "Reserv'd for Caesar, and ordain'd by me" is "quite beside the Cushion," or interpolation.[47] Here, however, Dryden stresses the divine nature of true poetic endeavor as he had from his earliest works. In *To My Lord Chancellor, Presented on New-years-day* (1662), for example, he indicates that the poet's laws lie in nature, arguing that after 1660 "the Muses stand restor'd again / To that great charge which Nature did ordain" (23–24). Likewise in "To Anne Killigrew" he reminds his "lubrique and adult'rate age" that the muse's "Harmony was first ordain'd above" (63, 60). Dryden's games, then, (like Vergil's before his) are part of a greater "charge which Nature did ordain." As they are "ordain'd" here in the shadow of "mighty *Cæsar,*" Dryden probably also has in mind his recently translated description of the "Games decreed" by Apollo after the slaying of a tyrant. Appearing in "The First Book of Ovid's *Metamorphoses"* in the 1693 miscellany, the passage concludes by emphasizing that "The Prize was Fame" (601). As Dryden now considers the setting of his own games (or poetic endeavors) he turns again to the subject of "Fame," implicitly contrasting Caesar's wars with the peaceful triumphs honored by Apollo's divine laurel.

As he imagines himself "with Olive crown'd" (32), Dryden does not turn, as Vergil does, "with joy to lead the solemn procession to the shrine to look upon the sacrificed heifers" (Ruæus, 22–23). Rather, he considers,

> Ev'n now methinks the publick shouts I hear;
> The passing Pageants, and the Pomps appear.
> I, to the Temple will conduct the Crew:
> The Sacrifice and Sacrificers view.
>
> (33–36)

While Vergil's sober religious procession becomes distant "publick shouts" and then "passing Pageants" and "Pomps," the sacrifice itself is mocked as a "Crew" (a word used of Milton's pandemonium) is led to the temple where "Sacrifice and Sacrificers" equally provide a spectacle. The poetic sentiment is that of detached observation and recalls the opening of Dryden's 1685 translation of Lucretius's second book. There the poet reflects how "sweet" it is to look down from "Vertues heights, with wisdom well supply'd, / And all the *Magazins* of Learning fortifi'd" on "humane kind, / Bewilder'd in the Maze of Life, and blind" (8–11). In view of the reminder of the divine nature of poetry just supplied by the image of poet as ordainer, the Lucretian philosophy behind these lines (and behind Dryden's *Georgics* as a whole) also offers Christian comfort. The "passing pageants," like "This crumbling Pageant" at the end of the "Song for St. Cecilia's Day, 1687," will be devoured by "the last and dreadful hour," yet the "heavenly harmony," which can be glimpsed in poetry, will ensure that "Musick" shall have the last word as it "untune[s] the Sky" (3:203.55–63).

Just as Dryden probably had the chaotic situation of 1687 in mind as he referred to "This crumbling Pageant" in the "St. Cecilia" song, the "passing pageants" here take on contemporary significance when considered in the context of the following lines. Dryden now turns to "Where the proud Theatres disclose the Scene: / Which interwoven *Britains* seem to raise, / And shew the Triumph which their Shame displays" (37–40). The poet's irony and bitterness belong to a world entirely different from that of Vergil's "proud Theatres" where Roman victory is glorified as "Th'inwoven Britons lift the purple fold" to mark "the turning scenes."[48] Dryden's notion of "shame" is his addition. Noting the British perspective which this gives the lines, Milbourne objected, "as if it had been so great a shame for a *little Island*, under a great many *petty Kings* of *different Interests*, to be worsted by the *Veterane united*

Armies of the Roman Empire."[49] Dryden's interest in Williamite rather than ancient Britain, however, is signalled by the introduction of seeming British victories. The subsequent rendition of Vergil's naval triumphs, which emphasizes the contemporary implications of the passage, reinforces the possibility that the "Scene" Dryden has in mind is the Battle of the Boyne (and perhaps the victory off Barfleur in 1692) in which Britons could be considered "interwoven" in Dutch William's foreign campaigns. The "triumph" at Boyne, after all, was at the price of much English and Irish suffering and hardship, and most of the commanders of William's troops in Ireland were Dutch not English.[50] In the following lines English "shame" is presented as a characteristic of Williamite England.

Again Dryden stresses ignominy rather than glory as he describes the scenes from Caesar's wars depicted "o're the Gate":

> The Crowd shall *Cæsar's Indian* War behold;
> The *Nile* shall flow beneath; and on the side,
> His shatter'd Ships on Brazen Pillars ride.
> Next him *Niphates* with inverted Urn,
> And drooping Sedge, shall his *Armenia* mourn;
> And *Asian* Cities in our Triumph born.
> With backward Bows the *Parthians* shall be there;
> And, spurring from the Fight confess their fear.
> A double Wreath shall crown our *Cæsar's* Brows;
> Two differing Trophies from two different Foes.
> *Europe* with *Africk* in his Fame shall join;
> But neither Shoar his Conquest shall confine.

(42–53)

The focus here is on the suffering and destructiveness of war. Dryden notes the Parthians' fear rather than their cowardice ("fidentemque fuga"). Likewise, mourning Niphates "with inverted urn / And drooping Sedge" is a very sympathetic version of Vergil's proud "pulsumque Niphaten" (routed Niphates). The description also draws a parallel between this scene and the one sketched by the stage directions at the opening of *Albion and Albanius*. There Thamesis, who is mourning over the national devastation caused by Augusta's unfaithfulness, is framed by "broken Reeds, Bullrushes, Sedge, &c. with his Urn Reverst" (15:20). The same concern for the nation expressed there is inherent here in the victory itself, which is undermined from the start by the interpolated image of "shatter'd Ships." It is further mocked by the subject matter of the moment when the focus turns to the triumphant procession: "Asian Cities in our Triumph born." The honor involved in such a conquest (from an English point of view) is indicated by Dry-

den's glorification of Prince Rupert and the Duke of Albermarle in
Annus Mirabilis: "With them no riotous pomp, nor *Asian* train, / T'infect
a Navy with their gawdy fears" (205–6).

Audiences used to Dryden's self-references and repeated themes and
images could not have failed to note the difference in tone between this
cynical rendering of Vergil and such poems as *Annus Mirabilis* where
Vergilian allusions glorify English history and conquest. The passage as
a whole, for example, can be contrasted with the solemn and glorious
procession in "To His Sacred Majesty," which Vergil's third *Georgic*
seems to have influenced. There Dryden uses his classical allusion to
celebrate Charles' semidivine kingship:

> Next to the sacred Temple you are led,
> Where waites a Crown for your more sacred Head:
> How justly from the Church that Crown is due,
> Preserv'd from ruine and restor'd by you!
>
> (45–48)

Clearly Dryden's own *Georgic* is diametrically opposed to such a passage; besides, the publication of a such a translation soon after the spec-
tacular victory at Barfleur in 1692 is in itself telling. As the reaction to
his silence on the death of Queen Mary would demonstrate, what Dryden did not say was noted almost as much as what he did say, and his
refusal here to use Vergil to honor Barfleur surely did not go unno-
ticed.[51]

In fact, the nostalgic reminder of the glory days (for Dryden and, in
his view, for England) of *Annus Mirabilis* lurks behind this passage, and
yokes the nation's state of prosperity with its monarch. By rendering
"Gangaridum faciam, victorisque arma Quirini" simply "*Cæsar's Indian
Wars*," Dryden ignores the suggestion inherent in the word "Quirinus"
that Octavian is a second founder of Rome: a point which Ruæus elaborates on in a note (n. 27). The continuation into the eighteenth century
of seventeenth-century interest in the figure of Octavian or Augustus
as *pater patriae* is illustrated in (for example) Samuel Cobb's *Clavis Virgiliana* (1714).[52] Cobb stresses that Vergil's purpose in the *Georgics* is to
counsel his master "how to behave himself in his New Monarchy, so as
to gain the Affections of his Subjects, and deserve to be called the *Father
of his Country*."[53] Dryden was surely counting on his audience's awareness of the importance of the figure of founder at the center of the victories described. His replacement of Vergil's Quirinus with an ambitious
military commander makes a point about the type of regime in which
his own *Georgics* are composed. A telling contrast between this work
and his Vergilian poems of the 1660s is drawn through the echo of
Annus Mirabilis in these lines.

The depiction of *"Cæsar's Indian* Wars" above the flowing Nile provides a reminder of the picture at the end of *Annus Mirabilis* of a prosperous and imperial England scented with eastern spices. Portraying Charles II as the major reason for that prosperity, Dryden seems there to have had Vergil's *Georgics* III, lines 27–28, in mind as he described English subjects' love of their king: "So glad Egyptians see their Nilus rise, / And in his plenty their abundance find" (183–84). As these lines appear immediately before the section "Prince Rupert and Duke Albemarl Sent to Sea," in which "war, severly, like itself appears" impeded by "no riotous pomp, nor *Asian* train," it seems likely that Dryden was thinking back to that moment of English glory as he translated the above passage. Notably, Vergil's swelling Nile ("Atque hic undantem bello, magnumque fluentem / Nilum" [27–28]) is now simply the flowing Nile, its significance as an emblem of imperial bounty lost.

The "shatter'd ships" of *Georgics* III also appear first in *Annus Mirabilis*; there, however, they are enemy ships not Caesar's own (89). In effect, then, Dryden places the victors of this military triumph in the position of the Dutch enemy in *Annus Mirabilis*. In so doing he anticipates the notion of victor-vanquished, which lies at the heart of *Alexander's Feast*:[54] the victorious fleet celebrated in *Annus Mirabilis* (and depicted as the source of the triumph here) has become a point of shame, so that even victory now is a type of defeat. Although in 1694 the image of "shatter'd ships" must have brought to mind specifically the numerous defeats suffered by the English navy before Barfleur, the decline marked by the contrast between the two poems points to a larger comment about the shattering of national pride and glory.[55]

Just as in *Annus Mirabilis* English victory is traced ultimately to her king, so here the source of the shame is seen as the military conqueror who dominates the triumph. The implications of this for England are highlighted by the connection of the double-wreathed *"Cæsar"* with William III, particularly in the line referred to by Milbourne as "an *absurd addition"*: "But neither Shoar his Conquest shall confine." Simply to use the word "conqueror" or "conquest" in this way at a time when the debate over whether William's title should be founded on conquest or succession was still raging signals political comment. However, the unbounded ambition attributed to Caesar by the interpolated line links him even more closely with England's warlike king. In the pamphlet for which he was hanged, William Anderton (for example) argued explicitly that King William planned only "to serve his own Ambition, and unsatisfied Thirst after Empire in particular."[56] Many other Jacobites made the same complaint, while Dryden's own post-1688 plays often make oblique comments on William III through portraits of conquerors with uncontrolled ambition.[57]

As Dryden reflects upon the "Fame" and "Trophies" won by such a Caesar, however, he turns back to the question of poetic fame and the "Trophies" he himself "shall in Triumph [bring] / From conquer'd *Greece*." Overturning the tail end of Vergil's poetic plans so as to begin the conclusion of his own programmatic introduction, he focuses on ʳ   ʳigins as he offers some comfort for the historical decline he has juʃ̣ ʍighlighted. In the process he again points to the importance of his poetic labors in a postlapsarian age, while his denunciation of martial heroism puts him in the position of the Son in *Paradise Regained*:

> They err who count it glorious to subdue
> By Conquest farr and wide, to over-run
> Large Countries, and in field great Battels win,
> Great Cities by assault: what do these Worthies,
> But rob and spoil, burn, slaughter, and enslave
> Peaceable Nations. . . .[58]

Like those of Milton's "glorious Eremite," Dryden's toils demonstrate the patience needed in a fallen world, and place faith in the laws of bountiful nature.

Vergil declares he will grace his temple with "breathing statues of Parian marble" that trace the founding of Rome's Trojan ancestors to Jove himself: "Stabunt et Parii lapides, spirantia signa, / Assaraci pro-les, demissæque ab Jove gentis / Nomina: Trosque parens, et Trojæ Cynthius auctor" (34–36). His emphasis is again on a nation and its divine origins (demissæque ab Jove gentis), its founder (auctor) and its ancestry (proles). Dryden, however, is interested in a larger question of history and its relation to art:

> The *Parian* Marble, there, shall seem to move,
> In breathing Statues, not unworthy *Jove*:
> Resembling Heroes, whose Etherial Root,
> Is *Jove* himself, and *Cæsar* is the Fruit.
> *Tros* and his Race the Sculptor shall employ;
> And He the God, who built the Walls of *Troy*.

> (54–59)

The image of the deathless plant in these lines recalls the opening of *The Hind and the Panther* where the pursued Hind "view'd" her "half hu-mane, half divine" offspring and "their race renew'd; / Their corps to perish, but their kind to last, / So much the deathless plant the dying fruit surpass'd" (3:123.10, 21–24). By portraying Caesar as the "Fruit" of such a plant Dryden suggests here too that while individual heroes die, the "Race" is eternal, and the plant anchored in the heroic archetype will go on producing new Caesars. The job of the divinely-inspired artist to tend and cultivate the immortal plant is also emphasized.

The power Dryden attributes to the artist is enormous, and works to mark a distinction between fabulous heroes (the fruit of sculptors) and historical heroes (whose "Etherial Root" is also Jove—or the supreme sculptor). First, the interpolated assertion that the artist's handiwork is "not unworthy Jove" points to the assimilation of artist and deity suggested in *The Hind and the Panther*. Second, Dryden develops Vergil's "spirantia signa" so that the power of the artist dominates the lines, and the heroes themselves and Trojan history are seen as dependent for their presence here on the "resembling" creations of the sculptor. He not only indicates, then, that the ambitious military hero just portrayed is the (rotten and) dying fruit of a plant which will bear new heroes (or that he is part of the "passing Pageants" of history), but that "*Cæsar's*" fame rests on the artist's presentation of him to posterity. Underlying this is surely a contrast between the ephemeralness of the "Trophies" won by the "double-crown'd" military victor and the lasting benefits of the poet's double crown "of profit and delight" (4:61). For, the connection of history and art made through the image of the plant also points to the artist's power to affect the course of history by providing heroes designed to advise historical heroes how to behave and how not to behave.

What Dryden has in fact achieved by this point is a recreation of sorts of a Jonsonian world. The inclusion in a setting embellished by grazing flocks, cooling streams and waving reeds of the issues of "Fame" (52), poetry and history and the figures of sculptors is reminiscent of Jonson's final masque, *Chloridia*. There, as Orgel points out, in the midst of a pastoral setting appears "the very uncharacteristic figure of Fame" as well as "personifications of Poetry, . . . History, and the city arts of Architecture and Sculpture, all uniting to sing the praises of the Caroline monarchy." The effect, he argues, is a "vision of nature controlled by human intellect," which is "a central way of expressing the sovereign's place in the Renaissance universe." The abandonment of pastoral otium to include figures who are the "source of laborious days" also emphasizes human toil.[59] In Dryden's *Georgics* the sovereign of Vergil's works and Renaissance poetry has been overthrown by a Caesar whose ambition is seen as antithetical to and disruptive of the arts celebrated in Renaissance poetry. The void left by the true sovereign has been filled, however, by the poet himself, whose work is anchored in nature and guided by the supreme artist as it toils to cultivate and control through the exercise of human intellect.

As Dryden translated the lines quoted above he also surely had in mind his recent comments from the "Discourse" where he explicitly links sculpture, poetry and their benefits. I can do most justice to Horace's satires, he says,

> by comparing them to the Statues of the *Sileni*. . . . They were Figures, which had nothing of agreeable, nothing of Beauty on their out-side: But when any one took the Pains to open them, and search into them, he there found the Figures of all the Deities. . . . [So] when we take away [Horace's] Crust, and that which hides him from our sight; when we discover him to the bottom, then we find all the Divinities in a full Assembly: That is to say, all the Virtues, which ought to be the continual exercise of those, who seriously endeavour to Correct their Vices. (4:74)

Here, perhaps, he solves the problem of having to blight his poetic gardens with the figure of a warlike Caesar. While the images of Caesar presented in *Georgics* III (for example) may have "nothing of Beauty on their out-side," lying under the Crust (by implicit contrast) are the divinely-informed patterns of Caesars presented by other artists and periods in history: "That is to say, all the Virtue, which ought to be the continual exercise of those, who seriously endeavour to Correct their Vices." The idea of finding in art "all the Divinities in a full Assembly" informs the decision announced at the end of the first part of *Georgics* III to "pursue the Silvan Lands" (67).

In the last section of his programmatic piece, Dryden again denounces the present, and puts faith in a future time:

> A time will come, when my maturer Muse,
> In *Cæsar's* Wars, a Nobler Theme shall chuse:
> And through more Ages bear my Soveraign's Praise;
> Than have from *Tithon* past to *Cæsar's* Days.
>
> (79–82)

In the 1693 "Discourse" he quotes the original lines behind these to describe his history of satire: "—nomen fama tot ferre per annos, / Tithoni prima quot abest ab origine Cæsar" (4:76). This, he says, is Vergil's address to Augustus. Given the distinction in his translation here between "*Cæsar*" and "my Soveraign" it seems possible that Dryden is addressing his own true Augustus (James II or, perhaps, the Stuart monarchy), and again pointing to his power by declaring that he will ensure the fame of his "Soveraign" through a longer period than has already passed "from Tithon" to these degenerate times. It is significant that the framework by which he measures time (both in the "Discourse" and here) is mythical, for his point in the passage immediately prior to these lines—the point that ultimately distinguishes Dryden's

Vergil from Vergil's—is that history can be redeemed by communing with past storytellers.

He begins by declaring that he "must pursue the Silvan Lands,"

> For such, *Mæcenas*, are thy hard Commands.
> Without thee nothing lofty can I sing;
> Come then, and with thy self thy Genius bring:
> With which Inspir'd, I brook no dull delay.
> *Cytheron* loudly calls me to my way;
> Thy Hounds, *Taygetus*, open and pursue their prey.
> High *Epidaurus* urges on my speed,
> Fam'd for his Hills, and for his Horses breed:
> From Hills and Dales the chearful Cries rebound:
> For Eccho hunts along; and propagates the sound.
>
> (67–72)

Unlike Vergil, Dryden had no financial supporter at the time of this *Georgic*. He was not to find a patron for the *Georgics* until the translations were complete (*Letters*, 86), and in his dedication of *Examen Poeticum* he indicates that he has no financial backing from its dedicatee, Lord Radcliffe: "Without Flattery, my Lord, you have it in your Nature, to be a Patron and Encourager of Good Poets, but your Fortune has not yet put into your Hands the opportunity of expressing it" (4:369). As Dryden considers patronage there in terms of moral support, so here his Maecenas is a spiritual one.[60] The source of his "inspiration" is to be "Genius": a word he uses over and again of poetic creativity. Although this poem is an "Example" of the planned complete Vergil, the particular poetic "Genius" that he seems to have in mind is Ovid: the master storyteller.

Immediately after praising Radcliffe in the dedication, Dryden observes that of all his translations the Ovid is the best for he "was more according to my Genius" (4:369).[61] As he introduces fragments of stories here his mind was perhaps on his bitter comments in "To Sir Godfrey Kneller": "Thy Genius bounded by the Times like mine, / Drudges on petty Draughts, nor dare design / A more Exalted Work, and more Divine" (147–50). Yet he must also have been thinking of the recently translated "First Book of Ovid's *Metamorphoses*." There, with Ovid, Dryden also traces history "from Nature's Birth to *Cæsar's* Times" (6), and the same theme of begetting from "Ungodly Times" a new age "ordain[ed]" from Jove's "wondrous Principles" is inherent in his plans here (320–41).[62] As in the Ovid translations, this is to be achieved by tracing history, through stories, to its divine roots; for in the Silvan woods "Eccho" ensures that the voices from past ages are heard and propagates sounds from the past for the benefit of posterity.

Clearly, Vergil's *apologia* for his *Georgics* and plans for epic have become Dryden's *recusatio*: his own "Ungodly Times" prevent him from attempting "A more Exalted Work, and more Divine." In its inconsistency and fragmentation—a preview of the complete *Vergil*—the opening of the third *Georgic* reiterates Dryden's observation immediately after his condemnation in the Kneller poem of "Ungodly Times": "what a Play to *Virgil's* Work wou'd be, / Such is a single Piece to History" (152–53). At a time when fundamental national institutions and traditions were threatened, Dryden's impulse, as his renewed georgic efforts and undertaking of the Vergil translations indicate, was to call upon the aid of Vergil, the husbandman and great political poet. Unable any longer to see—or to construe—history as a "piece," he intuitively reverted, however, to Ovidian epic within which (as in Vergil's epic) were incorporated the "Divinities in a full Assembly," yet which saw life not as a sustainable whole but as a series of plays, of stories, which continually repeat and revive one another.

This dependence on retold stories in a search through history for the primitive anticipates Benjamin's point that the "sphere of life" (*der Umkreis des Lebens*) must be determined starting from history, not from nature (*von der Geschichte, nicht von der Natur aus*).[63] The significance of both Dryden's and Benjamin's emphasis (in each case at a time of political chaos) on the reworking of past material lies in their parallel belief that the translator can "release in his own language that pure language [the language of nature and the sky] which is under the spell of another"—and obscured by historical dress.[64] At the beginning of *Georgics* III, Dryden also demonstrates—as Benjamin would later argue—that "for the sake of pure language" the translator must "break through the decayed barriers of his own language." In a much criticized line, Dryden announces the decoration of his temple gate "in Elephant and Gold" (42). By its absurdity, this rendering of Vergil's "solidoque elephanto" ("pure ivory") draws attention to the difference between Vergil's text and Dryden's. Yet it also argues that both texts derive from the same root for "the significance of fidelity as ensured by literalness is that the work reflects the great longing for linguistic complementation."[65] By using "Elephant" in a context that does not work in English, Dryden marks the distance between Vergil's fresher, younger world and his own. In the former, nature and art (the animal and its product) appear to—or are retrospectively thought to—converge in language. In the latter, language tries to obstruct access to that realm enjoyed by Vergil. In the dedication of *Examen Poeticum* he had argued that

our Language is both Copious, Significant, and Majestical; and might be reduc'd into a more harmonious sound. But for want of any Publick En-

couragement in this Iron Age, we are so far from making any progress in
the improvement of our Tongue, that in a few years, we shall Speak and
Write as Barbarously as as our Neighbours. (4:372)

His translation here illustrates the same desire to clean and refine the
English language as it attempts to reunite itself with Vergil's text in that
transcendent realm from which they both ultimately derive. The nostalgia for a pristine world where a true artist's powers shine forth brilliant
and unencumbered is powerful. At the same time, however, the humor
inherent in Dryden's line parodies Vergil's world, acknowledging the
demands of the present, albeit an "Iron Age." Such double-play, which
pervades the Vergil translations, is what brought upon Dryden the
wrath of Swift who saw a failed attempt to emulate the purity and the
power of the Ancients. Yet the tension makes Dryden's *Vergil* a true
document of its age, for generating it is the struggle at the center of
the generically-confused plays and burlesques of the period: an author's
simultaneous acknowledgment of a still-powerful idealized heroic world
and recognition of the needs of a world in which such idealism has no
place.

Dryden's *Georgics* as a group take on the toils outlined at the beginning of *Georgics* III, and, as they work their way toward the *Aeneis*, develop the methodologies Dryden was exploring even in this preliminary
work. As the following chapter will demonstrate, Dryden continues (as
he will in his *Aeneis*) to feel the force of the *imitatio Vergilis* tradition as
it had been cast by Spenser especially. He also therefore continues to
weave contemporary political and social issues into his translations,
thereby setting them in historical time and imbuing them with the urgency that is embedded in his didactic political poems. Simultaneously,
however, he apprehends the redundancy of his and others' time-honored toils even as he turns to them for authority. The study as a whole
focuses on the way in which first the *Georgics* and, increasingly, the *Aeneis* reveal Dryden's sense of bewilderment: his inability suddenly to
explain (or, perhaps more accurately, to explain away), as he had in the
past, events not just of recent history but of the turmoil that plagued
Stuart kingship. Unable to offer advice for the future yet still convinced
of the georgic powers of his poetry, informed as it is by others' tales told
in times of crisis, he invokes the spirit of Ovid, the arch-storyteller, in
his translations of Vergil. His apprehension that the right mode for the
age was Ovidian, not Vergilian epic would not be acknowledged until
Fables.

2

Studying Nature's Laws

CELESTIAL HEAT

Whence, but from *Heav'n*, cou'd men unskill'd in Arts
In several Ages born, in several parts,
Weave such *agreeing Truths*?

—Dryden, *Religio Laici*

The first line of Dryden's *Georgics* I is described by Milbourne as a "stumble at the Threshold."[1] William Benson, less charitably, calls it "dogmatical, and vulgar, and mean."[2] Both object to Dryden's disregard of Vergil's reverent address to his patron at the outset of "a very necessary Work" undertaken "for the Service of his Prince, and his Country."[3] Like the programmatic introduction of his third *Georgic*, however, the first sections of *Georgics* I and II announce, in *Hugh Selwyn Mauberley*–fashion, not classics in paraphrase, but what the age demanded. They again demonstrate that Dryden's own *Georgics* undertake a "very necessary Work" in the service of his prince and country, and that his task involves not Vergilian glorification of the present but the setting of his own "Inferiour Times" against the eternal laws of nature.

As he introduces his *Georgics* as a body, Dryden again presents himself as the nation's husbandman:

> What makes a plenteous Harvest, when to turn
> The fruitful Soil, and when to sowe the Corn;
> The Care of Sheep, of Oxen, and of Kine;
> And how to raise on Elms the teeming Vine:
> The Birth and Genius of the frugal Bee,
> I sing, *Mæcenas*, and I sing to thee.
>
> (1–6)

Vergil announces a song about "joyous crops" and about labors guided by heavenly signs and supported by a beneficent patron, whom he honors at the heart of the second line. Dryden's opening lines provide no such assurance of a caring Providence and patron; his focus (as Milbourne complains) is on "the Husbandman's Care," and the husbandman he has in mind is himself.[4] By suspending the main clause and thereby propelling the list of tasks toward the "I sing" of the final line, he yokes the "Poet's and the Ploughman's Cares," which he will ask "propitious *Cæsar*" to guide at line 61. The nature of the work undertaken and its consistency with his life-long toils are suggested by the echoes here of previous descriptions of his work both in England's fruitful soil in the reign of Charles II and in the blighted soil of the late 1680s and early 1690s.

His plans to continue weeding the land through satire are signalled by his interest in "What makes a plenteous Harvest" (Vergil has "what makes crops joyous"), which recalls the lament in the dedication to *Eleanora* over the plentiful "Harvest" to be reaped from an "extraordinary Crop" of vices (3:234). The statement also perhaps echoes his programmatic first Juvenal translation where a series of "What . . ."s, initiated by "What ever since that Golden Age was done," culminates in "Shall this Satyrical Collection fill" (129, 132). *Georgics* I goes on to portray the type of degeneracy that fills the Juvenal "Collection"; here, however, Dryden outlines his husbandry, and points to his own poetic power.

The interpolated image of sowing and the extension of "*cultus . . . pecori*" to include sheep emphasize the poet's role (portrayed in Dryden's works from *Annus Mirabilis* on) as cultivator of national fruitfulness and as shepherd (especially in the absence of Pan or the rightful king). The relevance to his task of the "Birth and Genius of the frugal Bee" (rather than "apibus quanta experientia parcis" [4]) is perhaps, then, that of his "lab'ring Bee" to the poetic endeavors of the 1690s. Again, "Genius" is the word applied continually by Dryden to true poetic spirit. Also, as he indicates in his references to himself and his fellow poets as bees and in his description of the "clust'ring Swarm of Bees" that might distil their "golden Dew" on Anne Killigrew's "sweet Mouth" (50–51), Dryden clearly felt that poets shared the special power of bees: "in their Mouths reside their Genial Pow'rs, / They gather Children from the Leaves and Flow'rs" (293–94).

These lines come from the fourth *Georgic*, but they are Dryden's own; Vergil has simply "Tantus amor florum, et generandi gloria mellis" ("so great is their love of flowers and the glory in generating honey") (205). They are followed by a point on which Dryden clearly conceded: "some have taught / That Bees have Portions of Etherial Thought: / Endu'd with Particles of Heavenly Fires: / For God the whole created Mass inspires" (321–24). The assimilation in these lines of the bees' genial powers and those of earth's "heavenly Fires" also underlies the por-

trayal of vibrant seething earth interpolated at the start of *Georgics* I by
means of the "teeming" vine (4) and the "teeming" earth struck by Neptune's trident (15). The development of poetry from this heavenly and
life-engendering force is the opening subject of *Georgics* II. There, having reestablished his position as national poet in *Georgics* I, Dryden
draws attention to the sacred nature of his poetry, emphasizing its regenerative power in the wasteland that is contemporary England.

His own concerns are evident from the introductory lines:

> Thus far of Tillage, and of Heav'nly Signs;
> Now sing my Muse the growth of gen'rous Vines:
> The shady Groves, the Woodland Progeny,
> And the slow Product of *Minerva's* Tree.
> Great Father *Bacchus!* to my Song repair;
> For clustring Grapes are thy peculiar Care:
>
> . . . .
>
> Come strip with me, my God, come drench all o're
> Thy Limbs in Must of Wine, and drink at ev'ry Pore.
> Some Trees their birth to bounteous Nature owe:
> For some without the pains of Planting grow.
> With Osiers thus the Banks of Brooks abound,
> Sprung from the watry Genius of the Ground:
> From the same Principles grey Willows come;
> *Herculean* Poplar, and the tender Broom.
> But some from Seeds inclos'd in Earth arise:
> For thus the mastful Chestnut mates the Skies.
> Hence rise the branching Beech and vocal Oke,
> Where *Jove* of old Oraculously spoke.
> Some from the Root a rising Wood disclose;
> Thus Elms, and thus the salvage Cherry grows.
> Thus the green Bays, that binds the Poet's Brows,
> Shoots and is shelter'd by the Mother's Boughs.
> These ways of Planting, Nature did ordain,
> For Trees and Shrubs, and all the Sylvan Reign.
>
> (1–6, 11–28)

While Vergil begins his second *Georgic* with an address to the deity
whose powers he will sing ("Nunc te, Bacche, canam" [2]), Dryden
opens with a reminder of the poet's inspiration by a celestial power:
"Now sing my Muse" (2). The rest of the introduction demonstrates
that the force pervading his song is part of the spirit permeating not
only "bounteous Nature" (13) but the songs of others before him. He
first blends Vergil's natural world into the realm of poetry and mythology. The interpolated "shady Groves" and "Woodland Progeny" create
from Vergil's rich autumn fields a semimythical "Sylvan" land (28).

Likewise the rendering of Vergil's "slow growing olive" (the symbol of peaceful triumph with which the poet was crowned in *Georgics* III) as the "slow Product of *Minerva's* Tree" suggests that Dryden is concerned as much with "Magazins of Learning" or the fruit of wisdom as with trees themselves (3:46.9). *"Minerva's* tree" is now made to bear new fruit as the invocation to Bacchus calls also upon the wisdom and beauties of former poets. The image of "clustring Grapes" is transmitted not from Vergil's text but from (for example) Horace's "paternal field" in "Epod. 2d." (31) and from Ovid's mythical garden in "The Fable of Acis, Polyphemus, and Galatea From the Thirteenth Book of the *Metamorphoses*" (107). The bacchic rites exhorted point to the common source of the poetic fruits.

In the hope of a bountiful harvest, Vergil invokes the spirit of "Father Lenaeus," requesting that he remove his "buskins," "In new sweet wine to dip thy bared thigh."[5] Dryden, however, attempts to capture the primal energy behind both his poem and Vergil's. He urges, "Come strip with me, my God, come drench all o're / Thy Limbs in Must of Wine, and drink at ev'ry Pore" (11–12). The religious fervor of the lines provides a reminder of his discussion of poetry's roots in the "Discourse Concerning . . . Satire." There Dryden argues,

> Mankind, even the most Barbarous, have the Seeds of Poetry implanted in them. The first Specimen of it was certainly shown in the Praises of the Deity, and Prayers to him: And as they are of Natural Obligation, so they are likewise of Divine Institution: Which *Milton* observing, introduces *Adam* and *Eve*, every Morning adoring God in Hymns and Prayers. The first Poetry was thus begun, in the wild Notes of Nature, before the invention of Feet, and Measures. . . . Festivals and Holydays soon succeeded to Private Worship. (4:29)

By emphasizing worship and freedom from constraint, Dryden looks beyond the formal control of his lines to their roots in divinely-inspired worship and ceremony. The underlying conviction that poetry is "of Divine Institution" offers similar comfort to the thought which inspires Cuddie in the "October" song of *The Shepheardes Calendar*:

> Thou kenst not *Percie* howe the ryme should rage.
> O if my temples were distaind with wine,
> And girt in girlonds of wild Yuie twine,
> How I could reare the Muse on stately stage.[6]

Dryden's passage is closer to this than to Vergil's original, on which Spenser is also drawing. Since the "October" song, like Dryden's *Georgics* as a whole, laments "the contempte of Poetrie" and traces "the causes thereof,"[7] it seems likely that Dryden had the passage in mind when he translated the lines. If so, he demonstrates that Vergil's, Spenser's and his own text are various fruit of the same root. In any case, he is again portraying poetry itself as a deathless plant that can survive the blights of time, for "Nature is the same in all places," and people will go on singing the same songs (4:30).

Later in *Georgics* II Dryden returns (this time with Vergil) to the subject of poetry's development from worship and festivals (525–43). Again, however, while Vergil is intent upon explaining fertility rituals of the countryside, Dryden's emphasis is on the development of art from the festivities of "Country Villages," and his lines are closer to the "Discourse Concerning . . . Satire" than they are to Vergil's text. His reason for raising the topic at the beginning of *Georgics* II is its relation (for his purposes) to the subsequent discussion of the "birth" and characteristics of trees. Once more he unites the realms of poetic endeavor and "bounteous Nature," and ultimately traces the roots of both to the "Seeds inclos'd in Earth" (19). Omitting Vergil's first line, which notes nature's inconsistency, Dryden plays down his focus on plants' different origins and modes of growth.[8] In effect, his own trees all arise from the "Genius of the Ground," their growth guided by the "same Principles" (16–17). By interpolating the concept of "Genius," used of the bee in *Georgics* I and used by him so many times of poetic inspiration, he links the "secret head" from which Vergil's natural trees spring with that from which arise the products of his toils as a "lab'ring Bee." These lines perhaps lie at the heart of Dryden's *Georgics*, which seem as a whole to pursue the special task outlined in *Religio Laici*: "Some few, whose Lamp shone brighter, have been led / From Cause to Cause, to *Nature*'s secret head; / And found that *one first principle* must be" (11–13). The search for first principles undertaken by Dryden's own "Sylvan Reign" (as he puts it at line 28) is then placed within the fabulous tradition of English poetry.[9]

Interpolating freely, Dryden claims that rising "from Seeds inclos'd in Earth," the "mastful Chestnut mates the Skies. / Hence rise the branching Beech and vocal Oke, / Where Jove of old Oraculously spoke" (19–22). Behind these lines is a history of "an ancient forest system" previously employed by Dryden himself.[10] His interpolated image of Jove's oracular "Oke" recalls his glorification of Charles II in *To His Sacred Majesty, A Panegyrick on His Coronation* (1661):

> Thus from your Royal Oke, like *Jove's* of old,
> Are answers sought, and destinies fore-told:
> Propitious Oracles are beg'd with vows,
> And Crowns that grow upon the sacred boughs.
>
> (129–32)

Behind both passages is Ogilby's grove of trees in his fable 36, "Of the Husband-man and the Wood."[11] There

> highly honour'd stood the sacred Oke,
> Whom Swains Invoke,
> Which Oracles, like that of Dodon, spoke.[12]

The note to this line and the earlier reference to "*Esculus* the Delight of *Jove*" single out the oak as Jove's special tree. The talking oak appears also in Spenser's "February" tale of the "Oake" and "Brere," which, as Annabel Patterson points out, is behind Ogilby's fable.[13] That story too is placed in an ancient tradition through the narrator's note, which observes, "This tale of the Oake and the Brere, he telleth as learned of Chaucer, but it is cleane in another kind, and rather like to Æsopes fables" (1:27). That Dryden in fact had Spenser's fable in mind here is suggested in his description of the chestnut as "mastful": a word chosen by Spenser for his oak, which "mochell mast to the husband did yielde" (109). The Spenserian parallel aside, Dryden's own use of such a notably germanic word (another Teuton monosyllable) emphasizes the Englishness of his grove.[14]

In both *Don Sebastian* (1689) and *Cleomenes* (1692), Dryden had again described kingship in terms of a forest: in both cases to convey bitterness and disillusionment.[15] Here too he surely has in mind the former glory of his "Royal Oke" as he invokes the fables of Spenser and Ogilby, whose groves "clearly [portray] the English political system."[16] The "Royal *Cedar*" which is deceived and cut down in Ogilby's story represents the king, and is "distinguished from the 'sacred Oke' (the national church or its greatest representative, Archbishop William Laud)."[17] In his description of the "mastful Chestnut" whose crown "mates the Skies," Dryden draws on Ogilby's portrayal of the cedar before its tragic downfall:

> This wealthy Grove, the Royal *Cedar* grac'd,
> Whose Head was fix'd among the wandring Stars,
> Above loud Meteors and Elements Wars,
> His root in th'*Adamantine* Centre fast.

> (85)

However, his line also recalls his description in "The First Book of Ovid's *Metamorphoses*" of "*Parnassus* . . . whose forky rise / Mounts through the Clouds, and mates the lofty Skies" (428–29). The notion of lofty height and lower strength (implied in the tree's origins in earth's genial seeds) also dominates Dryden's discussions in the 1690s of what poetry should be.[18] By implicitly equating his fruitful chestnut with immortal and inviolable Parnassus and by implicitly contrasting it with Ogilby's ephemeral cedar, Dryden again suggests that in England's Lycæan woods poetic authority and protection (as symbolized by the tree) have replaced monarchical. He perhaps also has in mind the Son's rejection of earthly power in *Paradise Regained*: "Know therefore when my season comes to sit / On *David's* Throne, it shall be like a tree / Spreading and over-shadowing all the Earth" (4:146–51).[19] If so he is making the same "bold assimilation of poet to savior" as he does in *The Hind and the Panther*.[20] The sanctity and antiquity of poetry are highlighted by the retelling itself of this ancient story, which was planted first by oral tradition and, like *The Hind and the Panther*, speaks the language of the sky. These qualities are stressed, however, by Dryden's last comment here: "Thus [from the seeds buried in earth] the green Bays, that binds the Poet's Brows" (25). This line (Vergil has "*Parnassus laurus*" [18]) provides a reminder of the games ordained by Apollo in "Book One of Ovid's *Metamorphoses*" where "The Lawrel was not yet for Triumphs born; / But every Green, alike by *Phoebus* worn" (603–4). In both cases the point is surely that the poet's laurels (the "peaceful Triumphs of the Gown") predate the military hero's, and are more fruitful.

Whether consciously or not, Dryden is asserting his own divinely-informed and sanctioned powers as poet over those of William III, whose roots in England are by no means in an "Adamantine Centre."[21] In *Georgics* I he draws attention to the contrast between nature's eternal laws and mutable human laws. After listing what the "Genius of the Soil" produces best in different places Dryden declares,

> This is the Orig'nal Contract; these the Laws
> Impos'd by Nature and Nature's Cause,
> On sundry Places, when *Deucalion* hurl'd
> His Mother's Entrails on the desart World.'
>
> (91–94)

Vergil's emphasis is also on nature's eternal treaties and the continuity of her laws from the time when Deucalion threw stones into the empty world creating a hard race: "Continuo has leges æternaque foedera certis / Imposuit natura locis, quo tempore primum / Deucalion vacuum lapides jactavit in orbem" (60–63).[22] By interpolating the notions of "Contract" and law imposed by a "Cause," however, Dryden also provides a reminder of the confused state of human laws in contemporary England due to the contract imposed by the Glorious Revolution and the chaos resulting from the "causes" of warring factions. The comfort offered here is that the true "Contract" is the "Orig'nal" one imposed by nature and maintained by nature's "Cause."

A reminder of his own Deucalion-like task of creating new life in a chaotic wasteland by following nature's laws perhaps underlies his replacement of Vergil's "lapides" with Mother Earth's "Entrails," which draws attention to the fecundity of earth's bowels.[23] The line recalls "The First Book of Ovid's *Metamorphoses*" where Deucalion and Pyrrha look out on a "dismal Desart, and a silent waste" and receive a divine order to "Throw each behind your backs, your mighty Mother's bones" (472, 517). As they obey, life rushes forth "from teeming Earth" for "The native moisture, in its close retreat, / Digested by the Sun's Ætherial heat, / As in a kindly Womb, began to breed" (559–62). Like Deucalion's, Dryden's mission in his translations is to ponder "mysterious words" (of ancient poets) for "some new sence" and to seek "Gods Command" in "dark Ænigma" (522–27). Like Deucalion too, he "moor[s] his little Skiff" on Parnassus's "Summet," and becomes an instrument for the production of new life from earth's "kindly Womb" (430–31); for poetry also issues from the genial seeds that are nurtured there (his *Georgics* demonstrate), and the same vigorous heat involved in natural procreation is needed for genuine poetic creation.

As a result of forgoing Vergil's advice concerning the various moods and laws of nature for an emphasis on first principles and the "Ætherial heat" involved in reproduction, Dryden's *Georgics*, like his selections from *Metamorphoses*, are much more Lucretian than Vergil's or Ovid's texts, which Lucretius also influences. Images of "teeming" earth vibrant with the "genial fire" of Lucretius' "Propitious Queen of Love" pervade both translations, and the beasts in Dryden's *Georgics*, like those in the 1685 *Lucretius*, are continually "stung" by Love's force.[24] The heavy sexual imagery that results deeply offended both Milbourne and Benson, yet its vigor serves to unite Dryden's verse with the natural world by pointing to the energy they share. As he did in *Sylvae*, in fact, Dryden explicitly connects the etherial fire inspiring his verse with the force that goads nature's plants, birds and beasts.

At the heart of the first Lucretius excerpt in *Sylvae* Dryden translates, "be thou my ayd: My tuneful Song inspire, / And kindle with thy own productive fire: / While all thy Province Nature, I survey" (32–34). This productive fire is the force at the heart of his (not Vergil's) apostrophe to his muse in *Georgics* II: "Ye sacred Muses, with whose Beauty fir'd, / My Soul is ravish'd, and my Brain inspir'd . . ." (673–74). The passage also recalls the dedication of *Eleanora* where Dryden excuses his delay: "We, who are Priests of *Apollo*, have not the Inspiration when we please; but must wait till the God comes rushing on us, and invades us with a fury, which we are not able to resist" (3:231). Both images anticipate Dryden's intensely-sexual rendering of Vergil's prophecying Sybil in *Aeneis* VI, a scene which will be discussed in chapter 5.

Throughout the 1690s, in the face of impending old age, Dryden continually points to the sexual vigor of his verse. Images of castration are used in the prologue to *Amphitryon* and the preface to *Cleomenes* to describe the restrictions imposed on his works by the times; yet he was still producing the biting satire that, he suggests in the "Discourse Concerning . . . Satire," was best suited to a "Manly" wit and vigor.[25]

In *Georgics* III Dryden again demonstrates that sacred fire still heats his verse as he sympathizes with Vergil's aged stallion:

> But worn with Years, when dire Diseases come,
> Then hide his not Ignoble Age, at Home:
> In Peace t'enjoy his former Palms and Pains;
> And gratefully be kind to his Remains.
> For when his Blood no Youthful Spirits move,
> He languishes and labours in his Love.
> And when the sprightly Seed shou'd swiftly come,
> Dribling he drudges, and defrauds the Womb.
> In vain he burns, like fainty Stubble Fires;
> And in himself his former self requires.
>
> (151–60)

As Sloman points out, Dryden undoubtedly has himself in mind. His sympathy for the horse has no grounds in Vergil, who, in a practical farmer-like manner, advises "nec turpi ignosce senectae" ("Nor pity his wretched old age").[26] The interpolated concept of gratitude, which was a catch-phrase of Stuart politics, perhaps suggests the gratitude Dryden felt he was owed for his lifetime of toil for his native land, while the vigor and nature of the verse here make the opposite point to the passage's statement about his declining powers. Dryden's ongoing cultivation of English poetry is illustrated by the strong and polished alliteration which places the passage firmly within an English tradition. The beauty and power still generated by his verse is especially notable in the line which declares their loss. The grating breathed fricative in the lament over "vain" efforts sparkles into energetic unbreathed plosive "f"s, while the stressed monosyllabic "Fires" ends the line with a blaze. In this way the poetry itself achieves a type of coitus at the moment it is denied.[27] As well, in each of the last three couplets here a noun is yoked to an active verb thereby producing from potential stasis an energy that belies the comment in the last line. Again too a dominance of "*Teuton* Monosyllables" not only reinforces the English tradition in which Dryden's verse is anchored, but consolidates the "muscularity" (to use Winn's word) of the lines.

Later in *Georgics* III, Dryden draws attention to the political and social significance of both the kind of control and the kind of divine energy he exhibits in these lines. Again his own verse helps him to make the point as he implicitly contrasts the "rage" of the female lion "stung" by lust with the "gen'rous Rage" of the bull defeated in a battle over love. When the "vanquish'd Bull" begins to "repair his Strength" in preparation for a second battle, Dryden both emphasizes and imitates the beast's control (346, 355):

> His Horns, yet sore, he tries against a Tree:
> And meditates his absent Enemy.
> He snuffs the Wind, his heels the Sand excite;
> But, when he stands collected in his might,
> He roars, and promises a more successful Fight.
> Then, to redeem his Honour at a blow,
> He moves his Camp, to meet his careless Foe.
>
> (360–66)

The notion of meditation and the bull's measured action are his additions. Vergil's bull, by contrast, "gathers his strength and, advancing his colors, rushes headlong into the unsuspecting enemy": "viresque receptæ, / Signa movet, præcepsq; oblitum fertur in hostem" (235–36). Dryden's emphasis on the psychological preparation of the bull, who "stands" to prepare himself and contemplate the enemy, is underscored by his employment in lines 363 and 365 of the logic words "But" and "Then" just as he replaces initial iambs with initial trochees. In both cases, the pause effected as the bull plans its next moves is reinforced by the caesurae that fall in the middle of both feet. Likewise, the caesura after the iambic "He roars" (sandwiched between these lines) stresses the "generous Rage" interpolated at line 350. After releasing pent-up anger, the bull's "generous" spirit allows him to stop and promise himself "a more successful fight"; his consideration of "honour" and the stealth and care with which he now proceeds are also Dryden's additions.[28]

The passage as a whole rings with political overtones. The incident is magnified into a state affair as Vergil's fight is labelled a "War," and an allusion is made to the present plight of James II when, "feeding in his Breast his ancient Fires, / And cursing Fate," Dryden's bull is "Driv'n from his Native Land, to foreign Grounds." There he laments "His ignominious Flight, the Victor's boast," and "Often he turns his Eyes, and, with a Groan, / Surveys the pleasing Kingdoms, once his own" (339–59). However, an echo of two earlier images in the subsequent description of the bull's controlled rage widens the frame of reference. First, the passage recalls a similar portrayal of the then Duke of York in *Absalom and Achitophel.* Advising Absalom to usurp the throne, Achitophel warns him about his uncle, the rightful heir, who already "markes" Absalom's "Progress in the Peoples Hearts":

> Though now his mighty Soul its Grief contains;
> He meditates Revenge who least Complains,
> And like a Lyon, Slumbring in the way,
> Or Sleep dissembling, while he waits his Prey,
> His fearless Foes within his Distance draws;
> Constrains his Roaring, and Contracts his Paws;
> Till at the last, his time for Fury found,
> He shoots with suddain Vengeance from the Ground.
>
> (445–52)

And, he concludes, "with a Lordly Rage, his Hunters teares" (454). The image is used again in *The Hind and the Panther* to describe the Hind's "boiling indignation":

> So when the gen'rous *Lyon* has in sight
> His equal match, he rouses for the fight;
> But when his foe lyes prostrate on the plain,
> He sheaths his paws, uncurls his angry mane;
> And, pleas'd with bloudless honours of the day,
> Walks over, and disdains th'inglorious Prey.
> So *JAMES*, if great with less we may compare,
> Arrests his rowling thunder-bolts in air;
> And grants ungratefull friends a lengthn'd space,
> T'implore the remnants of long suff'ring grace.
>
> (3:169.267–76)

All three passages emphasize a semidivine rage (emanating from a "mighty Soul" in pain) which is rationally controlled. The divinity inherent in the monarch's "mighty soul" is stressed in *The Hind and the Panther* by the comparison of James to the Hind. His Christ-like patience is even more marked as she comments "Be vengeance wholly left to pow'rs divine" (279). It is here that Dryden also suggests the kinship between the souls of "Saviour," monarch and poet. As the California editors note (3:415), he seems to have himself in mind as the Hind tells how she disciplines a son

> Whose uncheck'd fury to revenge wou'd run:
> He champs the bit, impatient of his loss,
> And starts a-side, and flounders at the cross.
> Instruct him better, gracious God, to know,
> As thine is vengeance, so forgiveness too.

That suff'ring from ill tongues he bears no more
Than what his Sovereign bears, and what his Saviour bore.

(3:170.298–304)

Such noble rage is contrasted with the "rage" of the female lion described almost immediately after the bull.

Perhaps remembering his description in "Lucretius: The Beginning of the First Book" of the "salvage Beasts" "Stung" by love's force (19–20), Dryden translates,

Love is Lord of all; and is in all the same.
'Tis with this rage, the Mother Lion stung,
Scours o're the Plain; regardless of her young:
Demanding Rites of Love, she sternly stalks;
And hunts her Lover in his lonely Walks.

(380–84)

The raging lioness' demand for "Rites of Love" has no basis in Vergil's text; it does, however, have precedent in Dryden's plays. In *Aureng-Zebe*, Nourmahal (whose rage is as uncontrolled and dangerous as that of the "Mother Lion") responds to her passion by asserting rites of love over the "Divine and Humane Rights" which Zayda reminds her about. "If names have such command on human Life," she declares, "Love's sure a name that's more Divine than Wife. / That Sovereign power all guilt from action takes" (12:203.366–68). Likewise, in *All for Love*, Cleopatra tells Octavia that "he whom Law calls yours, / . . . his love made mine." Octavia in turn complains that Cleopatra's "face" has "usurp'd my right" and "ruin'd my dear Lord" (12:69–70.433–36). The rage of Nourmahal, Cleopatra and the lioness can be contrasted with the refining effect love has on Almanzor in *The Conquest of Granada* and will have on Cymon in *Fables*. Almanzor feels the "flame" which "is in all the same," and his pain is such "As I were stung with some Tarantula" (11:56.329). He soon recognizes, however, that "There's something noble, lab'ring in my brest: / This raging fire, which through the Mass does move, / Shall purge my dross, and shall refine my Love" (11:58–59.422–24). Love is to have a similar effect on the high-born, but oafish Cymon, whose mind is "exalt[ed]" and behavior refined when beauty fires his blood. Underlying all of these examples seems to be a contrast between rational masculine and irrational feminine forces, which are connected with civilized humanity and animal passions respectively. In the same way (as Winn notes) an association of "men with reason, women with pleasure features frequently in [Dryden's] comparison of the arts, where the allegedly rational appeal of poetry allows him to define it as a masculine art superior to the more sensuous, bodily and feminine arts of music and painting."[29] By contrasting the reactions of the personified bull and lioness Dryden seems to highlight the point made in *Georgics* I (and present in many of his works) that the difference between humans and animals is the divine faculty of reason.[30] There, after agreeing with Vergil's "Not that I think their [birds'] Breasts with Heav'nly Souls / Inspir'd," Dryden interpolates a contrast with "Man, who Destiny controls" (563–64). As the subsequent portrayal of the birds "Compos'd by Calms, and discompos'd by Winds" demonstrates (568), his point, like that inherent in the controlled responses to love's sting of his bull and his heroes, is Ismeron's in *The Indian Queen*: " 'Tis Reason only can make the Passions less" (8:210.135).

If Dryden's Jacobite bull displays the rational and civilizing forces that Dryden associates with England's patriarchal monarchy in *Absalom and Achitophel, Annus Mirabilis* and *The Hind and the Panther* (for example), his raging lioness perhaps again figures London and her people as the embodiment of irrational and uncontrollable female passions. In *Astræa Redux*, the English people are represented as a lover repenting (as Winn puts it) her "affair with Cromwell" and longing to renew her "symbolic marriage to Charles."[31] Twenty-five years later in *Albion and Albanius* Augusta (or London) responds in sorrow to Mercury's rebuke over her unfaithfulness: "Ah 'tis too true! too true! / But what cou'd I, unthinking City, do? / Faction sway'd me, / Zeal allur'd me" (15:22.55–58). In the same "unthinking" way as Augusta, the lioness forgets her children and becomes a victim to irrational passions. The political implications of the passage are heightened by the subsequent references to the wild, destructive and "shapeless Bear" and to the "bristled Boar" (385–402), who also feature (in almost identical terms) in the catalogue of chaos-engendering beasts at the beginning of *The Hind and the Panther* (3:124.35–36, 43–52). As Sloman points out, however, female power was also "undeniably of interest at this time because of the very existence of the joint rule of William and Mary and because of the fact that Mary was indeed helping to govern England."[32] Dryden may, then, be illustrating the dangers of a regime subject to female powers: not only to a woman whose rage led her to usurp the throne from her father, but to the irrational forces of democracy and zeal (or law imposed by the people and their "Cause"), which, as Dryden's previous works have argued, are dangerous and chaotic. His warning is strengthened by the comparison of the present with the time of the Popish Plot, which is implicit in the echo of *Absalom and Achitophel* in the description of the outcast bull.

The association of his own divinely-inspired, "Manly" and civilizing powers with those of the rightful but (like himself, exiled) king suggests that he himself is maintaining his post and containing his rage. It also stresses that his poetry continues to uphold "th'Original Contract" in the face of laws imposed by William III and Mary II's government. As in *The Hind and the Panther* and *Britannia Rediviva*, where it first became central to his modus operandi, this confidence in the healing and sustaining powers of his own poetry buttresses his treatment of political issues in his *Georgics*—the subject of the next section. Having looked to Vergil's *Georgics* for authority again and again in his own political works, Dryden naturally approaches the political issues of Vergil's poems as he had previously, believing that the Roman poet can guide and validate his own advice to his contemporaries. Yet the Vergilian assurance that "labor omnia vincit" (which, as Sessions illustrates, is so central to the *imitatio Vergilis* tradition cultivated by Spenser) is displaced from the start by Dryden's emphasis on the immunity of poetry from time's corrosive powers—an emphasis resulting from his profound doubts over what, if anything, it was possible to do to mend history.[33] The absence in Dryden's translations, then, of that aspect of the *Georgics* which had made them such an important part of English poetic tradition—a tradition developed by his own Vergilian poems—signal changes to its Magna Carta that Dryden claims in his 1697 *Vergil* to uphold. Confused and irresolute over political and historical issues the importance of which they nonetheless acknowledge, these English *Georgics* undermine the heroic, thereby paving the way for the *Aeneis*—and for *Fables* and eighteenth-century novelistic modes.

HEAV'N WILL EXERCISE US TO THE LAST

> Think on the slippery state of human things,
> The strange vicissitudes and sudden turns
> Of war, and fate recoiling on the proud,
> To crush a merciless and cruel victor.
> Think, there are bounds of fortune set above,
> Periods of time, and progress of success,
> Which none can stop before the appointed limits,
> And none can push beyond.
>
> —Dryden, *Love Triumphant*

In *The English Georgic*, John Chalker notes how Dryden's *Georgics* stress "the sense—already present in Virgil—of the dignity and patterned rhythm of agricultural activities."[34] Indeed, Dryden's emphasis on natural rhythms makes his translations closer to *Britannia Rediviva* than to Vergil's originals, and the same bewilderment and desire for clarity that shape the 1688 poem permeate the *Georgics* published almost a decade later. As his rendering of Vergil's panegyrical address to Caesar at the start of *Georgics* I begins to illustrate, Dryden attempts, as he had through the typological underpinnings of *Britannia Rediviva* (and all previous political poems), to uncover historical patterns by weaving political events into temporal revolutions. Plagued by the same lack of conviction that made *Britannia Rediviva* an essentially different poem from, say, *Absalom and Achitophel*, however, the poet places faith in the turning of the seasons rather than the direction in which historical cycles are moving. This concern with transformation itself rather than future glory won by toils in the present betrays the essential Ovidianism of these Vergil translations. It also demonstrates that Dryden is already on the way to the philosophies of *Fables*, for the *Georgics* declare in effect what the poet would outline explicitly in "Of the Pythagorean Philosophy": that "chang'd by Nature's innovating Hand; / All Things are alter'd, nothing is destroy'd, / The shifted Scene, for some new Show employ'd" (387–89).[35]

Dryden had linked *Britannia Rediviva* with Vergil's *Georgics* from the start by using a quotation from *Georgics* I as an epigraph. At the beginning of his own first *Georgic* he recalls *Britannia Rediviva* as he introduces the figure of *"Cæsar."* He calls upon

> You, who supply the Ground with Seeds of Grain;
> And you, who swell those Seeds with kindly Rain:
> And chiefly thou, whose undetermin'd State
> Is yet the Business of the Gods Debate. . . .
>
> (28–31)

The anaphoric "And" unites the "thou" with those who supply the ground with seed and ensure its fertility. Like "th'Auspicious Heir" of *Britannia Rediviva* who "Betwixt two Seasons comes . . . / This Age to blossom and the next to bear" (17–18), the figure is in this way connected with the forces of natural regeneration. Like *Britannia Rediviva*, but unlike Vergil's text, he is not named straight away. The effect here is to allow Dryden immediately to consolidate a contemporary frame of reference.

Vergil first questions what company of Gods Caesar is soon to keep and whether he shall choose to watch over cities and care for the land (25–26).[36] Dryden's initial focus is on "undetermin'd State" and "after Times" (32). The interpolated image of "the Gods Debate" recalls the "strife in Heav'n" over the prince's name in *Britannia Rediviva* (193), while the hero's "undetermin'd State" associates him with *Threnodia Augustalis's* "Prince, long exercis'd by Fate" (430). There comfort is offered for James's toils by the same reminder of the inviolability of divine power that is implicit here: "In all the Changes of his doubtful

State, / His Truth, like Heav'ns, was kept inviolate" (485–86). As he continues to replace Vergil's Caesar with a conglomerate image of Stuart monarchy, Dryden describes his figure as "Pow'rful of Blessings" (36), a phrase used of Charles II in *To His Sacred Majesty* (41) and again in *Threnodia Augustalis* (297). He then asks, "wilt thou, *Cæsar*, chuse the watry Reign / To smooth the Surges, and correct the Main?" and reflects that if so, then *"Neptune* shall resign the Fasces of the Sea" (38, 42).[37] As in the reference in Aphra Behn's *The Rover* to an absent "Prince" who "reigns still lord of the wat'ry element,"[38] the concept here of a lord of "the watry Reign" wielding the "Fasces of the Sea" is almost certainly (as in Behn's play) an allusion to displaced Stuart monarchy. In *Astraea Redux* and *To His Sacred Majesty* Charles is presented as having "smooth[ed] the Surges and correct[ed] the Main": he is a second Caesar "Born to command the Mistress of the Seas" (1:35.99). By the end of *Threnodia Augustalis* the "Fasces of the Sea" have become a symbol of divinely-authorized Stuart empire. As James ushers in "A Series of Successful years," the "Ocean rears his reverand Head; / To View and Recognize his ancient Lord again: / And, with a willing hand, restores / The *Fasces* of the Main" (508, 514–17).

The passage perhaps suggests that even this late Dryden hopes for a Jacobite restoration—optimism which might also underlie his declaration at the end of the first section of *Georgics* III: "A time will come, when my maturer Muse, / In *Cæsar's* Wars, a Nobler Theme shall chuse." In any case, his reminder of the glory that was England's when the *"Fasces* of the Main" were in the hands of Stuart Caesars makes a telling comment on the "shatter'd Ships" of that poem's war-mongering Caesar. The presentation of a Jacobite Caesar is perhaps also a sly attack on the association of William III with Julius Caesar, which was current at the time.[39] Certainly, Dryden's point here (and the origin of his hope if there is any hope) is that the power of England's legitimate Caesar is shared by "Kindred Gods above" (54). The attribution of this true and "propitious" power to the Stuart line is underscored by the final vision of Caesar "seated near the Ballance . . . / Where in the Void of Heav'n a Space is free" (46–47). By translating Vergil's "between the virgin and the grasping claws" annotatively as "near the Ballance,"[40] Dryden stresses Caesar's association with Justice. He also again refers to *Britannia Rediviva*, which ends with an image of James as Justice embodied: "Your self our Ballance hold, the Worlds, our Isle" (361). Just above this line he had asserted, "Justice is Heav'ns self, so strictly He, / That cou'd it fail, the God-head cou'd not be" (355–56). The same thought seems to underlie the view here that Caesar's rightful place is not only with "the Ballance" but in "the Void" in heaven.

Dryden produces yet another echo from *Britannia Rediviva* as his rendering of Vergil's "more than ample space in heaven" (a literal translation) recalls the "naked void" which would have been left in England's fields by the death of the prince. The image there is part of a simile which compares the impact of the false news to the horror felt "when a sudden Storm of Hail and Rain / Beats to the ground the yet unbearded Grain" (259–60). Gardiner comments:

> The hopes of the loyal are like those of the farmer whose young wheat has been beaten down by a storm but has risen again by a clear sky. The "hopes of Harvest" have returned despite momentary despair. Dryden alludes to Genesis 1:2 when he calls the field without wheat a "naked void" (262). As in the allusion to Noah (101), the poet hints that without the wheat ripening to a future harvest, without James' policy of religious toleration and a young prince to ensure its continuity, England appears to be returning to a spiritual chaos.[41]

As Gardiner suggests of the purpose of the georgic imagery in *Britannia Rediviva*, Dryden's point here, perhaps, is that if the rightful and "propitious *Cæsar*" were to take his place, England would again flourish. Despite the unmistakably English context of Dryden's lines, however, the political allegory in its elusiveness and uncertainty offers neither consolation nor direction, and the real force is in the poet's confidence in divine and natural laws. A similar shift from interest in human endeavor to disinterest in the pettiness of human affairs occurs in the translation of Jupiter's theodicy later in *Georgics* I. Here Dryden sets out to offer comfort by evoking reminders of past storms, yet the overwhelming sentiment of the passage is weariness over pointless wars.

Low remarks that in "the great 'Jupiter theodicy,' which many consider to be at the heart of the *Georgics*, Vergil reveals the important interconnections among farming, the constructive arts, divine providence and civilization itself."[42] Dryden applies Vergil's general consolation closely to England's toils. After discussing the unpredictability of nature, he declares

> Nor yet the Ploughman, nor the lab'ring Steer,
> Sustain alone the hazards of the Year:
> But glutton Geese, and the *Strymonian* Crane,
> With foreign Troops, invade the tender Grain:
> And tow'ring Weeds malignant Shadows yield:
> And spreading Succ'ry choaks the rising Field.
> The Sire of Gods and Men, with hard Decrees,
> Forbids our Plenty to be bought with Ease:
> And wills that Mortal Men, inur'd to toil,
> Shou'd exercise, with pains, the grudging Soil:

> Himself invented first the shining Share,
> And whetted Humane Industry by Care:
> Himself did Handy-Crafts and Arts ordain;
> Nor suffer'd Sloath to rust his active Reign.
> E're this, no Peasant vex'd the peaceful Ground;
> Which only Turfs and Greens for Altars found:
> No Fences parted Fields, nor Marks nor Bounds
> Distinguish'd Acres of litigious Grounds:
> But all was common, and the fruitful Earth
> Was free to give her unexpected Birth.
> *Jove* added Venom to the Viper's Brood,
> And swell'd, with raging Storms, the peaceful Flood:
> Commission'd hungry Wolves t'infest the Fold. . . .
>
>   (177–99)

The interpolated invasion of foreign troops is unquestionably a glance at the Glorious Revolution. However, connected with the "glutton Geese" (Vergil has "improbus": "wicked" or "shameless" [119]) it becomes another version of the opening of the Hind's fable where "Glutton" pigeons invade and impoverish the otherwise peaceful farm of the "good" and pious husbandman-king (3:188.906). Most obviously, the birds in that fable represent the Anglican clergy maintained by a king who is "bound by Promise" (3:189.153)[43]; though, as the California editors note, they may also stand for the Reformation takeover by the English church of "the ecclesiastical structures originally designed" for Catholics (3:443.n.955). Here Dryden's "glutton Geese" is probably an attack on William's government, which is using up English resources in expensive continental wars. However, the fabulous structure framing both this story and the Hind's gives a timeless quality to a tale with immediate national relevance.

The image of weeds choking the fields, which Dryden expands from Vergil, also has a simultaneous immediacy and timelessness. It is, of course, a common-place biblical and literary metaphor for a sick land. It is also one that Dryden found particularly pertinent not only to post-1688 England (as evidenced by his complaint about the sowing of dragons' teeth) but to the Popish Plot: *Absalom and Achitophel* too employs an image of weeds choking a promising field to describe the blighting of history (194–95). Dryden also draws earlier English history into his scene by calling Jove's silver age an "active Reign." The interpolated epithet looks back to *Astræa Redux* where even "*Jove* and *Heaven*" were "violated" in Charles's "too, too active age" (40, 111). A reference to the upheaval that plagued the post-Restoration period is then made through the image of the Viper's venomous "Brood" (Vergil's Jove "put deadly venom in black serpents" [129]). In *Absalom and Achitophel*, rebels like Achitophel (who "sheds his Venome") are at the end portrayed as a "Viper-like" brood tearing "their Mother Plot" (229, 1013). Likewise, in *The Medall*, Shaftesbury is twice described as a viper spreading his poisonous "Venom" through the land (264, 267). Descriptions of political chaos as "raging Storms" swelling a once "peaceful Flood" also pervade Dryden's political poems.

The particularly English character of this postlapsarian world is stressed not only by the self-referentiality of Dryden's timeless images, but by the introduction of litigation into Vergil's Lucretian lament for the Golden Age "Ante Jovem" ("before Jove") when "nulli subigebant arva coloni: / Nec signare quidem, aut partiri limite campum / Fas erat" ("no farmers subdued the land, nor was it lawful to mark out boundaries dividing up the field" [125–27]). Dryden's "Acres of litigious Grounds" points to the English debates and problems over enclosure. It also recalls the lament by Piers in Spenser's "Maye" tale: "The time was once," he wails, "When shepeheards had none inheritaunce, / Ne of land, nor fee in sufferaunce / But what might arise of the bare sheepe" (103–7). As well as highlighting the iterability of historical struggles, then, Dryden is also (again) placing his poem in a tradition of poetic toils and, specifically, of English poetic toils.[44]

The greater picture of stormy English history is narrowed to focus once more on the present as "hungry Wolves" are "Commission'd . . . t'infest the Fold." Such an image is used as a metaphor for William's government in *Love Triumphant* (published at the same time as this *Georgic* was probably written).[45] Here the language of contract makes a similar indictment on an age (or on a settlement!) which "commissions" dangerous predators to enter England's fold. However, the image is also a reminder of *Paradise Lost* where Satan is compared to a "Wolfe" climbing into "Gods Fould" as he enters the Garden of Eden (4:183–92). The scene in the *Georgics* with its particular contemporary relevance can be seen, then, as an antitype whose type is anchored in humanity's fall from grace. In effect, Dryden makes the same point here as he does in the 1693 "Discourse Concerning . . . Satire" when he attempts to mitigate contemporary woes by pointing to a poet's need always "to add the opposition of ill Spirits to the good" (see p. 15 above). Yet the weariness and bitterness permeating his reflection yet again on the repetitiveness with which predators and invaders have entered and will continue to enter England's fold diminish the importance of the national and historical concern suggested by the contemporary context. Ultimately (as would happen in the *Aeneis* and in eighteenth-century literature) the focus is on the individual.

Milbourne complains that Dryden "belyes old *Father Jupiter*, while he makes him the *Inventor* of the *Plow-share, and of Handy-Crafts, and Arts;*

and gives us a very impertinent Idæa of the *Silver Age.*"[46] Dryden's concern, however, is with the lonely toiler in a barren world. Stressing human "pains" and "Care," he *"Paraphrases Three excellent Lines of Virgil* with no fewer than *eight* of his *own."*[47] A focus on his own situation in particular (and perhaps by extension that of his fellow Jacobites) seems to underlie his first image here of the "Ploughman" and the "lab'ring Steer" sustaining "alone the hazards of the Year." The notion of isolated toil is interpolated, and earlier in *Georgics* I he had linked "the Poet's and the Ploughman's Cares" (61). While he was not to use the image of the "lab'ring Steer" again until *Fables* (where it seems to represent his life's toils) the adjective was one he readily applied to himself at this time. Nor is Vergil's land "grudging"; for Dryden the soil in which he was "lab'ring" at this time was.

Dryden's personal disillusionment again takes over as he turns to the politically-charged conclusion to Vergil's first *Georgic*. Once more, the lines are set in an obvious national and political context; once more the poet's call for national toil and patience becomes advice on personal endurance. Dryden again recalls *Britannia Rediviva* as he translates Vergil's description of the battlefield of Philippi and cry for an end to civil bloodshed, a passage Chalker calls "One of the most compelling images in Virgil's poem."[48] By omitting Vergil's explicit reference to "Philippi" (490), Dryden may have intended to draw attention away from Roman history and toward English. He then translates the passage used as an epigraph in *Britannia Rediviva* in a way closer to that poem than to Vergil's. Perhaps reflecting on his comment in the "Discourse Concerning . . . Satire" regarding the folly of the "Factious Quarrels, Controversies, and Battels amongst" Jewish Ministers "United in the same Design, the Service and Honour of their common Master" (4:20), Dryden pleads for "home-born Deities, of Mortal Birth" (perhaps the "Discourse's" "Guardian Angels appointed by God Almighty, as his Vicegerents, for the Protection and Government of Cities, Provinces, Kingdoms, and Monarchies" [4:19]) to unite with "youthful *Cæsar*" (668, 672). "Nor," he continues, "hinder him to save the sinking Age" (673). His former hopes that the young Stuart prince would provide such a savior for England's "sinking Age" are now echoed: "O! let the Blood, already spilt, atone / For the past Crimes of curst *Laomedon*!" (674–75). In the 1688 poem a similar lament over payment still being exacted for former civil crimes is interwoven with Dryden's hopes: "Let his Baptismal Drops for us attone; / Lustrations for Offences not his own" (188–89). His bitterness here is indicated not only by the echo of that couplet, but by the subsequent interpolation: "monstrous Crimes in ev'ry Shape are crown'd" (680).[49] The crowning of monstrous crimes derives, of course, from events of 1689, not from Vergil's text.

That Dryden had contemporary affairs in mind at this point becomes clear in his note to *Georgics* I, where he compares the "present [continental] Wars" to those "here describ'd . . . As if *Virgil* had Prophecy'd of this Age." He also excuses the "Crimes" of Vergil's Caesar, imputing blame to "his two Partners, *Anthony* and *Lepidus* . . . the Head-strong Horses . . . [who] hurried *Octavius*, the trembling Charioteer along, and were deaf to his reclaiming them" (6:814). This is surely a bitter attack on England's perpetrator of "monstrous Crimes," who, far from being pushed into the wars, is the driving force behind them. The age of hope in which Vergil was writing is in this way contrasted with Dryden's own age where "long plighted Leagues" (the alliance between France and England?) are "divided" in a world "wasted" by Mars' "Triumphs" (688–89). The only comfort Dryden seems to find here is in the thought with which he was concerned in the address to Caesar at the start: "after Times." To Vergil's evocative list of war relics and giant bones that farmers in later ages shall dig up in their daily labors and wonder at, Dryden adds "Antick Titles on the Stones" (666). While Milbourne effuses scorn,[50] Dryden is stressing the one thing that human beings can achieve through the "rowling Years" (5:233.717): fame preserved by "Antick Titles"—and handed down by poets. The same recognition that in the end only nature and time have true power dominates the equally-bleak ending of *Georgics* III.

Like the storms described in *Britannia Rediviva*, the plague at the end of *Georgics* III seems both natural and political. As Dryden's "Victor Horse" is struck by plague, the poet seems again to be thinking of himself: weakened bodily by illness and old age and suffering because of the sickness of the times. The horse's "abhor[rence of] the Flood" has political overtones (Dryden describes political chaos as a "flood" throughout his works), while the reference to the animal's "patient sobbing" and "manly Moans" recalls Dryden's many laments over his pain during the 1690s (747–48, 755). The lines are distinctly Dryden's own for Vergil's epithets and verse stress the physical rather than the psychological struggle of the horse. The passage also recalls *Britannia Rediviva*'s account of the natural disasters that plagued the year 1688 before the birth of the prince. There too Dryden may well have had himself in mind (and was probably thinking of this section of Vergil's *Georgic*) when he described how "The Strong-limb'd Steed beneath his harness faints, / And the same shiv'ring sweat his Lord attaints" (173–74).

If the "Victor Horse" succumbs to sickness and death, so too does the "Viper" found "dead, within her Hole" (810). The personal and political implications of this are linked to the association of the viper with William III, which is made just before the plague scene. For, given that "Snakes besieg'd [the] Young Divinity" of the prince in *Britannia Rediv-*

iva (56), it seems likely that Dryden was attacking the king brought up on boggy Dutch marshes when he wrote of the "Snake" bred in *"Calabria's* Woods" (647).[51] Like William, this snake eventually "leaves the Fens" in order to "rage in the Fields, and wide Destruction threat" (657, 660). The contemporary context in which Vergil's snake is set at that point is again evident as Dryden translates the lines immediately following the discovery of the dead viper: "'tis in vain," he says of the sick, to "trust to Physick; Physick is their Bane. / The Learned Leaches in despair depart; / And shake their Heads, desponding of their Art" (816–19). Objecting to Dryden's "learned Leeches," Benson wonders why "Mr. Dryden makes Virgil fall foul upon Physicians and Lawyers; which was exceeding improper."[52] The answer perhaps lies at the end of the preface to *Fables*. Dryden there responds to Milbourne's and Richard Blackmore's attacks on his translations, calling the latter "the City Bard or Knight Physician," and expressing resentment that Blackmore had stolen his plans from the "Discourse Concerning . . . Satire": "it was not for this Noble Knight that I drew the Plan of an Epick Poem on King *Arthur*, in my Preface to the Translation of *Juvenal*" (Kinsley, 1462). His cynical remark here in *Georgics* III is perhaps evidence that the undertaking of the "learned Leech" was in progress. The comment might also be simply another attack on those awarded "Honours of the Gown" despite possessing "as little learning and less Honesty than my self" (4:363). In either case, Dryden's point concerns the ultimate impotence of such mercenary artisans, and whatever consolation is offered by the plague scene is related to the futility of such victories as are won by a monarch's destructive rage. It is also related to the thought that (as Dryden would later put it at the end of his poem to his cousin John Driden) "The Soul returns to Heav'n, from whence it came; / Earth keeps the Body, Verse preserves the Fame" (208–9).

In failing to provide Dryden with a space within which to offer advice or solutions that can be carried out in historical time, then, his *Georgics* document the disintegration of his conviction—or concern—that history will work itself to an ordained end. Interestingly, just as Dryden's theories of translation find parallels in Benjamin's, so the attitude toward history finally presented in his *Georgics* resembles that of Benjamin, who also suffered through social and personal upheavals and consequently struggled (as Peter Demetz observes) "with the seeming incompatibility of the profane (or historical) and the Messianic (or divine) order":

Only the Messiah himself consummates all history, in the sense that he alone redeems, creates its relation to the Messianic. For this reason nothing historical can relate itself on its own account to anything Messianic. Therefore the

Kingdom of God is not the *telos* of the historical dynamic; it cannot be set as goal. From the standpoint of history it is not the goal, but the end.[53]

As the final section of this chapter will demonstrate, the impact on the poems as a group of Dryden's gradual emphasis on God as the end rather than the *telos* of history culminates in *Georgics* IV, which focuses on the powers of the poet and the need for individual endurance in the face of history's plagues and storms.

SAFE IN OURSELVES, WHILE ON OURSELVES WE STAND

> As in a Shipwrack some poor Sailer tost,
> By the rude Ocean, on a Foreign Coast;
> Vows to the Gods, he never more for Gain
> Will tempt the Danger of the Faithless Main:
> But hugs himself upon the friendly Shoar,
> And loves to hear the raging Billows Roar,
> That spend their Malice and can hurt no more.
> Just so the Wretch, who can no longer stand
> The Shocks of Fortune, and is wreck'd at Land;
> Lays down the Burthen of his Cares to find
> A Solitary Place, and Quiet Mind. . . .
> —"ON THE *Happyness of a Retir'd Life*, By Mr. Charles Dryden.
>   Sent to his Father from Italy"

Dryden described his "To My Honour'd Kinsman, John Driden" (1700) as "my Opinion, of what an Englishman in Parliament ought to be . . . a Memorial of my own Principles to all Posterity" (*Letters*, 120). While critics have pointed to the poem's roots in Horace's second epode and in the seventeenth-century retirement poem tradition, the "Principles" it lays out can be traced to Dryden's *Georgics*. Here he begins to explore what the individual should do when confronted with overwhelming national and historical upheaval. Accordingly, the connections between, on the one hand, individual self-control, toil and happiness and, on the other, national stability, industry and prosperity that are made in "To John Driden" are first apparent in these translations.[54]

The view that national greatness begins with the individual was not, of course, new to Dryden's thinking. His heroic plays and tragedies (by their nature) are concerned with the establishment of political stability through the personal virtue of the hero. In a much more local way, he also deplores the political and national situation which gave rise to *The Medall* by echoing Vergil's exhortation to farmers, so that the lines he quotes in the dedication of his own *Georgics* ("O Fortunatos nimium,

bona si sua norint / Agricolas" [143]) appear first in his works as "Too
happy *England*, if our good we knew" (2:46.124). The emphasis in his
Georgics on the importance both to the individual and the nation of
studying God's and nature's laws also has precedence not only in the
poet's apostrophe in *Annus Mirabilis* to the Royal Society, which "great
in search of God and Nature grow[s]" (658), but in Dryden's two great
religious poems. However, the worse the national situation got (or at
least the more ostracized and cut off from political affairs Dryden felt)
the more emphasis he placed on the exercise of conscience by educated,
informed and reasonable individuals.[55]

The philosophical stance of his *Georgics* is outlined in the dedication
prefaced to them. Dryden ends by denouncing "the present War of the
Christians against the Turk" and contrasts that public turmoil with the
composed lifestyle and mind of his dedicatee, Philip, Earl of Chesterfield. Comparing him to "the happy Old *Corycian*, whom my Author
describes in his fourth *Georgic*; whose Fruits and Salads on which he
liv'd contented, were all of his own growth, and his own Plantation,"
Dryden praises Chesterfield's reason and learning:

> 'Tis but half possession not to understand that happiness which we possess:
> A foundation of good Sense, and a cultivation of Learning, are required to
> give seasoning to Retirement, and make us taste the blessing. God has be-
> stow'd on your Lordship the first of these, and you have bestow'd on your-
> self the second. *Eden* was not made for Beasts, though they were suffer'd to
> live in it, but for their Master, who studied God in the Works of his Cre-
> ation. (5:143–44)

Written after his *Georgics* were complete, these comments summarize
the emphasis throughout the poems on measured, persistent and lonely
toil in the study and cultivation of God's works for the good not only or
perhaps even primarily of nation but of self too.

The passage of Vergil alluded to in *The Medall* and in the first sentence
of the above quotation becomes, in Dryden's second *Georgic*,

> Oh happy, if he knew his happy State!
> The Swain, who free from Business and Debate,
> Receives his easy Food from Nature's Hand,
> And just Returns of cultivated Land!
>
> (639–42)

The Latin here is "O fortunatos nimium, sua si bona norint, / Agricolas!
quibus ipsa, procul discordibus armis, / Fundit humo facilem victum
iustissima tellus" (458–60). William Benson's translation demonstrates
that Vergil was thinking specifically of the recent Italian civil wars:

> O! happy Swains! did they their Bliss but know!
> To whom *the Earth*, releas'd from all the Woe
> Of *Civil Broils*, gives with a lib'ral Hand
> *An easy Plenty*, at their just Demand.[56]

Dryden's mind, however, is on the present. Rather than envying the "Swains'" distance from the sounds of war (an evil which he clearly saw as affecting all of England at this time), his translation promotes self-extrication from public strife. In this way, it anticipates the portrayal of John Driden, who "studying Peace, and shunning Civil Rage" (3) benefits others with his wisdom and reason. It also highlights the change in Dryden's attitude toward his native land since the Glorious Revolution. Vergil's last line here, which portrays liberal earth pouring forth her plenty unasked, is that on which Dryden drew in the "Account" of *Annus Mirabilis* to celebrate a time of golden-age bounty: "Omnia sponte sua reddit justissima tellus" (1:52) (see p. 28 above). Now not only is the soil "grudging," but its fruitfulness depends on a commercial transaction. In fact, as Donald Johnson argues, Dryden's *Georgics* establish "a practical business-like relationship" between the individual and the "potentially fruitful land," on the basis of which "the husbandman receives a reward from his land in direct proportion to the amount of labor he invests."[57] Here in *Georgics* II Dryden points to the central features of that relationship, which allows the individual freedom from "Business and Debate" and means that "Man [his own] Destiny controls." For, in accordance with "th'Original Contract" the land will repay with "just Returns" the toils of cultivation. The assurance of these returns and the importance of working within nature's rhythms are the focus of the panegyric to the "Old *Corycian*" in *Georgics* IV.

There Dryden first establishes a more intimate relationship between the old farmer and the poet. Whereas Vergil watches from a distance ("I recall having seen an old Corycian," he reminisces [125–27]), Dryden asserts "I chanc'd an Old *Corycian* Swain to know" (188). That he had Chesterfield in mind is suggested not only by the dedication but by the subsequent interpolated attribution of "Care" to the "Swain" (200). This, of course, suggests personal sympathy on the part of the "Care"-ridden Dryden trying to survive in his own "barren" land (189). In fact, as Gardiner points out, Chesterfield's situation was very similar to Dryden's. He had gone into self-imposed isolation at the Glorious Revolution, and when called on to take part in the new regime had refused at great risk to himself; after "voting for a regency, [he] left to cultivate his gardens at Bretby."[58] When Dryden finally asked Chesterfield to accept the dedication of his *Georgics* it was because "'Tis suitable to the retir'd life, which you have chosen, and to your studies of Philosophy"

(*Letters*, 86). In the dedication itself he again praises the earl because he "may properly be said to have chosen a Retreat; and not to have chosen it 'till you had maturely weighed the advantages of rising higher with the hazards of the fall" (5:142). It is perhaps with Chesterfield in mind, then, that Dryden makes his Corycian consciously compare his lifestyle with that of the court: he "wisely deem'd the Wealth of Monarchs less" (197). (In Vergil the comparison of the farmer's "wealth" to that of kings is made by the poet.)

Whether or not his swain represents Chesterfield (as seems to be the case), Dryden's point is that contentment can be attained even in a "barren" land. In effect the lifestyle of his Corycian is founded on the philosophy pronounced by Cleomenes as he confronts political and social chaos: "My mind on its own Centre stands unmov'd, / And Stable as the Fabrick of the World, / Propt on it self . . ." (16:88.3–5). The structure itself of the passage highlights the steadfastness both of the swain's self-conduct and nature's laws (or "the fabric of the world"). By stressing completed action in the past, the proliferation of active perfect verbs suggests just rewards (the swain's present happiness) for past labors. Emphasis is placed on the way in which these toils are conducted according to seasonal restrictions and knowledge of the land ("He knew," for example, "to rank his elms in even rows" [213]), and the sense of method pervading the lines is intensified by a scattering of logic words: "for," "because," "therefore." The climax of Dryden's semimoral story is marked by a triplet:

> He therefore first among the Swains was found,
> To reap the Product of his labour'd Ground,
> And squeese the Combs with Golden Liquor Crown'd.
>
> (206–8)

The interpolated middle line again stresses guaranteed returns for honest toil, while the triumphant "Crown'd," which completes the majestic triplet, emphasizes the dignity of the work and the value of its rewards. Perhaps also present here is an implicit contrast with the "Cares" and woes which go with the honors of political crowns.

In *Georgics* I, consistent toil of the sort by which the Corycian swain controls his life is presented as a potential antidote to political chaos. Dryden insists that Ceres will not regard the "Labours" of the "Peasant" with "a grudging Eye" (139–40):

> Nor his, who plows across the furrow'd Grounds,
> And on the Back of Earth inflicts new Wounds:

> For he with frequent Exercise Commands
> Th'unwilling Soil, and tames the stubborn Lands.
>
> (141–44)

His rendering of Vergil's instructions about cross-ploughing evokes not only the fallen world of "Book One of Ovid's *Metamorphoses*," but political chaos as it is depicted in *Absalom and Achitophel*. Enraged by the corruption of humanity, Dryden's Jupiter destroys the land by granting "new Command" to "Floods" and by inflicting a "wound" upon the earth with his mace (385–86, 389–90). In *Absalom and Achitophel*, the "sober part of *Israel*" shudders at the impending trouble, and, looking back at the civil wars, "Saw Seames of wounds, dishonest to the sight" (69–72). Meanwhile, the rebels are presented as "unwilling" and "stubborn." By injecting the same kind of politically-charged language into his description here of rustic labor, Dryden suggests that in this postlapsarian world the same principle applies in the public and political arena as in the private. That is, as a result of Jupiter's first "wound" (inflicted in the cause of human betterment), it is only through "frequent Exercise"—or ongoing toil in the interest of the land's health—that human beings have any kind of command or can "tame" "stubborn" and opposing forces. *Georgics* II and IV especially place firmly within the context of 1690s England and Dryden's own poetic endeavors the argument presented both here and in the story of the Corycian that it is possible for the individual to retreat from public strife.

In the passage that seems to lie at the heart of his *Georgics*, Dryden asserts:

> Happy the Man, who studying Nature's Laws,
> Thro' known Effects can trace the secret Cause:
> His Mind possessing, in a quiet state,
> Fearless of Fortune, and resign'd to Fate.
> And happy too is he, who decks the Bow'rs
> Of Sylvans, and adores the Rural Pow'rs:
> Whose Mind, unmov'd, the Bribes of Courts can see;
> Their glitt'ring Baits, and Purple Slavery:
> Nor hopes the People's Praise, nor fears their Frown,
> Nor, when contending Kindred tear the Crown,
> Will set up one, or pull another down.
>
> (698–708)[59]

Even Milbourne notes the attack here on William III and Mary II instead of again merely abusing Dryden for mistranslation.[60] As he evokes the horrors of recent history, however, Dryden also repeats his pronouncement from the dedication: "I commend not him who never knew a Court, but him who forsakes it because he knows it" (5:142). The philosophical self-control of the passage suggests that the poet himself, having witnessed such corruption, is resigned to fate and is content to possess his mind "in a quiet state." His attitude is that of the observers in Dryden's versions of the beginning of Lucretius's Second Book (1–11) and Pythagoras's discourse from the "Fifteenth Book of the *Metamorphoses*" (215–220). As David Hopkins puts it, these narrators reveal a desire

> to look down on mankind not "without interest and without emotion" but, rather, having attained a comprehensive view of life, encompassing both sympathetic involvement and objectifying distance, in which the pains and glories, follies and pleasures, pathos and comedy, of the human condition could all be given no more and no less than their due, and could thus be contemplated and enjoyed in untroubled calm.[61]

Dryden's treatment of the bees in *Georgics* IV reveals just this sort of Democritean stance.[62] Here, more than anywhere else in the *Georgics*, there is a very strong sense that the poet is watching life as if it were a play, laughing at its follies but at the same time "study[ing] God in the Works of his Creation."

The announcement of subject matter at the beginning of *Georgics* IV also introduces the poem's double-fold perspective. The poet says he will sing of "Embattl'd Squadrons and advent'rous Kings: / A mighty Pomp, tho' made of little Things. / Their Arms, their Arts, their Manners . . . " (4–6). In other words, the portrayal of apian life is also to be a study of human life with all its arms and arts and manners.[63] True to his promise, Dryden does, like Vergil before him, use the bee society as a vehicle for a sober treatment of the "important Concerns of Mankind" (as Addison puts it of Vergil's poem [5:152]). Yet, as David Hopkins also observes, the "location of human habits, personalities, laws and history in the miniature environment of the hive can, rather, serve to impress upon us the littleness of human affairs, allowing us to 'look below on humankind' with something of the philosophical detachment which Dryden's Lucretius found so pleasurable."[64] By "mingling human and apian attributes" (as Hopkins notes) Dryden not only establishes a "genuine sympathy and admiration" in his observations on the "mighty Pomp . . . of little Things" but effects "a certain detachment from, even amusement at, the events portrayed."[65] The tension which pervades the poem as a result of this simultaneous distance from and involvement and interest in human affairs can be seen as a product of Dryden's view of the poet's ambivalent role in society as both participator and spectator.

Dryden begins his account of the bee state by watching admiringly from a distance:

> The winged Nation wanders thro' the Skies,
> .   .   .   .
> They skim the Floods, and sip the purple Flow'rs.
> Exalted hence, and drunk with secret Joy,
> Their young Succession all their Cares employ:
> They breed, they brood, instruct and educate,
> And make Provision for the future State.
>
> (73, 76–80)

In *Georgics* II the poet had reflected that a "free Soul" unrestrained by "heavy Blood" can fly "to the Height / Of Nature, and unclouded Fields of Light" (685–87). The joys imagined there (to which, he suggests, his own heavy soul cannot aspire) are those experienced here by the bees, and their bliss is closely tied to a political situation which clearly allows them the life "void of Care and Strife" that the poet there declares he must look for in solitude (688–90). The passage is at once celebratory and didactic, timeless and immediate, distant from and involved in the problems of the 1690s; Dryden exults in the divine pleasures of the soul, yet he projects his scene into contemporary affairs by presenting sure succession as the key to stability in society and therefore to personal happiness.

He is again just as distant and philosophical as he is impassioned and concerned with his own times when he later describes the conflict between "two contending [bee] Princes" (121). The contemporary overtones which pervade his rendering of Vergil's civil conflict are unmistakable.[66] There is no doubt as to the identity of the "grizly Prince" hoping to depose the "Monarch" who is of "Regal Race," while the exhortation to the bees, "to the lawful King restore his Right," is as charged with loyalty to the Stuarts as any of Dryden's great political poems (134–45). Yet despite the gravity of his subject material, Dryden gently mocks the tiny creatures; for, as Hopkins observes of his descriptions of the contenders for the throne, "we remember" that their " 'narrow' bodies and 'Chaps' are . . . the minute mandibles and abdomens of insects, and there is something comically futile as well as touchingly grand about the fighting monarch's 'obstinacy.' "[67] Dryden's air, then, is one of an amused onlooker: of a Democritus daily supplied with occasions of laughter. However, he also seems strongly aware that his poem has a purpose within the society from which his observations derive.

As part of the description of "the Nature of the Bees" (220), he asserts:

> Such are the Bees, and such their busie Care:
> Studious of Honey, each in his Degree,
> The youthful Swain, the grave experienc'd Bee:
> That in the Field; this in Affairs of State,
> Employ'd at home, abides within the Gate:
> To fortify the Combs, to build the Wall,
> To prop the Ruins lest the Fabrick fall.
>
> (257–63)

This idealized hive is, in effect, a miniature of those equally-idealized portraits of England which have special importance in *Annus Mirabilis* and *Absalom and Achitophel* as incentives to national unity and peace. Here again Dryden seems to be advising, as he did in *Absalom and Achitophel*, that it is a citizen's duty "To Patch the Flaws, and Buttress up the Wall" when "ancient Fabrics nod, and threat to fall" (801–2).[68] The importance of his own place in society as a "grave experienc'd Bee" propping "the Ruins lest the Fabrick fall" is suggested by the echo itself from what is in his own reckoning his best social satire. Such an echo is not only a reminder of his own experience "in Affairs of State" but points to his continuation of a social task undertaken long before. The Aristæus episode with which the *Georgics* end again focuses attention on the importance of Dryden's work.

As he introduces Aristæus, Dryden seems to own a special affinity with him. While Vergil begins by presenting "pastor Aristæus" (317), the "shepherd" makes an appearance in Dryden's text as "Sad Aristæus" and then himself stresses the injustice of his suffering as a poet (451). Vergil's protesting son expresses doubt over his paternity as he addresses his mother,[69] but Dryden's complains, "What boots it, that from Phoebus Loyns I spring, / The third by him and thee, from Heav'ns high King?" (458–59). His subsequent lament over his "bitter Fate" and lack of those things which "The needful Aids of Human Life allow" has an intensity that points to genuine empathy on the part of the poet himself. In fact, in his hands the Aristæus epyllion seems to become not only an exposition of the poet's role in society but an explanation for his own *modus operandi* in these translations. The assimilation of his poetic task and Aristæus's mission is suggested not only by the unequivocal attribution to Vergil's shepherd of Apollo's paternity, but by the interpolated concern with lineage in the lines quoted above as well as in Arethusa's speech to Cyrene, where Aristæus's ancestry is traced to his "Paternal Stream" and beyond that to "Heav'n" (503–8). This concern with the poet's kinship with heaven and descent through a legitimate line from Apollo looks back to the preceding *Georgics* and beyond them to *The Hind and the Panther*. Here too seems to lurk the point implied earlier in the *Georgics* (which has seeds in the connection between poet and savior made in *The Hind and the Panther*) that, in a state where lawful monarchic succession has failed, protection and nurture of the land falls into the hands of the nation's leading poet. Just as Dryden's own divinely-sanctioned task involves transformation and the birth of new life from old material (or retold stories) for the benefit of his native land so the poet-shepherd will use his divine gifts to create a new race of bees from a corpse and release his land from blight. And just as Dryden—or any true poet—must have access to the "crystal Flood" yearned for by the poet in *Georgics* II so Aristæus's mission begins at the mouth of "Crystal" streams (690, 515), where, because of his kinship with Apollo, he is permitted "To view the Secrets" of the "deep Abodes" (511–12, 514).

In his efforts to relieve his lands from plague, Aristæus is in effect seeking to "trace the secret Cause" which lies in "Nature's Laws"—and which, *Georgics* II declares, can be found through the study of "known Effects." This kind of search is, of course, not only Dryden's prescription for personal contentment, but the task undertaken in his own *Georgics*, where the "known Effects" examined are drawn from distant and recent history and the works of his poetic ancestors. The first instruction given to Aristæus by his mother can be seen, therefore, as crucial not only to his success but to that of Dryden's own poetic endeavors. It can also be seen as the source of true quiet of mind for the individual and for the nation. Cyrene informs her son that before all else he must "Implore [the] Aid" of Proteus, who "only knows / The secret Cause and Cure of all thy Woes" (569–70). In *The Hind and the Panther* Proteus is the embodiment of "Conscience," which, when espoused by those like the trimming Panther, is "never to be ty'd" (3:185.818). The importance of confronting and pinning down conscience before taking action which will have future national consequences is stressed by the Hind as she pinpoints "*Camelion* hew[ed]" conscience as the source of the present upheaval in England and ruefully concludes, "Immortal pow'rs the term of conscience know, / But int'rest is her name with men below" (3:184–85.788, 823–24). She is careful to note, however, that alongside "*Phoebus*," "*Homer*, who learn'd the language of the sky" is among those powers who "know" the term. The same suggestion that poetry can provide access to truth or at least a quiet of mind in which the individual can begin a search for truth underlies Aristæus's journey to Proteus' abode.

The place where the "Goddess guides her Son" is "a Mountain's hollow Womb" where lies

> A large Recess, conceal'd from Human Eyes;
> Where heaps of Billows, driv'n by Wind and Tide,

In Form of War, their wat'ry Ranks divide;
And there, like Centries set, without the Mouth abide:
A Station safe for Ships, when Tempests roar,
A silent Harbour, and a cover'd Shoar.
Secure within resides the various God.

                                                    (603–13)

Dryden's detail about the cave's concealment "from Human Eyes" is
his addition, and his "silent Harbour" seems closer to the description in
the dedication of a composed mind than to Vergil's original:

> A good Conscience is a Port which is Land-lock'd on every side, and where
> no Winds can possibly invade, no Tempests can arise. There a Man may
> stand upon the Shore, and not only see his own Image, but that of his
> Maker, clearly reflected from the undisturb'd and silent waters. (5:143)

If Aristæus is to end his woes, Dryden suggests, he must first achieve
that quiet of mind, which is secure from history's winds and tumultuous
billows; for there, in "silent waters," he may discover "secret Causes."

The significance to history of Aristæus' confrontation with Proteus—or his own conscience—lies in his request to the "Prophet and
. . . God" for "Thy Help, my perish'd People to restore" (558, 650).
Vergil has "Venimus huc, lapsis quæsitum oracula rebus": "I come seeking oracles for my weary fortunes" (449). Manipulating chronology,
Dryden makes his Aristæus sound like Aeneas, although the plea could
easily be his own or that of any Jacobite. The point is that like Homer's
Menelaus, who secures Proteus and learns about the past fate of his
fellow Greeks and his own future,[70] like Aeneas, when he is guided by
the Sybil to the underworld, and like Dryden as he undertakes translation and fable, Aristæus must face a mythical past before taking action
which will affect his own future and that of his people. Having made
his way into the cave and pinned down the "Seer," Aristæus is informed
that the cause of his troubles is, in effect, his "lawless Lust." For, he is
told, he is being hounded by the curse of Orpheus, on whose bride he
"intended Rape" (651, 660–61). Proteus now tells the tale of Orpheus,
whom Dryden (not Vergil) calls "the Poets King" (787) and whose
music could move rocks to pity, make trees bend their heads, and
"Fierce Tygers [couch] around, and [loll] their fawning Tongues"
(740–41). Despite his great powers, Orpheus meets his downfall when
"strong Desires th'impatient Youth invade," and "Forgetful of the Law,
nor Master of his Mind," he violates the pact he made with "Hell" by
"cast[ing] his Eyes behind" for a glance at Eurydice (702–13). Aristæus's lesson, then, is about the tragedy that befalls when there is a lack
of control over the destructive and irrational forces that threaten human

life. Now, after confronting Proteus and listening to his tale, he is able to make amends for the past and for his own lust and to secure the future. Clearly, as in the programmatic introduction in the third *Georgic*, enormous power is attributed to poets in this story of the poet-shepherd. There is also a strong awareness of the responsibility that goes with such power, for Dryden points to the poet as society's means to salvation.

Significantly, he ends his *Georgics* by again contrasting his own peaceful toils with William III's destructive campaigns:

> Thus have I sung of Fields, and Flocks, and Trees,
> And of the waxen Work of lab'ring Bees;
> While mighty *Cæsar*, thund'ring from afar,
> Seeks on *Euphrates* Banks the Spoils of War:
> With conqu'ring Arms asserts his Country's Cause,
> With Arts of Peace the willing People draws:
> On the glad Earth the Golden Age renews,
> And his great Father's Path to Heav'n pursues:
> While I at *Naples* pass my peaceful Days,
> Affecting Studies of less noisy Praise.
>
> (807–16)

This conclusion is distinguished from Vergil's by Dryden's particular interest in "lab'ring Bees" as well as by the omission of Vergil's direct naming of himself. Placed, in this way, firmly within the context of his own rather than Vergil's *Georgics*, the ironic treatment of Caesar here becomes even more apparent. The figure presented in line 812, who draws a willing people with arts of peace, is not only inconsistent with the Caesar portrayed at the beginning of *Georgics* III, but is undermined by the interpolations which reveal him seeking "Spoils of War" and asserting "conqu'ring Arms." Dryden seems to be measuring England's war-mongering Caesar (a concern of his own *Georgics*) against the ideal embodied by Vergil's peace-oriented Augustus and by the son at the beginning of *Paradise Regained*: "[I] held it more humane, more heav'nly first / By winning words to conquer willing hearts, / And make perswasion do the work of fear" (1:221–23). As he then replaces Vergil's apology for his "ignoble leisure" with a contrast between the works of his own "peaceful Days" and the strife-ridden and strife-engendering arms of England's Caesar, Dryden in fact allies his toils with the arts of peace that should also be the concern of the nation's leader. In other words he ends his *Georgics* by pointing to his own fitness to undertake epic and William III's inelegibility to be his hero.

This tension between, on the one hand, Dryden's conviction in the healing powers of great poetry and his own powers in particular, and,

on the other, his view that the 1690s were not an age for great poetry is
at the heart of his *Aeneis*, where, Aristæus-like, he forces the nation to
confront its conscience as he himself does. Both the personal process
and the task of negotiating between old ideologies and a new world continue and are extended in the *Aeneis*; however, the ground work for
Dryden's unheroic epic is completely laid in his Georgics with their rejection of Spenserian-style toils and the traditions associated with those
toils. Accordingly, as they have been outlined here, the key features of
Dryden's *Georgics* anticipate prevailing characteristics of eighteenth-
century literary forms: emphasis on the poet's rather than history's redeeming powers, uncertainty about the future or the importance of political and historical issues, and concern ultimately with the individual.
These are the building blocks too, of course, of the *Aeneis*, where the
more obvious failure of the heroic is manifested in the poem's emphasis
on moral truth and individual survival and virtue over the cultivation
of national history and a national hero.

3

Towards a Carmen Perpetuum

THE *MAGNA CARTA* OF HEROICK POETRY

> When first young *Maro* in his boundless Mind
> A Work t'outlast Immortal *Rome* design'd,
> Perhaps he seem'd *above* the Critick's Law,
> And but from *Nature's Fountains* seem'd to draw:
> But when t'examine ev'ry Part he came,
> *Nature* and *Homer* were, he found, the *same*:
> Convinc'd, amaz'd, he checks the bold Design,
> And Rules as strict his labour'd Work confine,
> As if the *Stagyrite* o'erlook'd each Line.
> Learn hence for Ancient *Rules* a just Esteem;
> To copy *Nature* is to copy *Them*.
>
> —Pope, "An Essay on Criticism"

In order to fortify her argument concerning the authority and rights of the Anglican church, Dryden's Panther employs Vergil's myth wrongfully to claim ownership "By long possession" (like Latinus) of "all the land" and to accuse the Hind of coming, like Aeneas, with her "exil'd Gods" and "intruding line, / To share my sceptre, which you call to join" (3:523.766–80). As Zwicker remarks, what is interesting about this passage from the point of view of the *Aeneis* is that Dryden "should already in 1687 have conceived its central action not as imperial destiny but as invasion and conquest." He also points out that all the issues with which the Panther is here concerned—"invasion and conquest," "property and propriety," "political deceit and political legitimacy"— would be raised again throughout Dryden's *Vergil*.[1] Equally important, however, is the function in the translation of the type of "veil" with which the Panther accuses the Hind of covering her "intended wrong" but which, ironically, applies to her own use of Vergil's fable (3:184.777). Like this episode of *The Hind and the Panther*, Dryden's *Aeneis* employs Vergil's tale of Aeneas's arrival in Latium not to provide answers by analogy but to pose probing questions about contemporary

political and ecclesiastical issues. Again, too, the comfort offered is in
the method itself, which depends upon the poet's sacred powers.

In response to the Panther's manipulation of Vergil in the interest of
her "*Proteus* Conscience," the Hind asserts faith in "What *Phoebus* from
the *Tripod* shall disclose" (3:185.819).[2] As the California editors point
out, she alludes here to Aeneas's plea to Helenus for guidance in Vergil's third book (3:437.n.819). In Dryden's own *Aeneis* III, Aeneas addresses Helenus as a "Royal Seer" "Whom *Phoebus* taught unerring
Prophecy, / From his own Tripod," and then decribes how "To *Phoebus*
next, my trembling Steps he led: / Full of religious Doubts and awful
dread" (458–62, 476–77). He sounds like Dryden himself at the beginning of *The Hind and the Panther* as he reflects upon the "doubts," which
resulted in a "manhood, long misled by wandring fires" (3:125.72–78).
In both *The Hind and the Panther* and the *Aeneis*, uncertainty and doubts
continue to plague the poet, this time as he confronts England's crises
of conscience. Yet inherent in each poem is a conviction that if the
"*Camelion* hew[ed]" kaleidoscope of contemporary politics and history
is set against the *Aeneid*, Vergil himself will provide the poet's "trembling
steps" with a guide to Phoebus's "Tripod" and its "unerring" disclo-
sures. The basis of such faith lies in the central theme of *Georgics*: that
underneath the elusive fable (or obscuring "veil") of Vergil's poetry are
Phoebus's laws, which are also the laws of nature—and outside historical time.

In the first metaphor of the dedication of his *Aeneis*, Dryden instructs
the epic poet as he would a builder:

> There is nothing to be left void in a firm Building: even the Cavities ought
> not to be fill'd with Rubbish, which is of a perishable kind, destructive to
> the strength: But with Brick or Stone, though of less pieces, yet of the same
> Nature, and fitted to the Cranies. Even the least portions of them must be
> of the Epick kind; all things must be Grave, Majestical, and Sublime: Noth-
> ing of Foreign Nature, like the trifling Novels, which *Ariosto* and others have
> inserted in their Poems. (5:267)

The same imagery and issues permeate the Hind's discussion of the
firmness of the Roman Catholic church. Louis Bredvold notes her scorn
"of a state church without any inner principle of authority"[3]:

> How answ'ring to its end a church is made,
> Whose pow'r is but to counsell and persuade?
> O solid rock, on which secure she stands!
> Eternal house, not built with mortal hands!
>
> (3:137.491–94)

He might have contrasted this bitter comment with her defense of the infrastructure of the Catholic church:

> 'Tis said with ease, but never can be prov'd,
> The church her old foundations has remov'd,
> And built new doctrines on unstable sands:
> Judge that ye winds and rains; you prov'd her, yet she stands.
> Those ancient doctrines charg'd on her for new,
> Shew when, and how, and from what hands they grew.
>
> (3:156.587–92)

In the same way, too, as Dryden argues that an epic poem in "all things must be Grave, Majestical, and Sublime: Nothing of Foreign Nature," the Hind stresses unity and sublimity as inherent in the fabric of the Catholic church:

> One in herself not rent by schism, but sound,
> Entire, one solid shining Diamond,
> Not sparkles shatter'd into sects like you,
> One is the church, and must be to be true:
> One central principle of unity,
> As undivided, so from errours free,
> As one in faith, so one in sanctity.
>
> (3:154–55.526–32)

The building imagery was to be employed again in the preface to *Fables*. "I have built a House, where I intended but a Lodge: Yet with better Success than a certain Nobleman, who beginning with a Dog-kennil, never liv'd to finish the Palace he had contriv'd," Dryden observes in his opening paragraph (Kinsley, 1444). By describing his poetic endeavors in terms he had already used to outline the principles on which the authority of the Catholic church was based, Dryden underscores the extent to which he viewed tradition as fundamental to solid and lasting poetry. He also reveals that he held as sacred a poetic building whose fabric was drawn from the sublimities of past poets so that a "Grave" and "Majestical" structure stood "secure" on "old foundations," radiating light as "one solid shining Diamond."

It is unsurprising, then, that as well as launching his dedication with an *ars poetica* that reiterates *The Hind and the Panther*'s recognition of the sacred nature of the works of poetic forefathers, Dryden immediately acknowledges his own duty as a secular apostle. While George Noyes dismisses the opening sentence ("A heroick Poem, truly such, is undoubtedly the greatest Work which the Soul of Man is capable to perform") with a yawn,[4] the citation here of Rapin's well-known maxim places Dryden's translation in an epic and critical tradition from the start.[5] Such almost self-conscious intertextuality is maintained throughout, and probably most comments Dryden makes have a precedent in one or more of the numerous ancient and modern, Greek, Italian, French and English poets and critics on which he drew.

Not only does the method (which is, of course, that of all Dryden's works) attribute to the undertaking the authority of the past, however; as the *Georgics* had endeavored to do with poetry in general, it traces its roots to nature itself. This is emphasized when the dedication turns from the building metaphor to "touch . . . on some few of those many Rules of imitating Nature, which *Aristotle* drew from *Homers Iliads* and *Odysses*, and which he fitted to the Drama" (5:268–69). Dryden had made the same argument twenty years earlier in the preface containing "The Grounds of Criticism in Tragedy" attached to his *Troilus and Cressida* (1679). "If the Rules be well consider'd," he there observes, quoting Rapin, "we shall find them to be made only to reduce Nature into Method, to trace her step by step, and not to suffer the least mark of her to escape us: 'tis only by these, that probability in Fiction is maintain'd, which is the Soul of Poetry" (13:248).[6] In his "Author's Apology for Heroique Poetry; and Poetique Licence," prefixed to *The State of Innocence and Fall of Man*," published the previous year in 1677, he had argued that the reliability of the "rules" derives from the "force of Universal Tradition" or what has "generally . . . pleased, and through all ages":

> *Aristotle* rais'd the Fabrique of his Poetry, from observation of those things, in which *Euripides, Sophocles,* and *Æschylus* pleas'd: he consider'd how they rais'd the Passions, and thence has drawn rules for our Imitation. . . . Thus I grant you, that the knowledge of Nature was the Original Rule; and that all Poets ought to study her; as well as *Aristotle* and *Horace* her Interpreters. But then this also undeniably follows, that those things which delight all Ages, must have been an imitation of Nature. (12:91)

The reason for the rules and the importance of the "force of Universal Tradition" are also indicated in the preface to *Troilus and Cressida*: they guard against "the ridiculous mistakes and gross absurdities, which have been made by those Poets who have taken their Fancy only for their guide, [for] if this Fancy be not regulated, 'tis a mere caprice, and utterly incapable to produce a reasonable and judicious Poem" (13:248). The dedication begins, then, by again expressing for poetry the "absolute need for a final authority," that Donald Benson sees exhibited in *Religio Laici* and *The Hind and the Panther*.[7] The underlying belief that the "Apostolick" tradition of poetry (like that of the church) could lead him down its "stream" to the "native source" (or "truth") meant that Dryden could turn to Vergil for answers both in 1687, when the constitutional crisis was ecclesiastical, and in the 1690s, when it was monarchical (3:157.612–15).

As it searches the past for solutions to contemporary crises, however, Dryden's *Vergil* runs into problems that highlight the interwoven nature of historical and literary developments through the seventeenth and eighteenth centuries. Perhaps even more so than the *Georgics*, the *Aeneis* clings to time-honored traditions and rules, deriving its authority from them. Yet it simultaneously rejects the strictures of the past and explores new ways of treating old and new issues. William Frost pinpoints the source of the tensions inherent in the translation when he observes that in the *Aeneis* "Dryden confronts the past and present: the long echoing corridors of lettered Europe and the urgent immediate expectations of coffeehouse circles in modern Europe."[8] The result is not only conflict between the rules observed in those corridors and the demands of the present, but the adjustment of "traditional standards and beliefs" by "new modes of thought."[9] Dryden's *Aeneis* reflects the traditions, concerns and hallmarks of the seventeenth-century Royalist epic while exhibiting properties and characteristics that were to find a home in eighteenth-century literature.

The appropriateness of his *Aeneis* as a medium through which Dryden could perform his special task in the 1690s lay in Vergil's subject matter and task as they had been presented by seventeenth-century French and English royalists and neoclassicists. The "*Truths*," as Bossu puts it, which the "general *Fiction*" of the *Aeneid* "disguises, [and which make] up the *Fable* and Life of the Poem" are concerned with "the establishment of a new Empire" (to quote Rapin) and (to quote Segrais) with "la Religion" or "des Dieux qu'Enée eût dû apporter en Italie."[10] Bossu asserts, therefore, that Vergil "ought to instruct *Augustus* as the Founder of a great Empire, and to inspire into him as well as his Successors, the same Spirit and Conduct which had rais'd this *Empire* to such a Grandeur."[11] Likewise, when Dryden recalls that "*Augustus* is . . . shadow'd in the Person of *Æneas*" and that Vergil's duty was to advise Augustus "how to behave himself in his new Monarchy, so as to gain the Affections of his Subjects, and deserve to be call'd the Father of his Country," he is echoing another commonplace of neoclassical criticism: that which recognizes both the mission of the poet in a time of national crisis and the special quality of the *Aeneid*. The ultimate authority on the matter was Aristotle, who, observes Rapin, "saith" that the "end" of the "*Epopoea*" is "the *instruction* of *Princes* and *Grandees*."[12] However, when Dryden begins to consider the instructions he should lay out as poet, the rules and assumptions of his predecessors fray under his fingertips.

Underlying the givens of heroic theory transmitted from Aristotle is a conflict pointed to by the elder Scaliger when he based his *Poetices libri septem* on two major convictions: "Nature imposes one set of conditions upon poetry; the needs of the audience another." (For Scaliger, as for Dryden and others, Vergil is nature and his works inspired by that "universal [soul] of which he speaks" [see p. 34 above].)[13] These contradictory premises are reflected in the works of all the major neoclassical critics on which Dryden was drawing. Both English and continental discourses as well as Dryden's own earlier discussions of heroic theory, for example, render perfunctory the statement at the beginning of the dedication that the purpose of an "heroick Poem" is to present ideals designed "to form the Mind to Heroick Virtue by Example" (5:267). Likewise, the essay's equally urgent emphasis on temporal, political and social difference merely reiterates what all Dryden's Italian, French and English predecessors recognized: that "the Instructions, which [Vergil] ought to give both to Prince and People, were quite different from those Homer left his Countrymen."[14] The extent of the differences between the situation confronting Vergil and that confronting Dryden, however, meant that Dryden was forced to probe too deeply into the gap between platonic ideal and historical reality glossed over by his predecessors. As a result the *Aeneis* threatens the foundations of traditional neoclassical and royalists models and marks the demise of their reign as a social and literary force.

Sixteenth and seventeeth-century poets and critics could use glorified Roman history as a basis for their undertakings because of Augustus's reputation as a benevolent and civilizing leader. Vergil's marriage of an historically-legitimate Augustus to a platonic "idea of a Prince or accomplish'd Person in general" is outlined by Rapin: "So that out of the vertues of *Augustus*, and an infinite number of perfections distributed and scattered among divers other Heroes, *Virgil* fram'd his; in as much as the true Heroick vertue is a combination of all the vertues, as *Aristotle* affirmes in his Ethicks" (18, 24). Bossu also stresses Augustus's piety, and defends his political actions against Tacitus's accusations when he argues, "*Augustus Cæsar* did nothing to settle himself upon the Throne, but what his *Piety* put him upon undertaking; or at least he had a mind the World should think so."[15] In the interest of presenting an ideal of leadership, Dryden's dedication appears to uphold Augustus's reputation. Like Bossu's, its overview of Roman history from the Tarquins to Augustus works to defend the Augustan settlement as the only solution to civil strife. While Bossu concludes, "Thus *Augustus* destroyed nothing, he only re-established a tottering State,"[16] Dryden observes that "the Commonwealth," "lost without a ressource," was "turn'd into a Monarchy, by the Conduct and good Fortune of *Augustus*" (5:280). Like his predecessors, too, Dryden attributes the success of Augustus's regime to his character. He even felt Segrais's summary of the Roman's virtues worthy of being interpolated into his own essay, "Translated literally" (5:288).

To this extent, Dryden is able to follow Bossu and others in maintaining Vergil's platonism while setting the *Aeneid* in the context of Roman history and Vergil's own time. However, problems arise as soon as he begins to impose the needs of his own audience by situating the dedication and his *Aeneis* in the context of English history and, specifically, the 1690s. For, in "endeavour[ing] to make Virgil speak such English, as he wou'd himself have spoken, if he had been born in England, and in this present Age" he had somehow to reconcile Vergil's poem of national and historical glory with what he (as a Jacobite loyalist) viewed as an essentially unheroic age. The true English king was in exile (with little hope of being restored in 1697 when the dedication was composed), and Dryden had already implied that the leader at the helm of England's new regime was an Homeric-style figure: one of "those ungodly Man-killers, whom we Poets, when we flatter them, call Heroes; a race of Men who can never enjoy quiet in themselves, 'till they have taken it from all the World" (4:374). His solution is to present his Augustus and Aeneas in a way that at points revives the Tacitean version of Augustus, at others upholds the Roman's good reputation and sometimes does both simultaneously. His aim is to demonstrate the dangers of allowing a bad leader (for example William III) the powers, privileges and honors which were worked to fruitful ends by a leader of sound character.

As Zwicker observes, the presentation of "ancient figures in a language that [argues] the circumstances of William III's kingship" is unmistakable when Dryden launches his "long and peculiar passage on succession and title as they bear on Aeneas's claims to the Trojan office."[17] To label Aeneas an "Elective King" and to expound at length on why he "cou'd not pretend to be *Priam*'s Heir in a Lineal Succession" was just as daring on Dryden's part as many of the satiric punches in his post-1688 plays (5:283–84). Having made a connection between and contrasted the honesty of Augustus's and William III's titles, Dryden then enumerates the

> Manners which our Poet gives his Heroe; and which are the same which were eminently seen in his *Augustus*. Those Manners were Piety to the Gods, and a dutiful Affection to his Father; Love to his Relations; Care of his People; Courage and Conduct in the Wars; Gratitude to those who had oblig'd him; and Justice in general to Mankind. (5:285–86)

From the point of view of probably most English subjects, the only quality listed here which could be applied to William III was "Courage and Conduct in the Wars." Even then, an exhausted England might object, the king's "Conduct" was dubious, especially on the issue of a standing army. To be sure, "Piety to the Gods" was the excuse for William III's arrival in England, and the land had breathed a sigh of relief when Protestantism was firmly reestablished in 1688, yet in subsequent years the king's supposed "Piety" was subject to criticism. William Anderton, for example, angrily accused William III and his "*Latitudinarian Gang*" of having "dissolved the True Old Church of *England*, and erected a new One upon a mere civil Basis, such as 'tis, of Rebellion, Perjury and Usurpation, and rendered it impossible to retrieve the Discipline of the Church and her Sacred Offices during his Government here." Nathaniel Johnston, too, dedicated a whole section of his political pamphlet to "The uncertain State of our Religion."[18]

Given the continuous animosity between William and his parliament and the fact that the English never, in fact, ceased to view the Dutch prince as a foreigner, Dryden's consideration of Augustus's "Care of his People" may well be a bitter comment on the type of kingship established in 1688.[19] He may also be reminding William of the "Gratitude" he owed "to those who had oblig'd him" by inviting him to England and supporting his continental wars. If so, his criticism is intensified and his charge woven into the ongoing pattern of English politics through the notion of "Gratitude," which (again) was a catchphrase of Stuart politics. It also seems possible that Dryden mentions Augustus's "Love to his Relations" in order to comment on the reputedly cold relationship between William III and Mary II. If Dryden's focus really had been Augustus, he may have deemed it wiser to omit this quality; he had, after all, censored Augustus for incest with his daughter Julia in his 1680 preface to *Ovid's Epistles* (1:110). Certainly, positioned as it is between the discussion of Aeneas's respect for his father-in-law's title and the passage which dwells on Augustus's "Filial Love" and "Duty to his Father while he liv'd" (5:286), Dryden's praise of the Roman's "dutiful Affection to his Father" implicitly condemns William III's metaphorical patricide and regicide. While he here forgets his earlier condemnations of Augustus so as to present him as a paradigm against which to measure the monstrous Dutch prince, however, Dryden has nonetheless indicted him in the eyes of at least Jacobite readers by drawing attention to his status as a newcomer who could not claim "the proper Character of a King by Inheritance, who is born a Father of his Country" (5:284). He further darkens the picture, in effect placing Augustus irrevocably in the shadow of Tacitean history, by recognizing (and stressing) the need to clear his title from the charge of "Conquest" and by ominously warning that "what was introduc'd by force, by force may be remov'd" (5:284). The inconsistency of his presentation, like his slip in forgetting as he defends Augustus's title that he has already labelled him "Conqueror," points to the tension that pervades both the dedication and *Aeneis*. This tension is highlighted in that earlier incident.

Under the guise of discussing Vergil's position as national poet, Dryden contemplates his own:

> I say that *Virgil* having maturely weigh'd the Condition of the Times in which he liv'd: that an entire Liberty was not to be retriev'd: that the present Settlement had the prospect of a long continuance under the same Family, or those adopted into it: that he held his Paternal Estate from the Bounty of the Conqueror, by whom he was likewise enrich'd, esteem'd and cherish'd: that this Conquerour, though of a bad kind, was the very best of it: that the Arts of Peace flourish'd under him. . . . (5:281)

The "Conqueror" presented here invites a comparison between Augustus and Louis XIV and a contrast between both of them and William III. The passage recalls Dryden's praise of Louis' patronage of the arts in the "Discourse Concerning . . . Satire." There Boileau's work is described in the same coinage imagery as Dryden uses in the dedication for his own translation (5:334), and the value of the Frenchman's "Coin" is attributed in part to the monarch under which he was writing:

> What [Boileau] borrows from the Ancients, he repays with Usury of his own: in Coin as good, and almost as Universally valuable: For setting prejudice and Partiality apart, though he is our Enemy, the Stamp of a *Louis*, the Patron of all Arts, is not much inferiour to the Medal of an *Augustus Cæsar*. (4:12)

At this point in the dedication Dryden also seems to have his eye on Segrais, who observed, "Il [Vergil] passa sa vie sous le regne d'un Prince qui le combla de richesses, & qui a été l'un des plus grands hommes qu'on puisse proposer aux autres pour exemple." As Dryden also does here, Segrais pointed to Vergil's gratitude to a benevolent leader concerned with the peaceful arts of civilization: "Il faut donc le regarder en même-temps comme un sujet d'Auguste, obligé à son Maître, & comme un Romain charmé de la gloire de Rome." As Dryden could not, Segrais implies a parallel between Vergil's role and his own in his "traduction de l'Eneïde," which he entrusts to "la protection d'un Monarque, en qui l'on void éclater la grandeur des Cesars, et la vertu des Heros."[20] Behind Dryden's words, then, is the same bitterness with which, in 1694, he lamented living "in a stupid Military State," where "Pen and Pencil find an equal Fate" (4:463.51–52). Like his defense of

Octavian in the note to his first *Georgic* (see p. 75 above), his comments here seem designed to contrast Augustus's behavior as "Conqueror" with that of the new English king. Unlike the historical invader portrayed by Segrais and others, William III has not turned his conquest into a triumph of peace and civilization, choosing instead to drain the English treasury as he takes peace "from all the World." Even the tyrannical Louis XIV is a model king in comparison; he at least is aware of the value of "good coin" in national coffers—both literary and monetary!

However, by calling Augustus "Conqueror" so as to raise the issue of the Glorious Revolution, and by recognizing his settlement as indeed a conquest (which "though of a bad kind, was the very best of it"), Dryden draws attention to that aspect of his character which had been largely ignored in the seventeenth century.[21] In so doing he anticipates the eighteenth-century condemnation of Augustus and contempt for Vergil and Horace in particular as "*flattering, soothing* Tools / Fit to *praise Tyrants*, and *gull Fools*."[22] In fact, his discussion here embodies both the favorable Augustanism that was carried through into the eighteenth century from the seventeenth as well as the key elements of eighteenth-century anti-Augustanism. On the surface the passage upholds the seventeenth-century view of the *Aeneid* as an instruction manual for societies seeking a strong leader and settled government as an end to civil discord. T. W. Harrison remarks on the appeal of Vergil's blueprint for civic stability: "Even to the Roman Republican as well as to the seventeenth-century Royalists, and even some Parliamentarians, absolute monarchy was better than anarchy, democracy, or civil war."[23] This view lived on in the eighteenth century. Joseph Warton, for example, sees Vergil as "reconcil[ing] his countrymen to this almost necessary change of government," although he adds, with eighteenth-century hesitation, that the poet instructed "that if [Augustus] would reign ALONE, he should reign like an Æneas."[24] Nicolas Tindal, too, accepts the "best of a bad kind" philosophy; in his essay attached to Spence's *Polymetis* (1747), he declares,

Virgil wrote in the service of the new usurpation on the state; and all that can be said in his vindication, is, that the temper and bent of their constitution at that time were such, that the reins of the government must have fallen into the hands of some one person or another, who might possibly be less indulgent than Augustus was at that time.[25]

Echoes of Dryden's dedication in both Tindal's and Warton's essays suggest his influence on their thinking. Dryden's portrayal of Augustus as promoter and protector of the "Arts of Peace," and his implication that the Roman victory was that of civilization, also survived into the eighteenth-century. The sentiment behind Dryden's words is that pervading the passages of Cowley and Addison cited by Weinbrot as he outlines this aspect of Augustanism. In 1664, as he notes, Abraham Cowley "remarks that 'the Roman victory / Taught our rude Land, Arts and Civility.' " In 1713, Addison's Juba still feels confident in arguing that "A Roman Soul is bent on higher Views: / To civilize the rude unpolish'd World," and his action throughout *Cato* is based on "Roman" values.[26]

By presenting such an Augustus as a rebuff to William III's relentless military policies and neglect of the arts, Dryden also anticipates another eighteenth-century movement to which Weinbrot draws attention. "Addison's disgust with Achilles," he argues, "reflects a major cultural shift away from Homeric and towards more pacific ideals. The eighteenth century was ravaged by terrible and costly wars that nonetheless required anti-war psychology. . . ."[27] However, the same "pacific ideals" meant that Augustus was often viewed by eighteenth-century critics as a tyrant and destroyer of liberty, and the charges that were frequently laid against him also lie close to the surface of Dryden's text at this point. Perhaps thinking bitterly of the present state of the English nation, he suggests that the enslavement of the Romans—a product of centuries of discord—was confirmed with Augustus, who was able to impose his rule because "an entire Liberty was not to be retriev'd." He also draws attention to Augustus's (or Octavian's) crimes in the proscriptions and confiscation of old family estates when he mentions Vergil's gratitude at the return of his "Paternal Estate." Later in the dedication too, while he prefaces the lines by commenting "whether they will pass for Gospel now, I cannot tell," he nonetheless cites Ariosto's indictment of Augustus's involvement:

> Augustus Caesar was not such a Saint,
> As Virgil maketh him by his description.
> His love of learning scuseth that complaint,
> That men might justly make of his proscription.[28]

In essence, this is precisely the argument Dryden is making in the earlier passage under discussion. It is also interesting that, as Weinbrot notes, "This particular section [of Ariosto's *Orlando Furioso*] . . . was singled out as a gloss in the notes to Amelot de la Houssaye's translation of Tacitus (1690) and thus appeared as well in 1698 in 'Dryden's' version of Amelot."[29] At its most extreme, the criticism implied by Dryden becomes, in the eighteenth century, the kind of angry outburst that—as, again, Weinbrot notes—"Ambrose Philip's Briton Vanoc" aims at "the

Roman apologist Valens": "Came you, then, here, thus far, through Waves, to conquer, / To waste, to plunder; out of mere Compassion?"

Vanoc's concern at the end of his speech with precedent-setting crimes against princes is also present here in the dedication: did you come, he continues, "To lead in Bonds the generous, free-born Princes, / Who spurn, who fight against your Tyranny?" A common exception to Augustus in the Renaissance, and one which was "urged most forcefully in the eighteenth century," Weinbrot asserts, was that in destroying liberty although ruling well himself Augustus was "responsible for the bad leaders after him."[30] While the eighteenth-century Vanocs are concerned with the effects of tyranny, however, Dryden's objection to chains imposed on "generous, free-born Princes" involves the disruption of genealogical succession in monarchy. His ironic defence of Augustus's adoption by Julius Caesar ("the present Settlement had the prospect of a long continuance in the same Family, or those adopted into it") points to his fears about the precedent set by the Glorious Revolution. As any contemporary reader would know, Augustus had no heir (this is in fact remembered in *Aeneis* VI), and the decline of the Roman empire set in with his adopted successor Tiberius, who was evil, debauched and probably mad.

The paradox is, of course, that Dryden resurrects anti-Augustanism in the spirit with which it would be employed in the eighteenth century while clinging tenaciously to those seventeenth-century royalist convictions that the eighteenth century rejected. This is most obvious when he declares, "As for *Augustus*, or his Uncle *Julius*, claiming by descent from *Æneas*; that Title is already out of doors. *Æneas* succeeded not, but was Elected. Troy was fore-doom'd to fall for ever" (5:285). Dryden here presents the view that would become common in the eighteenth century: the fall of Rome can be traced to Augustus's reign. ("*Augustus*" is, after all, "shadow'd in the Person of *Æneas*" and Rome, as Vergil demonstrates, was to be a second Troy.) Yet, while Swift and others attributed Rome's decline to Augustus's tyrannical upsetting of balance in the state, Dryden pinpoints the beginning of that decline at the disruption of Priam's royal line.[31] His language threatens a similar fate for England if the genealogical rights of the Stuart household are rejected in favor of a king who "succeeded not, but was Elected."[32] Behind Dryden's manipulation of Roman history is his awareness that if Vergil will lead him through an historical spectrum to the truths disclosed at Phoebus's tripod, he must lead him as an Englishman. Like his *Georgics*, the dedication and *Aeneis* constantly set the eternal and unchanging laws of poetry against ephemeral laws subject to historical flux, and perhaps even more so than the *Georgics*, these works are conscious that they must counter England's imminent ruin by upholding fundamental English laws. In the process, they too contrast Dryden's work as poet and patriot with that of William III.

Dryden's discussion of civil wars during the Roman Republic, for example, recognizes the timeless and universal laws underlying his and Vergil's poems as well as the essential difference between Rome and England. In a statement that also points at the Glorious Revolution, he observes that Sylla, in his proscriptions, "had nothing but Liberty and Reformation in his Mouth: (for the Cause of Religion is but a Modern Motive to Rebellion . . .)" (5:278). Sylla's crime, he continues, contemplating the nature of Roman government, was to upset the balance between Senate and Commons so that "each destroy'd the Foundations of the other side: So the Fabrique of consequence must fall betwixt them: And Tyranny must be built upon their Ruines. This comes of altering Fundamental Laws and Constitutions" (5:279). Being careful to "affirm" that, despite bowing to "the Condition of the Times," Vergil was "still of Republican principles in his Heart," Dryden stresses that Rome was originally and fundamentally "an Elective Kingdom": "Kings of *Rome* were at first Elective, and Govern'd not without a Senate . . . " (5:280). He then (in another charged statement) notes vulnerability to "Overt Acts of Tyranny and Male-Administration" as the "Conditions" of such a government, renounces his authority on the matter ("I meddle not with others"), and declares,

> being, for my own Opinion, of *Montaign*'s Principles, that an Honest Man ought to be contented with that Form of Government, and with those Fundamental Constitutions of it, which he receiv'd from his Ancestors, and under which he himself was Born: . . . [I] am better pleas'd to have been born an *English* Man. (5:281)[33]

In *The Medall* he had dwelt at length on England's "Fundamental Constitutions": "Our Fathers," he says there,

> to destroy the seeds of Civil War,
> Inherent right in Monarchs did declare:
> And, that a lawfull Pow'r might never cease,
> Secur'd Succession, to secure our Peace.
>
> (112–16)

He ends the poem with a chilling picture of the "Poyson" that will infect "the Nations Health" if "true Succession from our Isle shou'd fail" (287–97). The dedication recognizes, then, that while Vergil's poem aimed at upholding different national laws and constitutions from Dryden's own, the same general principle informs both: rebellion is an ongoing problem but disaster "comes of altering Fundamental Laws and Constitutions."

Accordingly, Dryden not only declares himself "A Native of Parnassus, and bred up in the Studies of its Fundamental Laws," but states that he has followed his English predecessors as "the *Magna Charta* of Heroick Poetry; [for I] am too much an *English*-man to lose what my Ancestors have gain'd for me" (5:331). As the dedication suggests, the *Aeneis* is imbued with echoes from numerous English poets and translators. These voices from the past, especially those of Spenser and the Royalist translators, help him to explore the question of royal succession within an English tradition and according to English authority and laws. By placing himself, in this way, within a poetic ancestry, however, Dryden also demonstrates that while England's political monarchy has crumbled, the true poetic succession has not failed—despite the fact that "*Tom* the Second" has followed "*Tom* the first" (4:433.48).

As he puts faith in poetic succession and laws rather than monarchical, Dryden focuses on Vergil, as the eighteenth century did when it chose to praise him,[34] not as the product of Augustus's court or a particular moment in Roman history, but as the poetical son of Homer. The effect this has on the *Aeneis* is a new-found freedom and energy in his verse; the difference between this translation and Dryden's earlier Vergilian poems was noted by William Hayley as early as 1782.[35] In the "Notes to the First Epistle" of *An Essay on Epic Poetry*, he condemns Vergil and Dryden together: "the Roman Bard is supposed to have drawn a flattering portrait of his Emperor in the character of Æneas, and . . . the English poet has, with equal ingenuity, enwrapt the dissolute Charles the Second in the Jewish robes of King David." He goes on in "Epistle III" of the same essay, however, to celebrate Dryden's *Aeneis*:

> Of humbler mien, but not of mortal race,
> Ill-fated Dryden, with Imperial grace,
> Gives to th'obedient lyre his rapid laws;
> Tones yet unheard, with touch divine, he draws,
> The melting fall, the rising swell sublime,
> And all the magic of melodious rhyme.
> See with proud joy Imagination spread
> A wreath of honor round his aged head.
>
> (65–66.433–40)

The *Aeneis*'s "touch divine," "swell sublime," and "melodious rhyme" are evidence that it too was "design'd," as Pope put it of Vergil's *Aeneid* in 1711, "t'outlast," well, not "Immortal *Rome*" for Rome had already

fallen, but the ravages of time and national disasters. Sloman says of
Fables that its "poets form an historical continuum from the heroic age
in Greece to a civilized but still pagan Rome, to the fourteenth-century
Boccaccio and Chaucer, and finally to Dryden himself."[36] It is perhaps
more accurate to say that (in the *Aeneis* as well as in *Fables*) Dryden is
conscious of creating a poetic continuum, shaped and directed by history, but beyond the reach of time's and history's corrosive powers. The
timeless element bonding the works within that continuum as well as
the continuity between poets is also outlined in the dedication.

Contemplating his role as translator, Dryden observes,

> *Raphael* imitated Nature: They who Copy one of *Raphael*'s Pieces, imitate but
> him, for his Work is their Original. They Translate him as I do *Virgil*; and
> fall short of him as I of *Virgil*. There is a kind of Invention in the imitation
> of *Raphael*; for though the thing was in Nature, yet the Idea of it was his
> own. . . . Suppose *Apelles* and *Raphael* had each of them Painted a burning
> Troy; might not the Modern Painter have succeeded as well as the Ancient,
> tho' neither of them had seen the Town on Fire? For the draughts of both
> were taken from the Idea's which they had of Nature. (5:305)

He ends his argument about the originality of both translator and original poet by indicating that emulation inspires great works: "I may safely
grant, that by reading *Homer*, *Virgil* was taught to imitate his Invention."
Thus, he ponders, "I might imitate *Virgil*, if I were capable of writing
an Heroick Poem, and yet the Invention be my own" (5:306–7). The
theory espoused here bears the hallmarks of Longinus's discussion of
"[le] chemin . . . qui nous peut conduire au Sublime," which is "l'Imitation & l'emulation des Poëtes & des Escrivains illustres qui ont vescu
devant nous":

> Et certainement il s'en void beaucoup que l'esprit d'autrui ravit hors d'eux-
> mesmes, comme on dit qu'une sainte fureur saisit la Prestresse d'Apollon sur
> le sacré Trepié. Car on tient qu'il y a une ouverture en terre d'où sort un
> souffle, une vapeur toute celeste qui la remplit sur le champ d'une vertu
> divine, & lui fait prononcer des oracles. Des mesme ces grandes beautez
> que nous remarquons dans les Ouvrages des Anciens sont comme autant de
> sources sacrées d'où il s'éleve des vapeurs heureuses qui se respandent dans
> l'ame de leurs Imitateurs, & animent les esprits mesmes naturellement les
> moins échaussez.[37]

Near the end of his essay, Dryden concludes, "I Trade both with the
Living and the Dead, for the enrichment of our Native Language. We
have enough in *England* to supply our necessity; but if we will have
things of Magnificence and Splendour, we must get them by Com-

merce." (5:336). Unintentionally, the statement points to Dryden's own achievement: through commerce with "des Anciens" (or by breathing in their "vapeurs heureuses") and by cultivating "the Beauties of his Mother Tongue," he himself has produced a new English monument of "Magnificence and Splendour" (5:331).

His success is verified by the reception history of the *Aeneis*, which has been admired since its publication for its poetic achievement yet rarely commended for its faithfulness to Vergil. In a century obsessed with the sublime, Hayley was not alone in praising the *Aeneis*'s poetic fire and genius. Alexander Pope deemed it "the most noble and spirited Translation I know in any Language."[38] Joseph Trapp agreed with the sentiment but noted its status as a poem: "In many Places, where he shines most as a Poet, he is least a Translator: And where you most admire Mr. *Dryden*, you see least of *Virgil*." Tindal concurs, "In Dryden's translation of Virgil there is so much spirit, that it reads rather like an orginal than a translation. This makes us go on with so much pleasure, that the faults are scarcely minded."[39] Since the eighteenth-century, too, critics have admired its "force and energy" (Walter Scott, 1882), "individuality . . . of sufficient mark to interest and impress the reader" (John Conington, 1861) and "vitality" (Mark Van Doren, 1946); John Churton Collins called it "a work instinct with genius" and declared that Dryden had managed "to substitute a masterpiece of rhetoric for a masterpiece of poetry" (1895).[40]

By focussing its energy on its own poetic force and English achievement, Dryden's *Aeneis* not only anticipates the eighteenth-century emphasis on the sublime but participates in the movement outlined by Weinbrot, which saw veneration for classical excellence and ideals give way to recognition of the value of native English standards, ideals and literary traditions. Conviction in this process, as Weinbrot demonstrates, had shaped Dryden's thinking about the relation of ancient, modern, French and English poets to their own time and to each other as early as *An Essay of Dramatick Poesie* (1667). The skeptical method of that essay (indeed of all Dryden's works) is also at work in the same cause in the *Aeneis*; however, here it is part of the fabric itself of the poem, and its effect is quite different. Weinbrot points out that Neander's establishment of an English literary triumph over all other nations ancient or modern means that the "*Essay* itself is skeptical only in its methods, not conclusions. . . ."[41] Such is not the case with the *Aeneis* where there are no conclusions. The result is a disintegration of epic structure and closure as they were presented in the seventeenth-century heroic works on which Dryden was drawing.

MONUMENTS OF WOES

> in successive Course the Minutes run,
> And urge their Predecessor Minutes on,
> Still moving, ever new: For former Things
> Are set aside, like abdicated Kings:
> And every moment alters what is done.
> —Dryden, "Of the Pythagorean Philosophy"

The tensions inherent in the dedication can be felt in the opening paragraph of the *Aeneis*. Vergil's well-known *"arma virumque cano"* becomes,

> Arms, and the Man I sing, who, forc'd by Fate,
> And haughty *Juno*'s unrelenting Hate,
> Expell'd and exil'd, left the *Trojan* Shoar:
> Long Labours, both by Sea and Land, he bore,
> And in the doubtful War, before he won
> The *Latian* Realm, and built the destin'd Town;
> His banish'd Gods restor'd to Rites Divine;
> And setl'd sure Succession in his Line:
> From whence the Race of *Alban* Fathers come,
> And the long Glories of Majestic *Rome*.
>
>   (1–10)[42]

It is particularly striking that Dryden not only chooses to begin his translation of Vergil's great paean to Roman imperial destiny with an emphasis on displacement, but that the displacement is felt on the part of the poet himself.

The focus of Vergil's opening lines is new beginnings and the Homeric theme of *"nostos"* or homecoming. By the second line, he has already promised the arrival in Italy and, more specifically, on Lavinian shores, and his recognition of individual suffering is balanced with an assurance of a glorious national purpose to that suffering. Dryden, as Trapp complains, completely omits *"Italiam, Laviniaque Littora . . .* tho' necessary to the Design of the Poem."[43] It is not until his sixth line that he mentions the arrival in Latium, and even then there is no sense of the accomplishment at last of a divinely-guarded destiny: the *"Latian* Realm" here is "won" (a word suggesting chance) in a "doubtful War." He also undermines Vergil's emphasis on Aeneas's role as "auctor" or founder of a new nation from the ruins of an old, for, as Trapp also objects, "he leaves out a very material Word in the very *first* Line: And That too happens to be the Word *First*: As if That stood for Nothing, in *Virgil*'s Verse; and as if *First* would not have stood as well as *Forc'd* in his own."[44] Trapp also laments Dryden's "Tautology," which is "utterly unlike *Virgil's* Manner." His exception is to the three adjectives "of the same Signification agreeing with the same Substantive, all three to express the single Epithet *Profugus*."[45] In fact, in his first three lines, Dryden employs four verbs (even if three are used adjectivally) to stress his themes of banishment and displacement. The Jacobite implications of his own consequently violent and angry opening are obvious, of course, and his poem is further distinguished from Vergil's by the echo here of the Panther's complaint about the Hind's "exil'd Gods" and "intruding line." This first couplet also provides a parallel to that describing James's accession in *Threnodia Augustalis*: "A Warlike Prince ascends the Regal State, / A Prince, long exercis'd by Fate" (429–30). The contrast between the two passages in which the couplets appear highlights the bitterness in the 1690s of the poet who still believed that the true English nature of monarchic succession is by genealogy not victory won in a "doubtful War." As well as evoking contemporary issues and debates, however, Dryden seems, at this important moment, once more to suggest a parallel between his position and his rightful king's. The "who" in line 1 is, in effect, linked with "I sing" until the end of line 4, and the verbs employed in these first lines are equally applicable to the poet's own situation in the 1690s. By yoking the poetical and historical dilemma—or by pointing out that as a political exile he is unable (like his king) to glorify his country through "more Exalted Work, and more Divine"—Dryden begins his epic translation by rejecting the heroic mode. He also immediately and paradoxically situates himself within a line of English royalist poets and translators.

On their own, the Jacobite resonances place Dryden's poem in the tradition that employed Vergil's *Aeneid* to address contemporary problems. However, Dryden suggests a parallel between Spenser's poetic toils and his own as he substitutes "Long Labours" for Vergil's "multum . . . jactatus"[46] and so recalls *The Faerie Queene's* peculiarly Spenserian theme of "labours long" for "the glory of a new time."[47] That Spenser (the "poet's poet") was very much on Dryden's mind in the last half of his career is apparent in his own copy of the 1679 edition of Spenser. "Traces of Dryden's pen are found on about sixty-five pages," James Osborn points out. These annotations include corrections and emendations of rhyme, meter and vocabulary, as well as personal comments on both the *Shepheardes Calender* and the *Faerie Queene*—"jottings" which "preserve traces of Dryden's personality." Marginal allusions to Vergil indicate Dryden's interest in the connections between Vergil and Spenser.[48] So positioned at the beginning of the *Aeneis*, his own English epic, his Spenserian echo seems more than accidental and more than whimsical. By introducing "Labours" at the beginning of his poem, and by associating them (albeit ambiguously) with his task as poet, Dryden alludes (whether consciously or not) to the passage in Spenser's *Shepheardes Calender* where Cuddye outlines Vergil's poetic progression:

> Indeede the Romish *Tityrus*, I heare,
> Through his *Mecænas* left his Oaten reede,
> Whereon he earst had taught his flocks to feede,
> And laboured lands to yield the timely eare,
> And eft did sing of warres and deadly drede.
>
> (55–59)[49]

As Spenser did both in that poem and *The Faerie Queene*, Dryden seems here to declare that he will continue his georgic labors through epic as he follows Vergil's poetic course along the path beaten by Spenser. In any case, the allusion in itself suggests that the labors outlined in Spenser's glorious national epic still can be and are being pursued—in Dryden's own poetry if nowhere else. His invocation of an English and royalist framework is strengthened as "sure Succession" is yoked to "long Glories," providing a bitter reminder of Spenser's promise of an "antique Image [of] great auncestry."[50] The poem is drawn still deeper into English tradition by its seemingly conscious echo here of John Ogilby's 1654 translation of the *Aeneid*, which reworked his 1649 attempt with "an eye on events leading to the execution of Charles I."[51] No other translator appears to match his misplaced relative in line 1 and his "Fate-forc'd" Aeneas; no one else's Juno vents "persecuting Rage" (see Dryden line 14).[52]

The key issues of Dryden's introductory lines, then, are disruption (yet again) to the Stuart line and poetical continuity despite historical disaster. This movement away from Vergil's historical concern is reinforced as Dryden ends by replacing his tangible "altæ moenia Romæ" ("walls of lofty Rome") with "long Glories." At this point, he also again ignores Vergil's emphasis on foundation ("dum conderet urbem") as he unites "Gods restor'd to Rites Divine" and "sure Succession" as the source of "long Glories." Having implied that the only sure succession underlying his poem is that which connects him to Spenser and other predecessors, Dryden in fact equates poetry's traditions with those which have as both source and buttress the "banish'd" Hind by coupling its "sure Succession" with restored rites of exiled gods and by positing this basis as the guarantee of his poem's own immortality. In other words, in his opening statement, he implies that the "long Glories" of his poem, like those of the true church, will live on not only outside but in spite of history. The resulting tension between a concern for problems in the present and an indifference towards history's "tide" is developed in the subsequent passage.

Again, while suggesting the plight of James II, Dryden's lines seem also to glance at his own situation:

> O Muse! the Causes and the Crimes relate,
> What Goddess was provok'd, and whence her hate:
> For what Offence the Queen of Heav'n began
> To persecute so brave, so just a Man!
> Involv'd his anxious Life in endless Cares,
> Expos'd to Wants, and hurry'd into Wars!
> Can Heav'nly Minds such high resentment show;
> Or exercise their Spight in Human Woe?
>
> (11–18)

The description of "so just a Man" corresponds with Dryden's many complaints about his own hardships in the 1690s, while the last couplet's mournful rendition of Vergil's "Tantæne animis coelestibus iræ" (11) asks the question which surely haunted him at this time and which he had already posed in a different form in 1692 when Cleomenes cried out in despair, "But Virtue in Distress, and Vice in Triumph / Make Atheists of Mankind" (16:145.6–7). The contemporary problems which pervade *Cleomenes* (indeed all Dryden's post-1688 works) are also raised here yet again with the interpolation of "Crimes," which in fact recalls his condemnation of his age's crimes from 1660 on. Yet the poem now looks as far back into English history as the Reformation by echoing *Cooper's Hill*. The proximity of his language and sentiment to Denham's suggests that Dryden had in mind his plea, "Tell me (my Muse) what monstrous dire offence, / What crime could any Christian King incense / To such a rage?"[53] Denham's reference, of course, is to Henry VIII's pillaging and destruction of Catholic churches. Dryden's allusion here is particularly significant for it draws a parallel between the Reformation and the Glorious Revolution just after the echo of Ogilby with its reminder of the decapitation of Charles I. By placing events of 1688 in a line of major threats to fundamental English institutions (patrilineal monarchy and the original church), Dryden reduces their significance; they become merely another link in a chain of historical struggle, and he becomes another brave but care-ridden loyalist poet working to save his native land.

Through its fragmentation and its lack of conviction in and inability to uphold traditional heroic codes, however, Dryden's poem in fact admits the disintegration of the system it desperately wants to perpetuate. McKeon traces the gradual historical decline that Dryden would deny by highlighting the striking blow made to the patrilineal basis of England's "Fundamental Constitutions" by the three political events present here in the *Aeneis*. Citing Sir Henry Spelman, he argues that it was the "families of the nobility themselves that were enriched by the dissolution of the monasteries but to no lasting end: and 'the Greatness and Splendour of the Church being thus destroyed . . . in their places some Men of obscure Beginnings came into Action, and were advanced to Titles of Honour.' " Likewise, "If Charles was indeed restored to his aristocratic patrimony, the killing of the king had dealt a resounding blow to the royal succession, and the ensuing triumphs of Cromwell and William of Orange eloquently argued the superiority of industrious valour to mere lineage."[54] Underlying the conflicts of the *Aeneis* is one product of these social crises: the dialectic oscillation between birth as worth and honor derived from personal merit, which, McKeon demonstrates, grew more urgent in the latter part of the seventeenth century (and which, he argues, is a key feature in the development of the novel). Dryden's poem continues to stress lineage as the key to national stability while maintaining that the only way to establish personal integrity in the present age is through individual choice and endeavor. This tension is highlighted as he translates Vergil's well-known conclusion to his introductory piece.

The Latin emphasizes nationhood and family ("gens") and national roots ("condere") as the poet recognizes the cost of Roman glory: "Tantæ molis erat Romanam condere gentem" ("Such a great task was it to found the Roman race") (33).[55] Dryden has, "Such Time, such Toil requir'd the *Roman* Name, / Such length of Labour for so vast a Frame" (48–49). By maintaining the status of Vergil's epithet "Romanam" as almost a proper noun, Dryden indicates the concern for nationality and genealogy inherent in the original; through his Name/Frame rhyme and his use of "Time," "Toil" and "Labour" for "molis," he recalls Spenser's Arthurian myth. At the climax of the first book of *The Faerie Queene*, Spenser stresses his theme of ancestral labors for England's future glory. Showing Red Cross the "new *Hierusalem*," "heauenly *Contemplation*" assures him that

> *Cleopolis* for earthly frame,
> The fairest peece, that eye beholden can:
> And well beseemes all knights of noble name,
> That covet in th'immortall booke of fame
> To be eternized, that same to haunt,
> And doen their seruice to that soueraigne Dame,
> That glorie does to them for guerdon graunt.

He then tells him that "thou Saint *George* shalt called bee," and, as Vergil does in *Aeneid* I, points both to the cost and purpose of his and his nation's victory:

> thou springst from ancient race
> Of *Saxon* kings, that haue with mightie hand
> And many bloudie battailes fought in place
> High reard their royall throne in *Britane* land.[56]

However, as Dryden contemplates Spenser's vision, he is aware that his *Aeneis* lacks *The Faerie Queene*'s sense of national destiny.

He undermines the stability inherent in Vergil's line by replacing "gentem" with "Name" and by establishing it as the "Frame" and focus of the couplet. The same kind of subtle shift away from emphasis on lineage and towards earned reputation is embodied in "To my Dear Friend Mr. Congreve" (1693) and "To Sir Godfrey Kneller" (1694). Having lamented that Congreve, who is his poetical "Son" and "lineal to" his own "Throne," has not "descended" to the position left open by his deposition, Dryden commiserates, "Maintain Your Post: That's all the Fame You need: / For 'tis impossible you shou'd proceed." He ends by asking a fatherly favor of Congreve: "Let not the Insulting Foe my Fame pursue; / But shade those Lawrels which descend to You" (41–44, 64–75). Dryden's point is that the line of England's true poetic monarchy can be traced and maintained despite the crisis that has also deposed the rightful Stuart monarch. In the process, however, he dismisses external social structures (thereby undermining the social stability he spent his life upholding) and places the burden on individual talent and effort. In the end, the only continuity is that inherent in "Fame" (or name), and it is up to the individual to ensure that this is "shade[d]." The same thought concludes the poem to Kneller; although also a victim of "these Inferiour Times," Kneller's own "Genius" will ensure that "Time" shall "Retouch [his] Figures" and "To future Ages" his "Fame convey" (118, 176–80).[57]

The ultimate message of the Congreve and Kneller poems would culminate in *Fables*, where concern for name and personal virtue is all pervasive. In fact, the nature of that work as a whole is reflected in the final triplet of "To my Honour'd Kinsman, John Driden," which, in effect, dismisses the importance of the poem's political concerns: "For ev'n when Death dissolves our Humane Frame, / The Soul returns to Heav'n, from whence it came; / Earth keeps the Body, Verse preserves the Fame" (207–9). The importance of the *Aeneis* in the movement towards *Fables* (and its new epic mode) is indicated by the recurrence of the Name/Fame couplet ending, which occurs thirty-nine times throughout the poem: at least once in every book, and three, four or five times in eight of the twelve; in *Aeneis* IV it seems to be replaced (unsurprisingly) by Name/Shame, which is used three times.[58] No other single rhyme ending appears to be employed so emphatically and frequently. There are also many other variations on couplets ending in "Name" and a rhyming word, while the Name/Frame couplet employed here is used again once in each of *Aeneis* II, III, IV and XII. Clearly, Dryden wanted to "Frame" his *Aeneis*, as Spenser did his epic, on national glory and ancestry. Recognizing, however, that there was no "soueraigne Dame" (or king) to provide a center for the poem, he let his emphasis fall instead on the "fame" that could be won by the lonely individual and the "glorie" that his own poetry could "graunt." The same simultaneous espousal of seventeenth-century codes and admission of their loss lies at the heart of the storm scene in *Aeneis* I.

As if it were not enough to say that Aeolus was "Impos'd . . . with arbitrary Sway," Dryden adds a note to *Aeneis* I so as to make a connection between the storm he brews up at Juno's request and events of 1688 (93). Of Neptune's objection in line 196 ("The Realms of Ocean, and the Fields of Air / Are mine, not his") Dryden comments (after an unnecessarily long reflection on the matter) "To raise a Tempest on the Sea was Usurpation on the Prerogative of *Neptune*" (6:816–17). His choice of vocabulary and his previous depictions of James II as Neptune's vicegerent from the dedication of *The Conquest of Granada* through *Threnodia Augustalis* and *Britannia Rediviva* leave no doubt as to the satiric attack in the note and the contemporary overtones of the passage itself.[59] However, just as his note carries his complaint back beyond the 1690s, so Aeolus's tempest reverberates at every point with the political turmoil that assailed the Stuart monarchy throughout the seventeenth century.

The "Queen of Heav'n's" "persecut[ing]" "Spight" and "hate," which are blamed for the miseries announced as subject in the *Aeneis*'s opening lines, had already been portrayed as the source of James's woes in *Threnodia Augustalis*. There the poet compares James to Hercules, declaring that "Dangers and Toils, and *Juno*'s Hate / Even o're his Cradle lay in wait; / And there he grappled first with Fate." Later, he goes on, the "Furies" further "oppose[d]" his "Infant Arms" by means of "His Father's Rebels, and his Brother's Foes" (450–60). At this point in his *Aeneis* Dryden again wonders at the ongoing nature of the "Fury" directed by Juno at the Stuart family. As the storm hits, Vergil's "Eripiunt subito nubes coelumque, diemque, / Teucrorum ex oculis . . . " (88–89) becomes "sable Night involves the Skies: / And Heav'n it self is ravish'd from their Eyes" (129–30). The lines look as far back as *Astræa Redux* and the civil wars "Which storm'd the skies and ravish'd *Charles* from thence / As Heav'n itself is took by violence" (143–44). Yet Dryden had also used Vergil's image of a sky suddenly overcast in *Britannia Rediviva* when he described "the sudden blast" of the false news of the prince's death (228–29). There as well, the turbulence created by "dire Rebellion" against the Stuart regime is portrayed in terms of natural storms and disasters, which pervade the poem; however, Aeolus's tempest here perhaps evokes *Absalom and Achitophel* more strongly than any other of Dryden's works. "The Tyrant *Æolus*" who is here "Impos'd" on the winds "with arbitrary Sway" (93) embodies the same warning delivered earlier by *Absalom and Achitophel's* "God-like *David*" as he demanded "Would *They* [the rebels] impose an Heir upon the Throne?" (975). Likewise, as the Neptune of the first *Aeneis* teaches the "Audacious Winds" in their "Rebel Insolence" "obedience to my Reign" so as to protect "the thin remains of ruin'd *Troy*" (188–94), he repeats the lesson of David-Charles, who, "To guard the Small remains of Royalty," upheld the "Law" that would "teach Rebels to Obey" (990–92). Again too, the "hollow Wound" (122) inflicted in the ground by the *Aeneis's* Aeolus as an outlet for the rebel winds provides a reminder of England's many previous wounds, depicted in *Absalom and Achitophel* and throughout Dryden's work (e.g. 2:33.924).

Also like *Absalom and Achitophel*, the scene here is imbued with Miltonic echoes and images; Juno herself is presented as a satanic figure "lab'ring still, with endless discontent" (54). (She is also reminiscent of Nourmahal, Cleopatra and the lioness in Dryden's *Georgics* III when she "her Fury vent[s]" [55].) The effect of Milton's presence is to stress that England's storms should be seen in the context of the ongoing battle of "Evil Spirits contending with the Good": a battle which the "Discourse Concerning . . . Satire" declares a necessary element of epic (cf. p. 15 above) (4:21). In the same way, when Dryden labels Aeolus Juno's "Vicegerent" in his note, he recalls his point in the "Discourse" (also discussed earlier) that sometimes "Vicegerents" "appointed by God Almighty . . . for the Protection and Government of Cities, Provinces, Kingdoms and Monarchies" are imposed on nations as a temporary punishment (6:816; 4:19–20). Nor is the antidote to these periodic tempests presented any differently here than in earlier works.

Disturbed by the boiling waves, the *Aeneis's* "Imperial *Neptune*," "fearing for his Wat'ry Reign," rears "his awful Head above the Main: / Serene in Majesty" (176–80). As he then quells the wind and waves, he not only provides the same comforting image of power restabilized that James does at the end of *Threnodia Augustalis* and *Britannia Rediviva*, but he embodies the essence of Stuart kingship as it was presented by Jacobean, Caroline and Jacobite poets. Dryden captures the flow and majesty of Vergil's liquid lines and evokes an image from an English past as he recreates Vergil's picture of Neptune calming the sea and skimming away over the wave tops in his light chariot. He translates "et temperat æquor, / Atque rotis summas levibus perlabitur undas" (146–47) with "where e're he guides / His finny Coursers, and in Triumph rides, / The Waves unruffles and the Sea subsides" (210–12). As Orgel notes, in Jonson's and Jones' masque *Neptune's Triumph for the Return of Albion* (1625), James I is presented unequivocally as Neptune, and "Neptune appears in the masque 'Not as the lord and sovereign of the seas'—he is that in any case—'But chief in the art of riding' ":

> The mighty Neptune, mighty in his styles,
> And large command of waters and of isles,
> Not as the lord and sovereign of the seas,
> But chief in the art of riding, late did please
> To send his Albion forth. . . .[60]

The purpose of Jonson's allegory is to provide (at a time of political unrest) a public image of the king in full control of the reins of state and able through his *chevalerie* to bring "destructive energies . . . under control."[61] By providing a parallel portrait to Jonson's, Dryden again stresses the Stuart regime's special quality as the bulwark of a great naval power; by interpolating a line (and an alexandrine at that) which portrays the "Father of the Flood" as he had portrayed Charles II and James II throughout his career, Dryden also demonstrates that the type of kingship embodied by James I was carried on through the century to the reigns of his two grandsons: as Neptune departs, he "Majestick moves along, and awful Peace maintains" (225). Several echoes of vocabulary and couplet rhymes from both Ogilby and George Sandys also suggest that throughout this section Dryden had his eye on their versions, which celebrate the kingship of Charles I.[62] Certainly, like Dryden's, Sandys's Neptune is both "King and Father." He also exercises the kind of "*Commaund*" associated with the Neptune in Sandys' prefatory "A Panegyricke to the King," which makes an explicit connection between Vergil's myth and Stuart kingship.[63] The differences between Ogilby's 1649 and 1654 storm and Neptune indicate that the latter are colored by his royalist stance.[64]

The loyalism that frames Dryden's episode is both intensified and threatened, however, by the Aeneas he portrays in the middle and at the end of this storm. As is the case with Augustus in the dedication, the hero of Dryden's *Aeneis* is morally inconsistent and, as Anselm Bayly complained in 1789, displays no "leading action or principle."[65] He is also reminiscent at different points of different historical figures, including the Stuart monarchs, William III and Dryden himself. Here, as he is introduced in person, he manifests a type of leadership guaranteed to contrast with that of the Stuart monarchs and so highlight the dangers of England's current storm. As the storm hits, the limbs of Vergil's hero give out in a "chill of fear." He groans in pain and raises his hands piously to heaven: "Extemplo Æneæ solvuntur frigore membra. / Ingemit, et duplices tendens ad sidera palmas . . ." (93–94). Dryden's Aeneas, however, reacts as only a hardened soldier could: "Struck with unusual Fright, the *Trojan* Chief, / With lifted Hands and Eyes, invokes Relief" (135–36). He then laments the fact that he did not perish "in those bloody Fields, / Where *Simoïs* rouls the Bodies, and the Shields / Of Heroes, whose dismember'd hands yet bear / The Dart aloft, and clench the pointed Spear" (142–45). This bloody-minded and brash figure bears little resemblance to the bewildered, vulnerable and suffering hero introduced by Vergil and acknowledged by Dryden as vital to Vergil's overall design. In the dedication he devotes several pages to defending Aeneas against those "who accuse [him] for want of Courage" and who make him "little better than a kind of St. *Swithen* Heroe, always raining" (5:290–92). Quoting the two lines of Vergil cited above, he concludes, "But to this I have answer'd formerly; that his fear was not for himself, but for his People. And who can give a Soveraign a better Commendation, or recommend a Heroe more to the Affection of the Reader?" (292). The "formerly" referred to here is his 1692 "A Character of Saint-Evremond." Like the dedication, that brief essay discusses Roman politics in terms that evoke contemporary England, and it too labels Augustus "Conquerour." In stark contrast to the figure here in the translation, Aeneas is there (as in the dedication) celebrated for his humanity. Citing, as he would later, the Latin lines "where *Æneas* shows the utmost fear, in the beginning of a Tempest," Dryden proposes that, though acquainted with such storms, "At least, as a Father of his People, his concernment might be greater for them, than for himself" (20:10).

Dryden's approval of Vergil's anguished hero is also reflected in his plays. At the heart of his two final tragedies is the view expressed by Almahide as early as 1672 in *The Conquest of Granada, Part II*: "Heroes must live to succour the distrest" (11:132.42). During Don Sebastian's first appearance on stage, he breaks down and weeps: for gratitude at the "Loyalty" shown by his people and for pity at their plight (15:93–94.387–402). Likewise, the exiled king Cleomenes is introduced, like Vergil's Aeneas, as a soul in pain, and throughout the play his concern is for his family and his people. The humanity of these weeping kings was also displayed by that real-life "God-like Heroe," the Duke of York, at the news of Charles II's death: "He bent, he sunk beneath his grief: / His dauntless heart wou'd fain have held / From weeping, but his eyes rebell'd" (*Threnodia Augustalis*, 273–76).

The Aeneas who appears in the middle of Dryden's staunchly Jacobite storm scene, then, glaringly lacks the "Compassion, and tenderness of Nature" which leads Vergil's "perfect Prince" to weep at the same disaster (5:292, 298). Not only does his austerity differentiate him from the Aeneas in perhaps any other translation,[66] but it also marks the distance between him and the Stuart-ized Neptune.[67] His ignobility becomes even more apparent when Dryden concludes, "Thus . . . the Pious Prince his Fate bewails" (146). Unlike Vergil, who describes how Aeneas is assailed by an even fiercer blast as he "hurls forth such words,"[68] Dryden draws attention to Aeneas's complaint rather than his pain, and his ironic use of "pious" is all the more telling for its absence in Vergil. Vergil's point, in fact, is that Aeneas is not "pius" at this point for he does not yet realize that he must align his will with that of heaven and reject the ethos of the Homeric warrior, thereby becoming a new kind of hero. The importance of the poet's rejection of "pius" here where Aeneas laments not having died like a Hector is highlighted by Warton's 1778 defence of Vergil's ubiquitous and frequent use of the "epithet pius." It is, Warton claims, vital in making Aeneas "a far more amiable character than that of Achilles, or Ulysses"; in the same paragraph he also argues that "that epithet conveys with it the design of the whole poem, namely, that of founding a new state according to the dictates of Heaven."[69]

Dryden's first ironic use of the word, in contrast, "conveys with it the design of [his] whole poem," which is to highlight the threat to a state founded "according to the dictates of heaven" if it has such a leader at its center.[70] His satire is intensified by the suggestion of Aeneas's bloodthirstiness in the violent interpolation that looks forward to the one in the translation of Vergil's famous first simile where Dryden compares his Neptune to a "grave and Pious Man" able to "quench" an "angry" crowd's "innate Desire of Blood" (217–20). The result is an association of his Homeric Aeneas and the chaotic forces of the vulgar mob as both are set against the kingship represented by Neptune. The emphasis on blood and destruction perhaps has behind it the cry for an end to civil bloodshed in *Georgics* I, which (recalling *Britannia Rediviva*) Dryden translates, "O! let the Blood already spilt, atone / For the past Crimes of curst *Laomedon*!" (see p. 74 above). Certainly Aeneas's words here anticipate the poet's all-pervasive antiwar sentiment in *Fables*—and, as chapter 4 will demonstrate, in *Aeneis* VII–XII. A connection between his Homeric Aeneas and William III is suggested as Dryden transforms the speech delivered by Vergil's hero on the Trojans' arrival in Carthage.

While his weary men prepare dinner, their leader takes out the wine given them as they left Sicily, and

> Thus while he dealt it round, the pious Chief,
> With chearful Words, allay'd the common Grief.

Endure, and conquer; *Jove* will soon dispose
To future Good, our past and present Woes.
With me, the rocks of *Scylla* you have try'd;
Th'inhuman *Cyclops*, and his Den defy'd.
What greater Ills hereafter can you bear?
Resume your Courage, and dismiss your Care.

. . . .

Through various Hazards, and Events we move
To *Latium*, and the Realms foredoom'd by *Jove*:

. . . .

Endure the Hardships of your present State,
Live, and reserve your selves for better Fate.
These Words he spoke; but spoke not from his Heart;
His outward Smiles conceal'd his inward Smart.
The jolly Crew, unmindful of the past,
The Quarry share. . . .

                                       (275–94)

Again, Dryden's Aeneas bears little resemblance to Vergil's anxiety-ridden hero. In fact, he is here reminiscent of Milton's Satan addressing his "infernal Crew" at the beginning of *Paradise Regained* and allowing them no time "For long indulgence to thir fears or grief."[71] Given the conflation of William III and Satan in the "Discourse Concerning . . . Satire" (see p. 15 above), the allusion to Milton as an attack on the Dutch prince seems likely, the more so for being yoked with the exhortation "Endure and conquer!" The interpolated second imperative not only evokes the contemporary debate over whether or not William's title should be founded on conquest, but, like the introductory piece of *Georgics* III, provides a reminder of William's unsatiable thirst for conquest. Personalities aside, Dryden's unmistakable condemnation of the leadership displayed here can be seen by contrasting this cold soldier with the Duke of Albemarle in *Annus Mirabilis*. The Latin line translated here as "he spoke, but spoke not from his Heart; / His outward Smiles conceal'd his inward Smart" appears there after the Duke's speech to his men as "He sigh'd, but, like a Father of the War, / His face spake hope, while deep his sorrows flow" (291–92).

A comparison of Dryden's Aeneas's speech with that of Segrais's Aeneas suggests that Dryden's purpose here is again to argue the dangers for a state whose leader lacks essential qualities of the complete hero as outlined by Segrais in the passage quoted in Dryden's dedication. As Segrais's Aeneas addresses his men, "Il les anime tous, les plaint, et les console," calling them "Fidelles Compagnons de mon triste destin." He pleads with them, "Bannissez la terreur, Troyens, rasseurez-vous," yet

Ayant fini ces mots, il veut que l'allegresse
De son auguste front écarte la tristesse;

Qu'un doux soûris aux siens promette un sort meilleur.
Mais son coeur au dedans est pressé de douleur.[72]

In a way that Dryden's Aeneas could not, this anguished hero validates Segrais's claim that "Valour, destitute of other Virtues, cannot render a Man worthy of any true esteem." Dryden's reason for choosing to include from Segrais's long essay the passage where he illustrates his "preference [of] Piety before Valour" perhaps lies in the relevance to contemporary England of the last remark he cites. His own translation, after all, seems to repeat from within an English context the question posed by Segrais as he comments that a "man may be very Valiant, and yet Impious and Vicious," then asks if it is possible to "give the Praise of Valour to a Man . . . who shou'd abandon his Father, or desert his King in his last Necessity?" (5:289).

Buttressing the Stuart monarchy against political and social tempests had, of course, been Dryden's self-appointed mission since *Astræa Redux*, and the mode he employs in *Aeneis* I to contend with "Evil Spirits" is in essence that used in all his political poems. The difference between this poem and, say, *Absalom and Achitophel*, however, is that this lacks the ultimate political conviction and optimism inherent in that work despite the poet's prefatory wish that he were "the Inventour, who am only the Historian, [for] I shoud certainly conclude the Piece, with the Reconcilement of *Absalom* to *David*" (2:4). The kind of resolution and calm finally discovered by the *Aeneis* is in fact that which would underlie *Fables*; the translation's role in the transition between Dryden's poems of 1660–1688 and his last work is highlighted when the storm here is considered along side that in the story of Ceyx and Alcyone. Like those in *Aeneis* I, that fable's Aeolean winds "wage intestine Wars," and, agents of arbitrary power, "Are toss'd, and mingled as their Tyrants please" (113–14). Their wrath, too, seems directed at the ship of state, and they "Rush through the Ruins of her gaping Side" (150) leaving a victim who, "with last Looks," "seeks his Native Shoar," a figure of pathos "who late a Scepter did command" and "Now grasps a floating Fragment in his Hand" (192, 210–11). Yet the emphasis moves from the political to the human and personal as the poet reports of the dying Ceyx "his Consort is his greatest Care" (214). Dryden perhaps has in mind the royal family at St. Germain.[73] Whether he does or not is no longer important, however, for the focus of his fable is ultimately the transcendence of disaster and suffering, political or otherwise, through love and nature's restorative powers. Ceyx's last wish is simply for "his dead Body" to be "wafted to the Sands" that it "might have its Burial from [Alcyone's] Friendly Hands" (220–21). In a passage that exemplifies the new, heightened Ovidianism of Dryden's late verse in general, sympathetic nature looks on and weeps: "Bright *Lucifer* unlike himself appears / That night, his heav'nly Form obscur'd with Tears" (228–29). Moved by "Their conjugal Affection," nature finally releases Ceyx and Alcyone from their grief. When Alcyone spies Ceyx's body and plunges into the ocean in order to "join / Their Names remember'd in one common Line," she is turned into a bird (492, 432). Then, as she kisses her husband's corpse, "a present Miracle was shown" (489). Ceyx too becomes a bird, and the story ends with birth: Alcyone's father, Aeolus, calms the storm, "prepares his Empire for his Daughter's Ease, / And for his hatching Nephews smooths the Seas" (499).

Hopkins comments of the fable,

> In the most daringly witty stroke of all, Dryden makes play with his own Catholicism, in asserting that their transformation, the work of gods far removed from the God of Christianity, . . . is a 'present Miracle', a demonstration that, by mysterious means to which only the gods are privy, human grief can be transcended and overcome, just as the storms of Winter are transformed into the calm of the 'halycon days'.[74]

Emphasis on mystery, as it is described here by Hopkins, pervades *Fables* and has a touchstone in *The Hind and the Panther* where Dryden reasons the unreasonable:

> Can I believe eternal God could lye
> Disguis'd in mortal mold and infancy?
> That the great maker of the world could dye?
> And after that, trust my imperfect sense
> Which calls in question his omnipotence?
>
> (3:125.80–84)

The mind-set behind these lines, which go to the heart of Catholic faith, is clearly that which drew Dryden so frequently to Ovid after 1688. The rejection of worldly worries it entails helps to explain the Ovidianism that profoundly affects his *Vergil*. Foreshadowing the eclipse of the Aeolus episode in Dryden's Vergil by the less cynical Ovidian version in *Fables*, the storm of *Aeneis* I and the grief it embodies are ultimately transcended by the three Ovidian elements that would be so important in "Ceyx and Alcyone": trust in "Name," love and transformation. In the process, as *The Hind and the Panther* had done ten years earlier and as *Fables* was to do later, the *Aeneis* declares from the outset that its only certainty is faith in mysteries "to which only the Gods are privy."

The dark cynicism of the storm scene continues in Dryden's rendition of Jove's speech: a speech, which, in Vergil's text, performs the function that *Annus Mirabilis* did when it aimed to stir national pride and unity and concluded with a Vergilian-style promise of *"Imperium sine fine"* (empire without limits) for a chosen nation (279). As he contemplates the much-debated contemporary issue of "the role of fate in the disposition of governments,"[75] Dryden replaces Vergil's reassurances with the "sense of the precariousness of the human situation," that dominates "Ceyx and Alcyone" and most of the other fables.[76] Such coloring of Vergil's text so that (as Zwicker puts it) the "neutral future, the promised day, the destined land . . . and a number of Vergilian topoi are consistently darkened and undercut" has already occurred in *Aeneis* I where Aeneas offers his men "Realms foredoom'd by *Jove.*"[77] There the poet's cynicism derives from his implicit condemnation of disruption to the Stuart line by an Achillean newcomer. Here again, he traces the source of the nation's insecurity to the absence of a stable power base.

When Venus complains to Jupiter of the Trojans' woes and angrily demands, "is it thus that *Jove* his plighted Faith regards?"[78] she provides yet another bitter reminder of the stability of a realm where the king is God's anointed. Whether used ironically, as here and in *The Medall,* or as consolation, as in *Absalom and Achitophel,* the royalist notion of "plighted Faith," or the king's word as social bond, runs through Dryden's works.[79] Venus's Jacobite indignation becomes more bitingly satiric as she goes on,

> But we, descended from your sacred Line,
> Entitl'd to your Heav'n, and Rites Divine,
> Are banish'd Earth, and, for the Wrath of one,
> Remov'd from *Latium,* and the promis'd Throne.
>
> (340–43)

Even the California editors (who make such observations sparingly) point to the "political addition" to Vergil's text (6:969.n.343). While attempting to stir England's conscience, however, Dryden's Venus here reflects the Lear-like sense of desolation and bewilderment at heavenly indifference and cruelty that underpin *Don Sebastian, Cleomenes* and *Amphitryon* especially. As she wails over *"Troy . . . ruin'd in that cruel War,"* she asks "How is your Doom revers'd . . . ?" (326–27). By omitting the pleading vocative, *"genitor,"* and by interpolating "Doom," Dryden loses Vergil's image of a comforting caring father figure.[80] His own introduction of an unreliable and irrational Jove is developed when the god replies by promising that the Trojans

> In *Italy* shall wage successful War:
> Shall tame fierce Nations in the bloody Field,
> And Sov'raign Laws impose, and Cities build.
>
> (359–61)

After the descriptions of Aeolus and the Homeric Aeneas, this war-ob-sessed prophecy does not offer much peace of mind. Dryden's Jove also undermines the assurance of peace that is the *telos* of Vergil's text (at least as it was seen by seventeenth-century Royalists) when he ends his speech by declaring,

> *Janus* himself before his Fane shall wait,
> And keep the dreadful issues of his Gate,
> With Bolts and Iron Bars: within remains
> Imprison'd Fury, bound in brazen Chains:
> High on a Trophie rais'd, of useless Arms,
> He sits, and threats the World with vain Alarms.
>
> (402–7)

The Latin lines behind these are arguably among the finest in the epic:

> Claudentur belli portæ: Furor impius intus
> Sæva sedens super arma, et centum vinctus ahenis
> Post tergum nodis, fremet horridus ore cruento.
>
> (294–96)

A sense of finality is achieved by Vergil's verse itself, which dramatizes the last closing of the heavy gates of Mars. "Claudentur" and "intus," positioned at the beginning and end of line 294, enclose "Furor impius" as impenetrably as do the gates themselves, while the dominance of spondees and long vowels, sibilant 's' and harsh consonants means that the lines hiss, rattle and jolt like the monster in its brass chains.

Clearly, then, Dryden's notion of the continuation of "vain alarms" goes against the spirit of the original. His cynicism is intensified and the retaining powers of the gates rendered even more dubious as an echo from the opening of book 2 of *Paradise Lost* compares "Imprison'd Fury" to Satan as he "exalted sat," "High on a Throne of Royal State," "insat-iat to persue / Vain warr with Heav'n."[81] The highlighting of Janus as gatekeeper is also Dryden's addition. The significance of this will be-come apparent in *Aeneis* VII, which describes Aeneas's arrival in Lat-ium. As Zwicker notes, the themes of that book include "lineage, succession and conquest," and its first plate, which depicts Janus keeper of the gate, is assigned to Henry Viscount Sydney, in whose hand was written the invitation to William. Sydney was also one of seven who signed the invitation and "one of the few Englishmen whom William trusted over the whole of his administration."[82] Despite his deep pessimism, however, Dryden begins in the speech to work towards a transcendence of the "Human Miseries" that his Jove not only contemplates but seems instrumental in (311).

As he did in the opening passage he here lifts his poem out of temporal politics and into a realm where, as he would put it in "Of the Pythagorean Philosophy," "pure Particles of *Æther* flow, / Far from th'Infection of the World below" (290–91). When Vergil's "hominum sator atque Deorum"[83] becomes Dryden's "Father of th'immortal Race" and the Romans' future is fixed rather to their "immortal Line" than to Vergil's politically-based "Imperium sine fine," the *Aeneis* offers the view that Theseus would in "Palamon and Arcite":

> This Law th'Omniscient Pow'r was pleas'd to give,
> That ev'ry Kind should by Succession live;
> That Individuals die, his Will ordains;
> The propagated Species still remains.
>
> (1054–57)

Nature's assurance of the continuation of human life through succession (no matter what devastation has attacked the true monarchic line) is also at the heart of "Of the Pythagorean Philosophy," where another philosopher king declares, "Nor dies the Spirit, but new Life repeats / In other Forms, and only changes Seats" (229–30).[84] The subsequent emphasis Dryden's Pythagoras puts on the ebb and flow of nature as "she destroys her old, / And casts new Figures in another Mold" (264–65) is also anticipated here in the *Aeneis*, where the inexorable movement of time provides implicit consolation for political disaster by stressing that no external structure lasts forever.

By coloring Vergil's Jove's promise that Venus "shall bear up great-hearted Aeneas sublime to starry heaven" (259–60), Dryden draws the hero's fate into the inevitable cycle of seasons: "And, ripe for Heav'n, when Fate *Æneas* calls, / Then shalt thou bear him up . . ." (353–54). Then, even more so than Vergil does, he emphasizes the rolling of the ages as Jove outlines the history of Rome from Aeneas to Caesar. His focus on "rowling Years" (366) rather than imperial destiny is highlighted as his series of "Then . . . "s ends in mockery of the *imperium* that *Annus Mirabilis* had celebrated and forecast for England: "The subject World shall *Rome*'s Dominion own, / And, prostrate, shall adore the Nation of the Gown" (384–85). This cynical rendition of Vergil's proud "[Juno] fovebit / Romanos rerum dominos, gentemque togatam" (281–82)[85] recalls the satiric portrayal of the Asians and timid Parthians at the feet of an implacable conqueror in *Georgics* III. It also marks Dryden's movement towards *Fables*, for, like the speech as a whole, it admits the futility of earthly conquest and political victory in the way that Pythagoras would in observing,

> in successive Course the Minutes run,
> And urge their Predecessor Minutes on,

> Still moving, ever new: For former Things
> Are set aside, like abdicated Kings:
> And every moment alters what is done.
>
> (722–26)

Dryden also looks back at his *Georgics* and forward to *Fables* as he implies that the individual can achieve peace of mind in the midst of the worst historical disaster.

His Jove offers the reader comfort as well as Venus when he assures her, "lest new Fears disturb thy happy State, / Know, I have search'd the Mystick Rolls of Fate" (356–57). A submission to "the Mystic Rolls of Fate" as the key to a "happy State" not only has Catholic overtones but reflects on both *Sylvæ* and *Georgics* II. In "Horace. Ode 29. Book 3," Dryden chose to present Horace's view that "God has, wisely, hid from humane sight / The dark decrees of future fate" and that "He laughs at all the giddy turns of State" (45–46, 48). Because it is impossible to know what fortune has in store, the poem concludes, "Happy the Man, and happy he alone, / He, who can call to day his own" (65–66). As suggested earlier, the same philosophy lies at the heart of Dryden's *Georgics* and is expressed twice in *Georgics* II: when the poet envies the "happy State" of the "Swain . . . free from Business and Debate" (639–40), and when he declares "Happy the Man," who, "His Mind possessing, in a quiet state," is oblivious "when contending Kindred tear the Crown" (698–708).

However, the speech neither espouses the epicureanism that Weinbrot argues the English rejected as dangerous, nor is it nihilistic.[86] Conviction in the ultimate benevolence of "the Mystic Rolls of Fate" is borne out when Dryden soberly translates the prophecy of Caesar's apotheosis:

> Then *Cæsar* from the *Julian* Stock shall rise,
> Whose Empire Ocean, and whose Fame the Skies
> Alone shall bound: Whom fraught with Eastern Spoils,
> Our Heav'n, the just Reward of Human Toyls,
> Securely shall repay with Rites Divine.
>
> (390–94)

The notion of "just Reward of Human Toyls" is Dryden's addition and points to the need for individual effort and integrity.[87] A similar emphasis on personal endeavor and its reward occurs when Venus ponders Antenor's success in founding "*Padua*'s happy Seat"; here, she says, he "gave his *Trojans* a secure Retreat" and "renew'd their Name, / And there in Quiet rules, and crown'd with Fame" (336–39).[88] For his Spenserian-style labors,[89] Antenor has been granted the best that can be hoped for in 1690s England: a quiet retreat and "Fame" won by personal achievement. However, Dryden's own prophecy here also demonstrates his refusal to abandon the Stuart monarchy. In recalling *Britannia Rediviva*'s "Heir apparent of the Skyes" and by putting faith in "Rite Divine" (125), he yet again yields ultimate authority to England's divinely-appointed monarchy.

In fact, when Dryden turns to Aeneas after Jove's speech, the hero becomes an embodiment of persecuted Stuart monarchy, "forc'd," like the "Milk white *Hind*," forever "to fly, / And doom'd to death, though fated not to dy" (3:123.7–8). On encountering his divine mother in the Tyrian woods, Aeneas responds in sorrow to her questions,

> The Good *Æneas* am I call'd, a Name,
> While Fortune favour'd, not unknown to Fame:
> My houshold Gods, Companions of my Woes,
> With pious Care I rescu'd from our Foes.
> To fruitful Italy my Course was bent,
> And from the King of Heav'n is my Descent.
> With twice ten Sail I crost the Phrygian Sea;
> Fate, and my Mother Goddess, led my Way.
> Scarce sev'n, the thin Remainders of my Fleet,
> From Storms preserv'd, within your Harbour meet:
> My self distress'd, an Exile, and unknown,
> Debarr'd from *Europe*, and from *Asia* thrown,
> In Lybian Desarts wander thus alone.
>
> (521–33)

As well as providing a reminder of James II living in poverty and exile at St. Germain as he picks up the tone and concerns of the opening passage, Aeneas here represents embattled kingship. The adjective "Good" had been used by Dryden several times in strategic places of the piety of Charles II and James II, while the image of a storm-plagued figure following "Fate, and my Mother Goddess" as he protects the "thin Remainders" of a faithful few is quintessentially Jacobite and Drydenian. By reminding his audience that the king in exile is descended from "the King Of Heav'n," Dryden perhaps intended to render even more disconcerting the contrast between this truly pious Aeneas and the one who has just glibly told his men to dismiss their cares. More importantly, he prepares for the scene where Aeneas appears from a mist before Dido and the Carthaginians.

As Dido promises Ilioneus her people will search the shore-line for the Trojans' "wand'ring King" (807), Aeneas reveals his presence:

> The *Trojan* Chief appear'd in open sight,
> August in Visage, and serenely bright.

His Mother Goddess, with her hands Divine,
Had form'd his Curling Locks, and made his Temples shine.

(824–27)

The same lines from Vergil had been used in *Britannia Rediviva* just after
the prince was called "Heir apparent of the Skyes":

Not Great *Æneas* stood in plainer Day,
When, the dark mantling Mist dissolv'd away,
He to the *Tyrians* shew'd his sudden face,
Shining with his Goddess Mother's Grace.

(128–31)

There the metaphor has typological overtones as it works to verify both
the baby prince's divine roots and his authenticity as he appears in the
midst of stormy and dubious circumstances. Here, the same loyalty to
and faith in the Stuart family is restated as Aeneas James tells Dido
(and Dryden's audience) "He whom you seek am I" (834). He repeats,
of course, the Hind's response to the Panther's demand for a "mighty
Moyses of the chosen crew" (3:151.393, 398). In effect, then, Dryden
declares that the true Moses can never die for he will live on through a
legitimate line of heirs which can be traced to the divine Hind, and that
he can be discerned through any mists diffused by public and political
turmoil.

His argument in fact has a long tradition in the seventeenth-century
notion of the "inexpungeability of aristocratic nobility." This belief is
evident, McKeon relates, in the stories that describe Charles Stuart
wandering the English countryside after his defeat in battle by Cromwell. Despite covering his telltale white skin and concealing "his royal
nobility by dressing first as a 'Country-Fellow' and then as a 'Serveing-
man' and a 'Woodcutter,' . . . more than once [the prince's] true identity
is suspected and discovered by loyal subjects—'majestie beeing soe nat-
urall unto him'." Such stories, McKeon points out, became part of "a
venerable romance convention," and he argues that both the historical
phenomenon and its literary manifestations were part of the dialectic
between aristocratic ideology and its "progressive critique": a process
which led ultimately to the novel.[90] The *Aeneis*'s own skeptical method
leaves the reader to decide which of its Aeneases represent England's
true leaders, which its false, which uphold and which are destructive to
her traditions—while in fact admitting no choice. Again, however, no
political solutions are suggested (or even seem possible), and the real
regenerative power in the poem seems to lie with Aeneas' divine
mother.

As Dryden's Venus is introduced into his epic, it is, in effect, as the lusty goddess of *Sylvæ*, for in response to the goddess' "Fears" for her Trojans, Dryden's Jove promises her, "To thy desire / The Fates of thine are fix'd" (350–51). The evocative "desire" has no basis in Vergil whose verse stresses the steadfastness of the fates: "manent immota tuorum / Fata tibi" (257–58). ("Your fates remain unmoved for you.") Admittedly, the word is used in the sense of "wish"; however, its presence provides a fleeting reminder of what Venus represents. While, at this point, the connection of the fates to such a power by a dubious Jove seems further to undermine the gods' authority, eventually Venus begins to shine more clearly as she had in *Sylvæ* and would in *Fables* as a restorative energy: a "Creator *Venus*, Genial Pow'r of Love" who "mad'st the World, and dost the World repair" (129, 144).[91] Later in *Aeneis* I, for example, she declares to Cupid that she will counter Juno's rage by granting Dido "A Love so violent, so strong, so sure, / As neither Age can change, nor Art can cure" (948–49). Such pure, unadulterable love is completely Dryden's; Vergil's artful Venus wants to "ensnare the queen by guile" and "encircle her in flames so that no spirit may change her, but she may be held, like me, by a mighty love for Aeneas."[92] The heavenly nature of Dryden's Venus's love (which permeates nature) and therefore its guarantee as an ultimate healing power for worldly woes becomes apparent when she guides Aeneas in the woods.

As the "Care"-ridden Aeneas explores the Phoenician coast (421), his "Goddess Mother" appears before him as "A Huntress in her Habit and her Meen" though "Her dress a Maid, her Air confess'd a Queen" (434–36). She addresses him with a question: "have you lately seen, she said, / One of my Sisters, like my self array'd; / Who crost the Lawn, or in the Forest stray'd?" (443–45). Aeneas responds to her beauty: "O more than mortal fair! / Your Voice and Meen Coelestial birth betray!" (452–53). Dryden's scene invites a comparison between the goddess and his Hind. As Aeneas does Venus, the reader encounters the Hind in a hunt setting and is told she "Fed on the lawns, and in the forest rang'd" (3:123.2). She too is wandering alone in a kingdom that could be her own, and her beauty is praised in terms that anticipate the reaction of Dryden's Aeneas to his mother: "For truth has such a face and such a meen / As to be lov'd needs only to be seen" (33–34). The Roman Catholic overtones here in *Aeneis* I are reinforced at the end of the passage when Venus, turning away, reveals her identity, and Aeneas protests,

> Unkind and cruel, to deceive your Son
> In borrow'd Shapes, and his Embrace to shun:

Never to bless my Sight, but thus unknown;
And still to speak in Accents not your own.

(564–67)

It is tempting to read the lines as the cry of a faithful but distraught
Catholic who wants certain answers as he wanders lost in an uncertain
world. At any rate, the mystical overtones distinguish Dryden's lines
from Vergil's, and help to define his "Queen of Love" as heavenly love
and a guide to Truth (561).

As he would in "Ceyx and Alcyone" and other fables, Dryden also
puts a human face on the love embodied by his heavenly Venus when he
assigns "To her Grace Mary, Dutchess of Ormond" the plate depicting
Venus's appeal to Jove (5:354). In *Fables*, he was to describe the Duchess of Ormond as "*Venus* . . . the Promise of the *Sun*" (63); like Venus's
and the Hind's, her beauty would be seen as the face of truth, and her
pure, nurturing, humble love for her husband and her country as a healing power in war-ravaged Ireland: "So mighty Recompence [the Duchess'] Beauty brought" that her presence "Wip'd all the Tears of three
Campaigns away" (69, 67). Again, then, *Aeneis* I looks forward to *Fables*
as it suggests the achievements and consolation (and fame) that can be
won by individual effort in the face of historical disaster. It also looks
back to the 1693 Ovid, which, Sloman observes, "emphasizes the
themes of regeneration in nature, beneficent female power, and the possibility of real contact with the divine."[93] In another way, too, Dryden's
description of Venus underlines the poem's emphasis on transformation
while revealing both its Ovidian character and its faith in the power of
retold stories as a means of "real contact with the divine": that is,
through its consciousness of its own art.

In the same way as the Hind roams "lawns" and "forest" against a
backdrop of mangy, dangerous and destructive beasts, so Carthage's
"wild uncultivated Shoar" transforms twenty lines later, in Venus's
presence, into "Lawn" and "Forest" (425, 445). In both cases, the retreat into England's pastoral and lyrical past offered by the verse itself,
as well as its own consolatory and regenerative power for the nation,
are verified by the impact of passages like these on the eighteenth century. The young Pope remembered these particular lines in his translation of Ovid's "Fable of Vertumnus and Pomona": "How oft the *Satyrs*
and the wanton *Fawns*, / Who haunt the Forests or frequent the
Lawns. . . ." (21–22). Later, too, in his nationalist monument, *Windsor
Forest*, he would follow in the footsteps planted by Dryden as he set the
peaceful and plentiful land of "Lawns" and "Glades" where "a Stuart
reigns" against the "dreary Desart" and "gloomy Waste" of "Ages past"
(21, 42–44). The role played by the *Aeneis* (as by Dryden's other late

verse especially) as a bridge between the past and the future is particularly notable in the description of the Carthaginian inlet where the Trojans land.

The passage needs to be quoted in its entirety:

> Within a long Recess there lies a Bay,
> An Island shades it from the rowling Sea,
> And forms a Port secure for Ships to ride,
> Broke by the jutting Land on either side:
> In double Streams the briny Waters glide.
> Betwixt two rows of Rocks, a Sylvan Scene
> Appears above, and Groves for ever green:
> A Grott is form'd beneath, with Mossy Seats,
> To rest the Nereids, and exclude the Heats.
> Down thro' the Cranies of the living Walls
> The Crystal Streams descend in murm'ring Falls.
> No Haulsers need to bind the Vessels here,
> Nor bearded Anchors, for no Storms they fear.
> Sev'n Ships within this happy Harbour meet,
> The thin Remainders of the scatter'd Fleet.
>
> (228–42)[94]

Mark Van Doren says of these lines, "In these 'briny waters,' 'sylvan
scenes,' and 'crystal streams' are the beginnings of the stereotyped Nature which graced the verse of England for at least two generations. No
one can be held more strictly accountable for its vogue than Dryden,
whose *Virgil* was read by every poet and served as a storehouse, like
Pope's *Homer*, of cultivated phrases."[95] Yet, as William Frost notes,
quibbling over Van Doren's "beginnings," the lines look back as well as
forward. Frost points to Milton's "sylvan scene" in *Paradise Lost* (4:140)
as well as to Spenser's frequent variations on "Crystal Streams."[96] Another noteworthy Spenserian echo occurs when the ships enter the
"happy Harbour" and in so doing recall that in her restoration "To nat-
iue crowne and kingdome" Una was "As weather-beaten ship arriu'd
on happie shore."[97] The *"Sylvan* Scenes" recreated here also emanated
from Anne Killigrew's *"Arethusian* Stream," and, as their beauties provided relief from "steaming Ordures" of "This lubrique and adult'rate
age," so Dryden's lines here supply a haven from history's and literature's debaucheries (63–68, 108). In fact, a conscious effort to furnish
a retreat and respite for his readers as well as for the weary Trojans is
perhaps suggested by the proximity of this harbor both to Proteus' "silent Harbour," which provides a "Station safe . . . when Tempests roar,"
and to his description of a "good Conscience" as "a Port which is Land-
lock'd on every side, and where no Winds can possibly invade, no Tem-

pests can arise" (see p. 86 above). Certainly, the restorative power of literature and nature are equated in this scene as it looks to the past to revive the spirits of the "thin Remainders" of loyal Jacobites while providing a refreshing setting for the "thin Remainders" of the Trojan nation.[98]

The same emphasis on the transformative power of nature and literature closes *Aeneis* I. As Dido invites Aeneas to tell his story of "Flight" and "Wand'rings" and "Woes," Dryden interpolates a reminder of the cyclical process of the seasons; the book ends with the queen's reflection that since Aeneas left Troy "Sev'n times the Sun has either Tropick view'd, / The Winter banish'd, and the Spring renew'd" (1061, 1065–66). The notion of nature's renewal has no basis in the Latin and seemingly no precedent in earlier translations. The final couplet of book 1, in other words, illustrates the nature of Dryden's *Aeneis*. The translation's concern is not with the fulfilment of imperial destiny, but with the re-telling of the eternal story of human woe and history's disasters and with the regeneration that is inherent in nature and poetry. The resulting open-endedness both distinguishes it from Dryden's earlier poems treating national issues, and illustrates the degree to which it is embedded in the literary and historical landscapes out of which it arises. The inconsistencies and loose ends that shapes *Aeneis* I—and the rest of the epic—point not just to Dryden's own struggle to reconcile the irreconcilable as he had managed to do in the past but to the challenges and difficulties of world's of literature and politics that were worlds in between.

4

Thy Wars Brought Nothing About

WANDERING BETWEEN TWO WORLDS, ONE DEAD,
THE OTHER POWERLESS TO BE BORN

> The Sea of Faith
> Was once, too, at the full, and round earth's shore
> Lay like the folds of a bright girdle furl'd.
> But now I only hear
> Its melancholy, long, withdrawing roar,
> Retreating, to the breath
> Of the night-wind, down the vast edges drear
> And naked shingles of the world.
> —Matthew Arnold, "Dover Beach"

Hand-in-hand with the *Aeneis*'s rejection of imperial destiny as subject is a rejection of the framework of Vergil's epic.[1] Whereas books 1–6 of the *Aeneid* (Vergil's *Odyssey*) trace the hero's growing awareness of and conviction in his task as he travels from Troy to a new homeland, Dryden's Aeneas—or rather Aeneases—wander, from beginning to end of the translation, in an undefinable present against the backdrop of an idealized epic past. Likewise, Vergil's concern with the purpose behind the Latium wars of books 7–12 (his *Iliad*) has no place in the *Aeneis*, dominated as it is by the poet's sense of historical crisis and continual questioning of the type of conquest he had celebrated in Vergilian-style in *Annus Mirabilis*.[2]

Naturally, Dryden's dismissal of Vergil's key structural principle accentuates the nature of his own fragmented poem, in which, as *Aeneis* I demonstrates and as Sloman puts it, "separate sections . . . elicit whatever response seems appropriate for that section" and "virtually any character can become either [the] object or [the] mouthpiece" of his satire at any given moment.[3] The effect of this wandering narrative is to transfer to the poet himself the authority attributed by Vergil to history and the divine purpose, and the method anticipates that of *Fables* where

129

Dryden would move from author to author, work to work as the fancy took him and where the narrative of each translated piece is as fragmented as the work as a whole. If there is any progression within or between the travel books of the first half of the *Aeneis* and the war books of the second, in fact, it is propelled by and interwoven with the poet's own mounting disillusionment and it pushes the translation ever further from Vergil. This can be seen by juxtaposing *Aeneis* II and *Aeneis* VII–XII.

Dryden's second book opens as the first closed: by shifting Vergil's focus on suffering and history to the storyteller's role and the iterability of history's tales:

> All were attentive to the God-like Man;
> When from his lofty Couch he thus began.
> Great Queen, what you command me to relate,
> Renews the sad remembrance of our Fate.
> An Empire from its old Foundations rent,
> And ev'ry Woe the *Trojans* underwent:
> A Peopl'd City made a Desart Place.
>
> (1–7)

The interpolated epithet "God-like" endows Aeneas as speaker with the divinity that would be attributed to philosopher kings in *Fables*; in "Of the Pythagorean Philosophy," for example, Pythagoras is a "Man divine" whose people listen to him "with silent Admiration" "as they heard their God's Command" (87–88). Just as there Dryden is associated with his exiled king through Pythagoras when the storyteller is described as "Self-banish'd from his Native Shore, / Because he hated Tyrants, nor cou'd bear / The Chains which none but servile Souls will wear" (78–80), so here a chronicler's divine powers are equated with a king's as the portrayal of Aeneas recalls that of David-Charles at the end of *Absalom and Achitophel*: "Thus from his Royal Throne by Heav'n inspir'd, / The God-like *David* spoke: with awfull fear / His Train their Maker in their Master hear" (936–38).

Dryden's own presence can be felt in the echoes from his plays. Behind Aeneas's lament for "An Empire from its old Foundations rent" is Agamemnon's comment in *Troilus and Cressida* that when (the Stuartized) Hector fell, the Trojans' "Old foundations shook, their nodding Towers / Threatned from high" (13:353.306–7). His description of "A Peopl'd City made a Desart Place" recalls both the opening of *Oedipus* and the last act of *Cleomenes* (16:156.1). Since the first two plays reflect issues surrounding the Popish Plot and Exclusion Crisis and the last events of 1688–89, Dryden's purpose in echoing them here is surely to point again both to his own role and to the need to keep retelling the story of English civil discord. His greater emphasis on storytelling itself than the suffering involved in the tales is reinforced by his replacement of Vergil's "Infandum . . . dolorem" ("unspeakable pain") (3) with "the sad remembrance of our Fate." Again too, then, consolation is offered by the poet's knowledge that despite the sadness caused by fate's vicissitudes, yet he can offer posterity "matter of iust memory" as Spenser did before him.[4] Already apparent here is the tension established in the *Georgics* and *Aeneis* I between the poet's Lucretian detachment from political affairs and his acute awareness of his own epic mission. This is intensified as Aeneas's tale of "Woe" unfolds, transforming Vergil's instructions about the means to a glorious future into a reflection on the seemingly desperate state of English history. In a way that anticipates *Fables* as well as *Aeneis* VII–XII, however, any didacticism is now more profoundly undermined than previously in the *Vergil*, and, with a bitterness that seems to grow in proportion to the destruction depicted, Dryden heightens Vergil's pathos, stresses the cruelty and pointlessness of war and, finally, denies that anything may be accomplished through the struggles.

A connection between "Troy's disast'rous end" and that of Stuart England is made almost immediately as Dryden's Aeneas relates how the Greeks prepared for their invasion by sailing to "a faithless Bay" (29). Since "faithless" is a rather weak and ambiguous way of describing Vergil's bay which is a "statio malefida carinis" ("treacherous port for ships" [23]), it seems likely that Dryden had in mind Tor Bay where William III landed in 1688 to begin his journey to London. He had previously employed this notion of the land itself being more "faithless" than the sea in 1685 in *Albion and Albanius* where Albion-Charles refers both to his brother's role as Neptune's vicegerent and to the Exclusion Crisis when he addresses Albanius-James as "My Brother, and what's more, my Friend! / Born where the Foamy Billows roar, / On Seas less Dang'rous than the Shoar" (15:38.110–12). The introduction of events of 1688 at the beginning of Dryden's first war book is reinforced by the subsequent description of the first Trojan willing to lay open the city's defences: "*Thymoetes* first ('tis doubtful whether hir'd, / Or so the *Trojan* Destiny requir'd) / Mov'd that the Ramparts might be broken down" (42–44). While Vergil wonders whether it was treachery ("dolo") or the fates ("fata") behind Thymoetes' suggestion, Dryden again curses the present "Age of Gold" where "all Men wou'd be sold," and probably also sneers at those who argued that a providential Protestant wind had blown William III across the channel ("Or so the *Trojan* destiny requir'd").[5] Immediately, too, the mercenariness of William III's supporters is set against the loyalty of a faithful few by the introduction of Laocoön.

As Frost points out, the second plate of *Aeneis* II, which depicts the priest being strangled by the serpents from the sea for urging that the wooden horse be destroyed, is dedicated to James, Earl of Salisbury, who was impeached for high treason in 1689 as a popish recusant. Frost notes that like Laocoön, whose slain sons are depicted at his feet, Salisbury had male issue, and, arguing that the Englishman "could hardly have viewed the coming to England of William III with any more enthusiasm than Laocoön did the coming to Troy of the Trojan horse," he asks, "Is the fact that Laocoön was a priest relevant to Salisbury's faith (the illustration shows a corner of the altar at the left)? Are we to take the serpents as representing the House of Commons?"[6] In fact, even without the association between Salisbury and Laocoön, the incident highlights the problem (as Dryden saw it) at the heart of the Glorious Revolution settlement. The characterization of Laocoön as patriot is buttressed by his behavior as a father. Where Vergil relates that the snakes turn their attention to the priest after killing his sons, Dryden emphasizes both fatherly duty and the pathos of the father's plight as he describes "The wretched Father, running to their Aid / With pious Haste" (284–85).[7] Clearly, the priest represents an old-world piety of the sort stressed in *Aureng-Zebe* and directly associated with England's natural form of government in such poems as *Astræa Redux* and *Annus Mirabilis* where the king is portrayed as the nation's father. As Reuben Brower and Garrison have noted, Vergil is the origin of the piety espoused in Dryden's pre-1688 works,[8] and the emphasis on the father's "pious Haste" here where there is no basis for it in Vergil stresses its absence in the greater context of Dryden's poem—a world in which "all Men wou'd be sold." The downfall of the patriarchal system reflected in Laocoön's absolute piety is dramatized at the end of the scene when, having choked the priest, the snakes "tow'ring o're his Head, in Triumph ride" (289). By recalling the description in *Aeneis* I of Neptune riding "in Triumph" over seas he has just calmed (see p. 112 above), Dryden's line comments bitterly on the displacement of the peace-oriented Stuart regime by chaotic forces.

A similar admission of the irreversible demise of both the political system and worldview that the poet had propped for three decades comes at what is the climax of Vergil's second book. Looking down on the burning city, Aeneas realizes that Troy's last hour has come:

> *Troy* sunk in Flames I saw, nor could prevent;
> And *Ilium* from its old Foundations rent:
> Rent like a Mountain Ash, which dar'd the Winds;

And stood the sturdy Stroaks of lab'ring Hinds:
About the Roots the cruel Ax resounds,
The Stumps are pierc'd, with oft repeated Wounds.
The War is felt on high, the nodding Crown
Now threats a Fall, and throws the leafy Honours down.
To their united Force it yields, though late;
And mourns with mortal Groans th'approaching Fate:
The Roots no more their upper load sustain;
But down she falls, and spreads a ruin through the Plain.

(844–55)

Like the "royal" trees in Dryden's earlier poems (see pp. 59–61 above), this "Mountain Ash" seems to represent the Stuart monarchy. The echo from *Troilus and Cressida* as Aeneas again describes Ilium "from its old Foundations rent" reinforces the point that the regime's "Fall" and loss of (interpolated) "leafy Honours" end a long-sustained battle against the (also interpolated) "united Force" of attacks on its foundations. Both the focus on roots and the notion of the tree's daring "War" as it resists a series of assaults are Dryden's; Vergil is concerned with the visual and aural effect of his vignette as he describes the tree cracking and finally giving out under the axe strokes of energetic farmers. An association of the ash with James himself seems likely when it emits mournful "mortal Groans" at "th'approaching Fate." (Vergil has simply "supremum / Congemuit": "it gave a last groan" [630–31].) As well as establishing a parallel between this scene and the subsequent portrayal of King Priam (whose fall, as Dryden argues in the dedication, marks that of the Trojan line), the line recalls the prophecy of Cleomenes, whose plight also reflects that of the wretched English king:

> I will not go to Ground,
> Without a Noble Ruine round my Trunk:
> The Forest shall be shaken when I sink,
> And all the neighboring Trees
> Shall groan, and fall beneath my vast Destruction.
>
> (16:90.55–59)

In that play, the poet's own bewilderment is revealed by the form itself of the tragedy, in which almost only "good men suffer" and the absence of a final political resolution or any kind of *anagnorisis* means that there is no tragic *catharsis* and Sosibius's closing celebration of virtue is unconvincing. The same sense of helplessness on Dryden's part is indicated here both in the interpolation "nor could prevent" and, more emphatically, in the final alexandrine, which echoes Spenser's alexandrine at the decisive moment of Red Cross's victory over the dragon:

"So downe he fell, and like an heaped mountaine lay."[9] This bitter reminder of an event in Spenser's national epic that promises political and social stability through the reestablishment of a rightful king and the forces of good not only highlights the decline of English history but stresses that all Dryden can offer as Spenser's successor is a parodic version of his glorious vision.

Yet this tree is not the royal oak but a mountain ash. In Ogilby's fable 36, "Of the Husbandman, and the Wood," the ash is one of the trees that stands in the shade of the "Royal Cedar" and falls when it does.[10] Dryden may, then, be mocking William III for having assumed the role of a royal tree. If so, he prophesies his downfall. Yet the near-despair of the alexandrine is countered by Dryden's own poetry, which has the vigor of many of his finest pieces and, in its epic form, stresses the heroic nature of his efforts. The key point here, finally, is that whether lamenting the fall of the Stuarts, attacking William III, or doing both simultaneously, Dryden's lines embody a cynicism and uncertainty that are distinctly unheroic. The same simultaneous adherence to and rejection of the heroic are apparent in the lines immediately above these.

The tree simile follows hard on another Spenserian passage in which Venus, having appeared all radiance and "Charms" and having urged Aeneas to "Look if your helpless Father yet survive," assures him of her protection:

> Haste hence, my Son; this fruitless Labour end:
> Haste where your trembling Spouse, and Sire attend:
> Haste, and a Mother's Care your Passage shall befriend.
>
> (837–39)

In the same way as the triple anaphora and rhyming triplet of these lines place them unequivocally in the English epic tradition exemplified by Spenser and mourned as lost by Dryden in the next passage, so Venus's emphasis on Aeneas's family duties reveals the poet's immovable conviction in the royalist worldview, the fall of which he then describes. Yet, in the sympathy of Venus's speech it is possible to see the beginnings of a resolution to these conflicts between the epic structure and its satiric and disillusioned content, between a promotion of traditional Vergilian piety and a recognition of its anachronism in the world the *Aeneis* addresses. While the old public concerns underlie the essentially Drydenian focus on Aeneas's role as father, son and spouse, the human sentiment of the goddess' comforting words marks the shift from social laws to natural, which is discernible in *Aeneis* I and developed in *Fables*. Like those in the story of Ceyx and Alcyone, these sacred family bonds cannot be destroyed whatever the political chaos surrounding the family members. The conflicts apparent here maintain the same, if not greater, intensity where Dryden considers the plight of Priam's royal family and Aeneas' removal of his family from Troy.

The profundity of Dryden's commitment to the Stuart regime and what he viewed as its inherent stability is again manifest when Aeneas admonishes Anchises after the old man bids him (as James II might well have bid his supporters) "Make haste to save the poor remaining Crew; / And give this useless Corps a long Adieu" (870–71). Not using Vergil's proper nouns and still concentrating on family unity, Dryden's Aeneas relates how he orchestrated a scene reminiscent of that staged by Ventidius in *All for Love* to remind Antony of what piety demanded from him:

> My self, my Wife, my Son, my Family,
> Intreat, pray, beg, and raise a doleful Cry.
> What, will he still persist, on Death resolve,
> And in his Ruin all his House involve?
>
> (881–84)[11]

The lines also have a parallel in Dryden's "The Lady's Song" of the early 1690s where Phillis declares that the land can only be happy again if "*Pan*, and his Son, and fair *Syrinx*, return" (18). The possibility that here—even this late—there is a similar call to arms and a rebuke to James II is reinforced by Aeneas' next words to his father:

> Can I without so dear a Father live?
> You term it Prudence, what I Baseness call:
> Cou'd such a Word from such a Parent fall?
> If Fortune please, and so the Gods ordain,
> That nothing shou'd of ruin'd Troy remain:
> And you conspire with Fortune, to be slain;
> The way to Death is wide. . . .
>
> (891–97)

Both the argument that life is unliveable without his father and the distinction between "Prudence" and "Baseness" are peculiar to Dryden's hero; Vergil's asks "Mene efferre pedem, genitor, te posse relicto / Sperasti? tantumque nefas patrio excidit ore": "Did you expect, father, I could leave here without you? Can such profanity fall from a parent's lips?" (657–58). In effect, then, Dryden again puts greater emphasis on Vergilian piety than Vergil himself, this because his subject is its imminent loss whereas Vergil's is Aeneas's necessary departure from his homeland and renunciation of Homeric codes. Ultimately, Dryden's message is that a state's "way to Death" is the abandonment of a king

and father, and this is highlighted by the interpolation twice of "Fortune" as Aeneas accuses Anchises of being in conspiracy with fickle
forces.

The significance of Fortune's threatening presence here becomes
more apparent in light of Paul Hammond's observation on its importance as a theme in the *Aeneis*. "In his translation of the *Aeneid*," Hammond remarks, "Dryden increases the number of references to Fortune
from twenty-four in the Latin to ninety-two in his version."[12] He also
points out that when Aeneas trusts to Fortune in battle things go terri-
bly wrong; he highlights one passage in *Aeneis* II which has a telling
parallel in *Absalom and Achitophel*:

> Thus Fortune on our first Endeavour smil'd:
> *Choroebus* then, with youthful Hopes beguil'd,
> Swoln with Success, and of a daring Mind,
> This new Invention fatally design'd.
> My Friends, said he, since Fortune shows the way,
> 'Tis fit we shou'd th'auspicious Guide obey.
> For what has she these Grecian arms bestow'd,
> But their Destruction, and the *Trojans* good?
> Then change we Shields, and their Devices bear.
>
>   (518–26)

Hammond comments,

> The ruse only brings the Trojans trouble, but what is interesting here is that
> Dryden shows this to be an error not of tactics but of moral courage. The
> language which he adds to Virgil in description of Choroebus (1.520) re-
> minds us of Achitophel. Like Achitophel he . . . misuses Dryden's key word
> 'auspicious': the one thing Fortune is not is 'auspicious.'[13] (778–79)

He has in mind the speech where Achitophel addresses Absalom as
"Auspicious" by birth and urges him to seize the opportunity presented
by Fortune on the grounds that "Had thus Old *David*, from whose
Loyns you Spring, / Not dar'd, when Fortune call'd him, to be King, /
At Gath an *Exile* he might still remain" (262–64). Clearly, in *Aeneis* II,
the mistake charged against Anchises by Aeneas (and by Dryden
against the supporters of the Glorious Revolution) is that made by
Achitophel in attributing "David's call to be king . . . not to God but to
Fortune."[14]

Such juxtaposition of Fortune's fickleness and an image of a father
figure who can offer a stable center is, in fact, a central feature of *Aeneis*
V. There Dryden develops the point made in Aeneas's rebuke to Anchises by portraying the hero as an ideal father-king in a book which has

as one of its main subjects the suddenness with which Fortune's wheel can turn. The first example is the boat race. Dryden makes the most of Vergil's depiction of the four contesting crews, which one after the other appear poised for victory then meet with mishap. More so than Vergil, however, he stresses leadership as antidote to and consolation for the unpredictable. When the Chymaera loses its helmsman, Dryden translates, "The Ship without a Pilot yields the Prize" (289). Set against this is the success of Cloanthus's crew, who owe their victory to their leader's prayer, for after Cloanthus promises the "Gods of the liquid Realms" that "A Snow-white Bull shall on your Shore be slain," "old *Portunus*, with his breadth of Hand, / Push'd on, and sped the Gally to the Land" (305–14). The translation is fairly literal, but Dryden's Restoration vocabulary ("liquid Realms") and his subsequent portrayal of Aeneas's leadership suggest that he had in mind *Astræa Redux* where he observed, "To all the Sea-Gods *Charles* an Off'ring owes: / A Bull to thee *Portunus* shall be slain" for having "cast his shipwrack'd Vessel on the shore" (120–21, 124). The argument at the heart of that poem, that a divinely-sanctioned leader is in himself a haven safe from storms, is stressed at the end of Dryden's boat race when Aeneas offers consolation for the vicissitudes of the contest by rewarding all leaders: "Thus, all rewarded by the Heroe's hands . . ." (353). The emphasis on reward at "the Heroe's hands" is Dryden's; Vergil's passive "donati omnes" ("all were rewarded" [268]) focuses on the pride of the recipients. A reminder that this type of stabilizing leadership was offered by the Stuart regime is now effected through the prince's gratitude, which is a feature of Dryden's rather than Vergil's text (where Aeneas is "lætus" or "joyful" [283]): even the hapless Sergesthus is not forgotten as he brings his crippled ship back to shore, and "for his Gally sav'd, the grateful Prince, / Is pleas'd th'unhappy Chief to recompence" (369–70).

Dryden's even greater emphasis on his leadership theme in the next competition results in amendment not only of Vergil but of his 1685 *Sylvae* version of the Nisus and Euryalus episode. This time before the race even begins, the hero attempts to counter the inevitable cruelties of Fortune by promising the runners, "One common Largess is for all design'd: / The Vanquish'd and the Victor shall be join'd" (401–2). The last line has no basis in the Latin and does not exist in the *Sylvae* translation. Dryden subsequently alters a line from his 1685 text so as to echo Aeneas's words here and thereby associate the friendship of Nisus and Euryalus with the kind of magnanimity and dependability embodied by such a hero; when Nisus slips and catches the foot of Salius who is behind him, "*Euryalus* springs out," "The Victor to the Goal, who vanquish'd by his Friend" (439–41). (The 1685 line reads: "The Conqu'ror to the Goal, who conquer'd through his Friend" [3:21.68].) Aeneas then becomes more praiseworthy than his 1685 counterpart as he handles Salius's protest: "Let no Disputes arise: / Where Fortune plac'd it, I award the Prize. / But Fortune's Errors give me leave to mend, / At least to pity my deserving Friend" (454–57). The replacement of the 1685 indefinite article ("a Friend") with the possessive pronoun "my" strengthens Aeneas's bond with his men as friend and guardian, while the use of the verb "mend" rather than the earlier "amend" subtly suggests the hero's healing powers as God's anointed, an image which is now stressed. In both translations, "Th'indulgent Father of the People" smiles as he rewards Nisus too and then shares prizes among the other contestants; only in *Aeneis* V, however, does he "equal Justice, in his Gifts" express (470, 475). The fact that this action follows Nisus's plea, "Wou'd Fortune for my Fall so well provide!," further underscores Dryden's emphasis on Aeneas as consolation for and a counter to Fortune (467).

It is this apparent inability on the part of the poet to conceive life without the caring protection of an "indulgent Father of the People" to bestow "equal Justice" in a world plagued by misfortune that leads him to follow up Aeneas's rebuke to Anchises in *Aeneis* II with what seems to be an expression of hope for the Prince of Wales. Having finally been convinced that he too must leave Troy, Anchises declares that he will "follow where Heav'n shews the way," praying,

> Keep (O my Country Gods) our dwelling Place,
> And guard this Relick of the *Trojan* Race:
> This tender Child; these Omens are your own;
> And you can yet restore the ruin'd Town.
>
> (951–55)

By replacing "nepotem" ("grandson" [702]) with "tender Child" and "vestroq; in numine Troja est" ("Troy is in your protection" [703]) with "you can yet restore the ruin'd Town," Dryden reasserts the sentiment and faith at the heart of *Britannia Rediviva*. In this portrait of a promised child, however, the historical hope inherent in the vocabulary ("restore" and "ruin'd Town") is overwhelmed by the greater sense that (as Dryden put it in the 1688 poem) "God is abroad, and wondrous in his ways" as he "The Rise of Empires, and their Fall surveys" (75–76). Anchises' plea to "guard this Relick of the *Trojan* Race" is interpolated and embodies the kind of shift discussed earlier from concern with history to a focus on "after Times" and the assurance of natural succession. Then, as the old man declares himself "resign'd" and "prepar'd to go" (957), he expresses not the sudden conviction of Vergil's Anchises, but Christian patience for the "farther tryals and afflictions we are yet to undergo": the trials that Dryden resigned himself to in the dedication to the Queen, prefaced to *The Life of St. Francis Xavier* (1688) (19:3). The Christian overtones of the passage reach a climax when Aeneas agrees with Anchises that "One Death, or one Deliv'rance we will share" (965).

While *Aeneis* II (again, like *Aeneis* I) finally arrives at such a conclusion, the weight of its disillusionment and pessimism demonstrate the difficulty Dryden had in the 1690s coming to terms with the fact that (as he translated Pope Paul III's words in his *Life of St. Francis Xavier*) "the affairs of God, succeeded not, but by the ways of suffering" (19:33). In a way that seems to point to his own anguish at the cruelty and apparent pointlessness of the contemporary English situation, Dryden intensifies Vergil's Aeneas' pain at seeing his city burned and, in these passages, endows his hero with cynicism. At the height of battle, for example, Aeneas calls his men "Brave, alas! in vain," and wails,

> Come, finish what our Cruel Fates ordain.
> You see the desp'rate state of our Affairs;
> And Heav'ns protecting Pow'rs are deaf to Pray'rs.
> The passive Gods behold the *Greeks* defile
> Their Temples, and abandon to the Spoil
> Their own Abodes: we, feeble few, conspire
> To save a sinking Town, involv'd in Fire.
>
> (467–73)

Here Vergil's Aeneas displays the rage of the Homeric warrior: "si vobis audentem extrema cupido est / Certa sequi" (349–50). His speech is driven by passion ("cupido"), and he wants to demonstrate his daring ("audentem") by fighting to the bitter end for his country and family. In contrast, Dryden's Aeneas in effect expresses Cleomenes' view that "Devotion / Will cool in after times, if none but good Men suffer" (16:146.48–49). His remarks about heaven's deafness to prayers and the gods' passivity have no basis in the speech of Vergil's Aeneas who argues, "quæ sit rebus fortuna, videtis: / Excessere omnes adytis arisque relictis / Dii, quibus imperium hoc steterat" (350–51): "You see the chance; those kept this Realm, our Gods / Their altars have forsook, and blest abodes."[15] Likewise, the expression of horror at temples defiled with impunity has roots only in the historical event behind Cleomenes' tale of how "Victors robb'd the Shrines, polluted Temples": the destruction and pillaging of Roman Catholic churches after the Glorious Revolution (16:95.214).

The poet's own near despair here can again be seen by contrasting the passage with one in *To My Lord Chancellor* (1662), which has the same Vergilian lines behind it:

> When our Great Monarch into Exile went
> Wit and Religion suffer'd banishment:
> Thus once when *Troy* was wrapt in fire and smoak
> The helpless Gods their burning shrines forsook;
> They with the vanquisht Prince and Party go,
> And leave their Temples empty to the fo:
> At length the Muses stand restor'd again
> To that great charge which Nature did ordain.
>
> (17–24)

The difference between "helpless Gods" abandoning "burning shrines" and "passive Gods" watching intruders "defile" temples marks the difference between Dryden's sense of the typological significance of history's disasters in his earlier work and his own Cleomenes-like questioning after 1688. Yet, his insistence in 1662 that the Gods maintained allegiance to "the vanquisht Prince and Party" has been replaced here in *Aeneis* II by the interpolated image of a "feeble few" still conspiring to "save a sinking Town"; behind it is surely the thought that whatever the "Cruel Fates ordain" his own efforts as poet and those of others among the faithful few are at least working for "that great charge which Nature did ordain."

The mood of the speech (like that ultimately of *Cleomenes*) anticipates the stance of the author in "Palamon and Arcite" as he reflects on Arcite's accident:

> The vent'rous Knight is from the Saddle thrown;
> But 'tis the Fault of Fortune, not his own.
> If Crowns and Palms the conqu'ring Side adorn,
> The Victor under better Stars was born:
> The brave Man seeks not popular Applause,
> Nor overpow'r'd with Arms, deserts his Cause;
> Unsham'd, though foil'd, he does the best he can.
>
> (735–41)

This conflict between the poet's strong sense of the pointlessness of all endeavor and simultaneous refusal to desert the "Cause" that Dryden believed had its roots in what "Nature did ordain" becomes, of course, part of the fabric of *Fables*, not just a theme in "Palamon and Arcite." Yet, as is signalled by the emphasis here on personal dignity and integrity, ultimately in *Fables* Dryden's lifelong promotion of Vergilian *pietas* and its associated social codes is supplanted by the simple message that, as the narrator of the above passage continues, "Force is of Brutes, but Honour is of Man" (742). The significance of *Aeneis* II in helping Dryden to make the move towards *Fables* where the epic form itself concedes—if not accepts—the shift that English literature had now to make away from heroic codes and structures is highlighted in the description of Priam's fall. Shaped by the same conflict, this episode not only signals the process that would take place between the *Aeneis* and *Fables*, but, more globally, anticipates the dialectic oscillation between the old world and the new that was being reflected in the period's mockheroic and which had such a profound influence on the development of the novel.

As he introduces the scene, Dryden accentuates the pathos he finds in Vergil:

> Perhaps you may of *Priam*'s Fate enquire.
> He, when he saw his Regal Town on fire,
> His ruin'd Palace, and his ent'ring Foes,
> On ev'ry side inevitable woes;
> In Arms, disus'd, invests his Limbs, decay'd
> Like them, with Age; a late and useless aid.
> His feeble shoulders scarce the weight sustain:
> Loaded, not arm'd, he creeps along, with pain;
> Despairing of Success; ambitious to be slain!
>
> (691–99)

The California editors not only observe that there is no Vergilian equivalent for the "inevitable woes" of line 694, but point to the interpolated "grotesquely ironic and pathetic details" of lines 697–98 (6:985). Here too, Vergil's emphasis on the vanity of Priam's actions has become emphasis on decay,[16] and the last determined action of Vergil's king, who rushes headlong into the thronging enemy ("ac densos fertur moriturus in hostes" [511]), is now simply the despair of a creeping old man. The horrific implications for the state of such a picture are also heightened in Dryden's text by his connection of the king's personal situation with the monarchy's as he turns Vergil's "captured city" and "house" into a "Regal Town" and "ruin'd Palace."

The undoubted lament here for the downfall of England's time-honored institutions and for the treatment of the royal family also seems to underlie the subsequent equally pathetic image of Priam's consort:

> Here *Hecuba*, with all her helpless Train
> Of Dames, for shelter sought, but sought in vain.
> Driv'n like a Flock of Doves along the skie,
> Their Images they hugg, and to their Altars fly.
>
> (704–7)

The interpolation of a flight to "Altars" suggests that Dryden may have been thinking of the persecuted "Flock" in his Panther's tale, who "For succour to their helpless mother call, / She spread her wings; some few beneath 'em craul, / She spread 'em wider yet, but cou'd not cover all" (3:179.615–17). The California editors remark that the passage "shows Dryden's fear that the Catholic church will be unable to protect her brood when persecution returns to England" (3:430).

While the same old complaints and arguments lie behind this scene, however, its borderline despair means that there are no "Manners" to be learned: a prerequisite which Dryden stresses for the epic in his dedication and elsewhere (5:271). This is in marked contrast to Vergil's text where the pathos reinforces Priam's and Hecuba's role as sacrificial victims: the last adherers to the old-world Homeric warrior ethos which has no place in the nation's future. The displacement of Vergil's poignancy by a barren, nonproductive description is even more notable as Pyrrhus enters, drags "the trembling Sire, / Slidd'ring through clotter'd Blood, and holy Mire, / (The mingl'd Paste his murder'd Son had made)" and brutally slays him on "the Sacred Pile" (748–52). Violent as Vergil's scene is, it is not grotesque like this one, which has a precedent at line 635 when the palace roof caves in and "the *Greeks* beneath / Are piecemeal torn, or pounded into Death."

This over-the-top violence and bloodiness proliferates throughout the second half of the *Aeneis*, looking forward to *Fables* and its numerous gory brawls, which reach a climax with that started by the centaurs in "The Twelfth Book of Ovid." There, as here, "Foam and Brains, and mingled Blood" are mixed with "Chalices of Heav'n; and holy Things" in a way that is almost too absurd to be shocking (Kinsley, 335, 343).[17] More significantly, Dryden's disregard for Vergil's horror at the treatment of a king in favor of his unsettling picture of Priam amidst his "murder'd Son's" "clotter'd Blood" and "mingl'd Paste" marks the shift from seventeenth-century royalist certainties to the troubled world of fluctuating and elusive values manifest in such eighteenth-century works as *Tom Jones*. A reflection and product of the poet's own increasingly amoral (as opposed to immoral) world, Dryden's scene perhaps has a parallel in Fielding's church graveyard brawl where Molly Seagrim brandishes human thigh bones and trips over skulls as she wards off angry parishioners in a tussle involving her "honour." In both cases, the absence of a sense of the sanctity of human life means that there can be no horror, just laughter at the world represented in the scene. Dryden's simultaneous rejection of and veneration for the epic and its codes can also be compared to Fielding's use of the epic as both a base for his parody and a potential source of standards against which to measure contemporary behavior.[18]

It seems possible, in fact, to illuminate what has happened here in *Aeneis* II with Bakhtin's observations concerning the epic and novel.

Vergil's epic fabric, the "absolute past" or national traditions and the standards they provide for the (distanced) present, has been shredded by Dryden's obsession with contemporary reality. Having apprehended—even if he will not admit—that the codes have disintegrated by which he could once determine morality and immorality, Dryden rejects the high genre and the grandeur it receives from its "association with the past, the source of all authentic reality and value," and replaces it, necessarily, with 1690s "inconclusiveness," "indecision," "openness" and need for "re-thinking and re-evaluating."[19] Priam's speech to Pyrrhus before he is slaughtered highlights the extent to which the *Aeneis*'s contemporary overlay has undermined Vergil's heroic past, "a world," as Bakhtin puts it, "of 'beginnings' and 'peak times' in the national history, a world of fathers and founders of families, a world of 'firsts' and 'bests.' "[20]

While Dryden's king appeals to heaven, it is not with the confidence in his own position as the bulwark of divinely-sanctioned and protected laws that is displayed by Vergil's Priam, or by Dryden's kings in *Annus Mirabilis* and *Absalom and Achitophel*. Spluttering in rage, he assures Pyrrhus that the gods will "requite thy brutal Rage: / As sure they will, Barbarian, sure they must, / If there be Gods in Heav'n, and Gods be just" (729–31). The logic underlying the yoking of "just" and "must" is not particularly reassuring; more importantly, this assertion about what "must" be has replaced Vergil's Priam's appeal to divine "pietas" (536).[21] That the scene in fact reflects Dryden's own godless world is reinforced by the interpolated vocative "Barbarian." Derived from the Latin "barbarus," which was applied by the Romans to anyone non-Roman, the word draws attention to the foreignness of this brutal intruder. As Priam goes on, it becomes even clearer that the context of his speech is William III's mercenary England.

Having cursed Pyrrhus for daring "With a Son's death t'infect a Father's sight," the old man declares that not even Pyrrhus's "vaunted Sire"

> Thus us'd my wretched Age: The Gods he fear'd,
> The Laws of Nature and of Nations heard.
> He chear'd my Sorrows, and for Sums of Gold
> The bloodless Carcass of my *Hector* sold:
> Pity'd the Woes a Parent underwent,
> And sent me back in safety from his Tent.
>
> (735–41)

Priam replaces his Latin counterpart's invocation of a suppliant's traditional sacrosanct right ("jura fidemque / Supplicis" [541–42]) with a

nod towards "Laws of Nature and of Nations" as he appeals to Pyrrhus
rather in commercial language the invader can understand than in Vergil's language of *pietas*. In the Latin, the emphasis is on kinship ties and
the patriarchal system they uphold; Priam accuses Pyrrhus of falsely
claiming Achilles as his father, objecting that even he upheld sacred
codes, returned to him the bloodless body of his son and restored him
in his kingdom.[22] Caught up in Dryden's harsh world, however, the
helpless old man makes his plea through an image of a "Sums of Gold,"
perhaps suggesting another business transaction could be made, and
expresses weariness rather than indignation. In other words, as the *Aeneis* addresses the realities of Williamite England, Vergil's emphasis on
bloodline gives way to bloodshed and his promotion of time-honored
laws to overwhelming woes; princes become mercenaries and the old
centrality of king and kingdom ("mea regna") is lost in a desire simply
for personal "safety." If Bakhtin's litmus test for reliance on tradition
as "immanent in the very form of the epic" were applied here, then, the
Aeneis would fail to qualify as high genre, being forced to respond "not
at all" to the question about the degree to which its "represented world"
participates in the past.[23]

The displacement of the old world is driven home in the episode's
conclusion:

> Thus *Priam* fell: and shar'd one common Fate
> With *Troy* in Ashes, and his ruin'd State:
> He, who the Scepter of all *Asia* sway'd,
> Whom Monarchs like domestick Slaves obey'd.
> On the bleak Shoar now lies th'abandon'd King,
> A headless Carcass, and a nameless thing.

> (758–63)

As well as providing a parallel to the image of the falling ash and its
commentary on the history of the English monarchy, the passage, as
Dryden points out in a footnote, echoes Denham's *Destruction of Troy*:

> He, whom such Titles swell'd, such Power made proud
> To whom the Scepters of all *Asia* bow'd,
> On the cold earth lies th'unregarded King,
> A headless Carkass, and a nameless Thing.

> (546–49)[24]

While Denham's fragment was composed in 1636, these lines, which
are its climax and conclusion, must surely have evoked events of 1649
when the piece was published in 1656.[25] Through his vocabulary and
explicit allusion, Dryden once more, then, looks in anguish at the past.

No longer, however, can history offer any solutions, and, as England abandons its king, the poet himself seems alone on "the bleak Shoar," listening, as Matthew Arnold would a century and a half later, to the "Sea of Faith'"s "melancholy, long, withdrawing roar."

Dryden's own loss as to where to go next is, of course, directly responsible for the confusion that pervades *Aeneis* II. The problem at the heart of the book (indeed of the entire translation) is the difficulty of discerning, through the rubble of centuries of history and the smokescreens of contemporary debate, truths that the poet is sure can still be found. The crisis is highlighted in Dryden's portrayal of Vergil's Sinon, the Greek who tricked the Trojans into bringing the wooden horse within their walls. In a way that is at once universal and timeless and evocative of England's present quandary, Dryden uses the deceptive appearance and believable lies of this stranger and apparent friend to stress the vulnerability of a society where traditional codes and standards of behavior are not observed.

The foreigner captured on the beach by the Trojans has purposely "made himself their Prey, / T'impose on their Belief, and *Troy* betray" (77–78). The previous betrayal resulting from an imposition was that of *Aeneis* I when Jupiter "Impos'd a King, with arbitrary Sway" (see p. 112 above). The storm (with its contemporary political overtones) subsequently unleashed there hovers here too in the notion of altering fundamental constitutions, which is inherent in the stranger's threat to a people's "Belief." Vergil states simply that Sinon planned to employ guile: "versare dolos" (62). A possible connection between Sinon and William III is then made as Dryden passes up the chance to reproduce Vergil's hemistich (something he had imitated in his earlier works) and turns his warning ("accipe nunc Danaum insidias et crimine ab uno / disce omnis") into an expression of scorn: "Now hear how well the *Greeks* their Wiles disguis'd, / Behold a Nation in a Man compris'd" (83–84).[26] The sarcastic couplet is satiric not epic and recalls Dryden's third Juvenal translation where Juvenal's xenophobia is converted into an unmistakable attack on the Dutch prince's accession to England's top offices of church and state: "I hate," Dryden's Umbricius seethes, "To see the Scum of *Greece* transplanted here, / Receiv'd like Gods" (106–8); he then asks, "Riddle me this, and guess him if you can, / Who bears a Nation in a single Man?" (135–36). Like the interpolated "transplanted" and "Receiv'd like Gods," Umbricius's emphasis now on the foreigner's ugliness leaves no doubt that the "Man" bearing the nation in himself is the new king of England.

Having evoked his vitriolic *Juvenal* here in *Aeneis* II and suggested the contemporary social and political implications of the stranger's foreboding presence, Dryden then, however, proceeds to render Sinon's pleas

in terms that point to James II's position. The Greek's first words to
the Trojans "kindle" their "Pity": "Alas!," he says, "what Earth remains, what Sea / Is open to receive unhappy me? / What Fate a
wretched Fugitive attends, / Scorn'd by my Foes, abandon'd by my
Friends?" (87–90). The speech is intensely ironic; by omitting Vergil's
proper nouns, Dryden has created a scene which suggests that the sympathy the English should feel for their own wretched fugitive king has
been transferred to a menacing intruder. The irony intensifies as Sinon
continues. "What e're," he says,

> My Fate ordains, my Words shall be sincere:
> I neither can, nor dare my Birth disclaim,
> *Greece* is my Country, *Sinon* is my Name:
> Though plung'd by Fortune's Pow'r in Misery,
> 'Tis not in Fortune's Pow'r to make me lye.
>
> (97–102)

Vergil's Sinon declares that he will tell the truth (*"fatebor, / Vera"* [77–
78]); the emphasis on sincerity of "Words" is Dryden's, and it provides
a reminder that a world where the king's word is bond is not controlled
by Fortune. The irony, then, is that the rightful king's "birth" cannot
be disclaimed by any intruder, nor, indeed, is it in Fortune's power to
make anyone lie—and, as subsequent events demonstrate, both Fortune
and misery reign where lies do.

Sinon now concocts a story about his flight from his people that not
only reinforces Dryden's evocation of James' plight, but trembles with
a passion that suggests the poet's personal involvement:

> when *Ulysses*, with fallacious Arts,
> Had made Impression in the Peoples Hearts;
> And forg'd a Treason in my Patron's Name,
> (I speak of things too far divulg'd by Fame)
> My Kinsman fell; then I without support,
> In private mourn'd his Loss, and left the Court.
> Mad as I was, I could not bear his Fate
> With silent Grief, but loudly blam'd the State:
> And curs'd the direful Author of my Woes.
> 'Twas told again, and hence my Ruin rose.
> I threatn'd, if Indulgent Heav'n once more
> Wou'd land me safely on my Native Shore,
> His Death with double Vengeance to restore.
>
> (116–28)

The California editors remark on the late seventeenth-century overlay
of lines 117–18: "Dryden's transitional elaboration on Virgil, which has

no precedent in previous translations, associates Ulysses with the Restoration politician—a Shaftesbury or a Buckingham, e.g.—who sought, or was charged with seeking, popular approval" (4:979). In fact, the description of Ulysses also recalls the way Absalom-Monmouth, "furnish'd out with Arts," "glide[d] unfelt into [the people's] secret hearts" (2:26.692–93), and the related Exclusion Crisis is probably behind the "forg'd" "Treason," for Dryden seems again to be portraying the whole story of James' trials. The interpolated "left the Court," especially coupled with the also interpolated details of the exile's lack of "support" and endurance of his loss "in private," would seem, after all, to point to the hapless prince's necessary departures from England both in the late 1670s and then again in 1688.[27] The allusion to the latter incident is reinforced when Sinon describes his actual escape:

> Hid in a weedy Lake all Night I lay,
> Secure of Safety when they sail'd away.
> But now what further Hopes for me remain,
> To see my Friends or Native Soil again?
> My tender Infants, or my careful Sire;
> Whom they returning will to Death require?
>
>   (185–90)

While there is a basis in the Latin for all Dryden has here, the picture surely could not help but remind a loyal Jacobite of the English king's ignominious flight. It has a parallel, for example, in a 1689 engraving which depicts James fleeing Whitehall in a tiny boat, along the muddy banks of the Thames, in the dead of night.[28] The danger to the lives of the Stuart family was undoubtedly also of very real concern to Jacobites, and Dryden must have known about James's supposed instructions concerning his wife's and son's removal: "Arise, and take the young child and his mother, and flee into Egypt, and be thou there until I bring thee word: for Herod will seek the young child to destroy him."[29]

As he presents his king's plight, however, Dryden once more seems to include himself in the tale of woe. The speaker's proclamation that he "loudly blam'd the State" is perhaps most appropriate to the poet's stance as the Stuart regime's unwavering champion, while his comment about being "told again, and hence my Ruin rose" is an apt summary of Dryden's and James's disastrous adherence to their beliefs in the 1680s. The triplet at the end of the passage quoted, however, reverberates with the poet's wrath. The contemporary overtones of the rest of the passage place the vengeance referred to here in the context of the "Poetical Revenge" discussed in the dedication. There Dryden cites Horace's "genus irritabile Vatum" and warns, "When a Poet is thoroughly provok'd, he will do himself Justice, however dear it cost him, Animamque, in Vulnere ponit. . . . The Vengeance we defer, is not forgotten" (5:283). Though exiled on his own "Native Shore," Dryden is aware that his poetic vengeance will have more profound, further-reaching and longer-lasting consequences than the violence of the kind of bloody-minded invader in whose mouth he places the speech.

The contrast between the reality of Sinon's character and intentions and the old-world argument he presents to the Trojans is accentuated when he inadvertently allies himself with the Homeric Aeneas of the storm speech in *Aeneis* I by inviting his listeners to "Asswage your Thirst of Blood, and strike the Blow" (140). His blood-obsessed challenge has no basis in Vergil (whose Sinon bids "Take your vengeance immediately"[30]), and it indicates a brutality of character which is revealed again, tellingly, immediately before the speech describing how he hid in a lake. When faced with death, Sinon admits, "I follow'd Nature's Laws, and must avow / I broke my Bonds, and fled the fatal blow" (183–84). His adherence to natural rather than social laws connects him with Dryden's raging heroines and the lioness of *Georgics* III. His breaking of "Bonds" intensifies the distinction between him and the king whom he now evokes in the same way as Pyrrhus and Priam are contrasted later in *Aeneis* II.

The vulnerability of a society gulled by such a deceiver is then highlighted by Dryden in his poignant observation, "False Tears true Pity move" (197).[31] His horror at the thought of a society where such "true" and sincere feelings as "Pity" are completely at the mercy of false words is reinforced at the end of the scene in the anguished reflection that "easie Hearts" were won by "perfidious Arts" so that what neither "A thousand Ships, nor ten years Siege had done: / False Tears and fawning Words the City won" (259–63). The difficulty of combatting the kind of fickle but powerful forces depicted in this episode is pinpointed between the poet's two outbursts through Sinon's intensely ironic vow of loyalty to the Trojans. In a way that recalls Dryden's *Oedipus*, the arch-deceiver promises he will "Reveal the Secrets of the guilty State, / And justly punish whom I justly hate!" He then beseeches the king to "preserve the Faith you gave, / If I to save myself your Empire save" (212–15). The concern introduced here for the difficulty of seeing and therefore of being able to find a center on which to pin "Faith" and so save the "guilty State" becomes paramount in *Aeneis* VII and VIII where Dryden investigates Aeneas's leadership and status as invader.

BLOOD

A King can give no more than is his own:
The Title stood entail'd, had *Richard* had a Son.
Conquest, an odious Name, was laid aside,
Where all submitted; none the Battle try'd.
The senseless Plea of Right by Providence,
Was, by a flatt'ring Priest, invented since:
And lasts no longer than the present sway;
But justifies the next who comes in play.
                    —Dryden, "The Character of a Good Parson"

Blood flows through Dryden's *Aeneis* in torrents. The profusion of "gore," "purple streams," "crimson floods" and other metaphorical descriptions aside, the word "blood" itself (including such composites as "bloody") occurs 169 times in total: an average of 14 times in each book! Unsurprisingly, the word appears most frequently in *Aeneis* XI (25 times) and XII (22 times) where the Latian wars are at their height. *Aeneis* VII, however, is a close third with 21 references to "blood" and bloodiness. The effect of Dryden's sanguine insistence here, where the first blood is spilt over the Trojans' arrival, is to turn the focus of his own poem to the concern introduced in *Aeneis* II for the shift in 1690s England from a veneration for bloodline to the domination of bloodshed.[32]

As Zwicker observes, the attention in *Aeneid* VII "to foreign settlement, lineal descent, and the role of fate in politics" allows Dryden directly to question the Glorious Revolution settlement and (again) to wonder about the fate of the Stuart monarchy.[33] *Aeneis* VII's investigations reach a climax when Juno, having announced that the "Blood" is "already drawn, the War begun," prophesies, "A bloody *Hymen* shall th' Alliance join / Betwixt the *Trojan* and *Ausonian* Line" (756, 769–70). The poet's own confusion over the historical origins and implications of a union which sows "Seeds of Discord," "Frauds, Fears, and Fury" and "Causes of a lasting Hate" rather than sure succession and national peace dominates the rest of the translation (766–68). Most immediately, *Aeneis* VIII picks up the same questions in the same confrontational way, and, interestingly, the difference between *Aeneis* VII, with its more confident contrast of royalist values and 1690s impieties, and *Aeneis* VIII, which is shrouded in the type of veils that obscure the Panther's argument, reflects the general shift from the certainty of Dryden's pre-1688 works to the profound uncertainty that imbues everything he wrote afterward.

The series of contrasts that make up Dryden's seventh book begins

with the subject of fame. As Zwicker also points out, Dryden opens
what is Vergil's Iliadic section with an emphasis on name that is peculiar
to his own poem:

> And thou, O Matron of Immortal Fame!
> Here Dying, to the Shore hast left thy Name:
> *Cajeta* still the place is call'd from thee,
> The Nurse of great *Æneas* Infancy.
> Here rest thy Bones in rich *Hesperia's* Plains,
> Thy Name ('tis all a Ghost can have) remains.
>
> (1–6)

Zwicker notes that line 1 is "invention" and the mood is changed from
the conditional ("si qua est ea gloria" [4]) to the declarative in line 6.
As he comments, "[t]he change is slight, but not so the glory that at-
taches to name, a glory underscored by Dryden's insertion of 'still' in
line 3, and a glory that had come to have considerable force for Dryden
in the 1690s."[34]

Having prefaced the Trojans' arrival in Latium with a stress on personal fame that recalls his rejection of national glory in *Aeneis* I, however, the poet then addresses the muse of love in a style that renders
English Vergil's heroic. Sounding much like the Chorus in the prologue
to *Henry V*, in fact, he appeals, "Now, *Erato*, thy Poet's Mind inspire, /
And fill his Soul with Coelestial Fire. / Relate what *Latium* was, her
ancient Kings: / Declare the past, and present State of things."[35] He
then seems to reflect on Dryden's early work as he proposes to tell
"how the War began, / And how concluded by the Godlike Man." The
invocation ends with a recognition of the power of poetry that is both
characteristic of Dryden and again reminiscent of the *Henry V* prologue:
"A larger Scene of Action is display'd, / And, rising hence, a greater
Work is weigh'd" (52–67). This "greater Work" is now outlined: "*Latinus* old and mild, had long possess'd / The *Latian* Scepter, and his People bless'd" (68–69). The interpolation of "mild" (which was the king's
fault in *Absalom and Achitophel*) as well as the subsequent lengthy meditation on lineage reinforce the blending of Roman and English history,
which is suggested in the invocation to the muse (and, of course, pervades Dryden's early works). Dryden now argues, "King *Latinus*, in the
third Degree, / Had *Saturn* Author of his Family." The Restoration implications of the kingdom's problem are unmistakable: "But this old
peaceful Prince, as Heav'n decreed, / Was bless'd with no Male Issue
to succeed" (74–77).

In the same way as the book's opening sets the barren present with
its emphasis on individual fame against old-world poetic and historical

glories, however, this *Annus Mirabilis/Absalom and Achitophel*-style passage is countered by the entrance now of "foreign Men, of mighty Stature" whose "Habit" is "Uncouth" and whose "Name" is "unknown" (225–26). Cynicism takes over as the invading prince is labelled a "Pious Chief, who sought by peaceful Ways, / To found his Empire, and his Town to raise," but who then "designs / His new elected Seat" (203–4, 211–12). Juxtaposed with the discussion of Latinus's lineage (a piece highlighted in the dedication as Dryden reiterates, "He was descended from *Saturn*, and as I remember, in the Third Degree. . . . a King by Inheritance, who [was] born a Father of his Country" [5:284]), these ironic lines are as desolate as the politically-charged observation in the dedication that "*Æneas* succeeded not, but was Elected. *Troy* was fore-doom'd to fall for ever" (5:285). The irony and foreboding intensify as the poet states, "The King ordains their entrance" (227). Clearly, this is an indictment of William and his Dutch cronies, whose entrance, far from being "ordain[ed]" by a supreme authority, was debated by a nervous nation. Yet, it also highlights the fact that a prince who must depend on a "new elected Seat" is neither "Pious" (because he is not "born a Father of his Country"), nor (since his own position is not "ordain[ed]" by God) can he possess the kind of comforting, stabilizing power displayed here by Latinus.

This kind of opposition occurs again after the Trojans' appeal to Latinus for sanctuary. The portrayal of the old king "pond'ring future Things of wond'rous Weight; / Succession, Empire, and his Daughter's Fate" jars uneasily against his recollection of the prophecy that "A foreign Son-in-Law shall come from far, / (Such is our Doom) a Chief renown'd in War" (345–46, 371–72). Dryden's warning is heightened by Latinus's Lear-like pledge to Aeneas's envoys immediately before his comment about "our Doom": "Partake and use my Kingdom as your own; / All shall be yours, while I command the Crown" (359–60). Vergil's Latinus offers hospitality not regency as he promises "non vobis, rege Latino, / Divitis uber agri, Trojæve opulentia deerit": "Not while Latinus is king will you lack the wealth of rich soil or the bounty of Troy" (261–62). The probable contemporary implications of Dryden's Latinus's Lear-like proposition are illuminated when the passage is compared to *The Female Parricide* (1690); here the poet claims that we

> of unnatural daughters rarely hear
> 'Till those of hapless James and old King Lear.
> But worse than cruel lustful Goneril, thou!
> She took but what her father did allow;
> But thou, more impious, robb'st thy father's brow.[36]

At any rate, Dryden's insistence on Aeneas as a "foreign Son-in-Law" points a finger at James II's treatment at the hands of his daughter and her war-mongering husband. The poet himself makes the association with contemporary affairs as he remarks in a note to *Aeneis* VII that past critics have deemed it "odd" that "a King shou'd offer his Daughter and Heir, to a Stranger Prince, and a wanderer, before he had seen him, and when he had only heard of his arrival on his Coasts. . . ." Citing the oracle concerning the "foreign Son-in-Law" he continues, "Fathers, in those Ancient Ages, consider[ed] Birth and Vertue, more than Fortune, in the placing of their Daughters: Which I cou'd prove by various Examples: The contrary of which being now practis'd, I dare not say in our Nation, but in *France*, has not a little darken'd the Lustre of their Nobility" (6:826).

The threat to England's safety already implied in the earlier ironic description of the prince as "Pious" is also underscored in this interview between Latinus and the Trojans. As he requests safe haven, Ilioneus makes a promise on behalf of his people, and begs that Latinus "spare,"

> The common Water, and the common Air:
> Sheds which our selves will build, and mean abodes,
> Fit to receive and serve our banish'd Gods.
> Nor our Admission shall your Realm disgrace,
> Nor length of time our Gratitude efface.
> Besides, what endless Honour you shall gain
> To save and shelter *Troy*'s unhappy Train.
> Now, by my Sov'raign, and his Fate I swear,
> Renown'd for Faith in Peace, for Force in War.
>
> (313–22)

In its modesty and apparent humility, the request evokes the Hind's "mean retreat" which "did mighty *Pan* contain" and into which the Panther is invited as a "stranger" who is "amaz'd to see / Contempt of wealth, and wilfull poverty" (3:160.711, 714–15). Ironically, however, the speech also recalls the poet's reflection in *The Hind and the Panther* on those "happy Regions, *Italy* and *Spain*" where "The *Wolfe*, the *Bear*, the *Boar*, can there advance / No native claim of just inheritance" so that "Where birth has plac'd 'em" they "share / The common benefit of vital air" (3:131.291–98). Still more disconcertingly, Ilioneus's plea on behalf of his "banish'd Gods" and "unhappy Train" puts him in the dubious position of the intruders in the Panther's complaint to the Hind:

> Methinks such terms of proferr'd peace you bring
> As once *Æneas* to th'*Italian* King:
> By long possession all the land is mine,

You strangers come with your intruding line,

. . . .

    you bring your exil'd gods along;
And will endeavour in succeeding space,
Those houshold Poppits on our hearths to place.

                 (3:184.766–69, 778–80)

Subsequent events, of course, prove false the apparent innocuousness of Ilioneus's request to share "common Air" with the Latians, and the speech lurks hauntingly in *Aeneis* X when Juno taunts Venus,

    You think it hard, the *Latians* shou'd destroy
    With Swords your *Trojans*, and with Fires your *Troy*:
    Hard and unjust indeed, for Men to draw
    Their Native Air, nor take a foreign Law.

                    (112–15)[37]

Even here, however, the Trojan's promise is undercut and he himself ultimately put in the place of the equivocating panther who ends, "My gracious Sov'reign wou'd my vote implore: / I owe him much, but owe my conscience more" (3:184.784–85). Not only would Ilioneus's Jacobite-sounding assurance of lasting "Gratitude" as he swears by an invading "Sov'raign" "Renown'd for Faith in Peace, for Force in War" ring with irony in war-weary 1690s England, but Latinus's meeting with the Trojans is prefaced by the seer's prophecy that on Aeneas's arrival "War shall the Country waste, and change the State" (120). The "change" of state has no basis in Vergil but it does recall the poet's sober warning in *Absalom and Achitophel*: "All other Errors but disturb a State; / But Innovation is the Blow of Fate" (799–800).

What Dryden has done by this stage, in effect, is to dislodge both Vergil's emphasis on Aeneas's arrival in Italy as destined by Fate and his assurance that peace and stability will eventually supplant bloodshed and suffering. His personal horror at the displacement of England's own "Pious" prince by a stranger claiming a "new elected Seat" is accentuated when Juno announces,

    With Blood the Dear Alliance shall be bought;
    And both the People near Destruction brought.
    So shall the Son-in-Law, and Father join,
    With Ruin, War, and Waste of either Line.
    O fatal Maid! thy Marriage is endow'd
    With *Phrygian*, *Latian*, and *Rutulian* Blood!

                    (438–43)

It is possible that the same Vergilian lines are behind Spenser's account of Troy's "great genealogie"; when Aeneas finally arrived in Latium, Paridell observes, "he with cruell warre was entertaind,"

> Till he with old *Latinus* was constraind
> To contract wedlock, (so the fates ordaind)
> Wedlocke contract in blood, and eke in blood
> Accomplished. . . .[38]

There is a marked difference, however, between the darkness of Dryden's lines, which exaggerate the suffering and destruction admitted by Vergil, and Spenser's tale, which ends optimistically as Britomart eagerly interjects, "And *Troy* againe out of her dust was reard / To sit in second seat of soveraigne king, / Of all the world vnder her gouerning."[39] It seems difficult, in fact, to believe that, having posited Spenser as a polestar for English poets in his dedication, Dryden would not have been thinking of Britomart's vision of *"Troynouant"* washed by the waves of "wealthy *Thamis*" as he imbued Amata's subsequent appeal with unmistakable English overtones.

In her plea to Latinus, Amata not only echoes Juno's foreboding prophecy but provides Dryden's contemporaries with a warning as threatening as that issued by *The Medall* when it imagines an England where sure succession has failed:

> Think on a King's inviolable Word;
> And think on *Turnus*, her once plighted Lord:
> To this false Foreigner you gave your Throne,
> And wrong a Friend, a Kinsman, and a Son.
>
> (512–15)[40]

Vergil's Amata also points to the sanctity of her husband's promise that Turnus may marry their daughter ("tua sancta fides" [365]), stressing that the pledge was made with a kinsman and often reaffirmed by the king's right hand: "consanguineo toties data dextera Turno" (366). By rendering "sancta fides" as "a King's inviolable Word," however, Dryden again evokes a reminder of the social stability inherent in the Stuart regime. In effect, his Amata accuses Latinus of behaving in the same way as the dishonorable plantation governor in Southerne's enormously popular *Oroonoko* (1695). There Blanford demonstrates clear Jacobite sensibilities as he cries out in disgust at his governor's treatment of Oroonoko:

> Remember, sir, he yielded on your word.
> Your word! Which honest men will think should be

> The last resort of truth and trust on earth.
> There's no appeal beyond it but to Heav'n.[41]

The world presented here in *Aeneis* VII, where "a King's inviolable Word" and the bonds of friendship and kinship are meaningless and where society is at the mercy of the whim of a "false Foreigner" (who has been "given" a throne),[42] is not essentially different from *Oroonoko*'s mercenary world and was surely intended to have the same impact on a 1690s audience.

Yet again in *Aeneis* VII, Dryden seems to try to explain the upheaval depicted in terms of the ongoing opposition to England's rightful church and monarchy. This happens in the episode describing Ascanius's wounding of the pet deer of Silvia, the daughter of "*Tyrrheus*, chief Ranger to the *Latian* King": the event which sparks the war between the Latians and Trojans (676). Dryden portrays the animal's reaction to its wounding in a way that reflects *The Hind and the Panther*'s influence rather than Vergil's: "The bleeding Creature issues from the Floods, / Possess'd with Fear, and seeks his known abodes; / His old familiar Hearth, and household Gods" (695–97). Vergil's stag "flees back to a familiar roof and, groaning, makes its way into its stall."[43] Dryden's interpolated "Floods" evoke the numerous political "Floods" that wash through his works, while the image of a fearful creature seeking "an old familiar Hearth, and houshold Gods" has a parallel in the persecuted Hind's fear for her children as she wanders through "kingdoms, once Her own."

The theological framework is reinforced by echoes from *Religio Laici*. As they assemble to aid Silvia, Vergil's "hardy husbandmen" ("duros . . . agrestes" [504]) become "the clownish Neighbourhood" and "Churls," and then, as they snatch up weapons against the Trojans, convert from "Indomiti agricolæ" ("wild farmers" [521]) to "Clowns, a boist'rous, rude, ungovern'd Crew" (701–2, 724). Similarly, while Vergil describes how "Tyrrheus summons his bands" ("Vocat agmina Tyrrheus" [508]) and, breathing fury, snatches up an axe which was at hand because he happened then to be cleaving an oak in four,[44] Dryden's "*Tyrrheus*" becomes "the Foster-Father of the Beast," who, clenching "a Hatchet in his horny Fist," "held his Hand from the descending Stroke, / And left his Wedge within the cloven Oak, / To whet their Courage, and their Rage provoke" (708–12). In effect, Dryden has made the scene that gives rise to spilt blood and Juno's "bloody *Hymen*" a replica of the situation attacked in *Religio Laici* when

> The Book thus put in every vulgar hand,
> Which each presum'd he best cou'd understand,

The *Common Rule* was made the *common Prey*;
And at the mercy of the *Rabble* lay.
The tender Page with horney Fists was gaul'd;
And he was gifted most that loudest baul'd.

(400–405)

In his portrayal of Tyrrheus and his rabble precipitating chaos by taking matters into their own "horny" hands, then, Dryden seems to have
extended to matters of state his ecclesiastical argument from *Religio Laici*
and *The Hind and the Panther* about the dangers of the absence of a central authority. This linking of affairs theological (represented by the
"bleeding" deer) and monarchic is reinforced with the wedge left
"within the cloven Oak" in order to "whet" "Rage": an idea that has
precedents in Dryden's, Ogilby's and Spenser's royal oaks which are
assaulted by "Wars" and gradually weakened (as Dryden puts it in *Absalom and Achitophel*) by "Pious Subjects," who, in "secur[ing]" kingly
"Power," take it away (983–84) (see pp. 59–61 above).[45]
    As is also his wont, Dryden follows up this depiction of civil discord
by setting the chaos against a figure of a king:

With Fates averse, the Rout in Arms resort,
To Force their Monarch, and insult the Court.
But like a Rock unmov'd, a Rock that braves
The rageing Tempest and the rising Waves,
Prop'd on himself he stands: His solid sides
Wash off the Sea-weeds, and the sounding Tides:
So stood the Pious Prince unmov'd: and long
Sustain'd the madness of the noisie Throng.

(807–14)

As Garrison observes, "Vergil does not describe the Latian king as
pius," and these lines could be from any of Dryden's pre-1688 political
poems.[46] The most direct echo, though, is, of course, from *Cleomenes*
where the king confronts social turmoil and exile in his opening speech
and declares, "My mind on its own Centre stands unmov'd, / And Stable as the Fabrick of the World, / Propt on it self" (16:88.3–5).[47] In fact,
like the Priam episode in *Aeneis* II, the strong royalism of this scene now
yields, with Latinus, to *Cleomenes*-like weariness and submission to uncontrollable forces.
    Garrison also notes that Vergil's "*O miseri*" becomes "O more than
Madmen!" as Dryden's king gives up on his countrymen, and the same
shift from the political to the personal that is apparent in the earlier
books discussed is affirmed when the old man consoles himself that the
"guilt of Blood" is theirs but he himself can "to the Port of Death se-

curely tend" (821–22, 826). Dryden's empathy with the king undoubtedly shapes the philosophy that now asserts itself:

> He said no more, but in his Walls confin'd,
> Shut out the Woes which he too well divin'd:
> Nor with the rising Storm wou'd vainly strive,
> But left the Helm, and let the Vessel drive.
>
> (829–32)

Behind these completely Drydenian lines are one and a half in the Latin: "Nec plura locutus, / Sepsit se tectis, rerumque reliquit habenas" ("He said no more, but shut himself in his home and let go the reins of state" [599–600]). Garrison argues that by adding "the idea of Latinus as both visionary ('Woes which he too well divin'd') and realist ('Nor with the rising Storm wou'd vainly strive'), Dryden deflects blame from the Latian king who represents an idealism once but no longer possible."[48] In fact Dryden's Latinus here anticipates the pragmatic and "visionary" philosopher kings of *Fables*, who also know that it is useless to strive against "the rising Storm" and are willingly to let the ship of state "drive" without a helmsman.

By this point, in fact, it seems that *Aeneis* VII has advanced the philosophical shift established in *Aeneis* I and contended in *Aeneis* II; the conflict between the royalist tenets that Dryden refuses to relinquish from his politics or poetry and the contemporary reality that assails both is no less fierce here, but the disillusionment seems somehow more pervasive and the parallel generic shift more pronounced. Clearly, Dryden's revision of traditional heroism begins in the dedication with his split Augustus and Aeneas who substitute perhaps most obviously for Spenser's plural heroes. However, *Aeneis* VII as a whole reveals that there has been a movement away from even the exemplary element of Spenserian heroism, or the assumption that there can be clear outlines as to the way a hero should or should not behave. This movement in fact establishes itself in *Aeneis* IV (which will be discussed in the last chapter); its significance in *Aeneis* VII is that it directs the course of the war books to follow.

As Dryden's Aeneas penetrates further into Italy, he becomes less a Stuart figure to be praised or a William figure to be condemned than a forerunner to Gulliver or Tom Jones: a wanderer adrift in a world which one minute promotes time-honored, sacrosanct values, the next undercuts them. In the process, the epic skeleton on which Dryden has necessarily hung his poem (it is after all a translation) is clothed more and more in the garb of mock-heroic. The generic significance of this is perhaps again illuminated by McKeon's observations on the dialectic

constitution of the novel. Citing Fielding's mock-heroic as a product
and instrument of the complex relationship in the early eighteenth century between the "positive norm" supplied by ancient history and aristocratic ideology (the "heroic") and what he (McKeon) calls its
"progressive critique" (the "mock"-ery), he comments that the

> major effect of the asymmetry—the confusing conflation of terms (positive
> and negative, ancient and modern, hero and rogue) that have been posited
> in opposition to each other—is to emphasize what is a dominant feature of
> each strategy as it operates on its own: the sense of the collapse of catego-
> ries.[49]

In the *Aeneis*, a similar process is both propelled by and manifest in the
disintegration of *Aeneis* VII's series of sharp oppositions and historical
emphasis into the confusion of *Aeneis* VIII and its ultimate focus (in a
pre-Fielding way) on the narrative itself.

An indication of the direction the second part of Dryden's poem is to
steer is given near the beginning of *Aeneis* VII when the poet describes
the artwork depicted "Above the Portal" of Latinus's palace. A vision
not only of Rome's glorious past but of England's chaotic present mate-
rializes as Dryden portrays "Godlike Grandsires" alongside "ancient
Janus, with his double Face, / And Bunch of Keys, the Porter of the
place" (242–46). The mocking of England's guardian gatekeeper by the
assignment of the Janus plate to Viscount Sydney has already been discussed (see p. 120 above), and the contrast between "Godlike Grandsires" and the 1690s Janus is paralleled by the subsequent juxtaposition
of "Warlike Kings, who for their Country fought, / And honourable
Wounds from Battel brought" and "Captive Chariots, Axes, Shields,
and Bars, / And broken Beaks of Ships, the Trophies of their Wars"
(250–54). This last couplet is reminiscent of the temple engravings of
Caesar's "shatter'd Ships" in *Georgics* III and, in its emphasis on destruction, undermines the military prowess and historical glory embodied by the "Warlike Kings" and inherent in the Latin. Dryden perhaps
intended to intensify his subversion of Vergil's heroic by giving Janus
keys, a detail (objected to in Spence's *Polymetis*) which recalls *Macbeth*'s
drunken porter scene. At any rate, the distance between this scene with
its punctured heroic and allusions to contemporary chaos and Spenser's
epic vision (for example) is highlighted when it is compared with *The
Faerie Queene*'s promise of "A famous history" of "great *Troynouant*" to
"bee enrold / In euerlasting moniments of brasse."[50]

It is this jumble of past and present, kings and intruders, glory and
ignominy that opens *Aeneis* VIII. The summary of how "*Æneas* landed
on the *Latian* Coast, / With banish'd Gods, and with a baffled Hoast" is

as baffling to the reader as the problem confronting the Trojans. The clear polarities of *Aeneis* VII have disappeared, and the poet states that the newcomer

> now aspir'd to Conquest of the State;
> And claim'd a Title from the Gods and Fate.
> What num'rous Nations in his Quarrel came,
> And how they spread his formidable Name:
> What he design'd, what Mischiefs might arise,
> If Fortune favour'd his first Enterprise,
> Was left for him to weigh: whose equal Fears,
> And common Interest was involv'd in theirs.
>
>   (19–22)

The contemporary relevance of this picture of an invading conqueror trailing war with "num'rous Nations" is unmistakable, and the lines again attack through irony as Dryden scorns the title "claim'd" from "Gods and Fate." However, the rapidity of the oscillation between royalist convictions and the type of forces controlling contemporary England begins to obscure the polarities thereby producing (to use McKeon's phrase) a "sense of the collapse of categories." Most obviously, "Conquest" and "Fortune" are set against "a Title from the Gods and Fate." However, in quick succession a conqueror paradoxically "claims" a divinely-sanctioned "Title" and quest, which are immediately undermined by his enforcement of a (petty sounding) "Quarrel" involving "num'rous Nations" in the cause of his own "Name" (not national glory!). Yet again, the "formidable Name" of a leader was often the bulwark and support of states in the heroic past. Confusion mounts further still as he decides to depend on "Fortune" but is then pictured "weigh[-ing]" the people's "equal Fears" in a way that not only recalls the depiction of the Stuart kings in Dryden's early works but dissolves his selfishness and concern for his "Name" into "common Interest."

The portrait's complexity heightens yet again as the would-be conqueror becomes a replica of the kings in *Annus Mirabilis* and *Absalom and Achitophel* as they pondered the best course of action for the nation and people:

> This way and that he turns his anxious Mind;
> Thinks, and rejects the Counsels he design'd:
> Explores himself in vain, in ev'ry part,
> And gives no rest to his distracted Heart.
>
>   (30–33)

This blending of Aeneas and kingship-of-old is supported by the Tiber god's speech to him as he lies "on *Tyber*'s Banks, oppress'd with Grief," even in sleep (43). The god addresses the hero in semimystical terms that could be straight from *The Faerie Queene*: "Undoubted Off-spring of Etherial Race, / O long expected in this promis'd Place." He then informs him that his task now is to "restore" his "banish'd Gods" to "their Hearths, and old Abodes" for (again in Spenserian style) "This is thy happy Home" (51–55). Here it could again be argued that Dryden is setting old-world ideals against contemporary reality to shock the English into realizing what they have done by replacing England's rightful "Off-spring of Etherial Race" with a stranger who aspires "to Conquest of the State." And he is. But by now the conqueror and the "promis'd" newcomer have been confusingly blended—and, as any reader knows, the epic is to end with the victory that ensures Aeneas will remain in Italy.

Interestingly, not only does Dryden's treatment of Aeneas here (indeed throughout the translation) strongly anticipate what McKeon calls the "notoriously discontinuous quality of Gulliver's character," but in the next section, when the hero visits the Arcadian king Evander to request reinforcements, it could just as easily be him as Swift's hero that McKeon is describing when he also observes that

> throughout his travels Gulliver repeatedly assumes the role of the 'new man,' symbolically and unequivocally sundered from any past 'inheritance' by his status as a wandering alien who wades ashore willing and eager to serve the reigning prince and receive his due recompense.[51]

Still the codes and hallmarks of seventeenth-century royalism and its epics continue to be pinned on Aeneas as he makes his appeal to Evander. Not only (most notably) does the hero found his request on a reminder of "Our Fathers mingl'd Blood" (176),[52] but Dryden continually evokes the *Faerie Queene* theme of guest friendship (and its associated codes of behavior) by highlighting with epithets nearly all Vergil's references to Aeneas as "hospes." Yet, again, these attachments with the past are consistently—and insistently—undercut. Two lines after Pallas calls him a "welcome Guest," for example, Aeneas is referred to by the poet as a "Stranger Prince" and ominously (for Dryden's contemporary audience anyway) invited to "descend" "Upon our Shores" (162–65).

It is the scene where Evander lays out Latium's history to Aeneas, however, that points most clearly to the book's ultimate replacement of an exemplary or reprehensible prince with a hero who has more in common with the Bakhtinian novelistic hero: a figure who is not only (in Gulliver-style) "sundered from any past 'inheritance'," but who walks around on the same "time-and-value" plane as the poet rather than being separated and exalted by "epic distance."[53] As he passes through the city with Evander and Pallas,

> The Stranger cast around his curious Eyes;
> New Objects viewing still, with new Surprise:
> With greedy Joy enquires of various Things;
> And Acts and Monuments of Ancient Kings.

(412–15)

Here too the changes to Vergil's text are slight but not so the impact of the scene. Vergil stresses Aeneas's wonder ("Miratur . . . Æneas" [310–11]), and the Trojan's appreciation of the accomplishments before him clearly derives from a background that provides a means of association and comparison. Dryden's "curious" and "greedy" "Stranger," on the other hand, seems to have found himself in a place where even the concept of what he is viewing is a source of "new Surprise." The poet's own royalist and patriotic horror at the thought of a stranger who is about to become the nation's leader drinking in the unfamiliar sight and stories of "Acts and Monuments of Ancient Kings" is suggested as his Evander now recounts the history of Latium in a way that simultaneously reviews English history. In language that points unmistakably to Dryden's own tales from *Astræa Redux* to *Absalom and Achitophel* to *Britannia Rediviva*, the Arcadian king tells of a land that was the seat of "Silvan Pow'rs" before being beset by a series of troubled monarchies; it is a story of banishment, of "Laws ordain'd, and Civil Customs taught," of "Unduteous Son" 's and usurpation, of "mild Empire, Peace and Plenty," of "Avarice and Rage," "Arbitrary Sway" and oppression (417–40). The glorious means by which poets could once transmit these tales for the benefit of posterity is perhaps also alluded to as Evander's conclusion draws a parallel between him and Spenser's Una. Driven "from my native home," he reflects, and "Long toss'd on Seas I sought this happy Land: / . . . call'd by Heav'ns Command" (441–44).

This pitting of past against present is simply a continuation of the *modus operandi* that drives Dryden's *Vergil*. Yet here the gulf between the world of national history and tradition represented by Evander's Arcadia and the world of "flowing and transitory" contemporaneity (to use Bakhtinian terms) in which both poet and "Stranger Prince" are situated is one that neither the poet's loyalty nor his poetic powers can seem to bridge any longer. This impression is reinforced when the next part of the scene finally resolves itself (in the way announced in *Aeneis* I) into a focus on the healing powers of love and art.

Having completed his guided tour, Evander brings Aeneas to his own "Country Court," and

> thus the King bespoke his *Trojan* Guest.
> Mean as it is, this Palace, and this Door,
> Receiv'd *Alcides*, then a Conqueror.
> Dare to be poor: accept our homely Food
> Which feasted him; and emulate a God.
>
> (476–80)

Again here (as the California editors note), Dryden recalls the Hind's similar dare to the Panther:

> This peacefull Seat my poverty secures,
> War seldom enters but where wealth allures;
> Nor yet despise it, for this poor aboad
> Has oft receiv'd, and yet receives a god;
> A god victorious of the stygian race
> Here laid his sacred limbs, and sanctified the place.
> This mean retreat did mighty *Pan* contain;
> Be emulous of him, and pomp disdain,
> And dare not to debase your soul to gain.
>
> (3:160.705–13)

The noticeably Saxon vocabulary of the *Aeneis* piece suggests that Dryden also had in mind Sir Calidore's entreaty to his host in Spenser's "Book of Courtesie":

> Not that the burden of so bold a guest
> Shall chargefull be, or chaunge to you at all;
> For your meane food shall be my daily feast,
> And this your cabin both my bowre and hall.

Spenser's lines, however, follow the poet's assurance that "gentle bloud will gentle manners breed; / As well may be in *Calidore* descryde," whereas Dryden's are addressed to a would-be conqueror of foreign blood.[54] The *Aeneis* speech, then, is imbued with and underlined by cynicism (on the poet's part, not Evander's); not only has Dryden's "greedy," ambitious newcomer shown little evidence of a willingness to "be poor" and "accept . . . homely Food," but his conspicuous culture shock and ignorance of "Acts and Monuments of Ancient Kings" mean that he does not have the knowledge possessed by Sir Calidore or Dryden's Panther to allow him to uphold the social codes and traditions at the heart of both earlier English poems. It seems likely, in fact, that if this stranger-prince were to "emulate a God" it would be in the way the tyrannical Alexander "Assumes the God" in Dryden's *Alexander's Feast* (1697). Yet his role in the poem (like William III's apparent role in England) is unavoidably that of leader of a "Race," as Venus puts it in the subsequent episode, "doom'd to reign" in the country he has invaded (501).

Having hit this dilemma head-on, Dryden does here what he did in *Aeneis* I and subverts the historical issues by turning to love and literature for relief. The Venus who now appears "Couch'd with her Husband in his Golden Bed" invoking "his aid" through "Charms of Love" is even lustier and more seductive than the Venus in Dryden's 1685 *Sylvae* fragment "The Speech of Venus to Vulcan" (488–91). For a start, she is introduced as "Love's fair Goddess" rather than simply "Venus" as in 1685 and as in Vergil. The power of her charms in both a human and divine sense is then brought out in the description (included from the 1685 text) of how she

> her Arms, of snowy hue,
> About her unresolving Husband threw.
> Her soft Embraces soon infuse Desire:
> His Bones and Marrow sudden Warmth inspire;
> And all the Godhead feels the wonted Fire.
>
>   (512–16)

This Lucretianization of Vergil is even more notable in the conclusion to the scene, which outdoes its *Sylvae* counterpart in sensuality. As he does not do in 1685, Vulcan "trembles" as he grants Venus's request; he then "snatch[es] the willing Goddess to his Arms; / 'Till in her Lap infus'd, he lay possess'd / Of full Desire, and sunk to pleasing Rest" (535–38). The former "lovely Goddess" has become "willing" while Vulcan lies "in her Lap infus'd" rather than "infus'd in joy" (52–53). The heightened human quality of the *Aeneis* passage is added to when "The Goddess, proud of her successful Wiles, / And conscious of her Form in secret Smiles" (519–20). This picture of the god as a guileful woman smiling to herself over her victory has more psychological impact than the decorative 1685 version: "The Goddess pleas'd with her successful wiles, / And, conscious of her conqu'ring Beauty, smiles" (35–36). Most importantly for Dryden's purposes at this point, Venus's compassion is more marked than previously. As the California editors remark, in the *Sylvae* text, the goddess is not "anxious for her Son" as she is here, and she now calls Fate "Cruel" rather than "adverse" (486, 492; cf. 3:42.8). Also picking up Dryden's new emphasis on "after Times," she adds an expression of fear for the (interpolated) "Relicks of the *Phrygian* Kind" (509). What has happened between the Evander scene and this, in effect, is that the consolation and assurance once offered by the Hind and that Evander should be able to extend to Dryden's audience but cannot have been replaced by a reminder of the solace and regeneration inherent in the pleasures of secular love: a force which has its own divinity but which resides in the world of ordinary women and men. The transformative power represented by "Creator Venus" (which is reflected in the refreshment offered by the poetry itself!) substitutes for the theological transformation embodied in the Hind's speech and missing from Evander's; as the California editors note, "[t]he Hind's cell," as presented in the speech quoted above, "is represented as a Catholic chapel, which repeatedly *receives a god* in the doctrine of transubstantiation, which holds that Christ's body and blood are present in each Mass" (3:407.n.707–8).

While the energy of the scene indirectly equates Dryden's own healing powers as poet with Venus's, at the end he turns the focus to art itself by picking up his recurring theme of the god-like artist.[55] As Vulcan leaves Venus's bed to go to the smithy, he is labelled not "Lord of Fire" ("ignipotens" [423]) but "the forging Pow'r" (550). He subsequently informs his apprentice "Sons" that they must apply all their "forming Fire" in Venus's cause (579–82). Dryden then flaunts his own art as the divine blacksmiths apply their skills to the task:

> The hissing Steel is in the Smithy drown'd;
> The Grot with beaten Anvils groans around.
> By turns their Arms advance, in equal time:
> By turns their Hands descend, and Hammers chime.
> They turn the glowing Mass, with crooked Tongs:
> The fiery Work proceeds, with Rustick Songs.
>
> (591–96)

The aesthetic impact of the original has been fully exploited. Vergil has:

> alii stridentia tingunt
> Æra lacu: gemit impositis incudibus antrum.
> Illi inter sese multa vi brachia tollunt
> In numerum, versantque tenaci forcipe massam.
>
> (450–53)

Dryden's own sibilants and hollow syllables transfer to his piece the onomatopoeia of Vergil's description of the hissing steel and echoing grot, while the anaphora and perfectly regular pentameter of lines 593–94 substitute for Vergil's triple dactyl-spondee arrangement of line 453 in reproducing the rhythmical chiming of hammers and rotation of tasks. However, while he recreates for his audience the beauty and power of Vergil's art (thereby stressing his poetic ancestry with the Ancient), Dryden's addition of the accompaniment of "Rustick Songs" to the smiths' work weaves the piece firmly into the fabric of his own poem by aiding the movement away from Vergilian high seriousness. This introduction of folklore into a passage which has as its subject divine art (and in Dryden's text the transmission of that art from poet to poet) both reflects and draws attention to the emphasis on everyday, "low" life that becomes increasingly evident in the *Aeneis* and is especially noticeable in *Aeneis* VIII.

The first noteworthy example of the way the book punctures Vergil's heroic occurs, significantly, when the stranger-prince chances upon the Arcadians' "solemn" observation of a yearly national ritual. Having portrayed the "King and Prince" paying "their Off'rings in a sacred Grove," the poet then does what every Classics undergraduate would love to do in the final exam and depicts the sacrificers sizzling sausages on a barbeque: "Thick Clouds of Smoke involve the Skies: / And Fat of Entrails on his Altar fries" (137–42). Evander's narration of Hercules' exploits as he explains to Aeneas the god's importance to the Arcadians is similarly undercut at various points. In his battle against the monster Cacus, for example, Hercules is made to look like a cruel little boy as he "stands above; and from afar / Plies him with Darts, and Stones" (333–34). Rome's mighty river god fares no better in the dignity stakes, for, frightened at the commotion, "trembling *Tyber* div'd beneath his Bed" (320). The general chaos and bathos of the episode are accentuated by excessive violence and gore especially in the description of the monster slain—and mutilated—by the hero: a description entailing a wrung neck, "cripled Members bound" in a knot and eyeballs torn from their sockets (343–46).

Dryden's persistent mocking of the heroic in a piece whose original has aetiology and national history as its *raison d'être* illustrates the inexorability of the generic shift that is unfolding with the *Aeneis*. As Bakhtin observes, the "idealization of the past" belongs to high genres, to epic; it is the low genres (the mock-heroic, the novel), with their focus on the "transitory present," on "eternal continuation without beginning or end," that are the realm of "the common people's creative culture of laughter": a description which could well be applied to both the Hercules and Venus/Vulcan episodes of *Aeneis* VIII.[56] In fact, Bakhtin's claim that it is "precisely laughter that destroys the epic" is here borne out in the fact that Dryden's own Democritean laughter in the face of historical crisis has resulted in the transplanting of his own ostensibly epic work in the "comic world" where, Bakhtin observes, "there is nothing for memory and tradition to do."[57] As *Aeneis* I forecasts, then, it is in the realms of "popular laughter," of storytelling and of nature, where the fundamental laws are those of renewal and transformation, that Dryden ultimately finds release from seemingly insurmountable problems. Despite rejecting historical memory and tradition, however, his method still maintains his poetic imperatives (indeed is dependent on them) for it has as authority Ovid (whose style it perhaps most closely resembles), folklore (both Homeric and English) and the English fabulous tradition. (The use of the Saxon verb form "clomb" during Evander's story is one example of Dryden's attempt to make his own English voice felt [288].) Yet while the poet looks back, emphasizing his poetic and English roots, the *Aeneis* itself, positioned as it is on the brink of the eighteenth century, both reflects the artistic self-consciousness and social questioning inherent in the period's mock-heroic while anticipating the same features of Fielding's novels in particular.

Having reached a high point in *Aeneis* VIII, this ascendance of art over politics and history closes the book. Vergil's panegyric to Roman history and *imperium* (both the glory and the cost) in his description of the shield presented by Venus to Aeneas becomes, in Dryden's hands, a celebration of art itself and, again, a repudiation of military victory. Dryden opens this scene too by emphasizing the divinity of both the storytelling shield's art and its artist. While Vergil's hero wonders at the fabric of the shield, which to him is "inexplicable" ("et clypei non enarrabile textum" [625]), Dryden's "admires the Shields Mysterious mould" (829); Vergil's "ignipotens" (628) meanwhile becomes "the Heav'nly Smith" (831). The historical and mythical tales then related as Dryden peruses Vergil's shield are imbued with the same mixture of royalist nostalgia and cynicism for contemporary bloodshed that underlines the rendering of Evander's tales—and Dryden's own in the rest of the *Aeneis*. The victory of art over suffering and historical disaster rather than of Rome over the world comes at the end of the chronicles with the depiction of the festivities in honor of Caesar's triumph:

> All Altars flame: Before each Altar lies,
> Drench'd in his Gore, the destin'd Sacrifice.
> Great *Cæsar* sits sublime upon his Throne;
> Before *Apollo*'s Porch of *Parian* Stone:
> Accepts the Presents vow'd for Victory;
> And hangs the monumental Crowns on high.
>
> (956–61)

By this point in the *Aeneis* the mocking of the military figure through the "gore" which drenches the picture is almost to be expected. In this case, however, Dryden seems (once again) specifically to be pouring scorn on the military triumphs of England's "Great Cæsar" and reminding him that the real "monumental Crowns" are those offered from "Apollo's Porch." For, as Frost observes, "[p]erhaps the most obvious example of a plate that could not have been randomly assigned is the fourth illustration of *Aeneid* VIII, showing Venus delivering to Aeneas the new armor just made by Vulcan: at the center of the plate the hook-nosed hero is said to 'gaz[e] with vast delight' at the shield . . . . The inevitable dedicatee of the plate is Sir Godfrey Kneller, 'Principall Painter to his Majesty.' "[58] In effect, then, *Aeneis* VII and VIII's stranger-prince finds a parallel in this William III figure, and as the authority lies with Venus and the shield in the plate, so in England it lies with Kneller and Dryden, whose work will produce the English victory that the newcomer can never achieve.

JOVE WAS ALIKE TO LATIAN AND PHRYGIAN

What is that sound high in the air
Murmur of maternal lamentation
Who are those hooded hordes swarming
Over endless plains, stumbling in cracked earth
Ringed by the flat horizon only
What is the city over the mountains
Cracks and reforms and bursts in the violet air
Falling Towers
Jerusalem Athens Alexandria
Vienna London
Unreal

　　　　　　　　　　　　—T. S. Eliot, *The Waste Land*

By about the mid-eighteenth century, novels characteristically embodied the kind of tensions just outlined, tensions between veneration of the past and rejection of the past, between history and story-telling, between high and popular literature.[59] This said, Dryden was not of course consciously laying out the ground work for what would become the novel. What he was doing was responding to contemporary social forces, which themselves perverted the medium through which he was confronting them. In this, as Brean Hammond observes, the *Aeneis* can be seen as a vital document in the "broad tendency in post-Restoration writing towards the 'novelization' of all forms of imaginative writing, one product of which was the modern novel itself." Certainly, the *Aeneis*'s lapse into mock-heroic as it finds itself unable to reconcile old-world ideologies with contemporary reality strongly supports his proposition that the mock-heroic, which had its "moment" in the 1690s, perhaps acts as "missing link between the epic and the novel."[60] The mock-heroic elements of the translation, which have already been discussed, increase in number and strength in the battles of *Aeneis* IX–XII as Dryden's centerless epic disintegrates into bathos and confusion when Vergil's examples of heroism are called upon to supply standards while being transferred to a world where they find no parallels. In fact, as a unit, the last section of Dryden's translation perhaps provides another instance of the 1690s mock-heroic, for the emphasis of *Aeneis* IX–XII is rather on a (contemporary) world of inconsistencies and chaos than on the hero's response to historically-significant dilemmas.

The source of the Dryden's intensified animosity and bleakness in this last part of the translation is Vergil's subject matter: war. In his poems of the Stuart era, from *Astræa Redux* on, Dryden had employed Vergil as he portrayed England's wars as essential to her imperial destiny. *Annus Mirabilis* in particular perpetuates the myth consolidated by Spenser that London as Troynovant had been promised the same "imperium sine fine" that Vergil's Jupiter bestowed upon her predecessor Rome. The long and wasteful Dutch wars consequently become "a most just and necessary War" as Dryden works to unite his country people by reminding them that they have been chosen by God to be world leaders (1:50). Even in the darker poems of the later part of Charles II's reign and James II's brief and disastrous rule, he continues to present England's military might, specifically her navy under its royal generals, as the center of the nation's power and hope. After 1688, however, not only was the disheartened poet personally incapable of pronouncing a glorious future—or any future at all—for England, but the typology on which his former poems of destiny depended could not be employed to celebrate or to castigate a nation where the king was not anointed by God and where the course of history was now by no means clear.[61] Whereas his earlier poems turn national disaster and suffering into the pride and victories of a military nation, Dryden's plays and poems after 1688 paint dark pictures of the waste and destructiveness of war. In part these works ponder the apparent pointlessness of history's struggles, yet they are also a bitter reaction to William III's war-plagued kingdom. Not only was England once again internally divided and pitted against a foreign enemy, but the purpose of the enormously costly and draining Continental wars was, from an English viewpoint, profoundly dubious. Under the control of a cold and foreign king, English resources and troops seemed to be employed in a Dutch rather than an English cause. In the background too as a mark of national shame was the ignominious Battle of the Boyne of 1690. The deep disillusionment, even cynicism, felt by Dryden despite his laughing philosopher stance is especially evident in *Amphitryon*, written amidst the events that led to the confrontation of William's and James's forces on the muddy banks of an Irish river. The slapstick but sobering action of that play, which reflects English confusion over both the purpose and the outcome of the battle at Boyne, is developed in the last books of Dryden's *Aeneis*, and as the poet relinquishes his hold on the heroic his poem moves progressively towards the mode of *Fables*. In so doing, it also anticipates key features of the fiction of the next age, for Dryden's nervousness over the hero, which is at the heart of *Aeneis* VII–VIII, now gives way, and Turnus and Aeneas seem to be equated as victims of the way of the world rather than the world being the victim of a usurping, foreign invader.[62]

As his focus becomes the meaninglessness—indeed lunacy—of the wars plaguing Italy, Dryden is careful periodically to identify the world he is mocking with 1690s England. In *Aeneis* IX, for example, a specific attack on William III and his intimates is surely made when the Latian Numanus, cursing Aeneas's troops, dwells on a single detail in Vergil's original: accusing the Phrygians of "female Pride," Numanus jeers, "Go, less than Women, in the Shapes of Men. / Go, mix'd with Eunuchs . . ." (843–46). The California editors note that the "eunuchs are not mentioned by Virgil" (6:1073.n.847); however, neither are his Phrygians directly accused of "female Pride" or of being "less than Women." Dryden's elaborate charge arises from Vergil's Numanus's exclamation "O vere Phrygiæ, neque enim Phryges!": "O truly Phrygian women, for you are not Phrygian men" (617). Undoubtedly invective against William III, whose homosexuality and reputed affair with his handsome sidekick Hans Bentinck are the butt of much Jacobite satire of the period,[63] Dryden's attack perhaps also comments on the emasculation of England due to the replacement of a true "manly" king and father with the kind of fickle "female" forces (zeal and democracy) at the center of *Albion and Albanius* (see p. 67 above). The most bitter point, however, is made by the generic implications. Emphasis on sexual perversion is a feature of the mock-heroic, never of the heroic, and it functions as a marker of the fundamental perversion of the society in which it thrives.

When confronting the most persistent contemporary issue in these books, the destruction of peace by continual apparently pointless wars, however, Dryden's poetic voice is still more didactic than cynical, more the voice of *Absalom and Achitophel* than *Mac Flecknoe*. Yet it is weak. Jove's complaint to the council of Gods at the beginning of *Aeneis* X, for example, is also Dryden's lament:

> From whence these Murmurs, and this change of Mind,
> This backward Fate from what was first design'd?
> Why this protracted War, when my Commands
> Pronounc'd a Peace, and gave the *Latians* Lands?
>
> (9–12)

The "Murmurs," of course, recall the "Murmuring" Jews of *Absalom and Achitophel*. The emphasis on groundless "protracted War" as a re-

placement for divinely-sanctioned peace (embodied by the Stuart monarchy?) is also Dryden's, and his view of the backward slide taken by
English history is presented in his rendering of Vergil's "sententia
vobis / Versa" ("your change of heart" [6–7]) as "backward Fate."

The same questions are again the focus in the center of *Aeneis* XI.
Here, however, the speech of the Greek Diomedes, which is reported
by Venulus (Latinus's envoy to the city Argyripa, founded by Diomedes
after the fall of Troy), is permeated with a weariness equal to that of
Latinus in *Aeneis* VII, and it too displays a kingship both reminiscent of
Dryden's early poems and anticipatory of the stance of philosopher
kings in *Fables*. Refusing to supply the requested reinforcements and
chiding the Latians for becoming caught up in the wars, Diomedes essentially repeats Jove's puzzled protest:

> *Ausonian* Race, of old
> Renown'd for Peace, and for an Age of Gold,
> What Madness has your alter'd Minds possess'd,
> To change for War hereditary Rest?
> Sollicite Arms unknown, and tempt the Sword,
> (A needless Ill your Ancestors abhorr'd?)
>
> (386–91)

Vergil's Diomedes, by contrast, expresses sympathy that "Fortune"
"disrupts [the Latians'] calm and provokes them to initiate unknown
war": "O fortunatæ gentes, Saturnia regna, / Antiqui Ausonii: quæ vos
fortuna quietos / Sollicitat, suadetque ignota lacessere bella?" (253–4).
Dryden's Diomedes' charge of madness recalls Latinus's earlier condemnation of his people, while the annotative "Peace" and "Age of
Gold" (for Vergil's "Saturnia regna") and the indicting "alter'd Minds,"
"hereditary Rest," and "needless Ill" are also additions.

Dryden's Greek now outlines a philosophy of war that places all emphasis on its "needless Ill[s]." "Of [the] *Grecians*, who to Troy's Destruction came," all he has to say is that "Not one but suffer'd, and too
dearly bought / The Prize of Honour which in Arms he sought" (393,
396–97). Vergil's concern here is with suffering and the cost of war (his
"tantæ molis erat" theme); the mockery of the "Prize of Honour" is
Dryden's, and it is developed a couple of lines later. Instead of simply
listing the Greeks' sorrows, Dryden's Diomedes again stresses the emp-
tiness of seeming earthly prosperity so that what is in Vergil a reference
to "the overturned home of Idomeneus" ("referam, versosque Penates /
Idomenei?" [264–65]) becomes "Why shou'd I name *Idomeneus*, in
vain / Restor'd to Scepters, and expell'd again?" (408–9). He then begins the conclusion to his speech, which ends with advocacy of peace,

by undermining the whole ten-year war: "No Hate remains with me to ruin'd *Troy*. / I war not with its Dust; nor am I glad / To think of past Events, or good or bad" (430–33). Again the tone is different from the original, which celebrates peace rather than undermining the importance of "past Events": "Nec mihi cum Teucris ullum post eruta bellum / Pergama; nec veterum memini lætorve malorum": "Nor, since Troy fell, have I had any war with its people, and I do not dwell joyfully on old evils" (279–80). The cynicism of the piece as a whole is further accentuated if Diomedes' attitude towards Troy's dust is also contrasted with Britomart's (Vergilian-style) promise immediately after Paridell's prophecy of "Wedlocke contract in bloud, and eke in bloud / Accomplished": "*Troy* againe out of her dust was reard / To sit in second seat of soueraigne king / Of all the world vnder her gouerning."[64]

For Dryden's Jacobite readers at least, the bleakness of Diomedes' speech is perhaps momentarily relieved by the (on first appearances) didactic application of the Greek's advice to England's situation, which occurs when Drances takes his turn at addressing the assembled Latians. In a speech that unmistakably identifies the object of his wrath with England's war-obsessed king, he "load[s] young *Turnus* with invidious Crimes" (518):

> Your Interest is the War shou'd never cease;
> But we have felt enough, to wish the Peace:
> A Land exhausted to the last remains,
> Depopulated Towns, and driven Plains.
>
> .   .   .   .
>
> Mankind, it seems, is made for you alone;
> We, but the Slaves who mount you to the Throne:
> A base ignoble Crowd, without a Name.
> Unwept, unworthy of the Fun'ral Flame:
> By Duty bound to forfeit each his Life,
> That *Turnus* may possess a Royal Wife.
>
> (562–75)

Dryden here manages, as Brean Hammond notes, to get in his usual punch at "populist rabble-rousing politics."[65] It also seems likely that England itself is the "Royal Wife" acquired for this war-monger by "Slaves" who "mount [him] to the Throne." The greatest concern, however, is again with "protracted" or never-ceasing wars and a "Land exhausted to the last"—in King William's expensive continental wars. Drances' effusion of wrath, which is also Dryden's, is all the more venomous for the fact that it follows hard on Latinus' similar assessment of the (Latian and English) dilemma after Venulus returns from Diomedes without the hoped-for reinforcements:

> Our Hopes must center on ourselves alone.
> Yet those how feeble, and, indeed, how vain,
> You see too well; nor need my Words explain.
> Vanquish'd without ressource; laid flat by Fate,
> Factions within, a Foe without the Gate.
>
> (476–79)

Again, where Vergil creates pathos, Dryden depicts desolation, and the difference between the Latian and English situation is marked by his replacement of Latinus's praise of national unity ("toto certatum est corpore regni" [313]) with the desperate "Factions within, a Foe without." Yet by rendering "spes sibi quisque" ("each is his own hope" [309]) as "Our Hopes must center on ourselves alone" he does anticipate his own advice in "To John Driden, of Chesterton." There he appeals for native security to replace foreign endeavor, arguing "Safe in our selves, while on our selves we stand, / The Sea is ours, and that defends the Land. / Be, then, the Naval Stores the Nations Care, / New Ships to build, and batter'd to repair" (146–49).

Just as the conclusion of "To John Driden," with its emphasis on death and personal fame, ultimately undermines the work of Dryden's cousin and other "Patriots," who "assert the Peoples Right; / With noble Stubbornness resisting Might" (184–85), however, so the appeals of Latinus and Drances (and Diomedes), who act as fore-runners to these "Patriots," are overwhelmed both by the darkness of the world around them and by the *Aeneis'* ultimate conviction that real relief can now only be found in personal safety and fame won through personal endeavor. In fact, as Sloman points out, Drances' speech has a parallel in Dryden's "The First Book of Homer's Ilias," which, as she puts it, "shows a regression to a pre-Virgilian moral state. It is a concise epitome of a world of primitive violence which is nevertheless subject to the distortions of political involvement."[66] Achilles' condemnation of Agamemnon, which Sloman now cites, is as fraught with contemporary English meaning as Drances' indictment of Turnus:

> O, Impudent, regardful of thy own,
> Whose Thoughts are centr'd on thy self alone,
> Advanc'd to Sovereign Sway, for better Ends
> Than thus like abject Slaves to treat thy Friends.
> . . . .
> Thine is the Triumph; ours the Toil alone:
> We bear thee on our Backs, and mount thee on the Throne.
>
> (225–28, 238–39)[67]

The kind of "primitive violence" manifested in Dryden's "Ilias" and other fables is reinforced in the *Aeneis* XI scene by the refrain-like assertion " 'Tis a Destructive War," made by Drances to Turnus and later conceded by Turnus himself (552, 616). The world of *Aeneis* IX–XII as a whole (and by implication Williamite England) is converted into a pre-Vergilian world of Homeric brutality by the all-pervasive violence and gore and by the poet's own cynicism.

The battle scenes of *Aeneis* XI rival any in *Fables* for profusion of blood, mashed brains, crunched bones, bodies split down the middle and fields saturated with gore. Noteworthy passages occur in other books too. The slaying of Pandarus by Turnus in *Aeneis* IX is particularly graphic:

> the full descending blow
> Cleaves the broad Front, and beardless Cheeks in two:
> Down sinks the Giant with a thund'ring sound,
> His pond'rous Limbs oppress the trembling ground;
> Blood, Brains, and Foam, gush from the gaping Wound.
> Scalp, Face, and Shoulders, the keen Steel divides;
> And the shar'd Visage hangs on equal sides.
>
> (1013–18)

The dramatic and psychological impact is enhanced of course by the verse. In terms of grotesqueness, however, the lines are outdone by others in *Aeneis* X:

> For *Thimbrus* Head was lop'd: and *Laris* Hand
> Dismember'd, sought its Owner on the Strand:
> The trembling Fingers yet the Fauchion strain,
> And threaten still th'intended Stroke in vain.
>
> (551–54)

Also worthy of citation is the killing of Podalirius in *Aeneis* XII, a passage which rivals both of the above in onomatopoeia and grotesqueness and which is highlighted by an alexandrine:

> The broad Axe enters, with a crashing Sound,
> And cleaves the Chin, with one continu'd Wound:
> Warm Blood, and mingled Brains, besmear his Arms around.
>
> (464–66)

Each of these expands on its Vergilian basis.

At the same time blood and brains are being smattered everywhere, the poet draws constant attention to the meaninglessness of the slaughter and suffering. Turnus's (ironic) argument for going on with the wars in spite of Diomedes' refusal to help is in fact one of Dryden's central themes in his war books:

> Good unexpected, Evils unforeseen,
> Appear by Turns, as Fortune shifts the Scene:
> Some, rais'd aloft, come tumbling down amain;
> Then fall so hard, they bound and rise again.
>
> (656–59)

While treated more directly during the funeral games of *Aeneis* V, this victor-vanquished motif somehow has a more menacing and destructive impact on the translation as a whole as it is scattered through the final books, for the absence of a father-king to "mend" the pain and slaughter or of a cause to justify them renders them at best meaningless, at worst ludicrous. As Dryden lays out examples, his own cynicism can be felt in his verse. In the battle around the Trojan camp in *Aeneis* IX, for example,

> Brave *Cæneus* laid *Ortygius* on the Plain,
> The Victor *Cæneus* was by *Turnus* slain.
> By the same Hand, *Clonius* and *Itys* fall,
> *Sagar*, and *Idas*, standing on the Wall.
>
> (778–81)[68]

The chiasmus and the heaping of names are imitated from Vergil's original; however, as members either of the crowd of eunuchs and transvestites subsequently conjured up by Numanus or of the band of blustering opponents, Dryden's victims of Fortune cannot even claim to have met their ends honorably, and his epithets "Brave" (which is interpolated) and "Victor" serve merely to mock. In *Aeneis* X, the point behind these lines is made explicit, and again Dryden's verse intensifies the impact:

> Thus equal Deaths are dealt with equal Chance;
> By turns they quit their Ground, by turns advance:
> Victors, and vanquish'd, in the various Field,
> Nor wholly overcome, nor wholly yield.
>
> (1071–74)

The first three lines of the translation are fairly literal; however, even there Vergil's pathos is undermined by the omission of "luctus" ("woes"), and his concern (again) for the cost of Rome's glory is eradicated by Dryden's last line which mocks the entire endeavor as it replaces "neque *his* fuga nota, neque illis": "neither side knew flight" (755–57).

The barrenness of the world he has created means that the lines following these merely emphasize its desolation rather than offering comfort as they do in Vergil: "The Gods from Heav'n survey the fatal

Strife, / And mourn the Miseries of Human Life" (1075–76). Frost observes that "Dryden's deities are, in fact, the lusty inhabitants of a kind of perpetual Olympian alehouse, whose walls re-echo with salty personal invective or loud roars of drunken mirth."[69] The comment is made most immediately of Dryden's "Ilias," yet its accuracy with regard to the late translations in general and to the last books of the *Aeneis* in particular means that most declarations of the gods' concern for human miseries (especially against this kind of background) can only be read ironically. As suggested earlier, it is precisely the absence in the *Aeneis* of a center, or a sense of a divine purpose to the suffering, that renders Vergil's heroic mock-heroic, and the amorality shaping the last books in particular can be traced ultimately to a completely detached Jove.

Given the chaos of Dryden's wars, his chief deity's announcement at the beginning of *Aeneis* X that "Equal and unconcern'd I look on all" is utterly convincing (166). The comment is made again later in the same book where Pallas asserts that "*Jove* is impartial, and to both [sides] the same" (633). Here the statement echoes Dryden's own in the prologue to *Don Sebastian* ("*Jove* was alike to *Latian* and to *Phrygian*" [15:73.15; italics reversed]), and the same vacuum of codes of behavior and standards of action, which results in that play's disintegration into the low-life world of Antonio and Moryama as it fails to resolve the heroic plot, can be more keenly felt in *Aeneis* IX–XII because of the absence of a hero. To be sure, both Turnus and Aeneas are sporadically attributed with old-world heroic qualities during episodes that struggle, like the Latinus, Diomedes and Drances episodes, to assert heroic values in the midst of confusion. As the warriors prepare themselves for battle in *Aeneis* XII, for example, the nobility of both is suggested as Turnus becomes the kingly bull of *Georgics* III when "Proudly he bellows, and preludes the fight" by "meditat[ing] his absent Enemy," and not "less the *Trojan*, in his *Lemnian* Arms, / To future Fight his Manly Courage warms; / He whets his Fury, and with Joy prepares, / To terminate at once the ling'ring Wars" (159–68) (cf. pp. 64–67 above). Yet both are also called a "new *Achilles*" and, as precipitators and instruments of its mindless violence, play such roles in this "pre-Vergilian" world (see 6:672.1002; 6:742.674).

Perhaps what keeps the last books from collapsing completely into mock-heroic is the fact that the poet himself has not lost respect for human life and is sensitive still to its suffering and "woes." The grief expressed by Euryalus' mother in *Aeneis* IX, for example, does not belong in the realm of the mock-heroic:

> Thus then, my lov'd *Euryalus* appears;
> Thus looks the Prop of my declining Years!

Was't on this Face, my famish'd Eyes I fed?
. . . .
Nor was I near to close his dying Eyes,
To wash his Wounds, to weep his Obsequies:
To call about his Corps his crying Friends,
Or spread the Mantle, (made for other ends,)
On his dear Body, which I wove with Care.

(637–39, 647–51)

Likewise, powerful poetic compassion and feeling pervade Aeneas's
recognition of how Evander's friendship has been repaid:

These are my Triumphs of the Latian War;
Fruits of my plighted Faith, and boasted Care.
And yet, unhappy Sire, thou shalt not see
A Son, whose Death disgrac'd his Ancestry:
Thou shalt not blush, old Man, however, griev'd:
Thy *Pallas* no dishonest Wound receiv'd.

(79–84)

Here Aeneas is portrayed as a Duke of Albemarle or James II as Dryden prefaces the speech by replacing Vergil's "Ipse . . . lacrymis ita fatur
obortis" (39–41) with "First, melting into Tears, the pious Man / De-
plor'd so sad a sight, then thus began" (57–58). Yet the emphasis is on
human suffering not heroism, and such isolated examples of a "pious
Man" have not power enough to redeem the barren world in which all
are trapped. The incongruity also present in Aeneas's suggestion that
somehow honor can be won through participation in the violence is
highlighted in other places where paradox results from Dryden's attempt to uphold within his essentially unheroic poem the value of Vergil's examples of piety.

When the focus turns from Aeneas' to Evander's reaction to Pallas'
death, for example, the simultaneous praiseworthiness and pointlessness of the young warrior's act are in much greater conflict. "O *Pallas*!"
the grieving father exclaims,

thou hast fail'd thy plighted Word!
To fight with Caution, not to tempt the Sword:
. . . .
O curst Essay of Arms, disast'rous Doom,
Prelude of bloody Fields, and Fights to come!
Hard Elements of unauspicious War,
Vain Vows to Heav'n, and unavailing Care!

(230–31, 236–39)

Aeneas, however, has just made clear that Pallas "no dishonest Wound receiv'd" and that his death will consequently bring glory to his ancestry. The paradox of Evander's claim that his son has broken his "plighted Word" through an act which in fact honors his plighted bond with his family is Vergil's and serves to accentuate the father's pain.[70] Dryden's own paradox is a product of his insistence on "bloody Fields," "unauspicious War" and an indifferent heaven: Pallas's old-world and (in the poet's view) laudable loyalty to the last to his ancestry takes place in and helps perpetuate "bloody" war, waged in an amoral world. The same kind of oxymoron underlies Aeneas' outburst in *Aeneis* XII. Here, however, the irony is deeper and perhaps overwhelming:

> The Prince, whose Piety had long repell'd
> His inborn ardour, now invades the Field:
> Invokes the Pow'rs of violated Peace,
> Their Rites, and injur'd Altars to redress:
> Then, to his Rage abandoning the Rein,
> With Blood and slaughter'd Bodies fills the Plain.
>
> (719–24)

By positing "Piety" (which has no basis in Vergil) as the source of "Blood and slaughter'd Bodies," sacrificial offerings to the (ironic) cause of "violated Peace" rather than a "broken treaty" ("læsi . . . foederis aras" [496]), Dryden displays a cynicism, which perhaps suggests that it is no longer possible even to define "Piety."

As the final books plunge ever deeper into darkness, there are fewer moments of relief than previously, and release rather than regeneration is usually the basis of those moments. Ultimately, as would happen in *Fables*, the poet pinpoints personal fame and integrity as worthy of pursuit—indeed as all that can be pursued in such an environment. Significantly, the line which completes the couplet when Pallas recognizes "*Jove* is impartial, and to both the same" is "Alive or dead, I shall deserve a Name" (632–33). Jove himself then verifies Pallas's claim that even amidst this chaos there is still honor in a name by assuring Hercules, who is mourning Pallas's battle with Turnus, "Short bounds of Life are set to Mortal Man, / 'Tis Vertues work alone to stretch the narrow Span" (656–57). Behind these passages, of course, is the notion of the free soul invulnerable to worldly woes and absurdities, and it is this thought that ends *Aeneis* X, is the climax of *Aeneis* XI and closes *Aeneis* XII—and with it the epic. The paradoxes and pains of the father/son relationship, a central concern in *Aeneis* XI, are cushioned in advance by Dryden as the parallel Lausus/Mezentius episode in *Aeneis* X is resolved when the poem concludes as Mezentius's "disdainful Soul came rushing thro' the Wound" (1313). Dryden's interpolation here of "disdain" gives the couplet the same power as its counterpart in *Aeneis* XI, which releases the dignified Camilla from the bloodshed and slaughter of that book: "In the last Sigh her strugling Soul expires; / And murm'ring with Disdain, to *Stygian* Sounds retires" (1209–10). When the line from *Aeneis* X is transferred to the end of *Aeneis* XII, where it has even less basis in the Latin, it is perhaps possible to feel that along with Turnus's, the poet's own "disdainful Soul" has come "rushing thro' the Wound" (1377).

5

Thy Lovers Were All Untrue

TRAGEDY IS FOR THE PASSIONS

Albion shall his love renew:
But oh, ungrateful Fair,
Repeated Crimes beware,
And to his Bed be true!

— Dryden, *Albion and Albanius*

One of the first topics Dryden raises in his dedication, and a subject which occupies several pages, is the neoclassical notion of the common roots of epic and tragedy. While he is careful to privilege epic as the oldest, most venerable genre ("the Original of the Stage was from the Epick Poem" [5:269]), he also stresses that "Tragedy is the minature of Humane Life; an Epick Poem is the draught at length"; therefore, "*Homer* [is] the common Father of the Stage" and "Heroick Poetry" (5:269, 272). The investigation undertaken here of the connections between epic and tragedy is continued in *Aeneis* IV, which, as it provides a tragedy within the greater "draught" that is Dryden's translation, seems founded on the observation also in the dedication that "the Epick Poem is more for the Manners, and Tragedy for the Passions" (5:271). Yet, as it places the spotlight on the problem at the heart of the *Aeneis*, the Dido episode not only itself suffers a sea change in attempting to use tragedy to explore the overruling of reason, custom and stability by irrational, uncontrollable forces, but it reflects and (possibly) propels the generic shift that takes place within the translation as a whole. As suggested earlier, the *Aeneis*'s gradual movement away from earlier seventeenth-century (relative) certainties and its progressive questioning of whether it is even possible any longer to define standards of behavior perhaps begin in earnest in *Aeneis* IV.

Near the beginning of his discussion of Vergil's "Love" episode, Dryden stresses that the fourth book of the *Aeneid* is a direct product of Vergil's patriotism and awareness of his duty as a poet:

179

he thought himself engag'd in Honour to espouse the Cause and Quarrel of
his Country against *Carthage*. He knew he cou'd not please the Romans better, or oblige them more to Patronize his Poem, than by disgracing the
Foundress of that City. He shews her ungrateful to the Memory of her Husband, doting on a Stranger; enjoy'd, and afterwards forsaken by him. This
was the Original, says he, of the immortal hatred betwixt the two Rival Nations. (5:298)

He then dwells at some length on the liberties taken by Vergil "in making *Æneas* and *Dido* Contemporaries. For 'tis certain that the Heroe liv'd
almost two hundred years before the Building of *Carthage*" (5:299). Because of Vergil's "Divine Wit," which could "draw Truth out of Fiction,
after so probable a manner, with so much Beauty, and so much for the
Honour of his Country," Dryden argues, Apollo decided that "any
thing might be allow'd to his Son *Virgil* on the account of his other Mer-
its; That being a Monarch he had a dispensing Power, and pardon'd
him" (5:301, 299). "To Moralize this Story," he continues, "*Virgil* is the
Apollo, who has this Dispensing Power. His great Judgment made the
Laws of Poetry, but he never made himself a Slave to them. . . ." As far
as the rules go, then, Vergil "might make this Anachronism, by super-
seding the mechanick Rules of Poetry, for the same Reason, that a
Monarch may dispense with, or suspend his own Laws, when he finds
it necessary so to do; especially if those Laws are not altogether fundamental" (5:300–301).

Both Dryden's language and the universalized comment which prefaces this discussion illustrate that his mind is on his own powers as
much as Vergil's. He introduces the section by stating that "To love our
Native Country, and to study its Benefit and its Glory, to be interested
in its Concerns, is Natural to all Men"; however, a "Poet makes a farther step; for endeavouring to do honour to it, 'tis allowable in him even
to be partial in its Cause; for he is not ty'd to truth, or fetter'd by the
Laws of History" (5:298). The subject of monarchical dispensation or
suspension of laws, especially if they are "not altogether fundamental,"
is as topical and caustic as his earlier consideration of Aeneas's titles
and claims. Likewise, the emphasis on a poet's duty to his country, ancestry to Apollo and divine powers of creation and glorification are undoubtedly intended once again to assert Dryden's own authority as the
nation's guardian over that of the present king, who is both suspending
and altering laws in a land which is not his own.

Ironically, however, it is his simultaneous rejection of the kind of
"truth" that is "fetter'd by the Laws of History," and assertion that a
poet's "Fiction" contains "Truth," which is in fact attached to a nation's
history and works for its "Honour," that push a wedge into the gap

between supposed poetic platonism and historical legitimacy less easily discerned elsewhere in the essay. In other words, perhaps here can be found a center for the tensions which pervade both dedication and translation and which incapacitate Dryden's own heroic—and so destroy any attempt on his part at national glorification or honor. Accordingly, while the conflict inherent in the discussion at this point is obscured by the fervent praise of Vergil and his heroic mode, *Aeneis* IV itself disintegrates into confusion and a kind of tragicomedy when Dryden draws on Apollo's divine laws in the cause of his own country's honour by retelling Vergil's story in an English context. For, despite reviving the "rules" as he attempts to apply Vergil's blueprint and tragedy's laws to his own tale, he does so only to reject them as he addresses the needs of his own audience and fetters his story to the historical realities of a period in which time-honored laws are being abandoned by kings. Because his tale is therefore inherently unstable generically, Dryden's Dido becomes as fragmented a figure as his Aeneas, the more so as she intermittently and inconsistently represents both the plight and the guilt of England.

As he drew attention to the political and historical background to Vergil's fable, especially after contemplating a citizen's love for and poet's duty to a native country, Dryden surely could not have helped but reflect on his own previous use of the "Punic curse" myth. In *Annus Mirabilis*, of course, the "immortal hatred betwixt the two Rival Nations" is reenacted in the "second Punick War" between England ("Rome") and Holland ("Carthage") (17–20). In fact, Vergil's myth seems to have been current again at the time Dryden's translation was under way because of English resentment at and duress due to Dutch trade aspirations on the continent. In the anonymous *Delenda Carthago: Or, The True Interest of England, in Relation to France and Holland* (1695), the subject of how English "Interest stands as to *Holland*" is couched in terms of Dido's fated love for Aeneas. Declaring that "Nations do not fall in Love with one another, as particular Persons do for their Beauty," the author points out that the "*Interest* and *Life* of *Holland*, all the World knows is *Trade*" and that "*England* has been their only mighty *Rival* for the *Trade* of the World." The crux of his argument depends on a reminder of England's Punic curse: "*The States of* Holland *are* England's *eternal Enemy, both by Interest and Inclination* . . . because we are *their only Competitor for* Trade *and* Power *at Sea, and who only stand in their Way to an* universal Empire, *as great as* Rome."[1]

That Dryden's Dido episode should employ the well-established connection between English/Dutch and Roman/Carthaginian rivalry to attack William III and his Dutchification of England is perhaps to be expected given the political overlay of the rest of the translation. In fact,

Aeneis IV not only looks back to *Annus Mirabilis*; it provides another example of a standard Dryden technique: the anthropomorphization of England as a fickle woman prone to disastrous affairs and chronically unfaithful to her "Lawfull Lord."[2] The first example of this, as observed earlier, occurs in his first poem after the Restoration (see p. 67 above), while the notion introduced there of a faithless England repenting her affair with a false lover provides the framework for *Albion and Albanius*. The motif also runs through *The Medall*, where supporters of such "usurping Brave[s]" as Shaftesbury and Cromwell are described as having "Their Mayden Oaths debauch'd into a Whore" in forswearing "Justice and Religion" to raise "Men . . . by Factions" (152–54). The most significant 1690s example is, of course, *Amphitryon*, where England is the victim of a rapist-usurper rather than a fickle lover. In that daringly topical and vitriolic play, Amphitryon curses the tyrannical Jupiter as a "base Usurper of my Name and Bed" (15:307.144), and, as Bywaters points out, Jupiter himself describes his affair with Alcmena "in appropriate political terms":

> In me (my charming Mistris) you behold
> A Lover that disdains a Lawful Title;
> Such as of Monarchs to successive Thrones:
> The Generous Lover holds by force of Arms;
> And claims his Crown by Conquest.
>
> (15:258.83–87)[3]

In its own attack on the 1688 invasion of England's marriage-bed of state, Dryden's fourth *Aeneis* is more complex than even this elusive play, for not only does Aeneas at points represent the kind of threat that Jupiter does in *Amphitryon*; he is also intermittently the "Lawfull Lord" of *Absalom and Achitophel* and other Dryden poems, while Dido is the faithless female lover of *Astræa Redux* and *Albion and Albanius*. Unsurprisingly, it is *Amphitryon* that *Aeneis* IV ends up most closely resembling in terms of its irresolution and confusion; it is *Albion and Albanius*, however, that it most immediately evokes.

In the opening scene where she reveals to her sister Anna that her "Soul" is "lab'ring" "With strange Ideas of our *Trojan* Guest," Dryden's Dido presents her guilt over her vows to her former husband in a way that recalls Augusta's crime (12, 14). She first admits that "since *Sichæus* was untimely slain, / This onely Man is able to subvert / The fix'd Foundations of my stubborn Heart," but then invites Jove to blast her to hell "Before I break the plighted Faith I gave," declaring that "he who had my Vows, shall ever have" (26–29, 37–38). This devoted Dido could provide a moral lesson to the Augusta who appears at the beginning of

Albion and Albanius lamenting the absence of her "Plighted Lord" and being reprimanded by Mercury for "Forsak[ing her] Faith, and break[-ing her] Nuptial Vow" (15:20–21.17, 53–54). Her resistance to a sub-version of the "fix'd Foundations of my stubborn Heart" not only recalls and functions as a contrast with Augusta's admission that De-mocracy "allur'd my Heart away" (15:22.78), but is slightly different from Vergil's Dido's battle with an increasingly "irresolute soul" and stirred "emotions": "Solus hic inflexit sensus, animumque labantem / Impulit" (22–23).[4] Likewise, her emphasis on "plighted Faith" and "Vows" is not the same as Vergil's Dido's concern with the violation of shame ("Pudor") and its laws ("tua iura") that would result from a be-trayal of the man who "first joined me to himself and stole away my heart": "Ante pudor quam te violo, aut tua jura resolvo. / Ille meos, pri-mus qui me sibi junxit, amores / Abstulit" (27–29). Her kinship with the allegorical Augusta is strengthened by her resolution "against the Yoke / Of hapless Marriage," a comment which recalls the "foreign Yoke" that Achitophel tried to fit on Israel/England (177).

The connections with *Albion and Albanius* are developed as Dryden's Anna assumes the role held in the masque by Zeal and Democracy. Re-minding her sister that "This little Spot of Land . . . / On ev'ry side is hemm'd with warlike Foes," Anna prays,

> Propitious Heav'n, and gracious *Juno*, lead
> This wand'ring Navy to your needful Aid;
> How will your Empire spread, your City rise
> From such an Union, and with such Allies!
>
> (62–65)

While the speech is fairly close to the Latin, it also in effect repeats both Democracy's warning that since "The People are Arming" Augusta should "Reject thy old, / And to thy Bed receive another Lord" and Zelota's exhortation to the city to "leave a Husband for a Friend" (15:36.27–36). Immediately after that temptation scene, Albion ob-serves "Then Zeal and Common-wealth infest / My Land again: / The fumes of madness that possest / The Peoples giddy Brain, / Once more disturb the Nations rest" (15:37.55–59). Dryden's similar objection here is suggested by the "Fury" Anna's words "added" to Dido's "kin-dled Flame" (74) and, more significantly, by the way her speech antici-pates Amata's enraged and politically-charged outburst in *Aeneis* VII when she demands of Latinus, "Shall . . . / A wandring Prince enjoy *Lavinia's* Bed" (501–2). The connection (that will later become appar-ent) between the "wandring" stranger-prince of *Aeneis* VII–VIII and this threatening newcomer with his "wand'ring Navy" is reinforced a few lines later when Aeneas is referred to as a "wandring Guest," a label that anticipates Amata's insistence on the dangers imposed by Aeneas's similarity to Paris: "A Guest like him, a *Trojan* Guest before, / In shew of friendship, sought the *Spartan* Shore; / And ravish'd *Helen* from her Husband bore" (509–11).

At the heart of *Albion and Albanius*, of course, is a concern for the havoc wreaked on genealogical succession in monarchy and therefore the nation's stability by such unfaithfulness as Augusta exhibits. As he establishes the connections with his 1685 masque, Dryden seems to reinforce this theme in *Aeneis* IV by also invoking Spenser's emphasis on genealogy in *The Faerie Queene*. The stress on "plighted Faith" and "vows" and on Aeneas's status as an unknown "Guest" is especially reminiscent of the last canto of Spenser's first book. There Red Cross soberly "plight[s]" his "faith" to both Una's father and the "great Faerie Queene" only to be undermined by Archimago, who turns up in disguise and warns the king to

> be aduized for the best,
> Ere thou thy daughter linck, in holy band
> Of wedlocke to that new vnknowen guest:
> For he already plighted his right hand
> Vnto another loue, and to another land.[5]

In effect, (both here and throughout the translation) Dryden is voicing the same concern over William III's attempt to join himself "in holy band / Of wedlocke" to England, and the contrast between his shadowy "wandring Guest" and Spenser's "new vnknowen guest," who has already proved his integrity, is rendered all the more foreboding as Venus focuses directly on the succession issue.

Agreeing with Juno's plans for a union between Dido and Aeneas, the god complains,

> The Doubt is all from *Jove*, and Destiny:
> Lest he forbid, with absolute Command,
> To mix the People in one common Land.
> Or will the *Trojan*, and the *Tyrian* Line,
> In lasting Leagues and sure Succession join?
> But you, the Partner of his Bed and Throne,
> May move his Mind. . . .

(154–60)

By conceding to Juno's power as "the Partner of [Jove's] Bed and Throne" Venus evokes the "mysterious pow'r of Bed and Throne" referred to by Aureng-Zebe and presented in that play as the key to social and private stability (12:186.356). However, by declaring that the "Doubt is all from *Jove*, and Destiny" (rather than "The Fates make me uncertain whether Jove wishes there to be one city . . ."),[6] Venus places her consideration of "lasting Leagues and sure Succession" in the context of *Aeneis* I where "haughty *Juno*'s unrelenting Hate" and Jove's indifference are responsible for "banish'd Gods" and disruption to "sure Succession" (2, 7–8). It is perhaps also useful to remember that the last time Juno featured in one of Dryden's plays, it was as a parodic version of the queen who made an appearance in *Albion and Albanius* in order to "reconcile the Quarrels of the Marriage-Bed" of Albion and the faithless Augusta/London (15:3). For, in the conversation that opens *Amphitryon*, Phoebus tells the audience that an unusual council (a convention parliament?) has been called; Mercury replies that it will address "some Petticoat Affair I guess" for Juno has threatened to "sue" Jove "in the Spiritual Court, for some Matrimonial Omissions; and he stood upon his Prerogative" (15:231–32.1–25). The kind of political overtones pervading that play, with its indictment of the "Conquest" of a bed by a usurper who "disdains a Lawful Title; / Such as of Monarchs to successive Thrones," become more apparent in *Aeneis* IV as the focus turns to the throne and bed of Dido herself. Accordingly, as considerations of succession are overwhelmed by destructive passions, the *Albion and Albanius*-style didacticism gives way to *Amphitryon*-style cynicism.

As King notes, Dryden turns the blame from Aeneas and Dido to Dido alone as he depicts the spreading of Fame's rumors after the cave incident:[7]

> She fills the Peoples Ears with *Dido*'s Name;
> Who, lost to Honour, and the sense of Shame,
> Admits into her Throne and Nuptial Bed
> A wandring Guest, who from his Country fled:
> Whole Days with him she passes in delights;
> And wasts in Luxury long Winter Nights:
> Forgetful of her Fame, and Royal Trust;
> Dissolv'd in Ease, abandon'd to her Lust.
>
>   (274–81)[8]

The (interpolated) yoking of "Name" and "Shame" as they are sacrificed to an act of lust in a royal bed has a parallel in Amphitryon's complaint about Jove's double usurpation "of my Name and Bed" (15:307.144). That this "Throne and Nuptial Bed," like those in *Astræa Redux*, *Albion and Albanius* and *Amphitryon*, in fact represent England's marriage-bed of state is suggested by the substitution (in a way that anticipates *Aeneis* VII–VIII) of "a wandring Guest, who from his Coun-

try fled" for Vergil's Aeneas of renowned bloodline ("Æneam Trojano
a sanguine cretum": "Aeneas sprung from Trojan blood" [191]).[9] This
implicit indictment of Dido as a second Augusta reinforces and is reinforced by the political overtones of the preceding description of the
"marriage" in the cave.

Vergil's condemnation of the private act of Carthage's "Foundress,"
who "calls [what happens in the cave] a marriage, and by that name
covers the sin" ("Conjugium vocat, hoc prætexit nomine culpam"
[172]), is tinged with social considerations in Dryden's version, where
Dido "call'd it Marriage, by that specious Name, / To veil the Crime
and sanctifie the Shame" (249–50). In view of the subsequent portrayal
of Aeneas as an wanderer from another land (and, near the end of the
poem, as an intruder bringing war to a peaceful nation), it seems likely
that the veiled "Crime" and sanctified "Shame" that Dryden has in
mind are those that made possible the Glorious Revolution settlement.
An attempt (again) to draw events of 1688–89 into a line of English
historical disasters and crimes also seems to underlie the echo here of
the poet's description of the Reformation in *The Hind and the Panther*:

> A *Lyon* old, obscene, and furious made
> By lust, compress'd her mother in a shade;
> Then, by a left-hand marr'age weds the Dame,
> Cov'ring adult'ry with a specious name:
> So schism begot. . . .
>
> (3:133.351–55)

The subsequent reflection there on this precedent-setting "heresie" by
the Lyon (Henry VIII), namely that "Gods and kings rebels have the
same good cause, / To trample down divine and humane laws" (357–
58), also seems to hover here in *Aeneis* IV as this to-all-appearances state
"Marriage" is depicted as a second fall from grace: "From this ill
Omend Hour, in Time arose / Debate and Death, and all succeeding
woes" (245–46). It is worth noting here too that Eve in Dryden's *The
State of Innocence* also (Dido-like) "plight[s]" her "inviolable Faith" to
Adam and later calls him "partner of my bed" before revealing she has
committed the crime from which would ensue all succeeding woes
(12:112.76; 12:134.6).

The portrayal of Dido as another Eve through the Miltonic overtones
of this politically-charged passage can be seen even more clearly as another panel in Dryden's narrative tapestry of English monarchic woes
if it is juxtaposed with his poem *Eleanora* (1692). There, as Gardiner
points out citing Alan Roper, the Countess of Abingdon's "true wifely
submissiveness" is presented as "the pattern for the people's obedience
to the king":[10]

Love and Obedience to her Lord she bore,

. . . .

    taught by his Indulgence to obey.
Thus we love God as Author of our good;
So Subjects love just Kings, or so they shou'd.

(176–81)

Eleanora is also a "second *Eve*." The difference between her, the Genesis Eve, Milton's Eve, Dryden's Eve and Dido, however, is that "Had she been first, still Paradise had bin, / And Death had found no entrance by her sin" (170, 172–73). For the same reason too (it would seem) as the story of Britomart's ancestry is placed at the heart of Spenser's "Book of Chastitie," Eleanora's "fidelity in marriage," as Gardiner also observes, is specifically "related to succession" and "the passage about [her] union leads to remarks about her imperishable line of descendants."[11] The issue is given more weight and Eleanora in a way mythologized by the reference to Vergil's fable that occurs when the Countess "resembles Anchises in Hades, 'numb'ring o'er his future Roman Race' and Cybele on the mountain top viewing her 'Sons and Daughters of the Skie' (198–202)."[12] The panegyric ends unconventionally, however, as the poet admits struggling to prevent his "rage" from "break[ing] loose on this bad Age" and grieves having "to sing [Eleanora's] Praises, in a Clime / Where Vice triumphs, and Vertue is a Crime: / Where ev'n to draw the Picture of thy Mind, / Is Satyr on the most of Humane Kind" (363–68). The same frustration and cynicism over the succession problem and general dishonesty of the age begin to take over in *Aeneis* IV when Dryden turns to the consequences of Dido's (or England's) "specious" marriage—and the impact of his transformation of Vergil's heroine is perhaps greater if Eleanora is kept in mind as a contrast.

Leaving the "lustful Pair in lawless pleasure drown'd" (as opposed to simply "oblitos famæ melioris" or "forgetful of better fame" [221]), Dryden's Jove reflects on Venus's son:

    Hers was a Heroe, destin'd to command
    A Martial Race; and rule the Latian Land:
    Who shou'd his ancient Line from *Teucer* draw;
    And, on the conquer'd World, impose the Law.

(336–39)

Again, after both the cynicism of *Aeneis* I (with its Jove who will "Sov'raign Laws impose" after "bloody" war [359–61]) and the presentation here of Aeneas as a "wandring Guest" seemingly cut-off from any past inheritance, these lines look forward to the dilemma confronted in

Aeneis VII and VIII when a would-be conqueror shows up and takes
the job reserved for a "Heroe" who can trace "his ancient Line from
Teucer." Dryden's own bewilderment also again seems evident as the
following lines turn the conquering invader into a James II figure in
the same confusing way that Sinon represents both the false and true
English kings in *Aeneis* I.

It seems probable that the wronged Prince of Wales is on Dryden's
mind as his Jove objects, "Yet why shou'd he defraud his Son of
Fame; / And grudge the *Romans* their Immortal Name" (342–43).[13] It
seems more than probable that he was thinking of James "ling'ring on
a hostile Shore" as he translated the rebuke that has a precedent in his
own "The Lady's Song":

> What are his vain Designs? what hopes he more,
> From his long ling'ring on a hostile Shore?
> Regardless to redeem his Honour lost,
> And for his Race to gain th'*Ausonian* Coast?
> Bid him with Speed the *Tyrian* Court forsake;
> With this Command the slumb'ring Warrior wake.
>
> (344–49)

The "vain Designs" and "Honour lost" are Dryden's additions, and his
evocation of England's dilemma (from a Jacobite point of view) is supported by the interpolated images of a court that must be forsaken and
a "slumb'ring Warrior" that must be woken. Vergil's Jove commands
Mercury, "Naviget: hæc summa est, hic nostri nuntius esto": "Let him
set sail; this is the sum. Let this be my message" (237). The complexity
of the allegory by this stage, however, means that the poet can offer no
answers despite applying Vergil's platonic blueprint to England's problems. By presenting Dido's "specious" marriage to a foreign stranger as
England's ill-fated marriage to a natural enemy, while simultaneously
using the figure Aeneas to beg for redemption of lost honor and the
recall of England's rightful "Warrior" and his son, Dryden attacks, as
he did through Sinon in *Aeneis* I, the destruction of time-honored standards and codes by the Glorious Revolution settlement. Yet as he con-
founds Vergil's allegory to make his point about the difficulty of seeing
in such a world, he obscures any didacticism in his own text, which is
overwhelmed by the confusion unleashed with the simultaneously political, social and private act at the center of *Aeneis* IV. This confusion
heightens when the unlawful union begins to disintegrate.

Not only does Dryden's cynicism over the instability of England's
1690s constitutional *status quo* surely fuel the intense irony that permeates Dido's fury at Aeneas's imminent departure, but it places the

scene—with its contemporary overtones—among the most chaotic in his plays:

> Base and ungrateful, cou'd you hope to fly,
> And undiscover'd scape a Lover's Eye?
> Nor cou'd my Kindness your Compassion move,
> Nor plighted Vows, nor dearer bands of Love?
> Or is the Death of a despairing Queen
> Not worth preventing, though too well forseen?
>
> (441–44)

The (interpolated) notion of ingratitude and the "plighted Vows" connect the outburst with Dido's Jacobite-tinted speeches at the beginning of *Aeneis* IV and draw attention to the fact that the queen has, after all, committed Augusta's crime. Her refusal to see her own sin is highlighted by her (ironic) use of the same phrase ("plighted Vows") to condemn Aeneas as she used to pledge her unswerving loyalty to Sichaeus in the opening scene. If the speech is viewed within Dryden's overall political allegory, then, it can be seen as his indictment of those who refuse to recognize that the nation has repeated the crime committed by its "affairs" during the Interregnum and Exclusion Crisis. Dryden's bitterness at the chaotic, lawless world that is a product of such fundamental dishonesty and amorality manifests itself in his conversion of Vergil's heroine into another Nourmahal or Cleopatra as he shifts Vergil's emphasis on the suffering that was the cost of Rome's glory to his own contemporary concerns.

Ruæus points out that Vergil's Dido's entreaty to Aeneas here is presented as a rhetorical oration (n.305); however, in a move that denies his Dido the tragic stature and pathos of Vergil's heroine, Dryden seems consciously and methodically to overturn the structure and reasoning of the speech. The *"Propositio"* of the original lecture, Ruæus demonstrates, is Dido's assertion that "non esse Æneæ clam fugiendum" (Aeneas will not be able to achieve a secret flight). Her proposed subject is dissimulation and its treachery, and she enhances her attack on Aeneas's deceitfulness through an image, heightened by her scornful whispery tones, of the hero sneaking away from her land in silence: "Dissimulare etiam sperasti, perfide, tantum / Posse nefas, tacitusque mea decedere terra?" (305–6).[14] On the lips of Dryden's furious queen, however, this proud scorn becomes an outburst of "unrelenting Hate" and persecution of the kind attributed to and displayed by Juno in *Aeneis* I. Her opening abuse of Aeneas as "Base and ungrateful" is as futile as Nourmahal's sudden impatient dismissal of Aureng-Zebe as "Dull and ingrateful" (12:212.111); it has not the dignity and power of Ver-

gil's Dido's "perfide" (traitor), which serves to reinforce her initial condemnation of Aeneas's deceit. Similarly, the Fury-like assurance that
Aeneas will not "undiscover'd scape a Lover's eye" not only contrasts
starkly in its choppy contorted pentameter to Vergil's smooth and controlled "Posse nefas, tacitusque mea decedere terra," but it replaces a
significant element of the original "proposition" with an uncontrolled
and mindless promise of persecution.

The parallel between Dryden's Dido and his Nourmahal established
in the first couplet is developed in the subsequent inquiry, "Nor cou'd
my Kindness your Compassion move[?]". The demand has no basis in
Vergil, but it does recall Nourmahal's appeal to kindness as she attempts to win over Aureng-Zebe (12:214.159). The emphasis on natural
laws over social inserted here by the interpolation not only consolidates
the conflation of Dido and the raging heroines of Dryden's tragedies
but initiates the deliberate destruction of Vergil's "*Confirmatio*" and its
logic. The dismantling of the body of the oration is in fact achieved with
Dryden's coverage of the first three of the five points outlined by
Ruæus and addressed in the passage cited above. Dido's argument,
Ruæus demonstrates, is substantiated by appeals first and foremost to
love, to former pledges of faithfulness in that love and to *pietas*: "1. *Est
Amor*. 2. *Data dextera et fides*. 3. *Pietas in morituram* crudeli funere."
(n.305; italics reversed).[15] (The last two points involve the unsuitability
of the season for travel.) This reasonable, convincing and seemingly wa-
tertight argument is overwhelmed, however, when Dryden's Dido specifically privileges the kind of lawless love espoused by Nourmahal and
Cleopatra over the (lawful and social) bonds of pledges: "Nor plighted
Vows, nor dearer bands of Love." The use of the comparative in effect
achieves the point made by Cleopatra when she tells Octavia "he whom
Law calls yours, / . . . his love made mine" and by Nourmahal both
when she informs Zayda "Love's sure a name that's more Divine than
Wife. / That Sovereign power all guilt from action takes" and when she
assures Aureng-Zebe, "Custom our Native Royalty does awe; / Promis-
cuous Love is Nature's general Law" (12:213.131–32; cf. p. 66 above).
Ruæus' recognition of *pietas* at the heart of Dido's third point, which
concerns her certain death if Aeneas leaves, is similarly undercut by the
lawless abandon of Dryden's heroine, who is clearly already a victim of
despair: "Or is the Death of a despairing Queen / Not worth prevent-
ing, though too well foreseen?"

The suggestion that the destructive and uncontrollable passions governing Dryden's Dido and overriding the laws that uphold social bonds
and order are those governing William and Mary's England is reinforced in the center of what is in Vergil's text the "*Peroratio*." The original, Ruæus points out, is founded on an appeal to Aeneas's sympathy

for the queen's "extinctum pudorem" and "famam amissam" ("destroyed shame" and "lost fame" [n.305]). While the conclusion reached
by Dryden also hinges on the consideration of "Fame" and "Shame," it
seems to summarize (a Jacobite view of) England's predicament as
much as it does Dido's:

> For you I have provok'd a Tyrant's Hate,
> Incens'd the *Lybian*, and the *Tyrian* State;
> For you alone I suffer in my Fame;
> Bereft of Honour, and expos'd to Shame:
> Whom have I now to trust, ungrateful Guest,
> (That only Name remains of all the rest!)
>
> (463–68)

This time Dryden achieves a political overlay by abbreviating rather
than expanding Vergil's Latin. The "Tyrant's Hate," which derives from
Vergil's "Nomadumq; tyranni" ("Nomad chiefs" [320]), surely glances
at Louis XIV, whose "Hate" for England has been provoked by the nation's "ungrateful [Dutch] Guest." Certainly Dryden's bitterness would
account for his use of the evocative "Tyrant" (almost a phonetic pun)
as he finds a contemporary equivalent for Vergil's "Tyranni," a word
employed by the Latin-speaking Dido in its primary sense ("chiefs,"
"monarchs")—even if they are hostile chiefs. Dryden's anger and his
political framework would also explain his near eradication of the pathos of Vergil's Dido's cry, "Extinctus pudor, et, qua sola sidera
adibam, / Fama prior: cui me moribundam deseris, hospes; / Hoc solum
nomen quoniam de conjuge restat" (322–24). Segrais translates,

> Et pour toi j'ai perdu le plus grand bien de tous,
> L'irreprochable honneur, la renommée entiere,
> Qui me faisoit marcher si superbe & si fiere.
> Ah! Prince (puis qu'enfin la peur de ton couroux,
> Interdit à ma voix le charmant nom d'époux)
> A qui me laisses-tu desolée, & mourante?
>
> (*Traduction*, vol. I, 309)

Dryden's elimination of the once proud queen's reflection that her
lost "fama" was the means "alone" by which she was "making her way
to the stars" allows him to stress lost "Honour" in a way that is closer
to his nationalistic concern for a leader's and nation's "Honour lost" at
line 346 (discussed above) than to Dido's anguish over her personal
situation. Likewise, by reducing her lament that he whom she once
knew as "husband" can now only be called "hospes" to a bitter realization that only the name of "ungrateful Guest" "remains of all the rest,"

Dryden dehumanizes the passage in a way that allows room for an allegorical comment on England's vulnerability in her new "affair." Such a
reading of the lines is supported by a passage in the dedication, which,
followed up as it is, by an argument that a translation is a product of a
poet's own time, seems also to point to what England can expect from
her Dutch "Guest." In language strongly anticipatory of the unmistakably political *Aeneis* VII, Dryden there reasons Aeneas's position from
Aeneas's point of view: "If I took my pleasure, had not you your share
of it? I leave you free at my departure, to comfort yourself with the next
Stranger who happens to be Shipwreck'd on your Coast. Be as kind an
Hostess as you have been to me, and you can never fail of another Husband" (5:303). If this is a sarcastic comment on England's "promiscu-
ity," it also has a parallel in Dryden's attack on the "senseless Plea of
Right by Providence" in his fable "The Character of a Good Parson"
where he the poet asserts that such a claim "lasts no longer than the
present sway; / But justifies the next who comes in play" (119–20).

Just as the breakdown of Vergil's rhetorical oration at every stage
into a shapeless effusion of rage reflects (what is in Dryden's view) the
breakdown in England of civilizing, authoritative and peace-ensuring
structures by fickle, Whiggish forces, so in Dido's subsequent condemnation of Aeneas, Dryden portrays a world which seems to correspond
with his own view of life in the 1690s. "Of Man's Injustice," Dido demands of herself as much as Aeneas, "why shou'd I complain?"

> The Gods, and *Jove* himself behold in vain
> Triumphant Treason, yet no Thunder flyes:
> Nor *Juno* views my Wrongs with equal Eyes;
> Faithless is Earth, and Faithless are the Skies!
> Justice is fled, and Truth is now no more;
> I sav'd the Shipwrack'd Exile on my Shore:
> With needful Food his hungry *Trojans* fed;
> I took the Traytor to my Throne and Bed:
>
> . . . .
>
> I rave, I rave: A God's Command he pleads,
> And makes Heav'n accessary to his Deeds.
>
> (531–43)

Ironically (again), it is Dido's own actions which are to blame for her
predicament, and her imitation of Augusta's reaction ("I rave, I rave")
when she finds "my *Albion*'s Heart is gone" serves to reinforce the connection between the two faithless characters (15:35.5–9). However, the
passage is less didactic than cynical and in effect expresses—with
greater intensity—the sentiment voiced by Aureng-Zebe in the midst of
his woes: "When I consider Life, 'tis all a cheat" (12:210.33). As King

notices, "in Dryden's version [as in Vergil's], Dido stops for the reflec-
tive comparison between human and divine justice. . . ."[16] From that
point, however, Dryden darkens Vergil's original into the bleak world
of his late plays where the absence of human justice is a direct product
of divine indifference. Vergil's two half and one full lines become five
desolate ones as he translates "jam jam nec maxima Juno, / Nec Satur-
nius hæc oculis pater aspicit æquis. / Nusquam tuta fides": "Even now
neither mighty Juno nor the Saturnian father look on these things with
just eyes; nowhere is faith safe" (371–73). King also points out that
Dryden's "Faithless is Earth, and Faithless are the Skies" imitates Godolphin's "The earth is faithless, faithless are the skies,"[17] yet the
emphasis on the gods' "vain" observation (as opposed to non- interven-
tion) along with the addition of "Triumphant Treason" and the flight of
justice and truth weave the speech unequivocally into the body of Dryden's late works. His wonted insistence on political chaos as the source
of the woes described is evident here in his translation of Dido's
"egentem / Excepi, et regni demens in parte locavi": literally, "I received him in his desolation, mad as I was, and made him a part of my
kingdom" (373–74). Dryden adds his recurrent (political) image of
"Throne and Bed," and his likely attack on the plea of right by Providence as his Dido also throws in a condemnation of Aeneas for "mak[-
ing] Heav'n accessary to his Deeds" reinforces the impression given by
the passage as a whole that the poet himself has given up waiting for a
divine thunderbolt to strike down the "Traytor" who has most recently
invaded England's "Throne and Bed."[18]

The element of didacticism struggling nonetheless to assert itself
above the cynicism of this speech has a moment of triumph when the
focus switches to Aeneas's reaction to Dido. In his steadfast resistance
to the raging queen, Dryden's hero at this point both rebukes a faithless
England and provides the example Dryden's Eve says that Adam
should have when she chides him "You should have shown th' Authority you boast, / And, Soveraign-like, my headlong will have crost"
(12:139.33–34). As he elaborated Dido's rage, so Dryden expands Vergil's comparison of Aeneas to a "Mountain Oak" beaten and bent by
winds:

> Unmov'd the Royal Plant their Fury mocks;
> Or shaken, clings more closely to the Rocks:
> Far as he shoots his tow'ring Head on high,
> So deep in Earth his fix'd Foundations lye:
> No less a Storm the *Trojan* Heroe bears;
> Thick Messages and loud Complaints he hears;
> And bandy'd Words, still beating on his Ears.

Sighs, Groans and Tears, proclaim his inward Pains,
But the firm purpose of his Heart remains.

(644–52)

By calling Vergil's oak a "Royal Plant" (as Vergil does not) and by adding the detail of its mocking the winds' "Fury," Dryden deposits into
his translation yet another example of a favorite image of stable Stuart
monarchy battling irrational forces. The addition too of both "fix'd
Foundations" and "the firm purpose of his Heart" reinforces the political role assigned to Dryden's Dido by providing—at the same time they
are being codified as qualities of Stuart monarchy—a direct contrast
between Aeneas's dependability and her inability to resist the subversion of the "fix'd Foundations of my stubborn Heart." This image of
reason's conquest over passion with its tight-knit political and human
elements also provides a telling and poignant contrast to Ventidius' description of an Antony torn between passion and duty in *All for Love*:
"How sorrow shakes him! / So, now the Tempest tears him up by
th'Roots, / And on the ground extends the noble ruin" (13:30.215–17).
Yet, just as Antony and Cleopatra do sacrifice all for love, so in *Aeneis*
IV passion is ultimately omnipotent, and not only is the "Royal Plant"
image rendered ineffectual by the overwhelming chaos of the rest of the
poem, but there is no final sense of a controlling public and divine order
as there is in *All for Love*—and in Vergil's fourth book of the *Aeneid*.

While Dryden's Dido stands for political chaos and a fickle England,
she is also a suffering human being at the mercy of cruel, unfathomable
and uncontrollable forces. For all Dryden's contemporary satire, the
powerful human element of the "Faithless is Earth" speech (for example) is undeniable and Dido there, despite her Nourmahal-like lack of
control, as pitiable as the noble but helpless Don Sebastian and
Cleomenes. In fact, a concerted effort to convert this otherwise *Amphitryon*-like scene into a *Cleomenes*-like world, where human effort and
kindness (notably the princely behavior of princes themselves) are either punished or go unrewarded, is indicated by Dryden's lengthening
of Vergil's Dido's reminder of what she has done for Aeneas. As King
points out, elsewhere too Dryden adds "details which emphasize Dido's
kindliness and generosity," and this all-pervasive poetic sympathy ultimately prevents Dido from fully becoming simply another unendearing
Nourmahal or Augusta.[19] This is perhaps true even during the speech
which replaces Vergil's rhetorical oration, for while there is no immediately apparent distinction between Dido and Nourmahal at that point,
Dido's appeal to "Kindness" and "Compassion" has as close a kinship
with the qualities she has already displayed as monarch and sufferer as
with Nourmahal's desperate lawlessness. Her argument that "bands of

Love" are "dearer" than "plighted Vows" also becomes less reprehensible when it is seen as an imitation of Godolphin's "bands of vows, and dearer bands of Love," a line which embodies the overall focus of his translation on Dido's tragic love, its pathos and its pain.

As suggested at the beginning of this chapter, what Dryden seems to be doing here is investigating the chaos of his own world—a chaos ensuing from the political situation—through tragedy, which has the passions as its basis. His *modus operandi* is highlighted by a passage which falls between Dido's politically-charged "Faithless is Earth" speech and the even more politically-charged simile portraying Aeneas in terms used by Dryden and other loyalists to describe the Stuart monarchy. Dido's irrational and turmoil-precipitating behavior, which is instrumental in the "Faithless" world that is the source of her pain, is suddenly attributed by the poet to irresistible and unavoidable laws: "All pow'rful Love, what Changes canst thou cause / In Human Hearts, subjected to thy Laws!" (595–96). This outburst not only has a precedent in *Sylvæ*, where Dryden repeats Lucretius's argument that "the race of every living thing, / Obeys [Love's] pow'r" (3:44.28–29), but imitates (and expands upon) Godolphin's "All-conquering Love! who can resist thy sway?" (Vergil has "Improbe amor, quid non mortalia pectora cogis": "Tyrant Love, to what do you not drive mortal hearts?" [412].) Having associated the passions of his chaos-invoking Dido with those universal laws that render reason and human laws impotent, Dryden places her dilemma firmly in the realm of tragedy in a way that is accentuated by a parallel with *Tyrannick Love* (1670). Ironically evoking Maximin's realization that "Fates dark recesses we can never find" (a conclusion which leads him to rely on "Fortune" [10:118.63–64]), Dido now asks her sister to search "The dark recesses of [Aeneas's] inmost Mind," the "Secrets" of which will decide her own Fate, for their disclosure will decide "if I must live or dye" (609–12). As she then urges Anna to request "A short delay" and "an interval from Woe" she also (again ironically and tragically) echoes Maximin's subsequent reflection that "Th'unlucky have but hours, and those they lose" (626–27; 10:118.66).

The incongruity between the pitiable and tragic figure here and the raging, futile, semicomic character elsewhere in the poem is highlighted in Sloman's observation that "Dryden's Dido is like a tragedy queen adrift in the wrong kind of play, a Mrs Loveit or a Lady Wishfort."[20] The source of the poem's confusion lies surely in Dryden's attempt to employ the heroic codes inherent in Vergil's mode (and translated into Restoration tragic terms) to answer questions about the essentially unheroic world of which his Dido is both agent and victim. Yet, despite being a product of the tension between Dryden's efforts to be a Vergil for his age and his cynicism for that age, *Aeneis* IV can also be seen as less idiosyncratic than representative of its time if it is viewed in light of what was happening in the drama of the 1690s. Critics have noted the closing of the gap between tragedy and comedy during the last decade of the seventeenth century. Brean Hammond attributes this to a greater demand by readers for characters and situations resembling their own. He argues in particular for a trend in "late-century tragedy" to allow its characters (for example, Dorax in Dryden's *Don Sebastian* and Osmyn in Congreve's *The Mourning Bride*) "confessional, vulnerable modes that give intimations of a deeper psychology and are on the way to the forms of self display that are recognizably novelistic." So too "[f]rom the direction of comic theory and practice, there is a reciprocal move towards a less differentiated dramatic form that results from a readjustment of the relationship between punitive and sympathetic elements in the construction of comic characterisation."[21] Dryden's simultaneously reprehensible and sympathetic, tragic and futile Dido perhaps makes more sense then if the minidrama that is *Aeneis* IV is viewed from the perspective of this homogenization of genres and ousting of the heroic: trends that were products of the new social forces and demands of William and Mary's England.

Yet, Dryden's treatment of Vergil's *Aeneid* IV not only earmarks his poem as belonging to the 1690s, a period dominated by mixed-form works; it reflects changing attitudes toward and perceptions of the classical world.[22] The proliferation of mock-heroics in the first decade of the eighteenth century perhaps provides the strongest evidence of writers' troubled questioning of the relevance of the classics, especially epic, to contemporary life, yet the tensions and (ultimately) the rejection of the heroic that such questioning led to are already apparent in Dryden's dedication. Before launching into his consideration of the historical and poetic implications of Vergil's Dido episode, for example, Dryden somewhat nervously anticipates the reaction to Vergil's story by his female readers. The "Ladies," he says,

> will make a numerous Party against [Aeneas], for being false to Love, in forsaking *Dido*. And I cannot much blame them; for to say the truth, 'tis an ill Precedent for their Gallants to follow. Yet if I can bring him off, with Flying Colours, they may learn experience at her cost; and for her sake, avoid a Cave, as the worst shelter they can chuse from a shower of Rain, especially when they have a Lover in their Company. (5:294)

Like Pope's later letter to Arabella Fermor, this tongue-in-cheek advice at once recognizes the moral seriousness of the work under question and "mocks" the heroic by employing humor to undercut that serious-

ness. The changes in literary and social demands and tastes reflected in
Dryden's semihumorous moral here and affecting the shape of literary
output in the 1690s—changes that made epic an unfeasible mode to
Pope and his contemporaries—can be seen in action most clearly at the
end of *Aeneis* IV.

The poem's own Punic curse and death scenes highlight the incongruity from which its general confusion arises; Dryden demands that
his heroine fulfill a function requiring the moral high seriousness of
tragedy while denying her tragic stature as he makes her both agent and
victim of his own chaotic and amoral world. The historical and political
seriousness of this last section is acknowledged from the start as Dryden imbues Dido's pain at her desertion with royalist overtones:

> See now the promis'd Faith, the vaunted Name,
> The Pious Man, who, rushing through the Flame,
> Preserv'd his Gods; and to the *Phrygian* Shore
> The Burthen of his feeble Father bore!
> I shou'd have torn him piecemeal; strow'd in Floods
> His scatter'd Limbs, or left expos'd in Woods: .
> Destroy'd his Friends and Son; and from the Fire
> Have set the reeking Boy before the Sire.
>
> (857–64)

Dryden's adjective "Pious" is added, and, like the also interpolated
image of the prince "rushing through the Flame" to save his "Gods"
and family, emphasizes Aeneas's piety in a way that connects him with
the ideal princes in Dryden's early poems (perhaps most obviously
Annus Mirabilis). His Dido's emphasis on this piety and her anguish,
which has resulted from her opposition to it, would seem designed then
to do for Dryden's audience what Vergil's passage aimed to do for his.
Yet the poignancy (and ultimately the seriousness) of the original is
undercut by the queen's excessive violence. While Vergil's heroine also
advocates tearing Aeneas limb from limb and scattering him on the
waves, the "high and undisguised rhetoric" of her speech means she
retains the stature of the Greek tragic figures whose actions she is recalling.[23] Dryden, however, again punctures the rhetorical and literary
nature of Vergil's original, thereby denying his queen the mythical
standing of Vergil's. The added image of body parts "left expos'd in
Woods" is somehow more gruesome than the thought of them being lost
in the waves; equally disconcerting is Dido's use of "low" (and Saxon!)
vocabulary as she imagines tearing Aeneas "piecemeal" or serving him
up his "reeking" son.

When he comes to the curse itself, Dryden attempts to salvage the

historical and poetical usefulness of the passage by using Vergil's original to draw attention to England's problems. His Dido prays that if

> Th'ungrateful Wretch should find the *Latian* Lands,
> Yet let a Race untam'd, and haughty Foes,
> His peaceful Entrance with dire Arms oppose;
> Oppress'd with Numbers in th'unequal Field,
> His Men discourag'd, and himself expell'd,
> Let him for Succour sue from place to place,
> Torn from his Subjects, and his Son's embrace:
> First let him see his Friends in Battel slain;
> And their untimely Fate lament in vain.
>
> (879–87)

By introducing the notion of ingratitude (Vergil has "Infandum caput"
or "abhorrent wretch" [613]), Dryden again evokes a post-Stuart
world as he describes political and social disaster. The connections between this scene and Williamite England are strengthened as he adds
details which make the objectionable entrance "peaceful" (like the Glorious Revolution) and the subsequent war "unequal" (like the Battle of
the Boyne in which James's troops had been decimated). The pacifism
which permeates *Aeneis* IX–XII and *Fables* also seeps in here as he replaces Vergil's "indigna suorum / Funera" ("undeserving" or "cruel"
slaughter of his men) with the thought of friends meeting "untimely
Fate[s]" and the notion of "vain" lamentations.

Yet if any explanatory or beneficial point is being made (as the effort
to address a contemporary audience would imply), it is obscured as
Dryden again (letting his Jacobite horror get the better of him) blends
confusingly an attack on the Glorious Revolution and its aftermath with
images of a (rightful) king forced "for Succour [to] sue from place to
place, / Torn from his Subjects, and his Son's embrace." The shadow of
doubt cast in this way over the usefulness to his own poem of Vergil's
mode is further darkened during the climax of the curse when his Dido
loses completely the dignity she might have regained and becomes
(again) a replica of Augusta. In a speech saturated with venom, she too
gives "Hate the full possession of [her] Breast" (as Augusta did before
her), and in her obsession with this "Hate" displays a lack of control
that Vergil's Dido does not. What is in Vergil, then, a poignant and
grave event that will have a far-reaching historical and aetiological impact has been transformed by Dryden into another disillusioned effusion of wrath at the chaos that keeps plaguing English history—and
about which, it seems, nothing can be done. The movement away from
epic gravity and didacticism which has occured as a consequence is underscored by the death scene.

Having cursed the Trojan one last time, Dryden's heroine plunges the sword in her breast:

> She said, and struck: Deep enter'd in her side
> The piercing Steel, with reeking Purple dy'd:
> Clog'd in the Wound the cruel Weapon stands;
> The spouting Blood came streaming on her Hands.
>
> (950–53)

The graphic nature of the scene and its focus on the deed itself are entirely Dryden's. Vergil has: "Dixerat: atque illam media inter talia ferro / Collapsam aspiciunt comites, ensemq; cruore / Spumantem, sparsasq; manus": "She ended; and as she spoke her companions see her fallen on the sword, the blade foaming with blood and her hands smattered in it" (663–65). Dryden's anglicization of his scene is evident both in its Saxon vocabulary and in its proximity to Godolphin's: "With this the bloud came rushing from her side / Deep in her breast the reeking sword was dy'd." However, it also reflects the generic shifts that affect the entire translation. The classicist Richard Heinze points out that the stabbing itself is not seen in Vergil because in tragedy "we do not normally witness a death on the stage, but are only affected, like the hero's nearest and dearest, by the impact of the terrible event." Just so in Vergil, he observes, we are not permitted to watch as Dido stabs herself. The "narrative passes over the decisive moment: her handmaidens see her collapse under the blow," and we are forced to wait until wailing fills the halls. In this way, "we are made to feel the full significance of the death of a woman like Dido. . . ."[24] Once more, then, Dryden seems deliberately to have punctured the heroic. Again too the general novelization process, which picked up momentum in the 1690s, seems to be marked, for the description here of Dido's end has much in common not only with the mock-heroic style gore of the *Aeneis*'s war books but with the "attention to grisly realistic detail" in (for example) Behn's *Oroonoko* and *The Fair Jilt*: detail, which, as Brean Hammond also observes, is key among the features undermining and questioning the "romance motifs and assumptions" in Behn's writing.[25]

If, in the end, there is any comfort for Dryden's audience in *Aeneis* IV, it is that which is offered in the rest of the translation: a reminder of the freedom of the individual soul and of the ongoing nature of the story of human woes and history's disasters. Dido follows up her image of the "the reeking Boy [set] before the Sire" with the thought that "Events are doubtful, which on Battels wait; / Yet where's the doubt, to Souls secure of Fate?" (865–66). The emphasis on a soul's security from Fate is Dryden's; Vergil has "Quem metui moritura?": "What

have I to fear, being doomed to death?" (604). The release it offers both
the reader and Dido herself from the woes of her crazy and painful
world is stressed again in the alexandrine which ends the poem: "The
strugling Soul was loos'd; and Life dissolv'd in Air" (1009).

The poet's own release from the pain of the chaos he is describing is
also again achieved through Democritean laughter, the presence of
which of course stresses further the poem's dissolution of the epic form.
Trapp objects to Dryden's treatment of Vergil's comparison of Aeneas
to Apollo just before the hunt:

> If *Virgil* can be said to be remarkable for any one good Quality more than for
> Modesty, it is for his awful Reverence to Religion. And yet, as Mr. Dryden
> represents him describing Apollo's Presence at one of his own Festivals, he
> speaks Thus; Book iv. V. 210.
>
> > *Himself, on* Cynthus *walking, sees below*
> > *The merry Madness of the sacred Show.*
>
> *Virgil* says, He walks on the Top of *Cynthus;* That's all: The rest is Mr. *Dry-*
> *den*'s. And it is exactly of a Piece with a Passage in the Third Georgick; in
> which, without any sort of Provocation, or the least Hint from his Author,
> He calls the *Priest* the *Holy Butcher*.[26]

The reason why "Mr. Dryden" chooses here—as in his *Georgics*—to de-
pict the "merry Madness of the sacred Show" seems to be highlighted
in an interpolation near the beginning that describes Dido's response to
Aeneas's tale of Troy's fall: "still she begs to hear it once again. / The
Hearer on the Speaker's Mouth depends; / And thus the Tragick Story
never ends" (112–14). As he replaces Vergilian-style *imperium* with oft-
told woes as his subject matter, Dryden gradually and intermittently
realizes that Ovidian-style epic is what is needed in the 1690s—not Vergilian seriousness. By placing the emphasis in the translation as a whole
on "merry Madness," however, he also unwittingly contributes to the
larger movement taking place in the "mock-heroic moment" of the
1690s.

NOW LET US GO, WHERE *PHOEBUS* LEADS THE WAY

> The world was a fool, e're since it begun;
> And since neither Janus, nor Chronos, nor I,
> Can hinder the crimes,
> Or mend the bad times,
> 'Tis better to laugh than to cry.
>
> —Dryden, *The Secular Masque*

Just as *Aeneis* IV provides a kind of center for the generic shift that unfolds with the translation by offering a concentrated version of the "draught at length," so *Aeneis* III and *Aeneis* VI illuminate the process whereby the work as a whole becomes increasingly concerned with storytelling itself rather than the story being told: in other words, becomes Ovidian. Clearly, Vergil's *Aeneid* III, which traces Aeneas's wanderings before he settles in his new homeland, and his *Aeneid* VI, which outlines the glorious history of Rome and its heroes, would have posed a problem to Dryden after his rejection in *Aeneis* I of historical accomplishment and imperial glory as subject matter. In the end, it seems, he uses the two books to explore—more thoroughly than he can in the rest of the translation—the course he himself must take as poet as he navigates through the historical wasteland of the 1690s.

Both an English medieval and an Renaissance Italian tradition hold that the third book of the *Aeneid* in particular is an allegory for the wanderings of the soul.[27] Dryden was perhaps relying upon this legacy for authority in his own *Aeneis* III, which is imbued from the start by an otherworldly quality. Yet the poem is as firmly rooted in the problems of the 1690s and as satirical as any of the others. These seemingly disparate elements are yoked by the quest which lies at its heart: *Aeneis* III (again like the translation as a whole) traces Dryden's personal spiritual wanderings in the 1690s, but it also never loses sight of the fact that it has a role to play within the contemporary context from which it arises.

The twofold function of the poem is apparent in its opening lines:

> When Heav'n had overturn'd the *Trojan* State,
> And *Priam*'s Throne, by too severe a Fate:
> When ruin'd *Troy* became the *Grecians* Prey,
> And *Ilium*'s lofty Tow'rs in Ashes lay:
> Warn'd by Coelestial Omens, we retreat,
> To seek in foreign Lands a happier Seat.
>
> (1–6)

Dryden again turns Vergil's political concerns into his own as he substitutes "State" and "Throne" for "res Asiae" (the power of Asia) and "Priamique . . . gentem" (Priam's race) (1). His own view of political chaos being unable to extinguish a "gens" is, of course, a key element in the translation as a whole, and his replacement of Vergil's adjective "immeritam" ("undeserving"), which is used of Priam's people, with "too severe a Fate" points to his own bewilderment over the Glorious Revolution. The notion of a town falling "Prey" to a foreign enemy, which is embedded in his third line, is interpolated and provides yet another bitter comment on England's plight. The last couplet cited here is also essentially Dryden's, and it is this that turns the focus to what will be his central concern in *Aeneis* III: finding "a happier Seat" for himself (and perhaps his fellow Jacobites). The lines are essentially more positive than Vergil's Aeneas's dubious "Diversa exsilia, et desertas quærere terras, / Auguriis agimur divum": "We are driven on by divine signs to seek distant exile and waste lands" (4–5). Dryden's use of the adjective "happy," which permeates *The Faerie Queene*, suggests somehow that the solution is not to be found in a physical realm but in a spiritual or literary one. That the "foreign Lands" are translation—and most immediately this translation—becomes clearer as his Aeneas relates the first episode of his travels.

Having sailed from Troy to Thrace, the hero explains to Dido, the Trojans made their first false stop and thwarted attempt to build a town. Here one of the first things he did was go out "to crop the Silvan Scenes, / And shade our Altar with their leafy Greens" (34–35). As he pulled up plant after plant blood came rushing from the ground until finally

> From the Womb
> Of wounded Earth, and Caverns of the Tomb,
> A Groan, as of a troubled Ghost renew'd
> My Fright. . . .

(54–57)

The mystery is solved, of course, when the voice reveals itself to be Polydore, one of Priam's sons, who was slain by the Thracian king for the wealth he was carrying and whose body it is that the Trojans are rending as they tear up the plants. Dryden's changes to this tale suggest that his own concern is in fact with storytelling itself. By replacing "green shrubbery" ("viridemque . . . sylvam") with "Silvan Scenes" (the landscape of England's lyrical past), he surely points once more to his own literary endeavors, and the altar he has in mind seems to be Apollo's (Vergil's plural "aras" have become a single "Altar" [24–25]). For, the "Womb / Of wounded Earth," which is invention, draws this tale into Dryden's own mythological framework in a way that is highlighted by its proximity to his "First Book of Ovid's *Metamorphoses*," where Deucalion's and Pyrrha's goodness causes new life to spring from the "kindly Womb" of wounded earth (see pp. 61–62 above). Just as there the source of Dryden's Jove's wrath, which is responsible for the devastation, is quite clearly English political upheaval, so here the event which leads to the wounding of earth and cries from its womb is described in clear contemporary political terms. Aeneas relates what happened when Priam sent his son Polydore to Thrace:

> Loaded with Gold, he sent his Darling, far
> From Noise and Tumults, and destructive War:
> Commited to the faithless Tyrant's Care:
> Who, when he saw the Pow'r of *Troy* decline,
> Forsook the weaker, with the strong to join:
> Broke ev'ry Bond of Nature, and of Truth;
> And murder'd, for his Wealth, the Royal Youth.
> O sacred Hunger of pernicious Gold,
> What bands of Faith can impious Lucre hold?
>
> (73–81)

Beginning with the interpolated "Darling" and "faithless Tyrant," the passage becomes distinctly Dryden's own, and the story he tells becomes evocative of that of James II, Mary II (his "Darling") and William III (the "faithless Tyrant") rather than of Priam, Polydore and the Thracian king. At its center is the same bitterness towards a world described similarly in *Amphitryon*: "Our Iron Age is grown an Age of Gold: / 'Tis who bids most; for all Men wou'd be sold" (15:302.556–57).

In a way that epitomises the process that takes place in the *Aeneis* as a whole, however, the darkness of these lines and their concern with the present are quickly dissolved into larger, timeless issues. As Dryden's Aeneas recounts the travels of the third book, he seems to be a mouthpiece for the poet himself, and the narration of the next stage of the journey, unselfconsciously and unawares, reveals the process whereby Dryden's own anger and fears give way to faith in some unfathomable divine purpose and, perhaps more emphatically, to faith in the powers of poetry. Landing next in Delos, Aeneas visits Apollo's temple and requests that the god grant "a resting place,"

> To the sad Relicks of the *Trojan* Race:
> A Seat secure, a Region of their own,
> A lasting Empire, and a happier Town.
> Where shall we fix, where shall our Labours end,
> Whom shall we follow, and what Fate attend?
> Let not my Pray'rs a doubtful Answer find,
> But in clear Auguries unveil thy Mind.
>
> (114–21)

The Aeneas here sounds like that Aeneas in *Aeneis* I, who sounds like Dryden himself as he calls Venus "Unkind and cruel" and expresses frustration that she will never "bless my Sight, but thus unknown" nor "speak [but] in Accents not [her] own" (564–67). While the requests for a "Seat secure" and a "happier Town" have a basis in Vergil, the language used is again Dryden's own, and the final entreaty for answers that are not doubtful and for "clear Auguries" seems once more to be the cry of a distraught Catholic rather than a response to Vergil's Latin. However, the same confidence in his own Deucalion-like task of searching for answers to "dark Ænigmas," that he exhibited in his *Georgics* and "The First Book of Ovid's *Metamorphoses*" (see p. 62 above), informs his version of Apollo's answer to the prayer.

Here too the changes to the Latin are slight, but the piece unmistakably Dryden's. His Apollo charges, "go seek that Mother Earth / From which your Ancestors derive their Birth," and assures them that "Childrens Children shall the Crown sustain." His Aeneas concludes, "Thus *Phoebus* did our future Fates disclose" (127–28, 132–33). Inherent in these lines is the consolation offered first by *Aeneis* I and ultimately by the translation as a whole: relief is to be found in nature and poetry. The same reminder that the laws of natural succession can mend political devastation (or the destruction of the monarchic line), which is incorporated in *Aeneis* I and (later) in "Palamon and Arcite" (see p. 121 above), surely underlies the (interpolated) image of a crown in the assurance that "Childrens Children shall the Crown sustain." Likewise, the extension of Vergil's "Hæc Phoebus" ("And so Phoebus" [99]) reveals the poet's own immovable faith in Apollo's powers. As *Aeneis* III progresses, this conviction grows ever stronger. In the process, the poem comes to encapsulate the realization achieved by the translation as a whole concerning what Myers called "the wisdom of a surrender to the tide of history" and the need to confront the future "with the cheerful sense of the unimportance of great events" (see pp. 122 above).

In the same way that he assured Congreve and Kneller in the early 1690s that they could maintain their posts and achieve at least a little glory for the nation despite working in a sterile and "Brutal" environment, Dryden now seems to set himself up, as Apollo's instrument, as an antidote to both William III and, more generally, to historical devastation. Aeneas relates how he set off to find the "promis'd Land" and, having made yet another false stop in Crete, retreated to Delos to seek Apollo's advice. There, he says, he was visited by visions of the gods, whom he "from flaming *Troy* redeem'd" and who now conveyed to him the message from Apollo concerning Anchises' mistake over the two family lines. Dryden describes the hero's reaction to the divine revelation in the following way: "I started from my Couch; a clammy Sweat / On all my Limbs, and shiv'ring Body sate. / To Heav'n I lift my Hands with pious haste" (233–35). The "pious haste" is added and is perhaps intended to highlight the difference between this Aeneas and the hard, bloody-minded soldier who is momentarily thrown by the storm in *Aeneis* I: the Aeneas who "Struck with unusual Fright," "With lifted Hands and Eyes, invokes Relief"—and then conjures up images of dismembered body parts rolling in the waves (see p. 114 above). Just as this figure almost certainly represents William III, so the one here in *Aeneis* III seems associated with Dryden himself.

Anchises now addresses him, "O Son, turmoil'd in *Trojan* Fate" (243). While this is reasonably close to Vergil's "Nate Iliacis exercite fatis" (182), it also recalls Dryden's numerous laments over his own and his fellow Jacobites' plights. As it stands in relation to the rest of the passage (which as a whole advocates patience and faith in divine purpose), it also perhaps provides a parallel to the Hind's reminder to her "son" that in his "suff'ring" he "bears no more / Than what his Sovereign bears, and what his Saviour bore": the passage that Zwicker sees as being where Dryden first makes "the bold assimilation of poet to savior."[28] More importantly, however, the association of Dryden with the Aeneas of this poem is achieved through the pronounced emphasis on Apollo as the hero's guide. This episode ends with Anchises advising Aeneas, "Now let us go, where *Phoebus* leads the way" (250). Vergil has "Cedamus Phoebo, et moniti meliora sequamur": "Let us yield to Phoebus, and at his warning follow the better path" (188). The difference is that Vergil depicts Apollo as an adviser who can guide the Trojans onto the right path of destiny, whereas Dryden portrays him as the path itself. The heightened importance acquired by the god here and elsewhere in the poem effects the same kind of sea change in *Aeneis* III as the undermining of Dido's tragic status does in *Aeneis* IV, and Dryden's own interest in this change needs no explaining. His assimilation of himself to Aeneas is reinforced by the passage which has a precedent in *The Hind and the Panther*, where Vergil had provided a basis for the Hind's assertion of faith in "What *Phoebus* from the Tripod shall disclose" (3:185.819; see p. 90 above).

As noted at the beginning of chapter three, the image created by Dryden as Aeneas describes how the priest Helenus "To *Phoebus*" led "my trembling Steps," "Full of religious Doubts, and awful dread" associates the hero with the self-portrait of the poet at the beginning of *The Hind and the Panther* (476–77; see p. 90 above). The message subsequently conveyed through the priest includes the assurance that Apollo will "Teach thee to shun the dangers of the Main, / And how at length the promis'd Shore to gain" (485–86). Different in tone from Vergil's "quo tutior hospita lustres / Æquora et Ausonio possis considere portu" ("to traverse more safely the foreign waters and find a seat in Ausonia's haven" [377–78]), this promise reinforces the connection between Dryden and Aeneas by again addressing both the poet's and the Jacobites' dilemma in the 1690s. Dryden's continued confidence in his own ability to "shun the dangers of the Main" in the 1690s and to gain "at length the promis'd Shore" is demonstrated here through the idiosyncratic nature of his poetry as he reflects again upon some of these dangers.

Immediately after Anchises has advised "Now let us go, where *Phoebus* leads the way," Aeneas and his followers are thrown off-track by the onset of a violent storm:

> The face of Heav'n is ravish'd from our Eyes,
> And in redoubl'd Peals the roaring Thunder flys.
> Cast from our Course, we wander in the Dark;
> No Stars to guide, no point of Land to mark.
>
> (260–63)

The first couplet is closer to Dryden's previous descriptions of political upheavals than to Vergil's storm, and calls to mind most readily perhaps *Astræa Redux*, where the civil wars are portrayed as having "storm'd the skies and ravish'd *Charles* from thence / As Heav'n it self is took by violence" (143–44). The second couplet recalls the first and central image of *Religio Laici*. In view of the preceding couplet and the subsequent harpy episode, it perhaps also makes the same point about the contemporary political situation that Dryden had about both faith and affairs ecclesiastical in 1682: "Thus, *anxious Thoughts in endless Circles* roul, / Without a *Centre* where to fix the *Soul*" (2:110.36–37).

As the Trojans are washed up by the storm on the shore "where the foul Harpies reign," the contemporary overlay, which shapes this section as a whole, becomes more apparent (277). Dryden had used Vergil's harpy tale in *The Hind and the Panther*, and, by alluding to that poem, the changes to the original in his translation here develop its satire. He introduces the harpies as a plague sent by a wrathful heaven:

> Monsters more fierce, offended Heav'n ne're sent
> From Hell's Abyss, for Human Punishment:
> With Virgin-faces, but with Wombs obscene,
> Foul Paunches, and with Ordure still unclean:
> With Claws for Hands, and Looks for ever lean.
>
> (280–84)

Expanding Vergil's reference to the birds as "*ira deum*" (the wrath of the gods) so as to include the notion of "offended Heav'n" and "Human Punishment," the translation presents the harpies as the kind of "Evil Spirits contending with the Good," that, immediately after his discussion in the "Discourse Concerning . . . Satire" of God's unfathomable and intermittent "Debasing and Punishing of some Nations" and "Exaltation and Temporal Reward of others," Dryden declares as essential to epic (4:20–21). There an association between such spirits and William

III is made through the substantiating example pointing to "when God Almighty suffer'd *Satan* to appear in the Holy Synod of the Angels." Here the references to "Ordure still unclean" and "Looks for ever lean" recall the description in the Hind's fable of the evil forces punishing the English in the late 1680s. In her depiction of the internal politics plaguing the "just Estate" of the "Plain good Man," the Hind compares the (Protestant) pigeons to *"Harpy's,"* who "could scent a plenteous board," who "raven'd still for more," the "more they fed" and who "grudg'd that Modicum" granted the Doves (or Roman Catholics) (3:189.960–64; 191.1001). The "stench of ordures" in her story stems from the Buzzard, who, as the California editors note, most strongly represents William of Orange and who is portrayed as "a kind of harpy" (see notes to lines 1120–94 and 1159–62). Dryden must certainly have been reflecting on his Hind's words as he went on in the *Aeneis* III passage to refer yet again to "the hungry Harpies," their "loathsome Stench" and (a few lines later) "their loathsom Ordures," and subsequent passages seem to point if not to exactly the same matters at least to the same general concerns as the Hind's tale does (294–96, 306).

When Dryden's chief harpy Celaeno demands of the Trojans "Dare you with Heav'n an impious War maintain, / And drive the Harpies from their Native Reign?" (325–26), she may well be alluding to the Test Acts as the Hind does before her; or she may be making the same kind of argument as that put forth by the equivocating Panther in the speech where she manipulates Vergil's Aeneas myth. Yet the notion of maintaining an "impious War" with heaven (which is interpolated) and the question of a "Native Reign" (the Hind had earlier pointed out that the Buzzard, whom she calls the pigeons' "Prince Elect," had fled "his Native clyme" [3:197.1221; 195.1152]) have myriad implications for England of the 1690s. Likewise, Aeneas could be either referring to the question of Anglican loyalty to the throne that is at the heart of the Hind's moral, or expressing Dryden's own general weariness when he concludes resignedly,

> Hopeless to win by War, to Pray'rs we fall:
> And on th'offended Harpies humbly call:
> And whether Gods, or Birds obscene they were,
> Our Vows for Pardon, and for Peace prefer.
>
> (339–42)

What is important here, however, is the submission to God's unfathomable purpose inherent in this conclusion to a scene charged with contemporary social and political overtones. Yet, (to reiterate the point)

Dryden's allusions to his own previous works, which permeate the piece, indicate his confidence in his poetic powers to produce "Silvan Scenes" even in the face of the "loathsom Ordures" of contemporary history—in the same way perhaps that Anne Killigrew's *"Arethusian* Stream remain[ed] unsoil'd" enabling her to produce *"Sylvan* Scenes of Herds and Flocks" when the stage was being deluged by "steaming Ordures" (65–68, 108). Whereas in the past he had himself been in part responsible, as he recognizes in the Killigrew poem, for prophaning God's "Heav'nly Gift of Poesy" (57), his emphasis now is on the transcendental nature of his poetry. This is apparent in the *ars poetica* for the times to which the last part of *Aeneis* III is devoted.

Perhaps the most important piece of advice Helenus gives Aeneas concerns the demands he must make of the Sybil when he confronts her at Cumae. The priest concludes:

> But beg the sacred Priestess to relate
> With willing Words, and not to write thy Fate.
>
> . . . .
>
> She shall direct thy Course, instruct thy Mind;
> And teach thee how the happy Shores to find.
> This is what Heav'n allows me to relate:
> Now part in Peace; pursue thy better Fate,
> And raise, by strength of Arms, the *Trojan* State.
>
> (582–83, 587–91)

As the California editors note, there is no Vergilian equivalent for the admonition "not to write thy Fate," and the line looks back to *The Hind and the Panther* where the *insanum vatem* of *Aeneis* III becomes a "mad Divineress" whose cryptic writings the dunce Martyn stumbles across. The Martyn relates the incident:

> For he concluded, once upon a time,
> He found a leaf inscrib'd with sacred rime,
> Whose antique characters did well denote
> The *Sybil's* hand of the *Cumæan* Grott:
> The mad Divineress had plainly writ,
> A time shou'd come. . . .
>
> (3:175.486–91)

What the Martyn thinks "plainly writ" is, of course and as the California editors note, "muddled." Dryden's concern here, as in the Panther's faulty argument about the Trojans' arrival in Italy, is not only with the fallibility of the written word but with the inadequacy of logic and reason (the message of *Religio Laici*). In *The Hind and the Panther*, as in the

Aeneis, he both confronts and attempts to counter such problems by employing the fabulous mode, in the belief that underneath the obscuring veils of oft-told tales lay timeless truths that could somehow be unravelled by the storytelling process itself. It is this conviction that shapes the final triplet of Helenus's speech quoted above.

By translating Vergil's Helenus's "et ingentem factis fer ad æthera Trojam" ("exalt mighty Troy to the stars by your deeds" [462]) as "raise by strength of Arms, the *Trojan* State," Dryden seems once again to be mocking the endeavors of William III's "stupid Military State" and demonstrating wherein the true power of history resides. For, lying at the center of the triplet as a prerequisite almost to the advice to "pursue thy better Fate," the injunction to "part in Peace" not only offsets the reference to arms, but by acting as buttress to the yoking of "relate," "Fate" and "State," which is the force and focus of the lines, mocks it. The notion of the arts of peace, or (Ovidian-style) storytelling as a counter to military arts and a source of national continuity (and so, in a way, the nation's Fate) is reinforced as Dryden now adopts a noticeably more literary and fabular style, which dominates the rest of the travel log. Immediately after Helenus's speech, for example, Dryden verifies the priest's warning about the instability of the written word by translating Vergil's "ivory" as "elephant"; a rendition which is just as jarring to the reader's sense of complacency and security as the same use of the same word in the much-criticized line of the introductory piece to his programmatic third *Georgic* (see p. 53 above). Aeneas describes Helenus's generous farewell gifts: "Bounteous of Treasure, he supply'd my want / With heavy Gold, and polish'd Elephant" (494–95). The sumptuousness both of the verse and the artwork it describes continues as Andromache appears and also loads Aeneas with rich gifts, which she calls "Monuments of Love" (628). The process by which the political considerations behind these lines have been undermined as the poem shifts into an unmistakably literary and aesthetically and emotionally stimulating world is highlighted in the last major episode of *Aeneis* III: the stopover in the land of the Cyclops.

Like the predictions made indirectly in *Aeneis* I, this section illustrates how the *Aeneis* anticipates not only *Fables* but trends that were products of the phenomena that led to the demise of the epic as a feasible literary mode. Brean Hammond selects as his first example of how epic seriousness gave way in the 1690s and after to " 'carnivalised' representations of the classical world in burlesque even pornographic mutations" the description of the Cyclops given by Dryden's Achaemonides here in *Aeneis* III:[29]

Bellowing his Voice, and horrid in his Hue:
Ye Gods, remove this Plague from Mortal View!

> The Joints of slaughter'd Wretches are his Food:
> And for his Wine he quaffs the streaming Blood.
> These Eyes beheld, when with his spacious Hand
> He seiz'd two Captives of our *Grecian* Band;
> Stretch'd on his Back, he dash'd against the Stones
> Their broken Bodies, and their crackling Bones:
> With spouting Blood the Purple Pavement swims,
> While the dire Glutton grinds the trembling Limbs.
>
> (814–23)

Disconcertingly, this gorey and spine-chilling tale is followed closely by a Spenserian-style triplet depicting the cyclopes as shepherds in a kind of pastoral world where Polyphemus is king:

> Like him in Caves they shut their woolly Sheep,
> Like him, their Herds on tops of Mountains keep;
> Like him, with mighty Strides, they stalk from Steep to Steep.
>
> (844–46)

The horror inherent in the *Fables*-like violence of the first piece is surely a product of the same pacifism that pervades Dryden's last (and perhaps greatest) work. Just as *Fables* is a response to pointless wars and moral uncertainties, so too the disjointed nature of this episode reflects the poet's own fragmentary world. Dryden's nostalgia for Spenserian royalist certainties is apparent in his conspicuous employment of unmistakably heroic poetic techniques and moments, yet his recognition that such a world has crumbled forever is revealed in the overwhelmingly "carnivalesque" nature of this passage and others like it. The only comfort offered is that of a retreat into a literary world where old forms and modes are still discernible and where horrific realities are diffused by Democritean laughter. The realization achieved here, in fact (again, like that achieved ultimately by the *Aeneis* as a whole and like the stance assumed consciously by *Fables*), writes large the observation made by Dryden as early as 1694 in his tribute to Kneller: "what a Play to *Virgil*'s Work wou'd be, / Such is a single Piece to History" (152–53). It is this message that shapes *Aeneis* VI.

The opening of that book describes Aeneas's first action on arriving at Cumae:

> The Pious Prince ascends the sacred Hill
> Where *Phoebus* is ador'd; and seeks the Shade,
> Which hides from sight, his venerable Maid.
> Deep in a Cave the Sibyl makes abode;
> Thence full of Fate returns, and of the God.
>
> (11–15)

Unlike Vergil, Dryden presents the entrance into Italy as an entrance into a poetic realm. Vergil describes how "pius Æneas arces quibus altus Apollo / Præsidet . . . petit": "pious Aeneas seeks the heights, where Apollo presides on high" (9–11). Although only slight changes, Dryden's "sacred Hill" and "ador'd" Phoebus alter the tone of the lines, which, especially in view of the Miltonic overtones that unfold through the rest of the book, recall the opening of *Paradise Lost*. There, of course, the poet beseeches Urania, "Sing Heav'nly Muse, that on the secret top / Of *Oreb*, or of *Sinai*, didst inspire / That Shepherd," calling upon her to aid "my adventrous Song, / That with no middle flight intends to soar / Above th' *Aonian* mount" (1:5–6, 13–5). The kind of faith that Milton placed in the powers of the muse (as he too confronted political and historical devastation) is both the buttress and the focus of Dryden's sixth book. The effect of the Miltonic overtones and the emphasis on poetry is to convert Vergil's underworld episode into a spiritual journey of which the ultimate destination is not far from Satan's recognition in *Paradise Lost*: "The mind is its own place, and in itself / Can make a Heav'n of Hell, a Hell of Heav'n."[30] This transformation, in turn, undermines the importance of the historical issues (which are no less contemporized here than elsewhere throughout the translation) in a way that reinforces *Aeneis* I and III and prepares the way for the developments that occur between *Aeneis* VII and VIII.

Dryden's own convictions concerning the nature of poetic power also dominate the opening lines in a way that accentuates from the start his own subject matter. Where Vergil describes how Aeneas "sought the vast and hidden cave of the dread Sibyl, into whom the Delian priest breathes a mighty mind and soul, unfolding future things," Dryden makes the relationship between his Apollo and "venerable Maid" decidedly sexual.[31] The prophetic powers of his Sibyl are in this way indirectly connected with his own. As illustrated in chapter 2, Dryden was consumed in the early 1690s with demonstrating that his virility as a poet had not been diminished by his old age or by attempts to "geld" his plays, and he seems to have believed that the regenerative power of his verse lay in its "manly" nature—and that the (sexual) energy permeating it derived ultimately from Apollo himself. His portrayal of the Sibyl in the next section strengthens the correlation between this poem and *Aeneis* III, while developing the suggestion latent in *Aeneis* I and III (and the translation as a whole) that a poet—specifically Dryden himself—is the most fitting hero for the 1690s. It also reflects the theory of translation and imitation embodied in the dedication.

The scene in which the reader first encounters the Sibyl trembles with sexually charged energy. Having connected the priestess here with his sibyls in *Aeneis* III and *The Hind and the Panther* by referring to her as a "mad divining Dame" (54), Dryden describes what Aeneas and Achates witness as she calls upon Apollo:

> He comes, behold the God! Thus while she said,
> (And shiv'ring at the sacred Entry staid)
> Her Colour chang'd, her Face was not the same,
> And hollow Groans from her deep Spirit came.
> Her Hair stood up; convulsive Rage possess'd
> Her trembling Limbs, and heav'd her lab'ring Breast.
> Greater than Human Kind she seem'd to look:
> And with an Accent, more than Mortal, spoke.
> Her staring Eyes with sparkling Fury rowl;
> When all the God came rushing on her Soul.
>
> (70–79)

The California editors remark that "Dryden dwells upon the consequences of divine possession described by Virgil in vv. 47–48" and that "l. 73 has no equivalent in the Latin" (6:1029.n.71–74). Where these lines do have an "equivalent" is in Dryden's (again, not Vergil's) apostrophe to the muse in *Georgics* II ("Ye sacred Muses, with whose Beauty fir'd, / My Soul is ravish'd, and my Brain inspir'd . . .") and in the dedication to *Eleanora*, where he pleads, "We, who are Priests of *Apollo*, have not the Inspiration when we please; but must wait till the God comes rushing on us, and invades us with a fury, which we are not able to resist" (3:231; see p. 62 above). As also suggested earlier, it is this belief in a divine, timeless, universal energy imparted to poets alone that led to Dryden's arguments in the dedication and elsewhere regarding spiritual commerce between ancient and modern poets and the originality of both poet and translator. In the same way that the discussion in the dedication of Raphael, Apelles, Virgil and Dryden himself bears hallmarks of the Longinian sublime, so these lines (particularly the interpolated line 73) have a parallel in Longinus's view that "il s'en void beaucoup que l'esprit d'autrui ravit hors d'eux-mesmes [des Poëtes & des Escrivains qui ont vescu devant nous], comme on dit qu'une sainte fureur saisit la Prestresse d'Apollon sur le sacré Trepié. Car on tient qu'il y a une ouverture en terre d'où sort un souffle, une vapeur tout celeste qui la remplit sur le champ d'une vertu divine, & lui fait prononcer des oracles."[32] In the face of such forces *Aeneis* VI now demonstrates, historical disasters fade in significance.

As the Sibyl prepares to tell Aeneas his future, the sexual intensity of Dryden's episode heightens:

> Strugling in vain, impatient of her Load,
> And lab'ring underneath the pond'rous God,

The more she strove to shake him from her Breast,
With more, and far superior Force he press'd:
Commands his Entrance, and without Controul,
Usurps her Organs, and inspires her Soul.

(120–25)

Like the portrayal of Venus in *Aeneis* I, the effect of this passage is to stress the divinity as well as the human aspect of the Sybil's powers. Dryden also takes care to associate them with storytelling and fable. Immediately before the description of the Sibyl, Aeneas obeys the instructions given him by Dryden's Helenus in *Aeneis* III. Having outlined his woes, he begs her,

But, oh! commit not thy prophetick Mind
To flitting Leaves, the sport of ev'ry Wind:
Lest they disperse in Air our empty Fate:
Write not, but, what the Pow'rs ordain, relate.

(116–19)

The "empty Fate" and injunction to "Write not" but "relate" are interpolated, and the hero's plea directions for the 1690s, the horrors of which are now outlined. The disasters related, however, are presented as simply another tale in a long line of tales, and, in the shadow of both the Sibyl's and Dryden's creative powers, their importance is further diminished.

The Sibyl describes the Trojans' "empty Fate":

Wars, horrid Wars I view; a field of Blood;
And *Tyber* rolling with a Purple Flood.
Simois nor *Xanthus* shall be wanting there;
A new *Achilles* shall in Arms appear:
And he, too, Goddess-born: fierce *Juno*'s Hate,
Added to hostile Force, shall urge thy Fate.
To what strange Nations shalt not thou resort,
Driv'n to sollicite Aid at ev'ry Court!
The Cause the same which *Ilium* once oppress'd,
A foreign Mistress, and a foreign Guest.

(133–42)

Dryden's language and details point to the "empty Fate" of 1690s England and the "horrid Wars" waging on the Continent. The passage as a whole conveys the same resentment as his indictment of England's bloody-minded monarch in the dedication of *Examen Poeticum* where he refers to "those ungodly Man-killers, whom we Poets, when we flatter them, call Heroes; a race of Men who can never enjoy quiet in them-

selves, 'till they have taken it from all the World" (4:374). Like that of
the "Man-killers" referred to there, the identity of the "new Achilles"
appearing "in Arms" (Dryden's addition) is unmistakable, especially in
view of the description of the semidivine hero seeking "Aid" in foreign
courts. Even the California editors (who, again, make such observations sparingly) remark of Dryden's "ev'ry Court" that the "phrase in
both Dryden and Segrais recalls the plight of exiled monarchs in the
seventeenth century and, in Dryden, specifically the Stuart monarchs"
(6:1029.n.140). The "Court" that jumps most immediately to mind is,
perhaps, the French court, yet the point about the allusion in these lines
to a recurring seventeenth-century problem is a vital one.

As he did in Jupiter's speech in *Aeneis* I, Dryden here stresses the
iterability of historical struggles. The continuation of the Stuarts' troubles is also signalled through the reference to "*Juno*'s Hate" which recalls the poet's wonder at the queen of heaven's persecution of the royal
family both in *Threnodia Augustalis* (for example) and earlier in the *Aeneis*
(see pp. 111 above). While there is a basis in Vergil for the "new Achilles" and the renewal of a "same" "Cause," these details accentuate the
notion inherent in the passage that the contemporary woes alluded to
are simply part of an ongoing historical process—or no more than another episode in a series of oft-told tales. In effect, the prophecy recognizes that history lies in the hands of its chroniclers rather than those
of any particular Achilles, and Dryden's personal confidence becomes
suddenly apparent when his voice asserts itself at the end, drowning out
the Sibyl whose conclusion is clearly his own: "But thou, secure of Soul,
unbent with Woes, / The more thy Fortune frowns, the more oppose"
(143–44). The "secur[ity] of Soul" is completely Dryden's and the couplet recalls the ending of the preface to *Don Sebastian* where he concludes his tirade against the state of literature—and politics—in
England by alluding to the Latin lines behind the translation here:

> Certainly, if a Man can ever have a reason to set a value on himself, 'tis
> when his ungenerous Enemies are taking the advantage of the Times upon
> him, to ruin him in his reputation. And therefore for once, I will make bold
> to take the Counsel of my Old Master *Virgil. Tu, ne cede malis; sed, contra,*
> *audentior ito.* (15:72)

The same self-assurance and profession of faith in poetry at this point
in *Aeneis* VI also again establishes a contrast between Dryden and William III as potential heroes for the 1690s—and in so doing cushions the
opening of *Aeneis* VII.

While the Aeneas who tells the Sibyl to "Write not" but "relate" is
unmistakably associated with the poet himself, the one who commands

her just before this to reveal the "Event of things in dark Futurity" becomes, momentarily, the kind of William III figure that is satirized throughout the translation. That Aeneas demands,

> Give me, what Heav'n has promis'd to my Fate,
> To conquer and command the *Latian* State:
> To fix my wand'ring Gods; and find a place
> For the long Exiles of the *Trojan* Race.
>
> (101–5)

The lines obviously both reinforce and are reinforced by the subsequent passage concerning "horrid Wars." Zwicker remarks on their contemporary overtones:

> Virgil's Aeneas begs shelter and settlement; he specifically rejects empire. Dryden's Aeneas would "conquer and command the *Latian* State." Virgil's qualifications are ignored, and the whole passage is rendered in a language charged with the political currents of the 1690s. These are not random turns in the translation, but a consistent way of seeing Aeneas's entry as conquest and violation, not the gift of a benign heaven, but the will of unsearchable fate.[33]

Yet the strong presence of Dryden as an alternative Aeneas throughout this section and the promise offered by his poetic powers undermine the threat posed by such a figure. The resulting emphasis on the timeless rather than the historical is in fact reinforced by the Satanic element in the request. This Aeneas's "wand'ring Gods" have a counterpart in the "wandring Gods" that help make up Satan's pandemonium in *Paradise Lost*,[34] and the detail strengthens the presentation of the would-be conqueror and his wars as "Evil Spirits contending with the Good." It is Miltonic overtones and his own faith that add the final overwhelming argument to Dryden's rendition of the Sibyl's prophecy.

As the Sibyl comes to the end of her speech, the poet concludes:

> Th' ambiguous God, who rul'd her lab'ring Breast,
> In these mysterious Words his Mind exprest:
> Some Truths reveal'd, in Terms involv'd the rest.
>
> (150–52)

The Roman Catholic overtones are unmistakable, and Dryden's own resignation to what Zwicker calls the "will of unsearchable fate" becomes apparent yet again as Aeneas responds to the Sibyl's speech:

> Inur'd to suffer, and resolv'd to dare,
> The Fates, without my Pow'r, shall be without my Care.

> This let me crave, since near your Grove the Road
> To Hell lies open, and the dark Abode,
> Which *Acheron* surrounds, th' innavigable Flood:
> Conduct me thro' the Regions void of Light,
> And lead me longing to my Father's sight.
>
> (157–63)[35]

Dryden's lines correspond to the sentiment expressed ultimately by *The Hind and the Panther* and his *Life of St. Francis Xavier*; Vergil, by contrast, stresses toil not suffering: "Hic opus, hic labor est" ("This is the task, this the toil" [129]). Aeneas's expression of Christian patience and recognition of the need for individual effort is reinforced, of course, by his Miltonic statement regarding the road to hell, and Dryden's own commitment to the Christian faith inherent in the last couplet rests in its proximity to the central argument about faith in *Religio Laici*. Here, too, the notion of individual choice in the journey that could lead to the "Father's sight" is highlighted by the simultaneous proximity and distance of Aeneas's plea to Satan's address to "*Chaos* and *ancient Night*": "Alone, and without guide, half lost, I seek / What readiest path leads where your gloomie bounds / Confine with Heav'n."[36] The philosophy worked out in this first part of *Aeneis* VI is applied to and developed in the actual trip to hell that follows.

Unsurprisingly, Dryden uses Aeneas's sightseeing tour through hell's region of the damned to brandish once more his satirical sword. He seizes first upon Vergil's Salmoneus:

> *Salmoneus*, suff'ring cruel Pains, I found,
> For emulating *Jove*; the ratling Sound
> Of Mimick Thunder, and the glitt'ring Blaze
> Of pointed Lightnings, and their forky Rays.
> Through *Elis*, and the *Grecian* Towns he flew:
> Th'audacious Wretch four fiery Coursers drew:
> He wav'd a Torch aloft, and, madly vain,
> Sought Godlike Worship from a Servile Train.
>
> (788–95)

In *Astræa Redux*, the Salmoneus myth is alluded to in an attack on the Puritans' zeal; in *The Medall*, Dryden's "Satyre against Sedition," the Vergilian lines behind the first couplet translated above are used as an epigraph. Here Dryden's language and additions evoke the problems that plagued England throughout the seventeenth century, and the picture strongly recalls both *The Medall* and *Absalom and Achitophel* and their indictment of rabble-rousing politics. As Aeneas goes on, he encounters figures who clearly belong to recent English history. Zwicker draws attention to the most daring and caustic passage:

> Then they, who Brothers better Claim disown,
> Expel their Parents, and usurp the Throne;
> Defraud their Clients, and to Lucre sold,
> Sit brooding on unprofitable Gold:
> Who dare not give, and ev'n refuse to lend
> To their poor Kindred, or a wanting Friend:
> Vast is the Throng of these.
>
> (824–30)

From its Royalist and Jacobite horror to the element of self-pity on the part of the impoverished poet, the piece fortifies the recasting of Vergil's hell as England's and, more specifically, Dryden's own.[37] Yet the Elysium which the reader next enters, as Aeneas seeks out his father, is equally English and equally Drydenian, and not only offers relief once more from the debaucheries of history but again renders them insignificant.

This is the scene that Dryden's Aeneas views as he comes to the "long extended Plains of Pleasure" and the "blissful Seats of Happy Souls":

> Some, in Heroick Verse, divinely sing;
> Others in artful Measures lead the ring.
> The *Thracian* Bard, surrounded by the rest,
> There stands conspicuous in his flowing Vest.
> His flying Fingers, and harmonious Quill,
> Strike sev'n distinguish'd Notes, and sev'n at once they fill.
> Here found they *Teucer's* old Heroick Race;
> Born better times and happier Years to grace.
>
> (875–82)

The emphasis on "Heroick Verse" is Dryden's, and Vergil's portrait of the Thracian bard is heightened and extended as the careful artistry of the Latin verse is transformed into Dryden's own in a way that points once again to the kinship shared by the two poets. The strong consciousness here that the world of heroic verse and heroic ancestry are indistinguishable has a parallel in Dryden's reflection on Kneller's portrait of Shakespeare in his tribute to the painter in 1694. Claiming there to be "Proud to be less; but of his Godlike Race," Dryden declares, "His Soul Inspires me, while thy Praise I write, / And I like *Teucer*, under *Ajax* Fight" (76–78). His own place in the scene described above is reflected in the nostalgic lament for a lost world, which could be "grace[d]" (an interpolation) by poets and heroes. Yet, like the *Aeneis*

as a whole, Dryden's Elysium is itself proof of the inexpungeability of
the poetic line that can be traced to Vergil and beyond him to Homer
and Apollo, and it offers Dryden's own audience the kinds of pleasures
Vergil and Homer did theirs.

The appearance next of "Divine *Musæus*" argues for the continuation
of his presence in England. Having been called upon by the Sibyl for
directions, Dryden's "Sacred Poet" replies,

> In no fix'd place the Happy Souls reside.
> In Groves we live; and lye on mossy Beds
> By Crystal Streams, that murmur through the Meads.
>
> (912–15)

This is the landscape of the mind and of poetry. It has an equivalent in
the inlet where the Trojans land in *Aeneis* I, and its sanctity is accentuated not only by Dryden's insistence on Musæus' divinity but by its
proximity (both in its physicality and its role in Dryden's poem) to Milton's refreshing and fortifying retreat described at the beginning of the
third book of *Paradise Lost*:

> Yet not the more
> Cease I to wander where the Muses haunt
> Cleer Spring, or shadie Grove, or Sunnie Hill,
> Smit with the love of sacred Song; but chief
> Thee *Sion* and the flowrie Brooks beneath,
> That wash thy hallowd feet, and warbling flow.[38]

The power and impact of this episode provide a stabilizing center not
only for *Aeneis* VI but for the translation as a whole, and its function
with regard to the historical concerns that permeate the work is accentuated by its effect on the final section of the poem.

As is to be expected by this point in the *Aeneis*, Vergil's glorification
of history in his parade of heroes is completely undercut by Dryden,
who, instead, again reviews English history with a mixture of sorrow
and cynicism. Another direct attack on the 1690s is made when he takes
the opportunity to turn Vergil's relation of the disasters that must be
endured into an attack on a "Daughter's Husband [who] arms his Eastern Friends," while Anchises' subsequent plea, "Embrace again, my
Sons, be Foes no more: / Nor stain your Country with her Childrens
Gore" reiterates the entreaties in *Britannia Rediviva* and *Georgics* I to "let
the Blood already spilt, atone / For . . . past Crimes." However, as he
comes to the climax of Anchises' speech, the historical issues give way
to the message that lies at the heart of the *Aeneis*. As he did with Jove's
speech in *Aeneis* I, Dryden turns Vergil's emphasis on Rome's glory into

a comment on the vanity and ephemeracy of both historical disaster and accomplishment and earthly woes and honors:

> But, *Rome*, 'tis thine alone, with awful sway,
> To rule Mankind; and make the World obey;
> Disposing Peace, and War, thy own Majestick Way.
> To tame the Proud, the fetter'd Slave to free;
> These are Imperial Arts, and worthy thee.
>
> (1173–77)

Probably the proudest, most nationalistic moment in Vergil's Aeneid, the passage here, as Weinbrot observes, is decidedly "antiseptic."[39] In view of the contemporary framework just established through references to the destructive continental wars, it is also intensely ironic: the numerous recent ignominious defeats and hardships suffered by England would surely not be registered by any English subject as evidence of the nation's "Majestick" sway over the world. The prophecy is further undermined by the subsequent portrait of Marcellus, which both recalls Dryden's depiction of England as a new Rome in his poetry of 1660–1688 and recognizes the disintegration of that promise.

Vergil's moving portrayal of the ill-fated prince becomes Dryden's just-as-moving lament for the last hope of the Stuarts:

> This Youth (the blissful Vision of a day)
> Shall just be shown on Earth, and snatch'd away.
> The Gods too high had rais'd the *Roman* State;
> Were but their Gifts as permanent as great.
>
> . . . .
>
> No Youth shall equal hopes of Glory give:
> No Youth afford so great a Cause to grieve.
>
> (1202–5, 1210–11)

At once messianic and reminiscent of the poet's reaction to the unfounded rumors about the baby prince's death in *Britannia Rediviva*, this seems to be a cry of despair over the removal of the Prince of Wales from England and his ever-decreasing chances of being restored—like Charles II, perhaps—as England's "blissful Vision." Dryden's voice is strong, and, while his sorrow and bitterness are evident, there is also again a resignation to some unfathomable divine purpose. This is reinforced not only by the conviction he has already displayed in the divine powers of poetry but by the extension in this final section of the kind of consolation that is offered ultimately by the translation as a whole.

In the way anticipated in *Aeneis* I, emphasis on "Name" ousts Vergil's focus on historical glory and disaster as Dryden renders English Vergil's "long Procession of his Progeny," the sheer recurrence of the word drawing attention to it (1024). The climax of Dryden's own procession—indeed of the book—comes after the entrance of Romulus, who is described as "born to restore / The Crown that once his injur'd Grandsire wore" (1055–56). Just as attention is in this way again drawn to the devastations of English history, the scene lifts itself beyond such miseries. Dryden's Anchises describes the glories of Rome in a way that transforms Vergil's historical city:

> *Rome* whose ascending Tow'rs shall Heav'n invade;
> Involving Earth and Ocean in her Shade:
> High as the Mother of the Gods in place;
> And proud, like her, of an Immortal Race.
>
> (1065–68)

This Rome is unquestionably the immortal Roman church, and the "Mother of the Gods" surely Dryden's Hind. Juxtaposed with the reminder of seventeenth-century English toils, the vision in fact reiterates the faith inherent in the opening of *The Hind and the Panther*, where the poet reflects upon the Hind's "half humane, half divine" line:

> Their earthly mold obnoxious was to fate,
> Th' immortal part assum'd immortal state.
> Of these a slaughtered army lay in bloud,
> Extended o'er the *Caledonian* wood.
>
> (3:123.10–14)

The conviction shared by these two strategic passages—written a decade apart—demonstrate Dryden's unyielding commitment to the last both to the Stuarts and to his faith: a commitment, which, along with the reminder of the glory of the real immortal Rome, provides the foundation that holds the poem together.

Aeneis VI, then, provides a thematic as well as a physical center to the translation. Reinforcing and consolidating the themes, concerns and developments anticipated in *Aeneis* I, it looks forward as well to the second part of the translation and its inexorable movement toward a mode that would be refined in *Fables* and—by the hands of others—in the eighteenth century. While as fragmentary and discontinuous as the other books, the poem also acts perhaps as the lodestone around which the other fragments can revolve, and, in its distance from its Vergilian original, marks the individuality and self-sufficiency of Dryden's own epic. Essentially Ovidian in tone and function, though strongly and nostalgically aware of its Spenserian and Vergilian ancestry, Dryden's *Aeneis* places itself among the immortal songs of divine bards as it adds another English chapter to a universal *carmen perpetuum*.

Epilogue: Time To Begin Anew

Since finally Dryden offered no conclusions it seem inappropriate to do so here. Perhaps, then, the best point of departure in attempting some kind of closure is again the telling last lines of *The Secular Masque*:

> All, all of a piece throughout;
> Thy Chase had a Beast in View;
> Thy Wars brought nothing about;
> Thy Lover were all Untrue.
> 'Tis well an Old Age is out,
> And time to begin a New.
>
> (16: 273.86–91)

As the arguments above have attempted to demonstrate, the process which led Dryden reluctantly but ultimately to this viewpoint is a long and complicated one, and his submission to historical and literary open-endedness the completion of a difficult battle between history and ideology. The crises and struggles manifested in his *Vergil* did not, of course arise overnight—the night of James II's ignominious flight from London. The historical, political and generic issues embedded in the translation all have roots that go at least as deep as Charles II's troubled reign, if not to the Interregnum or further back into Stuart history. Yet the Glorious Revolution and the attendant financial revolutions in the mid-1690s changed forever relationships between monarch and subject, subject and subject, author and reader, thereby rendering problematic time-honored myths of patriarchal kingship and a hierarchical universe. As the nation's leading poet, satirist and playwright—national spokesperson in other words—Dryden was attuned from first to last to even the most subtle changes in the social and political climate and to audience and reader demands; his *Georgics* and *Aeneis* are therefore invaluable as maps of a crossroads in English literature and culture, and their neglect by scholars and teachers a lacuna in Restoration and eighteenth-century studies. The ultimate goal here, accordingly, is to point out that while Dryden's *Vergil* was unable to offer 1690s readers the kind of advice the poet perhaps initially thought possible, this watershed work can offer a twenty-first-century audience new insights into

221

the moods, debates and crises of an age of transition and the impact of
cultural uncertainties on literary forms and notions of genre.

Unquestionably, one of the major reasons why commentators on the
period and its literature charge right by Dryden's final, crucial works is
an inability to take translation seriously as a literary mode — this despite
emphasis in recent decades on so-called marginal writers and works.
Because of the perceived greater degree of authorial creativity and in-
dependence in Dryden's *Fables*, that work has received some attention,
but not much. As any catalogue of books published in the Restoration
and eighteenth century will reveal, however, translation was a major
not a marginal literary mode. In any case, when the field of study is an
age so glibly referred to as neoclassical, the importance of the frequency
and ways in which classical authors especially are translated, along with
the company they kept in the anthologies where they are often revived,
should not even need pointing out.

When it comes to the Ancients/Moderns debates and generic changes
and developments between the seventeenth and eighteenth centuries in
particular, translation provides a mine of information and insights.
Committed equally to the present and to the past, translation (as this
study of Dryden's *Vergil* has demonstrated) embodies a tension between
veneration for works somehow more sacred and endowed with timeless
truths, and validation of the demands of contemporary readers. From,
say, Marvell and Behn through, say, Fielding and Smollett, authors feel
the pressure of a still vibrant classical heritage even as they weave their
works into the politics and issues of the day. Examination both of translations produced at the same time as so-called original works and of
changing attitudes towards and uses of the classical world, especially
Homer and Vergil, can surely therefore shed important light on changing trends in literature and genre. In the ongoing discussion about the
origins or emergence of the novel especially, translation, as a meeting
point of the past and present, must offer an invaluable map in the search
for the paths whereby classical dominance and rigid literary forms lead
inexorably towards emphasis on native literary traditions and more
openended, personal, or "novelistic" literary forms. In other words,
read alongside literature that has become canonical, translation can
broaden and alter perceptions and understanding not merely of seventeenth and eighteenth century literature but of questions of genre and
the relationship between genre and its extra-literary contexts. As Dryden intended, then, the message of his *Vergil*, and of his late works in
general, is a timeless one, for the need to take stock of the past and to
begin anew is as relevant for an audience in the shadow of the twenty-
first century as it was for an audience facing the eighteenth century.

Notes

Introduction: All of a Piece

1. Swift, *Tale of a Tub*, 158.

2. Brean Hammond, *Professional Imaginative Writing*, 127.

3. The most significant work has been done by David Bywaters, William Frost, Anne Barbeau Gardiner, Earl Miner, Cedric D. Reverand II, Judith Sloman, James A. Winn and Steven N. Zwicker.

4. Dryden, *Works of John Dryden*, 4:21. All subsequent references to Dryden (except to *Fables* and letters) are to this edition and are cited parenthetically. Prose references are to volume and page numbers; drama references are to volume, page and line numbers; poetry references are to line numbers only, except in the case of *The Hind and the Panther*.

5. McKeon, *Origins of the English Novel*, 76.

6. Joseph Levine, *Battle of the Books*, 274–75.

7. Popkin, *Third Force*, 335.

8. Ibid., 335–37.

9. Cedric Reverand asserts that one "of Dryden's principal concerns in *Fables* is the heroic code," and he indicates that the poet's "experience in dealing with a changed and changing world" is the reason for the numerous instances of antiheroism, many of which he describes in his second chapter. See Reverand, *Dryden's Final Poetic Mode*, 5, 11. My chapters 3–5 will demonstrate how Dryden's profound questioning and obsessive probing of the heroic in his *Virgil* sets the mode for his *Fables*.

10. Judith Sloman observes that the "*Aeneis* is actually more disturbing than Dryden's satires for being an epic invaded by the psychology of satire." See Sloman, *Poetics of Translation*, 129.

11. McKeon, *Origins of the English Novel*, 88.

12. Brean Hammond, *Professional Imaginative Writing*, 112.

13. Ibid., 126.

14. Ibid., 112. These changes did not occur overnight, of course. In her study of Restoration drama, Susan Staves demonstrates how changing views of natural law throughout the second half of the seventeenth century affected generic stability and the presentation of the hero in drama. As she notes, "Partly because political experience had made a law dependent on God's will seem so untrustworthy and partly because nature itself began to feel less divine, less hierarchical, and less teleological, the later seventeenth century looked for a more secular idea of natural law. Philosophers tried to show how natural law could exist independently of the will of God and generally attacked the utopian character of the older tradition." See Staves, *Players' Scepters*, 313–14.

15. Indeed, placed in this way, within the social and political contexts of the late seventeenth and early eighteenth centuries, Hammond's claims support John Richetti's point that "[w]hat McKeon labels 'a crisis of categorical instability' that provokes the

223

eighteenth-century novel is . . . specifically the recognition in narrative by writers that their prevailing generic confusion about how to write a narrative is directly related to social-institutional (i.e., ideological) uncertainty." See Richetti, "Reply to David Richter," 207. The argument that the mock-heroic functions as a transitional point between the demise of one dominant literary mode (the heroic) and the establishment of another (the novel)—its allegiance, in other words, to an old world and a new—would also verify Hunter's observation that "[n]ovelists learned their craft in a world vibrant with a sense of loss, and they wrote for readers who, however restless about the present and ambitious about the future, needed to feel firmly grounded against uncertainty and flux." See Hunter, *Before Novels*, 138.

16. McKeon, *Origins of the English Novel*, 229.

17. Pocock, *Virtue, Commerce, and History*, especially chapter 5.

18. McKeon, *Origins of the English Novel*, 53.

19. Ibid., 214.

20. Ibid., 36.

21. Bakhtin, "Epic and Novel," 16.

22. Ibid., 13.

23. Ibid., 18.

24. Ibid., 13.

25. Probably the best discussion of the ways in which William III's European wars plunged England into political, social and economic upheaval is Robert Markley's essay on scarcity in the 1690s. See Markley, " 'Credit Exhausted.' "

26. Labelling *Fables* Dryden's "final poetic mode," Reverand too sees this new mode and the elusiveness of *Fables* as the product of Dryden's "experience in dealing with a changed and changing world, where the various systems of values he had long cherished are now crumbling, and he himself is caught in the trap of trying to reconcile the irreconcilable" (see Reverand, *Dryden's Final Poetic Mode*, 5).

27. Swift, *Tale of a Tub*, 157.

28. Barbara Benedict demonstrates how the same process is an integral part of the miscellanies of the period. The "emphasis on variety" in these works, she argues, "inscribes *différance* in the Derridean sense: a dislocation of meaning that traces value in dynamic comparison, contrast, and differentiation between similar or opposing forms and messages." See Benedict, *Making the Modern Reader*, 12.

29. McKeon spotlights the historical issue when he claims that in the seventeenth century "the assertion of historical truth aims to serve the end of inculcating Christian faith. In the early novels it will seek to aid the cause of teaching moral truth" (*Origins of the English Novel*, 89).

30. William J. Cameron, for example, sees the translation as pro-Williamite. See "John Dryden's Jacobitism." In his discussion of Dryden's *Essay of Dramatick Poesie*, Howard Weinbrot points out that Dryden's conclusions are not skeptical even if his methods are. This is true of all Dryden wrote before 1688, but of nothing he wrote after the Revolution. See Weinbrot, *Britannia's Issue*, 190.

31. Dryden, *Poems of John Dryden*, ed. Kinsley, 670–72. All subsequent references to *Fables* (poems and preface) are to this volume and are cited parenthetically as "Kinsley." References are to page numbers in the case of the preface, and to line numbers in the case of the poems.

32. Dryden, *Letters of John Dryden*, ed. Ward, 86. All subsequent references to Dryden's letters are to this edition and are cited parenthetically.

33. Dustin Griffin's discussion of Dryden's relationship to and attitude toward his patrons throughout his career highlights the poet's commitment to the last to the traditional seventeenth-century patronage system. In his efforts to demonstrate that patron-

age continued to thrive in the late-seventeenth and early-eighteenth centuries, Griffin attributes Dryden's continual efforts to "redefine his position in the patronage system" to his anomalous position within that system, not to the decline of the system itself—"it would last for another century" he claims. While Griffin argues in general for the ongoing "cultural authority" of a traditional, aristocratic patron class, he does illustrate the complexity and ambiguity of the patronage system in the eighteenth century and recognizes that "high culture became increasingly accessible to (and paid for by) large numbers of people, though in new cultural forms—subscription concerts, public exhibition of paintings, landscaped pleasure grounds." He also points to the 1690s as a crucial moment: the "so called 'financial revolution' and 'administrative revolution' concentrated greater power and resources in the hands of the crown (pensions and places) to reward their friends and promote their political programs in the emerging press." See Griffin, *Literary Patronage*, 82–83, 9–10, 6.

34. The echoes from numerous English, French and Classical poets in the translation will be illustrated throughout this study. The California editors (*Works of John Dryden*) point out that "During his Virgilian years . . . Dryden worked from a library full of Latin editions of Virgil's works and of sixteenth- and seventeenth-century Virgil translations into English, French and Italian." They also observe that he may have had access to "the work of at least eight or nine recent or fairly recent editors" (4:859).

35. See Losnes, "Dryden's *Æneis* and the Delphin *Virgil*, " 119. Losnes discusses the different editions available to Dryden and other translators.

36. Dryden, *Poetical Works of Dryden*, 1037.

CHAPTER 1: ON EQUAL TERMS WITH ANCIENT WIT ENGAGING

1. [William Benson,] *Virgil's Husbandry*, 1724, i–ii. References are distinguished from Benson's 1725 translation by date.

2. Milbourne, *Notes*, 105.

3. Ibid., 106, 108.

4. Arguing that by "the middle of the seventeenth century 'georgic economics' consistently bound the expansive aims of the individual to a celebratory vision of national achievement," Andrew McRae points out how Spenser's use of georgic in his *Faerie Queene* equates the national importance of poet and worker of the land. "In a thematic strain crucial to the poem as a whole," he observes, "Spenser infuses into the courtly ideal a sense of the value of labour as a force for individual and national honour. The activities of knight and poet symbolically collapse into the labours of the ploughman." See McRae, *God Speed the Plough*, 200, 201.

5. Note the link between divine husband and husbandman in Scripture: in Isaiah 5, for example.

6. Sessions, "Spenser's Georgics," 204.

7. Spenser, "October Song," *Poetical Works of Edmund Spenser*, ed. Selincourt, 96. All references to *The Shepheardes Calender* are to this volume.

8. The California editors point out that though "dated 1693, the translation appeared in the fall of 1692 and was advertised in the *London Gazette* for 24–27 October" (4:513).

9. Benjamin, "Task of the Translator," 71.

10. Sessions, "Spenser's Georgics," 203.

11. Ross, *Virgil's Elements*, 14.

12. Andrew McRae's discussion of the georgic and the pastoral in sixteenth and seventeenth- century England highlights how issues of the land and husbandry were

integral to English politics, economics and culture. In demonstrating how these fundamental issues were manifested in literature, McRae also observes that the "cultural significance" of those who wrote about the land and care of the land is "attested by their
remarkable popularity." "In the reign that fostered the genius of Sidney and Spenser,"
he notes, Tusser's *Five Hundred Points of Good Husbandry* "was the biggest selling book of
poetry" (see *God Speed the Plough*, 207).

13. Benjamin, "Task of the Translator," 72, 71.

14. Ibid., 73, 74.

15. At the beginning of his study of eighteenth-century imitations and translations,
Weinbrot claims that the "concept of general nature, a commonplace during the Restoration and eighteenth century, was one part of the matrix of Imitation. If the sins and
sinners of Augustan Rome are similar to the sins and sinners of 'Augustan' London,
then certainly the terms of castigation must be similar. The belief in general nature is
found in classical literature as well, and is exemplified in Juvenal's well-known first
satire: 'To these ways of ours posterity will have nothing to add; our children will do
the same things, and desire the same things that we do.' " Weinbrot also outlines the
"demand for modernization of 'dress' " that "soon became entrenched" as the theory of
"free translation" developed. See Weinbrot, *Formal Strain*, 2, 19.

16. Benjamin, "Task of the Translator," 75, 77.

17. *Religio Laici*, for example, ends with the comforting thought, "while from *Sacred
Truth* I do not swerve, / *Tom Sternhold's*, or *Tom Sha— —ll's Rhimes* will serve" (455–56).
See Sloman, *Poetics of Translation*, 16.

18. Both Emrys Jones and Paul Hammond point to Dryden's marriage of the sacred
and the aesthetic as he employs translation to commune with the souls of classical poets.
Jones remarks that in his translation of the atheistic Lucretius (1683), Dryden everywhere speaks with the same "unqualified urgency and sincerity—a religious sincerity"
that he does in *Religio Laici*. The "affinity" between Dryden's Lucretian translation and
his *Religio Laici* and *The Hind and the Panther*, Jones argues, is that they "are all about
matters of urgent import; they all have a bearing on man's stance with regard to ultimate reality." See Emrys Jones, " 'Perpetual Torrent,' " 50. Paul Hammond likewise
notes that "Dryden was one of those writers who could not confine themselves to a
Christian vocabulary when pondering life's larger questions." Hammond focuses especially on Dryden's reliance on classical poets to show how life is "often experienced as
a tragedy, a perception which cannot be spirited away by political optimism or Christian hope." Of Dryden's *Vergil*, Hammond notes that "both in the *Georgics* and in the
Aeneid," Dryden found a poetry which is "conscious of man's dependence on the powers
above him." See Paul Hammond, "Dryden's Philosophy of Fortune," 769, 772, 777.

19. Benjamin, "Task of the Translator," 78.

20. Ibid., 78.

21. See Lord, " 'Absalom and Achitophel,' " 159.

22. Dryden is not, however, as Miner proposes, simply "follow[ing] Virgil through
the *Georgics* with delight and the same gentlemanly knowledge of the sky, fields and
fold" (a statement which would have enraged William Benson). See Miner, *Dryden's
Poetry*, 173–74.

23. Zwicker, "Paradoxes of Tender Conscience," 863.

24. Zwicker argues that this happens at that "embarrassing moment in part 3 when
the masks seem inadvertantly to drop and the poet emerges in an unfamiliar voice to
claim 'That suff'ring from ill tongues he bears no more / Than what his Sovereign bears,
and what his Saviour bore' (2, 511, 304–5)." He points out that there is "throughout
the Hind's discourse, a political argument, an alignment of poet and monarch, a suggestion of protection from above." Here, he says, the "couplet argues that in his scandal

and suffering the poet bears no more contumely than James and Christ." See Zwicker, *Politics and Language*, 137.

25. In the prefatory address "To the Reader," Dryden looks for authority for his two satiric "fables" to "the times of *Boccace* and *Chawcer* on the one side, and . . . those of the Reformation on the other" (3:122).

26. Spinoza, *Chief Works of Benedict de Spinoza*, 19.

27. Ibid., 36.

28. Sloman points out that in the preface to *Fables* Dryden "separates the line of Chaucer, Spenser and Milton from the inferior one of Farifax and Waller." For, Dryden's "poetic community," she says, "seems to be modelled on Dante's hierarchically ordered circles of the blessed in paradise. There are unequal degrees of poetic intensity, although every poet revolves in heaven" (see *Poetics of Translation*, 16).

29. Quotations from the third *Georgic* in this chapter only are from the 1694 text, printed in volume 4 of the California Dryden; citations in other chapters come from the 1697 text, printed in volume 5.

30. Vergil, *P. Virgilii Maronis Opera*, 1–2. All Vergil citations are from this Delphin edition. J. McG. Bottkol discusses Dryden's use of various Latin texts but heavy reliance on the Delphin Vergil. He highlights several examples of Dryden's use of Ruæus's notes. See Bottkol, "Dryden's Latin Scholarship." Arvid Losnes argues for Dryden's use of the second London (1682) edition of the text, first published in Paris in 1675. See note 3 of the introduction. All translations, unless otherwise stated, are my own.

31. Maitland, *Works of Virgil*, 1–3. Lauderdale composed his translation at the same time as Dryden wrote his, and the two poets compared manuscripts. Lauderdale's translation was published posthumously by his family, who ignored his marginal notes, and in some places where the translations are similar it is impossible to know who influenced whom. See Boddy, "Dryden-Lauderdale Relationships."

32. Gardiner suggests that "May Day" was written in 1691 "in the hope of stirring up support in case of an actual landing of James and his troops on English soil" (49). She compares this loyalist poem, which is in Yale's Osborn collection ("A Collection of Loyal Poems, Satyrs and Lampoons"), with the shorter version: "The Lady's Song," printed in 1704 after Dryden's death. See Gardiner, "Jacobite Song by John Dryden."

33. Contrast Lauderdale's annotative translation: "You great Apollo from Thessalian Floods, / And Pan, who rules from Lycean Groves and Woods" (3–4).

34. Miner, "On Reading Dryden," in Miner, ed., *John Dryden*, 19. Dryden almost certainly had himself in mind in his translation of Juvenal's third satire, where he expanded Juvenal's complaint to lament, "Nor Place, nor Persons now are Sacred held, / From their own Grove the Muses are expell'd" (27–28).

35. Stephen Orgel discusses the development and political significance of the masque in the reigns of James I and Charles I. In *Pan's Anniversarie: Or, The Shepherds Holy-Day* (1620), for example, James I is presented as "Great *Pan*, the Father of our peace, and pleasure." See Orgel, *Illusion of Power*, 52. See also Jonson, *Ben Jonson*, 255. James I also presented himself as "Royall Pan" in his poem on Prince Charles' trip to Spain to woo the Spanish Infanta. See Craigie, ed., *Poems of King James VI of Scotland*, 2:192–93.

36. Cf. *Absalom and Achitophel*: "Yet of that Fate Propitiously Enclind, / Had rais'd my Birth, or had debas'd my Mind" (363–64) and "To Sir Godfrey Kneller": "Sure some propitious Planet then did Smile, / When first you [Kneller] were conducted to this Isle" (133–35).

37. May, trans., *Virgil's Georgicks*, 3. All subsequent references to May are to this edition.

38. Milton, *Poetical Works*, 1:14–17, 1, 8. All subsequent references to *Paradise Lost* and *Paradise Regained* are to this edition and are cited by book and line numbers.

39. Winn notes Dryden's "unmistakable" identification with Umbricius, remarking that details like "'so Base a Government' have no basis at all in the Latin, but an obvious base in Dryden's life since the Revolution." See Winn, *Dryden and His World*, 458.

40. It is also a central issue in "To Sir Godfrey Kneller."

41. See Winn, *Dryden and His World*, 434.

42. Sloman, *Poetics of Translation*, 14.

43. Ibid., 14

44. Winn, *Dryden and His World*, 490.

45. Milbourne, *Notes*, 175.

46. Winn's chapter on 1687–1694 (*Dryden and his World*, 428–70) provides a full discussion of Dryden's bitterness and hardships under a government which "wou'd have continu'd me what I was, if I cou'd have compl'd with the Termes which were offer'd me" (434). See especially 460 for Dryden's "irritation at seeing 'Wits of the Second Order' (IV, 364) elevated to his old places" (463).

47. Milbourne, *Notes*, 176.

48. Sotheby's translation (1800). See Sotheby, trans., *Georgics of Virgil*, 119.

49. Milbourne, *Notes*, 176.

50. Gardiner discusses Dryden's similar concerns and equally oblique mode of comment in *Love Triumphant* (1693). She points out that "Jacobites accused William, after 1688, of sacrificing English welfare to that of foreigners: of maintaining foreign mercenaries in England and in Flanders at a higher standard of living than the starving native troops, of placing foreigners in command of native troops with disastrous results, and of bringing about famine in England by the exporting of food to foreigners" (155). Gardiner's convincing and well-documented article lists several Jacobite pamphlets and documents which illustrate all aspects of Jacobite discontent highlighted here. See Gardiner, "John Dryden's *Love Triumphant*," 155.

51. While it is uncertain if *Georgics* III was in fact completed by the victory of 1692, Dryden would certainly have had time to make changes before its publication in 1694 if he had so desired.

52. Cobb, *Clavis Virgiliana*.

53. Ibid., 126. Weinbrot discusses the diversity and frequency of discussions of Octavian/Augustus in the eighteenth century. His fourth chapter, " 'Let Horace blush, and Virgil too': The Degradation of the Augustan Poets," considers those whose views concur with Cobb's. See Weinbrot, *Augustus Caesar in "Augustan England."*

54. In a way, then, he also anticipates the image of "hunter-hunted," which, as Rachel Miller argues, pervades *Fables* "as a direct reference to the violation of the Stuart succession." See Miller, "Regal Hunting," 184.

55. Sloman points to Dryden's special interest in the navy and his concern for it in William's reign. See *Poetics of Translation*, 133.

56. [Anderton,] *Remarks upon the Present Confederacy*, 8.

57. Muley-Moloch (*Don Sebastian*), Jove (*Amphitryon*) and Veramond (*Love Triumphant*) are all particularly notable as usurping tyrants who assert their power by conquest. David Bywaters discusses the political significance of the plays in detail in his *Dryden in Revolutionary England*. Gardiner offers the most detailed and informative political reading of *Love Triumphant* in her essay "John Dryden's *Love Triumphant*."

58. Milton, 3:71–76. Anthony Low discusses the influence of Vergil's *Georgics* on Milton's *Paradise Regained* and the poet's condemnation of military heroism. See Low, "Milton, *Paradise Regained*, and Georgic."

59. Orgel, *Illusion of Power*, 54.

60. Like Dryden, Edward Lord Radcliffe (1655–1705) was a Catholic excluded from public employment for his religion. See Gardiner, "Dryden's Patrons," 328.

61. David Hopkins demonstrates the extent and nature of this affinity in his examination of two of Dryden's translations in *Fables* from the *Metamorphoses*. Arguing that Dryden was drawn by his "sense of the sophistication and control exercised by Ovid," Hopkins shows how Dryden shares and recreates the "Ovidian vision, which allows readers to face, comprehend, and thus enjoy, in a state of untroubled equanimity and delight, a view of human life as simultaneously glorious and futile, dignified and absurd, precious and dispensable, ordered and arbitrary, the care of the gods and of no concern to them at all, at one in its transience with the rest of Nature, with which it is involved in a continuous process of transformation, metamorphosis and flux. . . ." See Hopkins, "Dryden and Ovid's 'Wit out of Season,' " 171, 190.

62. Dryden's heightened affinity with Ovid in the last part of his career is evident in the Ovidian influence on his *Fables*. Earl Miner highlights the way in which Dryden placed himself in Ovid's footsteps: as Dryden was "ending his work," he remarks, "he wrote Pepys about his having translated 'as many fables from Ovid, and as many novels from Boccaccio, and tales from Chaucer, as will make an indifferent large volume in folio.' Of the three possible terms, Dryden takes the one he associates with Ovid." See Miner, "Ovid Reformed," 84.

63. Benjamin, "Die Aufgabe des Übersetzers," 52.

64. Benjamin, "Task of the Translator," 80.

65. Ibid., 79.

CHAPTER 2: STUDYING NATURE'S LAWS

1. Milbourne, *Notes*, 108.

2. [William Benson,] *Virgil's Husbandry*, 1725, iv.

3. William Benson, *Virgil's Husbandry*, 1724, xiv.

4. Milbourne, *Notes*, 108. Noting Dryden's difference in tone but not in subject matter, William Benson's first objection is that Dryden proposes "the Practice of Husbandry to Mæcenas as if he was to get his Livelihood by it" (see *Virgil's Husbandry*, 1725, iv).

5. Thomas May's translation, 38.

6. *Shepheardes Calender* 109–12.

7. Ibid., p. 96.

8. Milbourne notes with sarcasm, "*Principio arboribus varia est natura creandis*. Was a *dull line*, and not worthy to be taken notice of by Mr. *D's exalted Genius*" (see *Notes*, 139). The line is translated by Lauderdale: "Kind Nature, Trees by sev'ral means supplies" (10).

9. Again Milbourne scorns, " *—And all the* Sylvan *Reign*. This Phrase is one of the *Elegentiae Drydeniae*, frequently *affected*, and downright *Nonsence*" (*Notes*, 140). However, as the following discussion will illustrate, the "Sylvan Reign" here seems to be part of the semimythical "Sylvan Lands" introduced as a subject in *Georgics* III.

10. Patterson, *Fables of Power*, 88. Beginning with the observation that rural poetry flourished in the crises of 1630–60, James Turner offers a detailed examination of the ways in which landscape "was often used for political purposes." He also outlines the various political implications and uses of trees as he argues that since "Traditional science graded all plants and animals according to their nobility so it was perhaps inevitable that they should become by-words for social hierarchy." See Turner, *Politics of Landscape*, 1, 96–99.

11. As Miner points out, John Ogilby's *The Fables of Æsop Paraphras'd in Verse* seems

to influence the mode of *The Hind and the Panther* as well as providing material for the two long tales in part 3. (See Miner, *Dryden's Poetry*, 157–58, 167–68.)

12. Ogilby, *Fables of Æsop*, 86.

13. See Patterson, *Fables of Power*, 88.

14. Dryden's vocabulary works hand-in-hand with his subject matter to reinforce his nostalgia for an idealized English past and English institutions: Turner notes that "topographia" (which he defines as "the literary depiction of rural places and the life they support") is "well suited to the emotive politics of the *ancien régime* for it allows the old order to seem permanent, orderly and universally agreeable." See Turner, *Politics of Landscape*, 1, 106.

15. *Don Sebastian*, 15:103.51–54; *Cleomenes*, 16:90.53–59.

16. Patterson, *Fables of Power*, 88.

17. Patterson, ibid.

18. In "To Congreve," for example, a tree-like image is used to describe Congreve's poetic temples: "Firm *Dorique* Pillars found Your solid Base: / The Fair *Corinthian* Crowns the higher Space; / Thus all below is Strength, and all above is Grace" (17–19).

19. Low cites these lines in his discussion of the georgic toils of *Paradise Regained*. See Low, "Milton, *Paradise Regained*, and Georgic," 166.

20. Zwicker, *Politics and Language*, 137.

21. If the ephemeral cedar does represent William III, Ogilby is not the only authority Dryden might call upon to back his use of this particular tree as a symbol of short-lived power. In his discussion of the social hierarchy associated with certain kinds of trees, Turner cites George D'Ouvilly's presentation of the cedar:

> In th'umble valley better be a shrubb
> With secure peace, than on th'aspiring top
> Of a proud hill, a Cedar, still expos'd
> To a certaine danger.

Turner also remarks that "Henry More's green chapel in *Psychozia*, an allegory of the state church is made up of a 'higher hedge of thickn'd trees' and 'a lower rank of lesser shrubs.' Cowley hails the 'old *Patrician* Trees, so great and good' and the '*Plebeian* underwood' ('Of Solitude')." See *Politics of Landscape*, 97.

22. William Benson translates these lines:

> Nature, these Cov'nants, these Eternal Bands
> Impos'd, immediate, on the sev'ral Lands,
> When first *Deucalion* thro the empty Space
> The Flints dispers'd. . . . (*Virgil's Husbandry*, 1725, 7)

23. Milbourne asks, "But, why *Entrails*? . . . The *Entrails*, or *Bowels*, are sometimes nam'd for *compassion*, and *tenderness*; and had the Oracle nam'd *Entrails*, instead of *Bones*, it would have puzzl'd *Deucalion*, as much as his *Wife*" (*Notes*, 112).

24. The influence of Dryden's *Lucretius* on his *Georgics* is clearly apparent, for example, in the following passages:

> The joyous Birds [Spring's] welcome first express,
> Whose native Songs thy genial fire confess:
> Then salvage Beasts bound o're their slighted food,
> Strook with thy darts, and tempt the raging floud:
> All Nature is thy Gift; Earth, Air, and Sea:
> Of all that breaths, the various progeny,
> Stung with delight, is goaded on by thee.
> ("Lucretius: The beginning of the First Book" [16–22])

> The Spring adorns the Woods, renews the Leaves;
> The Womb of Earth the genial Seed receives.
> For then Almighty *Jove* descends, and pours
> Into his buxom Bride his fruitful Show'rs.
> And mixing his large Limbs with hers, he feeds
> Her Births with kindly Juice, and fosters teeming Seeds
> Then joyous Birds frequent the lonely Grove,
> And Beasts, by Nature stung, renew their Love.
> (*Georgics* II [438–45])

25. For a discussion of the *Amphitryon* prologue, see Winn, *Dryden and His World*, 445.

26. Sloman, *Poetics of Translation*, 14. Dryden seems also to have himself in mind in a very similar passage in the fragment "Of the Pythagorean Philosophy" in *Fables*. There the speaker, like Dryden, is "Self-banish'd from his Native Shore, / Because he hated Tyrants, nor could bear / The Chains which none but servile Souls will wear" (78–80). As Dryden himself might of his lifetime toils, he argues ". . . with what Justice can'st thou hope / The promise of the Year, a plenteous Crop; / When thou destroy'st thy lab'ring Steer, who till'd, / And plough'd with Pains, thy else ungrateful Field?" (178–81). The images of toils and pain are those used by Dryden throughout the 1690s in complaints about his hardships.

27. Winn points out that in the *Essay of Dramatick Poesie* Neander, "the Dryden figure," argues that "artful rhyme, like dance and painting, is the best imitation of intense passion." In the passage in question, Neander claims, "I acknowledg the hand of Art appears in repartee, as of necessity it must in all kind of verse. But there is also the quick and poignant brevity of it (which is an imitation of Nature in those sudden gusts of passion) to mingle with it: and this joyn'd with the cadency and sweetness of the Rhyme, leaves nothing in the soul of the hearer to desire." Winn sees these comments as evidence of "an association between rhyme and orgasm at some level of Dryden's consciousness." See Winn, *When Beauty Fires the Blood*, 73–74.

28. Dryden's emphasis on control is even more apparent if his final couplet here is contrasted with those by which its rhyme words are influenced. Helene Maxwell Hooker claims that "there seems to be every reason for arguing a relationship between Dryden's 'Then, to redeem his honour at a blow, / He moves his camp, to meet his careless foe' and the couplet by the anonymous author of the translation of part of *Georgics* III also included in *Examen Poeticum*: 'Then with his force and strength prepar'd does go / With headlong rage against th'unwary foe'" (38–39). May's version (284–85) too, which, as Hooker notes, "seems closer to Dryden than does this middle source," stresses the unthinking nature of the bull's furious response: "And well improv'd, he doth with fury go / To meet again his not forgotten foe." Here the bull's "fury" is emphasized by the enjambment, which has a similar effect to Vergil's elision. These examples demonstrate that even when Dryden borrows a couplet ending, his own version can be essentially different from those of previous translators. See Hooker, "Dryden's *Georgics* and English Predecessors."

29. Winn, *When Beauty Fires the Blood*, 9.

30. The same distinction is made in *The Hind and the Panther*:

> One portion of informing fire was giv'n
> To Brutes, th' inferiour family of heav'n:
> The Smith divine, as with a careless beat,
> Struck out the mute creation at a heat:
> But, when arriv'd at last to humane race,
> The god-head took a deep consid'ring space:
> And, to distinguish man from all the rest,
> Unlock'd the sacred treasures of his breast:
> And mercy mix'd with reason did impart;

> One to his head, the other to his heart:
> Reason to rule, but mercy to forgive:
> The first is law, the last prerogative. (3:130.251–62)

31. Winn, *When Beauty Fires the Blood*, 256.

32. Sloman argues that "Dryden's emphasis on the feminine in his Ovid translations [for example the character Isis] can be seen as a tactful attempt to stay within the range of interests established by his contemporaries while treating the subject apolitically." She also notes the "ambivalence towards woman expressed in the conflict between" Juvenal's sixth satire and the argument to it (*Poetics of Translation*, 113). In his sixth satire, in fact, Dryden seems to issue the same warning as I think he does here about the dangers of a government which lacks a patriarchal basis.

33. Sessions, "Spenser's Georgics," 204.

34. Chalker, *English Georgic*, 31.

35. In his discussion of the essentially moralistic (as opposed to hermeneutical) nature of Dryden's *Fables*, Miner observes that "Dryden's later uses of types commonly tend more to involve individuals participating in the offices and imitation of Christ, as for example Anne Killigrew, Eleanora, and the Duchess of Ormond." This, he claims, "brings Dryden's practice in the use of typology closer to pre-Reformation usage, which is to say that it involves his greater use of the moral sense of Scripture (good works) and secular writing. Two major events appear to account for such a change: his conversion to Roman Catholicism and the Revolution of 1688." See Miner, "Ovid reformed," 99. For the mood expressed in "Of the Pythagorean Philosophy" see also Clingham, "Another and the Same," 151–52.

36. Lauderdale translates:

> Cæsar, since you with Fate and Pow'rs above,
> Conceal the Sphere, your Deity shall move:
> Shall you to Cities or Thrones give Law? (23–25)

37. Vergil has "*An deus immensi venias maris, ac tua nautæ / Numina sola colant*" (29–30): Or will you be "god . . . / Of the vast Sea" so that "thee alone the Saylors shall adore" (May's translation, 3).

38. Behn, *Rover*, 1.2.65–66.

39. Miner points out that in Williamite literature "Again and again William is compared to the great warrior kings Alexander the Great and Julius Caesar." See the introduction to his edition of *Poems on the Reign of William III*, iv. Dryden, of course, satirized the portrayal of William as Alexander in *Alexander's Feast* (1697). Evidence of the widespread and highly promoted nature of such portrayals of the king can be seen (for example) in the following advertisement in the newspaper *A Collection for Improvement of Husbandry and Trade* (Friday, 4 May 1694): "Large medals in Copper to be published with all possible speed: Representing several of the Kings and Princes etc of Europe, with regard to their remarkable Actions. . . ." Among these included one of "King William III and Julius Caesar for the Reverse."

40. Ruæus's note substantiates Dryden's translation: "Veteres diu Libram signum ignoverunt, medium inter Virginem et Scorpium" (n. 33). ("For a long time Ancient peoples did not know about the sign Libra between Virgo and Scorpio.")

41. Gardiner, "Dryden's *Britannia Rediviva*," 277.

42. Low, "Milton, *Paradise Regained*, and Georgic," 153.

43. As the California editors note, this promise is "James's word to the Privy Council . . . that he would preserve the civil and ecclesiastical government of England as established by law" (3:442.n.953).

44. *Shepheardes Calender* ll. 103–7.

45. See Gardiner, "John Dryden's *Love Triumphant*," 168.

46. Milbourne, *Notes*, 117.

47. Ibid.

48. Chalker, *English Georgic*, 3.

49. The California editors note the proximity of Lauderdale's translation with its parallel triplet: " *confound / resound / . . . crown'd*. Cf. Lauderdale: 'confound, / . . . sound, / And Villany in all its Shapes is Crown'd' " (6:918.n.678–80). Given Dryden's allusion to *Britannia Rediviva*, I would argue that Lauderdale noted and imitated the satirical content of Dryden's lines rather than vice versa.

50. "As if," he whines, "there had been *Tombs* or *Monuments*, *Stone-Henges* set up in the *Pharsalian* and *Philippic* Fields, which is a very fine fancy. But why should an antique Title amaze any body? Curious Men will go far to see 'em, and generally return from 'em sober enough, and not half so much as *Men of Sence* would be, to see a *flattering Inscription*, equal Mr. *D.* to *Denham*, *Waller* or *Cowley*" (137–38).

51. Cf. William Anderton's portrayal of the Prince of Orange in his fatal pamphlet, *Remarks upon the Present Confederacy*: "Was it not the P. of O's being joined with most of the Princes and States of Europe, that brought us into these Snares upon a parcel of sham Pretences, and Bugbear Stories, with his Bearskins and Laplanders, and the Devil knows what?" (37; italics eliminated).

52. William Benson, *Virgil's Husbandry*, 1724, xxii.

53. Benjamin, "Theologico-Political Fragment," in *Reflections*, xxiv, 312.

54. Carefully outlining the structure of the poem, Jay Levine demonstrates, in fact, that "Each of John Driden's activities in the first part of the poem has its equivalent in the policies advocated for England in the second part." See Jay Levine, "John Dryden's Epistle to John Driden," 447–48.

55. Donald Benson points out that while in *The Hind and the Panther*, as in *Religio Laici*, Dryden condemns the ascendancy of private reasons in public concerns, in the preface to the poem "he wholly concedes final authority for religious commitment to private conscience, as he had done in the answer to Stillingfleet": "I may safely say, that Conscience is the Royalty and Prerogative of every Private man. He is absolute in his own Breast, and accountable to no Earthly Power, for that which passes only betwixt God and Him" (3:120; Donald Benson, "Theology and Politics in Dryden's Conversion," 409.

56. William Benson, *Virgil's Husbandry*, 1724, 42.

57. Donald Johnson, "Proper Study of Husbandry," 99.

58. Gardiner, "Dryden's Patrons," 331.

59. This passage is cited by Maren-Sofie Rostvig in her study of the English *beatus ille* tradition: a tradition to which, she claims, Dryden's chief contribution lies in the realm of translation. See *Happy Man*, 238.

60. Instead he scorns Dryden's political views. Of lines 707–8, he remarks, *"Nor, when contending Kindred tear the Crown, / Will set up one, or pull another down — But a Republican* will pull *both down*; and of such, we have now, too many." He also notes that the subsequent references to "The Senates mad Decrees" and to those who "invade the Court" are "a *Flirt* at our *Parliaments* too" (see Milbourne, *Notes*, 718, 173). The line about "contending Kindred tear[ing] the Crown" can be compared to the attack on Mary II in *Aeneis* VI: "they, who Brothers better Claim disown, / Expel their Parents and usurp the Throne" (824–25). The contemporary implications of these lines are discussed by both Zwicker (*Politics and Language*, 202) and William Frost in "On Editing Dryden's Virgil," 100.

61. Hopkins, "Dryden and Ovid's 'Wit out of season,'" 181.

62. In the dedication of *Amphitryon*, Dryden declares, "The Merry Philosopher, is more to my Humour than the Melancholick; and I find no disposition in myself to Cry, while the mad World is daily supplying me with such Occasions of Laughter" (15:224).

63. Dryden is turning to his own ends a motif taken not only from Vergil but from English georgic tradition. Noting the significance of the "analogical use of bees" in English literature, McRae claims that by the seventeenth century the diligent labors of bees were employed in "representations of a thriving national economy" where prosperity is determined by "the accumulation of individual labours and energies" (*God Speed the Plough*, 222). Turner notes that "Bees and ants were taken seriously as 'Politicall creatures.' " See *Politics of Landscape*, 96.

64. Hopkins, *John Dryden*, 146.

65. Ibid., 148.

66. Even the California editors (who usually do note make such observations) discuss the political connotations of the passage. (6:936.n.137–51).

67. Hopkins, *John Dryden*, 148.

68. Hopkins notes the echo of *Absalom and Achitophel* in lines 262–63 of *Georgics* IV (*John Dryden*, 148).

69. "Quid me præclara stirpe Deorum / (Si modo, quem perhibes, pater est Thymbræus Apollo)" (322–23): "What good does it do me," he asks, "to be of the glorious race of Gods—if indeed, as you maintain, my father is Apollo Thymbraeus?"

70. Homer, *Odyssey*, 4:351–570.

CHAPTER 3: TOWARDS A CARMEN PERPETUUM

1. Zwicker, *Politics and Language*, 153–54.

2. It is at this point too that she refers to the authority of "*Homer*, who learn'd the language of the sky" and who can "unty" the "seeming *Gordian* knot" (3:185.821–22).

3. Bredvold, *Intellectual Milieu of John Dryden*, 126–27.

4. He calls it "a commonplace." Dryden, *Poetical Works of John Dryden*, 1010.

5. The opening line of René Rapin's *Observations Upon the Poems of Homer and Virgil* translates, "Of all the productions Man's mind is capable of, the *Epick Poem* is doubtless the most accomplished, in regard it involves all the perfections of the others" (1). Weinbrot points out that Rapin's *Comparaison des Pöemes d'Homère et de Virgile* (1664) "appears at least nine times between 1664 and 1731, four of these in English." See *Britannia's Issue*, 212.

6. Italics reversed. Pope, of course, was to repeat Dryden's comment in his "Essay on Criticism": "Those Rules of old *discover'd*, not *devis'd*, / Are *Nature* still, but *Nature Methodiz'd*" (see *Poems*, 89–90).

7. Donald Benson, "Theology and Politics in Dryden's Conversion," 407.

8. Frost, *Dryden and the Art of Translation*, 47.

9. I use the words of McKeon who argues that the "emergence of the rules, like that of poetic justice, represents not so much a renewal of traditional standards and beliefs as the onset of crisis and the ingenuous experimentation (although contemporaries thought differently) with new modes of thought." See *Origins of the English Novel*, 126.

10. Bossu, "Treatise of the Epick Poem," 29; [Rapin,] *Observations*; Segrais, *Virgile*, vol. 1, 47. Volume 1 of the Segrais translation contains the first six books of the *Aeneid*.

11. Bossu, "Treatise of the Epick Poem," 27.

12. Rapin, *Observations*, 8.

13. Bernard Weinberg points out that for Scaliger "Vergil is nature": "*Itaque non ex ipsius naturae opere uno potuimus exempla capere, quae ex una Virgiliana idea mutuati sumus.*" He translates, "Thus we could not take from any one work of nature herself the examples which we have borrowed from one work of Vergil." See Weinberg, "Scaliger versus Aristotle on Poetics," 349.

14. Bossu, "Treatise of the Epick Poem," 14.

15. Rapin, *Observations*, 18, 24. Bossu, "Treatise of the Epick Poem," 28. Weinbrot demonstrates that even in the sixteenth and seventeenth centuries when Augustus tended "to blend" with proabsolutist politics, the Tacitean view of him as tyrant and butcher surfaced from time to time, disseminated by means of the Italian Renaissance commentators. See *Augustus Caesar in "Augustan" England*, 36.

16. Bossu, "Treatise of the Epick Poem," 30.

17. Zwicker, *Politics and Language*, 184.

18. [Anderton,] *Remarks upon the Present Confederacy*, 20–21. [Johnston,] *Dear Bargain*, 2.

19. The ambivalent attitude of the English people toward their cold and foreign king is discussed by many historians of the period. Jane Garrett summarizes the situation neatly when she observes, "Tumultuous rejoicings greeted [Anne's] succession: once more England had a monarch who was both English and a Stuart. Their enthusiasm for Anne reflects both the xenophobia of the English and their emotional attachment to the [Stuart] dynasty." See Garrett, *Triumphs of Providence*, 264.

20. Segrais, *Traduction*, vol. 1 14, 15. For the last comment here see Segrais's prefatory *Epistre "Au Roy,"* A1.

21. The predominant seventeenth and eighteenth-century views and uses of Vergil and Augustus are outlined by, most importantly, Weinbrot (*Augustus Caesar in "Augustan" England* and *Britannia's Issue*) and by T. W. Harrison ("English Virgil"). The general pattern, Weinbrot argues, is that the favorable view of Augustus "rises and falls with royalism and absolutism; it reaches one normative peak as Charles is restored and certain historical parallels seem appropriate; it loses force later in the century, especially after 1688, but regains some vigor under Anne, the Peace of Utrecht in 1713, and apparent strength by a Stuart monarch" (*Augustus Caesar in "Augustan" England*, 51).

22. *Plain Truth, or Downright Dunstable: a Poem*, (London, 1740), 13. Cited by Harrison, "English Virgil," 2.

23. Harrison, "English Virgil," 3.

24. Warton, "Dissertation on the Nature and Conduct of the Aeneid," 4.

25. Nicolas Tindal, introduction, in Spence, *Spence's Polymetis Abridged*, 164.

26. For quotations and full discussion see Weinbrot, *Britannia's Issue*, 26.

27. Ibid., 27.

28. Canto 35, v. 26 of *Orlando Furioso*, trans. Sir John Harington, 3rd ed. (London, 1634), 292. Cited by Weinbrot, who points out that "The poem appeared in English in 1591 (John Harington), 1755 (William Huggins), and 1738 (John Hoole, abridged)" (*Augustus Caesar in "Augustan" England*, 66–67). Dryden quotes the lines in their original Italian (5:323). Weinbrot also observes that "Probably the ugliest and least ambiguous part of Augustus' background was his role in the triumvirate's proscription, a role even his partisans had to admit or lamely excuse (*Augustus Caesar in "Augustan" England*, 59).

29. Weinbrot, *Augustus Caesar in "Augustan" England*, 67.

30. *The Briton*, 37. Cited by Weinbrot, *Britannia's Issue*, 147.

31. In his *A Discourse of the Contests and Dissensions between the Nobles and Commons in Athens and Rome* (1701), Swift focuses on Augustus as Octavian the triumvir and villain. He calls his reign "the vilest Tyranny that Heaven in its Anger ever inflicted on a Corrupt and Poison'd People," and concludes, "Here ended all Shew or Shadow of Liberty in *Rome*. Here was the Repository of all the wise Contentions and Struggles for Power, between the Nobles and Commons, lapt up safely in the Bosom of a *Nero* and a *Caligula*, a *Tiberius* and a *Domitian*." Swift, *Discourse of the Contests and Dissensions*, 111.

32. The Englishness of Dryden's argument here is highlighted by McKeon's observation on the traditional association of English and Trojan lineage: "If 'history' was conceived during the Middle Ages as a branch of rhetoric, its principal trope was that of lineage. And this holds for romance as well, the truth of whose 'matter,' like that of all discourse, owed to the fact that it was inherited. . . . [In Britain, the] genealogy established at the fall of Troy . . . provided a national lineage not only for the followers of Aeneas but also, through Priam, for the barbarian tribes that roamed and settled the rest of Europe" (*Origins of the English Novel*, 36).

33. Cf. *Absalom and Achitophel*: "All other Errors but disturb a State; / But Innovation is the Blow of Fate" (799–802).

34. Harrison argues, "While the qualities of sublimity and pathos, and the passages of natural description, saved parts of the *Aeneid* from an almost total destruction [in the eighteenth century], and, though in the case of pathos particularly these parts might be quite extensive, the *Aeneid* remained a patchwork of 'capital beauties', something focused on intensely but also sporadically." Harrison cites several eighteenth-century comments on Vergil's sublimity (see "English Virgil," 87).

35. Hayley, *Essay on Epic Poetry*. Frost points out, "W. J. Courthope said of Dryden in the 1690s that he was 'no longer the poet-attorney of the Crown, but free representative of the nation.' " See Frost, *John Dryden*, 187.

36. Sloman, "Interpretation of Dryden's *Fables*," 199.

37. Nicolas Boileau-Despreaux, *Oeuvres diverses du Sieur D— —*, 134–35. I cite Boileau's 1674 translation, which Dryden would have used, because the passage will become important in a later discussion of *Aeneis* VI.

38. Pope, *Poems of Alexander Pope*, 22. All citations from Pope are from this Twickenham edition.

39. Trapp, *Preface to the Aeneis of Virgil*, 1. Spence, *Spence's Polymetis Abridged*, 156.

40. All comments are cited by Frost, who supplies a fuller discussion of reactions to Dryden's *Aeneis*. See Frost, *Dryden and the Art of Translation*, 4–6.

41. Weinbrot, *Britannia's Issue*, 190.

42. The unmistakable contemporary overtones have been noted by the California editors and Winn (6:965.n.3; *Dryden and His World*, 487–88). The corresponding lines in Vergil read:

> Arma, virumque cano, Trojæ qui primus ab oris
> Italiam, fato profugus, Laviniaque venit
> Litora: multum ille et terris jactatus et alto,
> Vi superum, sævæ memorem Junonis ob iram.
> Multa quoq; et bello passus, dum conderet urbem,
> Inferretq; Deos Latio: genus unde Latinum,
> Albanique patres, atque altæ moenia Romæ. (1–7)

Lauderdale's version, with its reference to "so just a Prince," is politically-tinged but by no means so embedded in current affairs or so angry as Dryden's:

> I sing the Warriour and his mighty Fame,
> Who driven by Fate from burning *Ilium*'s Flame,
> First led by *Trojans* to the *Latian* Coast,
> At Sea and Lands by Storms and Dangers cross'd;
> Rais'd by the angry Gods and wreakful Spleen
> Of *Jove*'s offended and revengeful Queen.
> Much in the Wars he suffer'd, long oppress'd
> E'er for his wand'ring Gods a place of Rest
> The Hero built; from whence the *Latin* fame,
> The *Alban* Fathers and the *Roman* name.
> O Muse, relate what Cause? what dire Offence?
> A Goddess urg'd against so just a Prince,
> And cou'd such worth in so much Toil engage,
> Are Minds Immortal fir'd with such a Rage? (78–79)

43. Trapp, *Preface to the Aeneis*, li.
44. Ibid., l.
45. Ibid., l–li.
46. Vergil has "multum ille et terris jactatus et alto": "he was much tossed about on land and sea." The California editors observe that this is not the only time "labours"

are interpolated: "Cf. *Aeneis*, III, 931: 'after endless Labours,' and VII, 171: 'And the long Labours of your Voyage end,' where the phrase is also introduced with nothing in the Latin corresponding to 'labours' " (6:965.n.4).

47. Arguing that the theme of "labor" is at the heart of Vergil's *Aeneid* as well as his *Georgics* and that it had an enormous (though previously unrecognized) influence on Spenser's *Faerie Queene*, Sessions points out that "There are ninety-nine references to 'labour' and its forms in the entire canon of Spenser. Twenty-five associate the word with "long," the greatest single association by far." ("Spenser's Georgics," 205, 216, n.27)

48. Osborne calls Spenser the "poets' poet." He also points out that Dryden's (and others') interest in Spenser really only surged after the publication of the 1679 edition of Spenser's works. As a boy, he observes, Dryden read Spenser in the 1611 edition and—as he confesses in the dedication of *The Spanish Fryar*—thought him a "mean poet" in comparison with Du Bartas. See Osborn, *John Dryden*, 241–45. Winn draws attention to the adeptness of Dryden's memory as he highlights the way in which the poet continually reworked the "fabric" of his own and others' earlier works. Congreve, Winn notes, "informs us that Dryden was 'happy in a Memory tenacious of every thing that he read.' " See Winn's introduction to *Critical Essays on John Dryden*, ed. Winn, 13.

49. Behind Spenser's lines, in fact, are four often attributed to Vergil and prefaced to *Aeneid* I—and rejected by Dryden in the dedication as "inferiour to any Four others, in the whole Poem" (5:338). Justifying his effort, "If there be not a tolerable Line in all these six, the Prefacer gave me no occasion to write better," Dryden translates them:

> I, who before, with Shepherds in the Groves,
> Sung to my Oaten Pipe, their Rural Loves,
> And issuing thence, compell'd the Neighb'ring Field
> A plenteous Crop of rising Corn to yield,
> Manur'd the Glebe, and stock'd the fruitful Plain,
> (A Poem grateful to the Greedy Swain.)&c. (5:339; italics reversed)

While Dryden might reject the lines as Vergil's, the poetic development they trace needs no defense.

50. Spenser, *Poetical Works of Edmund Spenser*, ed. Smith, 2.proem.iv. All citations from *The Faerie Queene* are from these volumes and are given by book, canto and stanza number.

51. Harrison, "Dryden's *Aeneid*," in *Dryden's Mind and Art*, ed. Bruce King (Edinburgh: Oliver and Boyd, 1969), 143. Harrison gives examples demonstrating how the 1654 translation is "a far more explicitly 'Royalist' version than the first."

52. Ogilby, trans., *Works of Publius Virgilius Maro*, (1654), 128.

53. Denham, *Expans'd Hieroglyphicks*, 117–19.

54. McKeon, *Origins of the Novel*, 215, 214.

55. Lewis, *Latin Dictionary* cites the root of *gens, gentis, f.* as "Gen, gigno, that which belongs together by birth or descent." The primary meaning of the word is "*a race or clan, embracing several families united together by a common name and by certain religious rites.*" *Latin Dictionary*, 808.

56. *Faerie Queene* 1.10.59, 1.10.65.

57. Zwicker also notes that throughout the *Aeneis* "name takes a new precedence over estate and over office. Place and name are not always antipodal, of course, but when Dryden now contemplates these themes, name is the bulwark against the vagaries of fortune; it has a substance beyond anything it had previously been invested with" (*Politics and Language*, 198).

58. This information was ascertained using an electronic text and basic word-processing tools. Text used: Dryden, trans., *Virgil's Aeneid*.

59. The point made in Dryden's panegyrical address to the Duke of York in the dedication of *The Conquest of Granada* about the insult to James as Neptune's appointee is almost identical to that made in his note to *Aeneis* I; while here it is William III, there

it is "the *Hollanders*" daring to "dispute the Soveraignty of the Seas" (11:4). The portrayal in *Threnodia Augustalis* and *Britannia Rediviva* of the Stuart monarchy (and particularly James II in his role as admiral) as the bulwark and base of England's naval power has already been discussed.

60. Orgel, *Illusion of Power*, 71, 75.

61. Ibid., 77.

62. These are noted by the California editors.

63. Sandys, *Ovid's Metamporphosis*, 536, 524–25.

64. Most notably, in 1649 Ogilby translated in an unremarkable way Vergil's simile comparing Neptune's calming of the waves to a politician calming an angry crowd; his 1654 version, however, evokes the English civil wars. It ends with a line not in the 1649 edition: "So did [Neptune's] Presence calm the troubled Main." The lament for Charles's absence is continued in the subsequent lines, which are again quite different from the earlier ones: compare the literal 1649 attempt, "Thus ceast all fragor of the Sea, which when / The father saw, carried through skies serene / He his blest Chariot drives, and turnes his horse" (6) with "Then through clear Skyes *Neptune* with gentle Reign / Wheels his swift Chariot, and well-manag'd Horse" (133).

65. Bayly quotes (without acknowledgment) Dryden quoting Segrais's list of Augustus's virtues when he says that Dryden "cut Æneas in pieces, making him civil, popular, eloquent, politic, religious, valiant, without any predominant leading action or principle; which piety certainly is not. . . ." Bayly, *Alliance of Music, Poetry and Oratory*, 143–44. The original title page reads: *The Alliance of Musick, Poetry and Oratory: Under the Head of Poetry is considered the Alliance and Nature of the Epic and Dramatic Poem as it exists in the Iliad, Aeneid and Paradise Lost.* (London, 1789).

66. Harrison quotes Edward Holdsworth's *Remarks and Dissertations on Virgil* (London, 1768) as he claims that Vergil, "along with his hero, Aeneas, enters the eighteenth century as the 'man of feeling' of antiquity." Harrison also contends that this typical eighteenth-century view developed from the typical seventeenth-century view, which he sees as summarized in *Verdicts of the Learned Concerning Virgil and Homer's Heroic Poems* (London, 1697), where Aeneas is a "weeping, blubbring, sighing, groaning, nay bawling Hero'" ("English Virgil," 85–86). While Harrison tends to posit a single view as representative of a century (his references to Dryden's dedication, for example, are misleading because they ignore Dryden's sources), his general points about Aeneas's character are valid for probably most imitations and translations through to the twentieth century. Note, for example, Thomas Phaer's 1558 Aeneas: "Eneas than in every lymme with cold beganne to quake, / With hands up throwen to heauens a loft his mone thus gan he make." Compare the sentiment of Mandelbaum's 1981 rendition: "At once Aeneas' limbs fall slack with chill. / He groans and stretches both hands to the stars." See Mandelbaum, trans., *Aeneid of Virgil*, 131–32.

67. Contrast Sandys's apparent attempt to draw a parallel between Neptune and Aeneas: as Neptune "o're the flood his sacred head erects" (536), he displays the same piety as Aeneas when "dismaid, / He sighs, and hand to heauen erecting, said. . . ." *Ovid's Metamporphosis*, 535.

68. Vergil has "Talia jactanti stridens Aquilone procella / Velum adversa ferit . . ." (102–3). In 1716 Nicholas Brady translates, "While thus He mourn'd, a rustling *Northern* Storm / Directly cross, shatters his Sails . . ." (9).

69. Warton, "Dissertation on the Nature and Conduct of the Æneid," 8.

70. Sloman notes how the *Aeneis'* "Drydenian overlay" often results in the ironic use of "pious." This happens, she observes, wherever Aeneas "appears as a butcher or a 'War-luck,'" and in book 4, where Aeneas behaves like a Dorimant" (see *Poetics of Translation*, 126).

71. *Paradise Regained* 1:107, 110.

72. Segrais, *Traduction*, vol. 1, 122, 123.

73. The comfort derived from their own company by the exiled royal family is perhaps indicated by the nickname given the baby princess born in St. Germain: La Consolatrice.

74. Hopkins, "Dryden and Ovid's 'Wit out of season,'" 189.

75. Zwicker in a discussion of the "providential view of the Glorious Revolution" and its opposition by Jacobites. As Zwicker points out, the "language" used to discuss fortune and fate in the *Aeneis* "suggests not so much the construct of historical analogy through which Dryden might intend to parallel the furies in English and Roman politics, but rather a general and philosophical point of view that I think could hardly be detained from expression." See Zwicker, "Reading Vergil," 297.

76. Frost actually makes this comment of Chaucer's "The Knight's Tale," adding that this sense "finds ready and convincing echoes in Dryden's rendition" (see *Art of Translation*, 79).

77. Zwicker, "Reading Vergil," 297.

78. Vergil has "Hic pietatis honos?": "Is this the reward for piety?" (253)

79. J. Douglas Canfield demonstrates the importance of the notion of word as bond not just in Dryden's works but in English literature from Beowulf through the Restoration period. Canfield in fact begins the foreword of his book by quoting Dryden's epilogue to *Albion and Albanius*:

> He Plights his Faith; and we believe him just;
> His Honour is to Promise, ours to Trust.
> Thus Britain's Basis on a Word is laid,
> As by a Word the World itself was made.

Canfield's probing discussion of *Absalom and Achitophel* in particular reveals the degree to which both Dryden and his fellow country people believed that "Britain's Basis on a Word is laid." See Canfield, *Word as Bond*.

80. Vergil's Venus sounds almost like a petulant child complaining "But Dad, you promised!": "Pollicitus: quæ te, genitor, sententia vertit?" (237).

81. *Paradise Lost* 2:1, 8.

82. Zwicker, *Politics and Language*, 203, 195.

83. "Father of humanity and Gods," 254.

84. Reverand points out that "In the second paragraph of his Preface [to *Fables*], Dryden calls special attention to this excerpt from Ovid by referring to it as 'the Master-piece of the whole *Metamorphoses*' (Kinsley, 4:1444). In addition, Dryden adds a headnote to his translation in which he describes both 'the Moral and Natural Philosophy of Pythagoras' as 'the most learned and beatiful Parts of the Whole Metamorphoses' (Kinsley, 4:1718)." See Reverand, *Dryden's Final Poetic Mode*, 164.

85. "Juno will protect the Romans, masters of the world and wearers of the toga."

86. Weinbrot, *Britannia's Issue*, 62–65.

87. Vergil's Jove says, "Hunc tu olim coelo, spoliis Orientis onustum, / Accipies secura: vocabitur hic quoque votis." (289–90): "One day you will receive him safely in heaven, loaded down with the spoils of the Orient, and he too will be invoked by prayers."

88. Dryden's emphasis on "Name" and "Fame" are his own. Vergil stresses the founding and settlement of a new city: "Hic tamen ille urbem Patavi sedesque locavit / Teucrorum, et genti nomen dedit, armaque fixit / Troïa: nunc placida compostus pace quiescit" (247–49). Ogilby's 1654 version reads, "Yet here he fix'd, and on this very Ground / *Patavium* Tow'rs did on the Waters Found; / *Trojans* new nam'd, and free from all Alarms, / Hung up now useless Consecrated Arms" (136)

89. That Dryden had Spenser in mind is suggested by his use of "happy," a word which permeates *The Faerie Queene*, usually in association with settlement or security of line.

90. McKeon, *Origins of the English Novel*, 212–13.

91. The story in which she appears is "Palamon and Arcite."

92. The Latin reads, "Quocirca capere ante dolis et cingere flamma / Reginam meditor, ne quo se numine mutet; / Sed magno Æneæ mecum teneatur amore." (673–75)

93. Sloman, *Poetics of Translation*, 109.

94. By contrast, Segrais (*Traduction*, vol. 1) begins by stressing the desertion and

savageness of the coast, then focuses on "Nature" rather than on creating a "Sylvan scene":

> Au lieu le plus desert de ce sauvage Bord,
> Sous sa pointe avancée une Isle fait un Port,
> Cache un Golphe paisable, où l'inconstant Nerée
> N'a jamais troublé l'Onde en tout temps azurée.
> Deux Montagnes autour s'élevent jusqu'aux Cieux,
> Et font taire des Flots les abbois furieux;
> Une haute Forest de ses feüillages sombres
> Couronne leur sommet, & porte au loin ses Ombres:
> La Nature au dessous forme un Autre plaisant,
> Où d'une eau claire & vive est le cristal luisant,
> Qui sur un gravier d'or excite un doux murmure,
> Alentour d'un long banc de mousse & de verdure,
> Où laissant quelquefois leur humide sejour,
> Les Nymphes à Thetis viennent faire leur tour.
> Jamais l'anchre en ce Bord n'enfonça dans les sables;
> Jamais Nef n'eut besoin d'y déployer ses cables;
> Avecque sept Vaisseaux de sa Flote restez. (119–20)

95. Mark Van Doren, *John Dryden* (New York: Holt, 1946), 55.
96. *Paradise Lost* 4:140; Frost, *Dryden and the Art of Translation*, 43.
97. *Faerie Queene* 2.1.2
98. Scaliger's view of the divine tranquillity offered by poetry corresponds both to Dryden's description of a good conscience and to his grove scene here: "Through poetry moreover the soul is reflected in itself and it draws forth from its celestial store whatever there is in it of divinity; which part indeed cannot be exhausted even by perpetual drawings off." (*"Per Poesin autem reflectitur anima in seipsam, atque promit è caelesti suo penu quod diuinitati inest: quae pars ne perpetuis quidem haustibus exhauriri potest"* [I. ii. 4].) See Weinberg, "Scaliger versus Aristotle on Poetics," 354.

CHAPTER 4: THY WARS BROUGHT NOTHING ABOUT

1. Anne King remarks that Dryden's reaction to Vergil in his dedication is "almost completely in terms of the style of the Latin poet. He never refers to the larger structural patterns of the *Aeneid*, and very rarely to its meaning." See King, "Translation from the Classics," 122.
2. Obviously, I disagree with James Garrison's claim that while "books 1–6 of the *Aeneis* recapture the optimism of the poems Dryden had written in the 1660s, books 7–12 reflect an impious age in the making from the Exclusion Crisis to the Revolution and after." See Garrison, *Pietas from Vergil to Dryden*, 239.
3. Sloman, *Poetics of Translation*, 131.
4. *Faerie Queene* 2.proem.1
5. The quotation is from *Amphitryon*; Dryden ironically reverses the myth of the ages so as to satirize the (in his view) Whiggish settlement of 1689: "Our Iron Age is grown an Age of Gold: / 'Tis who bids most; for all Men wou'd be sold" (15:302.556–57). While many historians record the widespread view that Providence was responsible for William's arrival in England, Garrett's *Triumphs of Providence* offers the best discussion of the ongoing part supposedly played by Providence in William's and Mary's reign. Quoting from such contemporaries as Burnet and Evelyn, she demonstrates how Providence was also seen as responsible for, among other things, the prevention of both a Jacobite restoration and a serious attempt on William's life in 1696.

6. Frost, "On Editing Dryden's Virgil," 110.

7. Vergil has "Post, ipsum auxilio subeuntem ac tela ferentem / Corripiunt . . .": "Next they seized Laocoön himself as he came bringing help, armed with weapons" (216–17).

8. Garrison, *Pietas from Vergil to Dryden*, 206; Reuben Brower states that "in the emphasis on 'piety' in the character of Aureng-Zebe, we feel that Dryden was emulating Virgli quite directly." See Brower, "Dryden's Epic Manner and Virgil," 127.

9. *Faerie Queene* 1.2.54

10. Ogilby, *Fables of Æsop.*

11. Ventidius appeals to Antony's knowledge of his public and private duties as he places the general's wife and children before him:

> *Ven.*   Was ever sight so moving! Emperor!
> *Dolla.*   Friend!
> *Octav.*   Husband!
> *Both Childr.*   Father!
> *Ant.*   I am vanquish'd: take me. (13:67.361–65).

12. Paul Hammond, "Dryden's Philosophy of Fortune," 778.

13. Ibid., 778–79.

14. Ibid., 773.

15. Ogilby, *Works of Publius Virgilius Maro* (1649), 36.

16. He uses the words "in vain" and "futile" in the same line as he describes how the aged Priam throws his long-unused armor over his trembling shoulders in vain and girds his useless sword: "Arma diu senior desueta trementibus ævo / Circumdat *nequicquam* humeris, et *inutile* ferrum / Cingitur" (509–11) (emphasis added). Literally: "In vain the old man shakily shouldered arms so long unused, and girded his futile sword."

17. Reverand too remarks on the bloodshed in Dryden's twelfth book of the *Metamorphoses*. Describing the scene at length, he points out that "the idea that bloodshed once begun knows no limits is what the Lapithae and the centaurs demonstrate, with bloody death after bloody death. . . ." He also cites Michael West's pertinent observation as he notes that this scene is not "merely parody, but is 'quite literally a grotesque of heroic literature.' " See Reverand, *Dryden's Final Poetic Mode*, 27. For West citation see West, "Dryden's Ambivalence as a Translator of Heroic Themes," 360.

18. In both cases, such a use would seem to validate McKeon's claim that the origins of the English novel entail the positing of a "new" generic category as a dialectical negation of a "traditional" dominance—the romance, the aristocracy—whose character still saturates, as an antithetical but formative force, the texture of the category by which it is being both constituted and replaced (*Origins of the English Novel*, 268).

19. Bakhtin, "Epic and Novel," 18.

20. Ibid., 13.

21. Ogilby's 1654 translation, in contrast, attempts to bring out the reassurance inherent in Priam's words by rendering "pietas" as divine ordination. There the king cries, "The Gods, if any of the Deifi'd / Such Deeds observe, shall just Rewards ordain" (217).

22.

> At non ille, satum quo te mentiris, Achilles
> Talis in hoste fuit Priamo: sed jura fidemque
> Supplicis erubuit; corpusque exsangue sepulchro
> Reddidit Hectoreum, meq; in mea regna remisit. (540–43)

Again, Ogilby's 1654 translation is much closer to the Latin:

> *Achilles*, whom thou Father falsly stil'd,
> Was no such Foe to me; he blush'd, when I

Implor'd the Law of Arms, nor did deny
Hector's pale Corps should have a Native Tomb,
And me sent with a Convoy home. (217)

23. Bakhtin, "Epic and Novel," 16, 13.
24. The California editors quote Denham's lines, observing that "Dryden footnoted his l. 763 as *'taken from Sir* John Denham' " (6:986).
25. [Denham], *Destruction of Troy*, 28.
26. Ogilby's 1654 translation of the Latin does reproduce the hemistich and reads: "Now hear *Greek* Treachery, from this one Crime / Let us all beware. / For . . ." (200).
27. In contrast to Dryden's politically-charged lines, Vergil's description puts emphasis on Sinon's feigned anguish: "Afflictus vitam in tenebris luctuque trahebam, / Et casum insontis mecum indignabar amici" (92–93). Literally, the lines translate, "In affliction, I dragged out my life in darkness and lamentation, full of wrath at the fall of my innocent friend." Ogilby (1654) has: "I my sad Life in Woe and Darkness spent, / And there my Princes unjust suffering mourn'd" (200).
28. This is in an untitled volume of plates on the theme of the Glorious Revolution, which is in the holdings of the William Andrews Clark Memorial Library, Los Angeles. The plate is reproduced by Harry T. Dickinson, "Glorious Revolution of 1688–89." Dickinson says that the engravings are by Adriaan Schoonebeck, most from designs by Pieter Pickaert, and date from around 1689 (1).
29. Cited by Baxter, *William III*, 242. Baxter records his source as B. M. Add. Ms. 32095, f. 306.
30. "Jamdudum sumite poenas" (102).
31. As the California editors remark, the "adjectives have no Virgilian equivalent" (6:979.n.197)137.
32. Sloman observes such a shift in *Fables*: in "Sigismonda and Guiscardo," she remarks, "Dryden plays on the various implications of the word 'blood,' adding disturbingly carnal overtones to the conception of noble descent" (*Poetics of Translation*, 140). See too note 17 above.
33. Zwicker, *Politics and Language*, 197.
34. Ibid., 197–98.
35. Ruæus's note states that *Erato* is the "Musa quæ versibus præest amatoriis, ab [era-o], amo. Hanc invocat, quia bellorum sequentium origo ex amore Turni et Æneæ in Laviniam": "Muse of love poetry, from 'era-o,' 'I love.' The poet invokes her because the origin of the subsequent wars is the love of Turnus and Aeneas for Lavinia." The explanation draws attention to the worthiness and nobility of the cause, a nobility which would seem to be honored in Dryden's translation here.
36. Cameron, ed., *Poems on Affairs of State*, 157.
37. Zwicker cites this passage in his discussion of Dryden's contemporary overlay (*Politics and Language*, 200).
38. *Faerie Queene* 3.9.42.
39. Ibid., 3.9.44
40. Canfield discusses in detail the importance to *The Medall* of the notion of the king's word as bond. See his *Word as Bond*, 272–79.
41. Southerne, *Oroonoko*, 105.
42. Both the adjective "false" and the gifted throne are interpolated.
43. "Saucius at quadrupes nota intra tecta refugit, / Successitq; gemens stabulis: questuque, cruentus" (500–501).
44. "Quadrifidam quercum cuneis ut forte coactis / Scindebat, rapta spirans immane securi" (509–10).
45. A direct association of the deer incident and its consequences with events of the 1690s is made through the assignment of the plate depicting the wounding to "Lady Mary Sackville daughter to Charles Earle of Dorset and Middlesex" (6:594). Zwicker observes that "Mary Sackville is the tenderhearted Latian maid and Dorset becomes '*Tyrrheus*, chief Ranger to the *Latian* King' . . . hence loyal retainer of Stuart monarchy, an allusion to a happier past that Dryden shared with Dorset" (*Politics and Language*,

193). Given the portrayal of Tyrrheus as precipitator of civil upheaval as he takes affairs into his own "horny Fists," however, it is also apparent that Dryden's tribute to Dorset is tempered by the same coyness present in the "Discourse Concerning . . . Satire" where he informs Dorset, "I must not presume to defend the Cause for which I now suffer, because your Lordship is engag'd against it" (4:23).

46. Garrison, *Pietas from Vergil to Dryden*, 241. Again, where I disagree with Garrison is in his argument that book 7 reaches an "ominously new conclusion" and is different in its treatment of *pietas* from books 1–6 (241).

47. Cf. too Dryden's Dedication of his *Don Sebastian*: "How much happier is he . . . who centring on himself, remains immovable, and smiles at the madness of the dance about him" (15:60)154.

48. Garrison, *Pietas from Vergil to Dryden*, 242.

49. McKeon, *Origins of the English Novel*, 384.

50. *Faerie Queene* 3.9.50

51. McKeon, *Origins of the English Novel*, 341.

52. There is a basis in the Latin for the statement, but the word "Blood" features in Dryden's text only.

53. Bakhtin, "Epic and Novel," 14.

54. *Faerie Queene* 6.9.32, 6.3.2

55. Clingham notes of Dryden's "Lucretius, The beginning of the First Book," lines 1–11 that the "sensuousness of Dryden's language, in excess of the Latin, inculcates an abundance, and it explicitly identifies the verse's energy with Venus' movement through nature." See "Another and the Same," 135.

56. Bakhtin, "Epic and Novel," 21.

57. Ibid., 23.

58. Frost, "On Editing Dryden's Virgil," 106.

59. Hunter also points out that while the novel "points forward in style, form, subjectivity, and its validation of the ordinary and everyday, it also longs for what is gone: its consciousness is borne back into a past where it searches for its origins and identity." See *Before Novels*, 140.

60. Brean Hammond, *Professional Imaginative Writing*, 107, 126.

61. Thomas Fujimura a long time ago pointed out how Dryden's late works especially have an extra edge that comes from the poet's intensely personal involvement in the issues he confronts. Noting the "almost obsessive character" of Dryden's personal themes, Fujimura remarks that even more so "than *Don Sebastian, Amphitryon* dramatizes Dryden's personal concern with the human condition. . . ." See Fujimura, "Autobiography in Dryden's Later Work," 22. See also Fujimura's "Dryden's Virgil." Phillip Harth meanwhile argues that while autobiography is indeed an important element of Dryden's works, the poet's public role dictates the shape and presentation of his arguments. Harth demonstrates how Dryden manipulates the historical events behind such poems as *Annus Mirabilis* for propagandistic purposes: "Dryden's portrait in these early public poems of a cohesive body of Englishmen united behind their beloved monarch is, of course, a political myth which substitutes the ideal for the actual." See Harth, "Dryden's Public Voices," 106.

62. I am thinking here of Brean Hammond's comment concerning generic changes in the drama of the period that "certainly in plays like Southerne's *The Wives Excuse* and Congreve's *The Way of the World*, [comedy] arrives at resolutions that generations of readers and spectators have perceived to be more adequate to the complexity of life as it is actually lived, by breaking the strict boundaries of established convention" (see *Professional Imaginative Writing*, 109–10).

63. See, for example, the vicious attack on William and his supporters cited in Cameron's *Poems on Affairs of State* (1688–1697):

> In love to his minions he partial and rash is,
> Makes statesmen of blockheads, and Earls of bardashes,
> His bed-chamber service he fills with young fellows,
> At Essex and Windsor which makes Capell jealous.

Numanus's accusations might also find a parallel in Ralph Gray's *The Coronation Ballad* (1689). Note especially the following stanza:

> He is not qualified for his wife,
> Because of the cruel midwife's knife,
> Yet buggering of Benting doth please to the life.
> A dainty [fine King indeed.]

As Cameron notes here, many of the cruelest attacks on William III occur in the poems in the MS anthology "Loyal Poems." See Cameron, *Poems on Affairs of State*, 37–38, 41–42.

64. *Faerie Queene* 3.9.64.
65. Hammond, *Professional Imaginative Writing*, 137.
66. Sloman, *Poetics of Translation*, 136.
67. Ibid., 137.

68.

> Ortygium Cæneus, victorem Cænea Turnus:
> Turnus Ityn, Cloniumque, Dioxippum, Promulumque,
> Et Sagarim, et summis stantem pro turribus Idam. (573–75)

Dryden has omitted a couple of names; perhaps so his victor/vanquished theme would not be overshadowed by the sheer number of deaths. Literally: "Caeneus slew Ortygius and Turnus the victor Caeneus. Turnus also slew Itys and Clonius, Dioxippus and Promulus, and Sagaris and Idas standing on the wall."

69. Frost, *Dryden and the Art of Translation*, 65.
70. Cf. the Lausus/Mezentius episode in *Aeneis* X. When Lausus throws himself across his father's body, Aeneas begs him to relent with a no-win argument: "Why wilt thou rush to certain Death, and Rage / In rash Attempts, beyond thy tender Age: / Betray'd by pious Love?" (1149–51).

CHAPTER 5: THY LOVERS WERE ALL UNTRUE

1. *Delenda Carthago*, 2–3. In Wing S2890. This is attributed by Wing to Anthony Ashley Cooper; if this is correct, the author must be the third earl of Shaftesbury and grandson to the Anthony Ashley Cooper who is the butt of Dryden's *The Medall*.

2. The motif of a marriage-bed of state in which the Stuart king is the rightful lord and the English people a fickle female lover or victim of a rapist usurper is not confined to Dryden's works, and was in fact popular in Jacobite literature at this time. In an extensively documented essay, Howard Erskine-Hill points out that (for example) the "sensational image of rape" employed by Jacobites to condemn William III's "conquest" was "also turned by Williamites to accuse James of violating the laws." See "Literature and the Jacobite Cause," 49.

3. Bywaters, *Dryden in Revolutionary England*, 66.

4. Cf. the same lines in the 1658 Godolphin-Waller translation of *Aeneid* IV, *The Passion of Dido for Æneas*, a text, which, as King points out, Dryden drew on throughout his translation:

> For, *Anna*, I confesse since funerall fire
> Embrac'd *Sichæus*, this first beame of Light
> Hath offered comfort to so dark a night,
> Unwonted motions in my thoughts retriv'd,
> I find and feel the brand of care reviv'd.

See Waller, *The Passion of Dido for Æneas*, B. [Wing V633] There are no page or line numbers, and subsequent references will give section letter. King points out that the "joint translation of Book IV by Sidney Godolphin and Edmund Waller was published as *The Passion of Dido for Aeneas*, in 1658, but it had actually been written much earlier. Godolphin's share, which runs from the beginning of the book to 1.434 of the Latin version, was probably written shortly before his death in 1643. Waller's part was known to Denham c. 1653" (see King, "Translation from the Classics," 179).

5. *Faerie Queene* 1.12.18, 1.12.26.

6. "Sed fatis incerta feror, si Jupiter unam / Esse velit Tyriis urbem, Trojaque profectis" (110–11).

7. King, "Translation from the Classics," 228.

8. Contrast Segrais's more literal translation, which places emphasis on Dido and Aeneas' unity through marriage and on their glory and great destinies:

> Elle dit hautement, qu'un second hymenée
> Avoit uni Didon, & le Troyen Enée;
> Que plongez dans le luxe, & parmi les festins,
> Indignes de leur gloire, & de leurs grands destins,
> Ils en font à l'amour de honteux sacrifices,
> Et consomment l'hyver dans les molles delices. (*Traduction*, Vol. 1, 298)

9. The Oxford Classical Text reads, "Aenean Troiano sanguine cretum."

10. Gardiner, "Dryden's *Eleanora*," 111. Gardiner cites Alan Roper, *Dryden's Poetic Kingdoms*, 112.

11. Gardiner, "Dryden's *Eleanora*," 112.

12. Ibid.

13. Dryden's first verb and its notion of fraud are interpolated; Vergil has "*Ascanione pater Romanas invidet arces?*": "Does he as father grudge Ascanius Roman towers?" (234). The hyphen in *Ascanio-ne* is a peculiarity of Ruæus's text.

14. Literally: You traitor! Did you hope to conceal such a crime and slip quietly away from my land?

15. An approximate translation of the points of Dido's argument that Ruæus enumerates is: 1. There is love to consider; 2. There was a pledge of faith sealed by the right hand; 3. There is piety to consider in the face of her imminent demise by a cruel death.

16. King, "Translation from the Classics," 225.

17. Ibid., 182.

18. Yet in the letter to the Earl of Chesterfield of February 1697 where he discusses his delay in publishing his Vergil, Dryden reveals that he does have residual hope that the *status quo* will somehow be rectified: "I have hinder'd [the publication of the translation] thus long in hopes of his return, for whom, and for my Conscience I have sufferd, that I may have layd my Authour at his feet: But now finding that Gods time for ending our miseries is not yet, I have been advis'd to make three severall Dedications . . ." (*Letters*, 85–86).

19. King, "Translation from the Classics," 154. King also notes that Dryden elaborates Dido's "succinct two and a half line summary of what she did for Aeneas . . . into a five line declaration" (225).

20. Sloman, *Poetics of Translation*, 132.

21. Hammond cites Brian Corman's study of generic change in English drama, *Genre and Generic Change in English Comedy*. See Brean Hammond, *Professional Imaginative Writing*, 108–9.

22. Brean Hammond also draws attention to the characteristically mixed forms of 1690s literature, positing the reason for this as the increasing dissolution of "boundaries between monologic discourses deriving from epic and dialogic, polyglossic, carnivalesque-comic discourses." He argues further for changes in "[s]tandards of plausibility and authenticity demanded by readers"; this "plausibility crisis," as he calls

it, "affects the way the classical world is represented in original writing and in the translation of the epic" (see *Professional Imaginative Writing*, 112).

23. The Latin reads: "Non potui abreptum divellere corpus, et undis / Spargere" (600–601). R.G. Austin points to the balanced structure of the speech and its *p* and *ſ* sounds, commenting that "Dido means she should have treated Aeneas like some victim in a Greek tragedy (so Medea killed her brother Apsyrtus and flung him overboard, and Atreus killed Thyestes' sons and served them up to him at table); but the allusions are secondary to the high and undisguised rhetoric." See Virgil, *P. Vergili Maronis Aeneidos Liber Quartus*, 175.

24. Heinze, *Virgil's Epic Technique*, 105–6.
25. Brean Hammond, *Professional Imaginative Writing*, 110.
26. Trapp, *Preface to the Aeneis*, lii.
27. This is discussed by Sessions in his article "Spenser's Georgics."
28. Zwicker, *Politics and Language*, 137.
29. Brean Hammond, *Professional Imaginative Writing*, 112.
30. *Paradise Lost* 1:254–55.
31. The Latin lines of the entire passage read:

> At pius Æneas arces quibus altus Apollo
> Præsidet, horrendæque procul secreta Sibyllæ,
> Antrum immane, petit; magnam cui mentem animumque
> Delius inspirat vates, aperitque futura. (9–12)

Segrais's translation is perhaps closest to Dryden's, as it too is charged with energy and has possible sexual overtones:

> Le Heros transporté du zele qui l'anime,
> Cherche au loin d'Apollon l'edifice sublime,
> Et de l'antre écarté les replis tortueux,
> Où l'antique Sibylle au port majestueux,
> Pleine dans sa fureur du grand Dieu qui l'inspire,
> Des destins absolus fait les ordres prescrire. (*Traduction, Vol. 1, 412*)

32. Boileau's 1674 translation, which Dryden would have used (134); see chapter 3, note 25.
33. Zwicker, *Politics and Language*, 201.
34. *Paradise Lost* 1:481.
35. The peculiarly English character of the lines can be seen by contrasting them with Segrais's translation where there is no mention of a road to hell lying open, of an innavigable flood, or of regions void of light:

> Ayant sû tout prévoir, rien n'abbat mon courage:
> Mais puisqu'en ce climat on ne peut voir l'Acheron,
> Et l'antre qui conduit au palais de Pluton;
> Montre toi favorable à ma juste prière;
> Fai moi jouïr encor des regards de mon pere. (*Virgile*, Vol. 1, 419–20)

36. *Paradise Lost* 2:975–77.
37. The California editors point out that "Lauderdale makes the same application as Dryden: 'Here those who Brothers for a Crown disown, / Turn out their Parents and usurp the Throne.' Dryden's application has long been recognized . . ." (6:1038.n. 824–25). In fact, Margaret Boddy, whose article the California editors also note, was the first to recognize that Lauderdale anticipated Dryden in his satirical attack. See Margaret Boddy, "Contemporary Allusions in Lauderdale's *Aeneid*," *N&Q* 207 (1962): 386–8.
38. *Paradise Lost* 3:26–31.

39. Weinbrot, *Britannia's Issue*, 238. Contrast Segrais' attempt to capture the pride of the Latin lines:

> Ton art, peuple Romain, ton illustre science,
> Sera d'asservir tout à ta vaste puissance,
> De te rendre en tous lieux dans la guerre & la paix
> L'effroi des ennemis, & l'amour des sujets. (*Traduction*, Vol. 1, 474–75)

Bibliography

DRYDEN AND VERGIL: ORIGINAL WORKS AND TRANSLATIONS

[Benson, William.] *Virgil's Husbandry, or an Essay on the Georgics: Being the First Book Translated into English Verse, to which are added the Latin Text, and Mr. Dryden's Version, with Notes Critical and Rustick.* London, 1725.

——. *Virgil's Husbandry, or an Essay on the Georgics: Being the Second Book Translated into English Verse, to which are added the Latin Text, and Mr. Dryden's Version, with Notes Critical and Rustick.* London, 1724.

Boys, John, trans. *Æneas his Errours, or his Voyage from Troy into Italy: An Essay upon the Third Book of Virgils Æneis.* London, 1661.

Brady, Nicholas, trans. *Proposals for Publishing a Translation of Virgil's Æneids in Blank Verse: Together with a Specimen of the Performance.* London, 1714.

——. *Virgil's Æneis Translated into Blank Verse.* London, 1716.

[Denham, Sir John.] *The Destruction of Troy: An Essay upon the Second Book of Virgils Aeneis.* London, 1656.

The Destruction of Troy: An Essay upon the Second Book of Virgils Æneis, Written in the Year, 1636. London, 1656.

Dryden, John. *Essays of John Dryden.* Ed. W. P. Ker. Oxford: Clarendon Press, 1900.

——. *John Dryden: Four Tragedies.* Eds. L. A. Beaurline and Fredson Bowers. Chicago: University of Chicago Press, 1967.

——. *The Letters of John Dryden: With Letters Addressed to Him.* Ed. Charles E. Ward. Durham, N.C.: Duke University Press, 1942.

——. *Letters upon Several Occasions: Written by and between Mr. Dryden, Mr. Wycherley, Mr. Congreve, and Mr. Dennis.* London, 1696.

——. *The Poems of John Dryden.* Ed. Paul Hammond. 2 vols. London: Longman, 1995.

——. *The Poems of John Dryden.* Ed. James Kinsley. Vol. 4. Oxford: Clarendon Press, 1958.

——. *The Poetical Works of Dryden.* Ed. George R. Noyes. 1909. Reprint, Boston: Houghton Mifflin, 1950.

——. *The Works of John Dryden.* Eds. Edward Niles Hooker, H. T. Swedenberg, et. al. 20 vols. Berkeley: University of California Press, 1955–.

——. trans. *Virgil's Aeneid.* The Harvard Classics 13. New York: P. F. Collier, 1909. Online at gopher://wiretap.spies.com./00/Library/Classic/aeneid.txt.

L'Estrange, Ro[ger], trans. *The First Book of Virgils Æneis: Made English.* London, 1687.

The Fourth Book of Virgil: Translated by a Person of Quality. London, 1692.

Harrington, James, trans. *Virgil's Æneis: The Third, Fourth, Fifth and Sixth Books.* London, 1659.

Maitland, Richard, Earl of Lauderdale. *The Works of Virgil, Translated into English Verse.* London, [1718].

Mandelbaum, Allen, trans. *The Aeneid of Virgil.* Berkeley: University of California Press, 1981.

May, Thomas, trans. *Virgil's Georgicks Englished by T. May.* London, 1628.

Ogilby, John, trans. *The Works of Publius Virgilius Maro.* London, 1649.

———. *The Works of Publius Virgilius Maro Translated, Adorned with Sculpture, and Illustrated with Annotations, By John Ogilby.* 2d ed. 1654. Reprint, London, 1668.

Phaer, Thomas, Esquier. *The Seven First Bookes of the Eneidos of Virgill, Converted into Englishe Meter.* N.p., 1558.

Pitt, [Christopher,] trans. *The Æneid of Virgil.* 2 vols. London, 1740.

———, trans. *The Works of Virgil in Latin and English: The Aeneid translated by the Rev. Mr. Christopher Pitt; The Eclogues and Georgicks, with Notes on the Whole, by the Rev. Mr. Joseph Warton; With Several New Observations, by Mr. Holdsworth, Mr. Spence, C. Heyne, and Others.* 3d ed. London, 1778.

Segrais, Jean Regnauld de. *Traduction de l'Eneïde de Virgile.* Vol. 1. 2d ed. Rev. Amsterdam, 1700.

———. *Traduction de L'Eneïde de Virgile.* Vol. 2. Paris, 1681.

Sotheby, William, trans. *The Georgics of Virgil Translated.* London, 1800.

Stanyhurst, Richard, trans. *Thee First Foure Bookes of Virgil his Æneis Translated intoo English Heroical Verse.* Leiden, Holland, 1582.

Virgil. *P. Vergili Maronis Aeneidos Liber Quartus.* Ed. R. G. Austin. 1955. Reprint, Oxford: Clarendon Press, 1963.

———. *P. Virgilii Maronis Opera.* Ed. and notes Carolus Ruæus. 2d ed. 1682. Reprint, London, 1827.

———. *Virgil.* Trans. H. Rushton Fairclough. 2 vols. Rev. ed. Cambridge: Harvard University Press, 1988.

———. *Virgil: Georgicks.* 2 vols. Ed. Richard F. Thomas. Cambridge: Cambridge University Press, 1988.

Waller, Edmund and Sidney Godolphin, trans. *The Passion of Dido for Æneas: As it is Incomparably Exprest in the Fourth Book of Virgil.* London, 1658.

OTHER WORKS CITED AND CONSULTED

Addison, Joseph. *The Miscellaneous Works of Joseph Addison.* Ed. A. C. Guthkelch. Vol. 1. London: G. Bell, 1914.

Alssid, Michael W. "The Impossible Form of Art: Dryden, Purcell, and *King Arthur.*" *Studies in the Literary Imagination* 10 (1977): 125–44.

[Anderton, William.] *Remarks upon the Present Confederacy, and Late Revolution in England.* N.p., 1693.

The Annual Miscellany for the Year 1694: Being the Fourth Part of Miscellany Poems, Containing Great Variety of New Translations and Original Copies, by the Most Eminent Hands. London, 1694.

Armistead, Jack. "The Mythic Dimension of Dryden's *The Hind and The Panther.*" *Studies in English Literature* 16 (1976): 377–86.

Austin, Norman. "Translation as Baptism: Dryden's Lucretius." *Arion* 7 (1968): 576–602.

Bakhtin, M. M. "Epic and Novel: Toward a Methodology for the Study of the Novel." In *The Dialogic Imagination: Four Essays By M. M. Bakhtin*, edited by Michael Holquist, translated by Caryl Emerson and Michael Holquist 3–40. 1981. Reprint, Austin: University of Texas Press, 1994.

Barnard, J. "Dryden, Tonson and Subscriptions for the 1697 Virgil." *Publications of the Bibliographical Society of America* 57 (1963): 129–51.

Bassnett-McGuire, Susan. *Translation Studies*. London: Methuen, 1980.

Bayly, Anselm. *The Alliance of Music, Poetry and Oratory*. 1789. Reprint, New York: Garland, 1970.

Baxter, Stephen B. *William III*. London: Longmans, 1966.

Behn, Aphra. *The Rover*. Ed. Frederick M. Link. Lincoln: University of Nebraska Press, 1967.

Bell, Robert H. "Dryden's 'Aeneid' as English Augustan Epic." *Criticism* 19 (1977): 34–50.

Benedict, Barbara M. *Making the Modern Reader: Cultural Mediation in Early Modern Anthologies*. Princeton: Princeton University Press, 1996.

Benjamin, Walter. "Die Aufgabe des Übersetzers." In *Illuminationen: Augewählte Schriften*, 50–62. Frankfurt am Main: Suhrkamp Verlag, 1977.

―――. *Reflections: Essays, Aphorisms, Autobiographical Writings*. Ed. Peter Demetz. Trans. Edmund Jephcott. New York: Schocken Books, 1986.

―――. "The Task of the Translator." In *Illuminations*, edited by Hannah Arendt, translated by Harry Zohn, 69–82. New York: Shocken Books, 1993.

―――. "Theologisch-politisches Fragment." In *Illuminationen: Augewählte Schriften*, 262–63. Frankfurt am Main: Suhrkamp Verlag, 1977.

Benson, Donald. "Space, Time, and the Language of Transcendence in Dryden's Poetry." *Restoration: Studies in English Literary Culture, 1660–1700* 8 (1984): 10–16.

―――. "Theology and Politics in Dryden's Conversion." *Studies in English Literature* 4 (1964): 393–412.

Boddy, Margaret P. "Contemporary Allusions in Lauderdale's *Aeneid*." *Notes and Queries* 207 (1962): 386–88.

―――. "The Dryden-Lauderdale Relationships, Some Bibliographical Notes and a Suggestion." *Philological Quarterly* 42 (1963): 267–72.

Boileau-Despreaux, Nicolas. *Oeuvres diverses du Sieur D― ― : Avec le Traite du Sublime ou du Merveilleux dans le Discours. Traduit du Grec de Longin*. Amsterdam: A. Wolfgang, 1677.

Bossu, René le. "Treatise of the Epick Poem." In *Le Bossu and Voltaire on the Epic*, introduction by Stuart Curran. 1695. Reprint, Gainesville, Florida: Scholars' Facsimiles and Reprints, 1970.

Bottkol, J. McG. "Dryden's Latin Scholarship." *Modern Philology* 40 (1943): 241–54.

Bowers, Fredson. "Dryden as Laureate: the Cancel Leaf in *King Arthur*." *Times Literary Supplement*, 10 Apr. 1953, 244.

Bredvold, Louis I. *The Intellectual Milieu of John Dryden: Studies in Some Aspects of Seventeenth-Century Thought*. Ann Arbor: University of Michigan Press, 1934.

Brower, Reuben A. "Dryden's Epic Manner and Virgil." *PMLA* 55 (1940): 119–38.

Brückmann, Patricia. "Catholicism in England." In *The Age of William III & Mary II:*

Power, Politics and Patronage 1688–1702, edited by Robert P. Maccubin and Martha Hamilton-Phillips, 82–88. Williamsburg: College of William and Mary; New York: Grolier Club; Washington D.C.: Folger Shakespeare Library, 1989.

Budick, Sanford. *Dryden and the Abyss of Light: A Study of Religio Laici and The Hind and the Panther*. New Haven: Yale University Press, 1970.

Burnet, Gilbert. *Bishop Burnet's History of his own Time*. 6 vols. Oxford: Clarendon Press, 1823.

Bywaters, David. *Dryden in Revolutionary England*. Berkeley: University of California Press, 1991.

Cameron, William J. "John Dryden's Jacobitism." In *Restoration Literature: Critical Approaches*, edited by Harold Love, 277–308. London: Methuen, 1972.

———, ed. *Poems on Affairs of State: Augustan Satirical Verse, 1660–1714*. Vol. 5. New Haven: Yale University Press, 1971.

Canfield, J. Douglas. "The Image of the Circle in Dryden's 'To My Honour'd Kinsman.'" *Papers on Literature and Language* 11 (1975): 168–76.

———. "*Regulus* and *Cleomenes* and 1688: From Royalism to Self-Reliance." *Eighteenth-Century Life* 12 (1988): 67–75.

———. *Word as Bond in English Literature from the Middle Ages to the Restoration*. Philadelphia: University of Pennsylvania Press, 1989.

Carnochan, W. B. "Dryden's Alexander" in *The English Hero, 1660–1800*, edited by Robert Folkenflik. Newark: University of Delaware Press, 1982.

Carver, Larry. "The Restoration Poets and their Father King." *Huntington Library Quarterly* 40 (1977): 333–51.

Chalker, John. *The English Georgic: A Study in the Development of a Form*. London: Routledge and Kegan Paul, 1969.

Clavis Virgiliana: Or, a Vocabulary of all the Words in Virgil's Bucolics, Georgics, and Æneid. By Several Hands. London, 1742.

Clingham, Gregory J. "Another and the Same: Johnson's Dryden." In *Literary Transmission and Authority: Dryden and Other Writers*, edited by Earl Miner and Jennifer Brady, 121–59. Cambridge: Cambridge University Press, 1993.

———. "Johnson's Criticism of Dryden's Odes in Praise of St. Cecilia." *Modern Language Studies* 18 (1988): 165–80.

Cobb, Samuel. *Clavis Virgiliana: Or, New Observations upon the Works of Virgil*. London, 1714. Reprint, New York: Garland, 1970.

A Collection for Improvement of Husbandry and Trade. Friday, 4 May 1694.

A Collection of Loyal Poems, Satyrs and Lampoons. N.p., n.d. Osborne collection b11, Beinecke Rare Books, Yale University.

Corman, Brian. *Genre and Generic Change in English Comedy, 1660–1710*. Toronto: University of Toronto Press, 1993.

Corse, Taylor. *Dryden's Aeneid: The English Virgil*. Newark: University of Delaware Press, 1991.

Cousins, A. D. "Heroic Satire: Dryden and the Defence of Later Stuart Kingship." *Southern Review: Literary and Interdisciplinary Essays* 13 (1980): 170–87.

Craigie, James, ed. *The Poems of King James VI of Scotland*. 2 vols. Edinburgh, 1958.

Delenda Carthago: Or, The True Interest of England, in Relation to France and Holland. [London, 1695].

Denham, Sir John. *Expans'd Hieroglyphicks: A Critical Edition of Sir John Denham's Coopers Hill.* Ed. Brendan O'Hehir. Berkeley: University of California Press, 1969.

Dickinson, Harry T. "The Glorious Revolution of 1688–89: A Revolution Made or One Prevented?" *The Clark Newsletter* 15 (1988): 1–4.

Dickson, P. G. M. *The Financial Revolution in England: A Study in the Development of Public Credit, 1688–1756.* London: MacMillan, 1967.

Doederlein, Sue Warwick. "*Ut Pictura Poesis*: Dryden's *Aeneis* and *Palamon and Arcite.*" *Comparative Literature* 33 (1981): 156–66.

Durling, Dwight L. *Georgic Tradition in English Poetry.* New York: Columbia University Press, 1935.

Duthie Elizabeth. " 'A Memorial of My Own Principles': Dryden's 'To My Honour'd Kinsman.' " *English Literary History* 47 (1980): 682–704.

Erskine-Hill, Howard. "Literature and the Jacobite Cause: was there a Rhetoric of Jacobitism?" In *Ideology and Conspiracy: Aspects of Jacobitism, 1689–1759*, edited by Eveline Cruickshanks, 49–69. Edinburgh: John Donald Publishers, 1982.

Ettin, Andrew. "The *Georgics* in *The Faerie Queene.*" *Spenser Studies* 3 (1982): 57–71.

Evelyn, John. *Diary.* Ed. E. S. de Beer. London: Oxford University Press, 1959.

Evremont, Saint. *The Works of M. de St. Evremont.* 2 vols. London, 1700.

Examen Poeticum: Being the Third Part of Miscellany Poems. Containing Variety of New Translations of Ancient Poets, together with Many Original Copies, by the Most Eminent Hands. London, 1693.

Fowler, Alistair. "The Beginnings of English Georgic." In *Renaissance Genres: Essays on Theory, History, and Interpretation*, edited by Barbara Kiefer Lewalski, 105–25. Harvard English Studies 14. Cambridge: Harvard University Press, 1986.

Frost, William. *Dryden and the Art of Translation.* New Haven: Yale University Press, 1955.

———. "Dryden and the Classics: With a Look at his 'Aeneis.' " In *John Dryden*, edited by Earl Miner, 267–96. London: G. Bell, 1972.

———. "Dryden's Virgil." *Comparative Literature* 36 (1984): 193–208.

———. *John Dryden: Dramatist, Satirist, Translator.* New York: AMS Press, 1988.

———. "On Editing Dryden's Virgil." In *Editing Poetry from Spenser to Dryden: Papers given at the Sixteenth Annual Conference on Editorial Problems, University of Toronto, 31 October-1 November, 1980*, edited by A. H. de Quehen, 99–126. New York: Garland, 1981.

Fujimura, Thomas H. " 'Autobiography' in Dryden's Later Work." *Restoration: Studies in English Literary Culture, 1660–1700* 8 (1984): 17–29.

———. "Dryden's Changing Political Views." *Restoration: Studies in English Literary Culture, 1660–1700* 10 (1986): 93–104.

———. "Dryden's Virgil: Translation as Autobiography." *Studies in Philology* 80 (1983): 67–83.

———. "The Personal Drama of Dryden's *The Hind and the Panther.*" *PMLA* 87 (1972): 406–16.

Gardiner, Anne Barbeau. "A Conflict of Laws: Consequences of the King's Inaction in *The Duke of Guise.*" *English Language Notes* 19 (1981): 109–15.

———. "Divine and Royal Art: History as Hand-Formed Artwork in Dryden's *Threnodia Augustalis* (1685)." *Papers on Literature and Language* 25 (1989): 398–424.

————. "Dryden's *Britannia Rediviva*: Interpreting the Signs of the Times in June 1688." *Huntington Library Quarterly* 48 (1985): 257–84.

————. "Dryden's *Cleomenes* (1692) and Contemporary Jacobite Verse." *Restoration: Studies in English Literary Culture, 1660–1700* 12 (1988): 87–95.

————. "Dryden's *Eleanora*: Passion for the Public Good as a Sign of the Divine Presence." *Studies in Philology* 84 (1987): 95–118.

————. "Dryden's Patrons." In *The Age of William III and Mary II: Power, Politics and Patronage 1688–1702*, edited by Robert P. Maccubbin and Martha Hamilton-Phillips, 326–32. Williamsburg: College of William and Mary; New York: Grolier Club; Washington D.C.: Folger Shakespeare Library, 1989.

————. "Dryden's *The Medall* and the Principle of Continuous Transmission of Laws." *Clio* 14 (1984): 51–70.

————. "A Jacobite Song by John Dryden." *Yale University Gazette* 61 (1986): 49–54.

————. "John Dryden's *Love Triumphant* and English Hostility to Foreigners 1688–1693." *Clio* 18 (1989): 153–70.

————. "*Religio Laici* and the Principle of Legal Continuity." *Papers on Literature and Language* 20 (1984): 29–46.

————. "The Roots of Authority: Fidelity to Inherited Laws in Dryden's *The Hind and the Panther*." *Clio* 11 (1981): 15–28.

Garrett, Jane. *The Triumphs of Providence: The Assassination Plot, 1696*. Cambridge: Cambridge University Press, 1980.

Garrison, James D. *Pietas from Vergil to Dryden*. University Park, Pa.: Pennsylvania State University Press, 1992.

Gillespie, Stuart. "The Early Years of the Dryden-Tonson Partnership: The Background to their Composite Translation and Miscellanies of the 1680s." *Restoration: Studies in English Literary Culture, 1660–1700* 12 (1988): 10–19.

Good and Seasonable Advice to the Male Contents in England: Shewing that it is neither the Duty, nor the Interest of the People of England to Re-call the Late King. London, 1689.

Griffin, Dustin. *Literary Patronage in England, 1650–1800*. Cambridge: Cambridge University Press, 1996.

Guibbory, Achsah. "Dryden's Views of History." *Philological Quarterly* 52 (1973): 187–204.

Hager, Alan. "British Virgil: Four Renaissance Disguises of the Laocoön Passage of Book 2 of *The Aeneid*." *Studies in English Literature 1500–1900* 22 (1982): 21–38.

Hammond, Brean S. *Professional Imaginative Writing in England, 1670–1740: 'Hackney for Bread.'* Oxford: Clarendon Press, 1997.

Hammond, Paul. "Dryden's Philosophy of Fortune." *Modern Language Review* 80 (1985): 769- 85.

————. "The Integrity of Dryden's Lucretius." *Modern Language Review* 78 (1983): 1–23.

————. *John Dryden: A Literary Life*. London: Macmillan, 1991.

Hardie, Philip R. *Virgil's Aeneid: Cosmos and Imperium*. Oxford: Clarendon Press, 1986.

Harrison, T. W. "Dryden's *Aeneid*." In *Dryden's Mind and Art*, edited by Bruce King, 143–67. Edinburgh: Oliver and Boyd, 1969.

————. "English Virgil: The *Aeneid* in the XVIII Century." *Philologica Pragensia* 10 (1967): 1–11, 80–92.

Harth, Phillip J. *Contexts of Dryden's Thought*. Chicago: University of Chicago Press, 1968.

———. "Dryden's Public Voices." In *Critical Essays on John Dryden*, edited by James Winn, 104–22. New York: G. K. Hall, 1997.

———. *Pen for a Party: Dryden's Tory Propaganda in its Contexts*. Princeton: Princeton University Press, 1993.

Hayley, William. *An Essay on Epic Poetry (1782)*. Introd. Sister M. Celeste Williamson. Gainesville, Florida: Scholars' Facsimiles and Reprints, 1968.

Heinze, Richard. *Virgil's Epic Technique*. Trans. Hazel and David Harvey and Fred Robertson. Berkeley: University of California Press, 1993.

Homer. *The Odyssey*. Trans. A. T. Murray and rev. by George E. Dimock. 2d ed. Cambridge: Harvard University Press, 1995.

Hooker, Helene Maxwell. "Dryden's *Georgics* and English Predecessors." *Huntington Library Quarterly* 9 (1946): 273–310.

Hopkins, David. "Dryden and Ovid's 'Wit out of season.' " In *Ovid Renewed: Ovidian Influences on Literature and Art from the Middle Ages to the Twentieth Century*, edited by Charles Martindale, 167–90. Cambridge: Cambridge University Press, 1988.

———. "Dryden's 'Baucis and Philemon.' " *Comparative Literature* 28 (1976): 135–43.

———. *John Dryden*. Cambridge: Cambridge University Press, 1986.

———. "Nature's Laws and Man's: The Story of Cinyras and Myrrha in Ovid and Dryden." *Modern Language Review* 80 (1985): 786–801.

Hunter, J. Paul. *Before Novels: The Cultural Contexts of Eighteenth-Century English Fiction*. New York: W. W. W. Norton, 1990.

Johnson, Donald R. "The Proper Study of Husbandry: Dryden's Translation of the *Georgics*." *Restoration: Studies in English Literary Culture, 1660–1700* 6 (1982): 94–104.

Johnson, W. R. *Darkness Visible: A Study of Vergil's Aeneid*. Berkeley: University of California Press, 1976.

[Johnston, Nathaniel.] *The Dear Bargain: Or, a True Representation of the State of the English Nation under the Dutch*. [N.p., 1688].

Jones, Emyrs. " 'A Perpetual Torrent': Dryden's Lucretian Style." In *Augustan Studies: Essays in Honor of Irvin Ehrenpreis*, edited by Douglas Lane Patey and Timothy Keegan, 47–63. Newark: University of Delaware Press, 1985.

Jonson, Ben. *Ben Jonson*. Eds. C. H. Herford, Percy and Evelyn Simpson. Vol. 7. Oxford: Clarendon Press, 1970.

Kelsall, M. M. "What God, What Mortal? *The Aeneid* and English Mock-Heroic." *Arion* 8 (1969): 359–79.

Kenyon, John P. *Revolution Principles: The Politics of Party, 1689–1720*. Cambridge: Cambridge University Press, 1977.

King, Anne Ruth. "Translation from the Classics during the Restoration with Special Reference to Dryden's Aeneis." Ph.D. diss., Cornell University, 1949.

Levine, Jay A. "John Dryden's Epistle to John Driden." *Journal of English and Germanic Philology* 63 (1964): 450–74.

Levine, Joseph M. *The Battle of the Books: History and Literature in the Augustan Age*. Ithaca: Cornell University Press, 1991.

Lewis, Charlton T., ed. *A Latin Dictionary*. Oxford: Clarendon Press, 1879.

Lord, George de F. " 'Absalom and Achitophel' and Dryden's Political Cosmos." In *John Dryden*, edited by Earl Miner, 156–90. London: G. Bell, 1972.

Losnes, Arvid. "Dryden's *Æneis* and the Delphin *Virgil*." In *The Hidden Sense and Other Essays*, 113–58. Oslo: Universitetsforlaget; New York: Humanities Press, 1963.

Low, Anthony. *The Georgic Revolution.* Princeton: Princeton University Press, 1985.

———. "Milton, *Paradise Regained*, and Georgic." *PMLA* 98 (1983): 152–69.

Maccubbin, Robert P. "The Ironies of Dryden's 'Alexander's Feast; or The Power of Musique': Texts and Contexts." *Mosaic* 18 (1983): 33–47.

MacLean, G. M. "Poetry as History: The Argumentative Design of Dryden's *Astræa Redux.*" *Restoration: Studies in English Literary Culture, 1660–1700* 4 (1980): 54–64.

Markley, Robert. " 'Credit Exhausted': Satire and Scarcity in the 1690s." In *Cutting Edges: Postmodern Critical Essays on Eighteenth-Century Satire,* edited by James Gill, 110–26. Knoxville: University of Tennessee Press, 1995.

Martin, R. H. "A Note on Dryden's *Aeneid.*" *Philological Quarterly* 30 (1951): 89–91.

Mason, H. A. *To Homer through Pope: An Introduction to Homer's Iliad and Pope's Translation.* New York: Barnes & Noble, 1972.

McKeon, Michael. *The Origins of the English Novel, 1600–1740.* Baltimore: Johns Hopkins University Press, 1987.

———. *Politics and Poetry in Restoration England: The Case of Annus Mirabilis.* Cambridge: Harvard University Press, 1975.

McRae, Andrew. *God Speed the Plough: The Representation of Agrarian England, 1500–1660.* Cambridge: Cambridge University Press, 1996.

Milbourne, Luke. *Notes on Dryden's Virgil, 1698.* New York: Garland, 1974.

Miller, Rachel A. "Physic for the Great: Dryden's Satiric Translations of Juvenal, Persius and Boccaccio." *Philological Quarterly* 68 (1989): 53–75.

———. "Regal Hunting: Dryden's Influence on *Windsor-Forest.*" *Eighteenth-Century Studies* 13 (1980): 53–75.

Milton, John. *The Poetical Works of John Milton.* Ed. Helen Darbishire. 2 vols. Oxford: Clarendon Press, 1962.

Miner, Earl. "Dryden's Eikon Basilike: To Sir Godfrey Kneller." In *Seventeenth-Century Imagery: Essays on Uses of Figurative Language from Donne to Farquahar,* edited by Earl Miner, 151–67. Berkeley: University of California Press, 1971.

———. *Dryden's Poetry.* Bloomington: Indiana University Press, 1967.

———. "Ovid Reformed: Fables, Morals, and the Second Epic." In *Literary Transmission and Authority: Dryden and Other Writers,* edited by Earl Miner and Jennifer Brady, 79–120. Cambridge: Cambridge University Press, 1993.

———, ed. *John Dryden.* London: G. Bell, 1972.

———, ed. *Poems on the Reign of William III.* Los Angeles: University of California Press, 1974.

Miscellany Poems Containing a New Translation of Virgills Eclogues, Ovid's Love Elegies, Odes of Horace, and other Authors, with Several Original Poems by the Most Eminent Hands. London, 1692.

Miscellany Poems upon Several Occasions: With an Essay upon Satyr, by the Famous M. Dacier. London, 1684.

Monod, Paul Kleber. *Jacobitism and the English People, 1688–1788.* Cambridge: Cambridge University Press, 1989.

Moore, John Robert. "Political Allusions in Dryden's Later Plays." *PMLA* 73 (1958): 36–42.

Myers, William. *Dryden.* London: Hutchinson & Co., 1973.

Nenner, Howard A. *By Colour of Law: Legal and Constitutional Politics in England, 1660–1689.* Chicago: University of Chicago Press, 1977.

Ogilby, John. *The Fables of Æsop Paraphras'd in Verse*. Introd. Earl Miner. 1668. Reprint, Los Angeles: University of California, 1965.

Orgel, Stephen. *The Illusion of Power: Political Theatre in the English Renaissance*. Berkeley: University of California Press, 1975.

Osborn, James M. *John Dryden: Some Biographical Facts and Problems*. Rev. ed. Gainesville: University of Florida Press, 1965.

Patterson, Annabel. *Fables of Power: Aesopian Writing and Political History*. Durham N.C.: Duke University Press, 1991.

Philips, Ambrose. *The Briton: A Tragedy*. London, 1722.

Pocock, J. G. A. *Virtue, Commerce, and History: Essays on Political Thought and History, Chiefly in the Eighteenth Century*. Cambridge: Cambridge University Press, 1985.

Pope, Alexander. *The Poems of Alexander Pope*. General ed. John Butt. Vol. 1. London: Methuen; New Haven: Yale University Press, 1939–69.

Popkin, Richard H. *The Third Force in Seventeenth-Century Thought*. Leiden: E. J. Brill, 1992.

Proffitt, Bessie. "Political Satire in Dryden's *Alexander's Feast*." *Texas Studies in Literature and Language* 11 (1970): 1307–16.

Proudfoot, L. *Dryden's Aeneid and its Seventeenth-Century Predecessors*. Manchester: Manchester University Press, 1960.

[Rapin, René.] *Observations on the Poems of Homer and Virgil*. Trans. John Davies. London, 1672.

Reverand II, Cedric D. "Dryden on Dryden in 'To Sir Godfrey Kneller.'" *Papers on Literature and Language* 17 (1981): 164–80.

———. *Dryden's Final Poetic Mode: The Fables*. Philadelphia: University of Pennsylvania Press, 1988.

———. "Patterns of Imagery and Metaphor in Dryden's *The Medall*." *Yearbook of English Studies* 2 (1972): 103–14.

Richardsoni, Ric. *De Cultu Hortorum ad Populares suos Carmen: Guilelmo Britanniarum Regi, Magno, Felici, Invicto, semper Augusto, Dicatum*. London, 1699.

Richetti, John. "Reply to David Richter: Ideology and Literary Form in Fielding's *Tom Jones*." *The Eighteenth Century: Theory and Interpretation* 37 (1996): 207.

Roper, Alan H. *Dryden's Poetic Kingdoms*. London: Routledge, 1965.

———. "Dryden's 'Secular Masque.'" *Modern Language Quarterly* 23 (1962): 29–40.

Ross, David. *Virgil's Elements: Physics and Poetry in the Georgics*. Princeton: Princeton University Press, 1987.

Rostvig, Maren-Sofie. *The Happy Man: Studies in the Metamorphoses of a Classical Ideal*. Vol. 1. 2d ed. Oslo: Norwegian Universities Press, 1962.

Sandys, George. *Ovid's Metamorphosis Englished, Mythologiz'd and Represented in Figures, [and] An Essay to the Translation of Virgil's Æneis, by G. S.* Oxford, 1632.

Schilling, Bernard N. *Dryden and the Conservative Myth: A Reading of Absalom and Achitophel*. New Haven: Yale University Press, 1964.

Schulte, Rainer and John Biguenet, eds. *Theories of Translation: An Anthology of Essays from Dryden to Derrida*. Chicago: University of Chicago Press, 1992.

Schwoerer, Lois. *"No Standing Armies!" The Antiarmy Ideology in Seventeenth-Century England*. Baltimore: Johns Hopkins University Press, 1974.

Scott. Sir Walter. *The Life of John Dryden*. Ed. Bernard Kreissman. Lincoln: University of Nebraska Press, 1963.

Sessions, William A. "Spenser's Georgics," *English Literary Renaissance* 10 (1980): 202–38.

Sloman, Judith. *Dryden: The Poetics of Translation.* Toronto: University of Toronto Press, 1985.

———. "Dryden's Originality in *Sigismonda and Guiscardo.*" *Studies in English Literature* 12 (1972): 445–57.

———. "An Interpretation of Dryden's *Fables.*" *Eighteenth-Century Studies* 4 (1970–71): 199–211.

Smith, Betty Adams. "Dryden's Translation of Virgil and its 18th-Century Successors." Ph.D. diss., Michigan State University, 1970.

Smith, Ruth. "The Arguments and Contexts of Dryden's *Alexander's Feast.*" *Studies in English Literature* 18 (1978): 465–90.

Southerne, Thomas. *Oroonoko.* Ed. Maximillian E. Novak and David Stuart Rodes. University of Nebraska Press, 1976.

Spence, Joseph. *Spence's Polymetis Abridged: Or a Guide to Classical Learning.* Introd. Nicolas Tindal. 6th ed. London, 1802.

Spenser, Edmund. *The Poetical Works of Edmund Spenser.* Ed. Ernest de Selincourt. Vol. 1, *Spenser's Minor Poems.* Oxford: Clarendon Press, 1970.

———. *The Poetical Works of Edmund Spenser.* Ed. J. C. Smith. Vols. 1 and 2, *Spenser's Faerie Queene.* Oxford: Clarendon Press, 1972.

Spinoza, Benedict de. *The Chief Works of Benedict de Spinoza.* Trans. R. H. M. Elwes. Vol. 1. Rev. ed. London: George Bell, 1891.

State Tracts: Being a Farther Collection of Several Choice Treatises Relating to the Government: From the Year 1660, to 1689. 1692. Delaware: Scholarly Resources, 1973.

Staves, Susan. *Players' Scepters: Fictions of Authority in the Restoration.* Lincoln: University of Nebraska Press, 1979.

Steiner, George. *After Babel: Aspects of Language and Translation.* London: Oxford University Press, 1975.

Steiner, T. R. *English Translation Theory 1650–1800.* Assen, Netherlands: Van Gorcum, 1975.

Swedenberg, Hugh T. Jr. "Dryden's Obsessive Concern with the Heroic." *Studies in Philology* 64 extra ser. 4 (1967): 12–26.

Swift, Jonathan. *A Discourse of the Contests and Dissensions between the Nobles and Commons in Athens and Rome: With the Consequences they had upon both those States.* Ed. Frank H. Ellis. Oxford: Clarendon Press, 1967.

———. *A Tale of a Tub: With Other Early Works, 1696–1707.* Ed. Herbert Davis. Oxford: Blackwell, 1957.

———. *The Theory of the Epic in England, 1650–1800.* University of California Publications in English 15. Berkeley: University of California Press, 1944.

Sylvæ: Or, the second Part of Poetical Miscellanies. London, 1685.

Tillyard, E. M. W. *The English Epic and its Background.* London: Chatto and Windus, 1954.

Trapp, Joseph. *The Preface to the Aeneis of Virgil.* Intro. Malcolm Kelsall. 1718. Reprint, Los Angeles: University of California Press, 1982.

Turner, James. *The Politics of Landscape: Rural Scenery and Society in English Poetry, 1630–1660.* Cambridge: Harvard University Press, 1979.

Van Doren, Mark. *John Dryden.* New York: Holt, 1946.

Verdumen, J. Peter. "Dryden's Cymon and Iphigenia at Century's End: Ploughshares into Swords." *Revue des Langues Vivantes* 44 (1978): 285–300.

Wallace, John M. "John Dryden's Plays and the Conception of an Heroic Society." In *Culture and Politics from Puritanism to the Enlightenment*, edited by Perez Zagorin, 113–34. Berkeley: University of California Press, 1980.

Ward, Charles E. *The Life of John Dryden*. Chapel Hill: University of North Carolina Press, 1961.

Warton, Joseph. "A Dissertation on the Nature and Conduct of the Aeneid." In *The Works of Virgil in Latin and English: The Æneid translated by the Rev. Mr. Christopher Pitt*, 3d ed., vol. 2, 1–18. London, 1778.

Watson, George. "Dryden and the Jacobites." *Times Literary Supplement*, 16 Mar. 1973, 301–2.

Weadon, Mark Preston. "The English Virgil: Dryden's *Aeneis* as an Augustan Epic." Ph.D. diss., University of Michigan, 1979.

Webb, Wm. Stanford. "Vergil in Spenser's Epic Theory." *English Literary History* 4 (1937): 62–84.

Weinberg, Bernard. "Scaliger versus Aristotle on Poetics." *Modern Philology* 39 (1942): 337–60.

Weinbrot, Howard D. *Augustus Caesar in "Augustan" England: The Decline of a Classical Norm*. Princeton: Princeton University Press, 1978.

———. *Britannia's Issue: The Rise of British Literature from Dryden to Ossian*. Cambridge: Cambridge University Press, 1993.

———. *The Formal Strain: Studies in Augustan Imitation and Satire*. Chicago: University of Chicago Press, 1969.

West, Michael. "Dryden and the Disintegration of Renaissance Heroic Ideals." *Costerus* 7 (1973): 193–222.

———. "Dryden's Ambivalence as a Translator of Heroic Themes." *Huntington Library Quarterly* 36 (1973): 347–66.

———. "Shifting Concepts of Heroism in Dryden's Panegyrics." *Papers on Literature and Language* 10 (1974): 378–93.

Wilkinson, L. P. *The Georgics of Virgil: A Critical Survey*. Cambridge: Cambridge University Press, 1969.

Williams, R. D. "Changing Attitudes to Virgil." In *Virgil*, edited by D. R. Dudley. London: Routledge and Kegan Paul, 1969.

Winn, James Anderson, " 'Complying with the Times': Dryden's *Satires of Juvenal and Persius* (1693)." *Eighteenth-Century Life* 12 (1988): 76–87.

———. " 'Dryden's Epistle before Creech's Lucretius': A Study in Restoration Ghost Writing." *Philological Quarterly* 71 (1992): 47–68.

———. *John Dryden and His World*. New Haven: Yale University Press, 1987.

———. "The Laureateship." In *The Age of William III and Mary II: Power, Politics and Patronage 1688–1702*, edited by Robert P. Maccubbin and Martha Hamilton-Phillips, 319–25. Williamsburg: College of William and Mary; New York: Grolier Club; Washington D.C.: Folger Shakespeare Library, 1989.

———. *When Beauty Fires the Blood: Love and the Arts in the Age of Dryden*. Ann Arbor: University of Michigan Press, 1992.

———, ed. *Critical Essays on John Dryden*. New York: G. K. Hall & Co., 1997.

Wykes, David. *A Preface to Dryden*. New York: Longman, 1977.

Zimbardo, Rose A. "The Late Seventeenth-Century Dilemma in Discourse: Dryden's *Don Sebastian* and Behn's *Oroonoko*." In *Rhetorics of Order/Ordering Rhetorics in English Neoclassical Literature*, edited by J. Douglas Canfield and J. Paul Hunter, 46–67. Newark: University of Delaware Press, 1989.

Zwicker, Steven N. *Dryden's Political Poetry: The Typology of King and Nation*. Providence, R. I.: Brown University Press, 1972.

———. "The Paradoxes of Tender Conscience." *English Literary History* 63 (1996): 851–69.

———. *Politics and Language in Dryden's Poetry: The Arts of Disguise*. Princeton: Princeton University Press, 1984.

———. "Politics and Literary Practice in the Restoration." In *Renaissance Genres: Essays on Theory, History and Interpretation*, edited by Barbara Kiefer Lewalski, 268–98. Harvard English Studies 14. Cambridge: Harvard University Press, 1986.

———. "Reading Vergil in the 1690s." In *Vergil at 2000: Commemorative Essays on the Poet and his Influence*, edited by John D. Bernard, 281–302. New York: AMS Press, 1986.

Index